John Matthews has been writing about and studying the Grail stories for over thirty years. He has written numerous books on the subject and many more on the Arthurian legends, esoterica and the British Mysteries. He lives in Oxford, England.

By the same author

The Celtic Shaman
The Grail: Quest for the Eternal
The Quest for the Green Man
The Song of Taliesin
Taliesin: Shamanism and the Bardic Mysteries of Britain
The Winter Solstice

at the Table of the Grail

No one who sets forth on the Grail Quest remains unchanged

Edited by

John Matthews

Watkins Publishing
London

This edition published in the UK in 2002 by
Watkins Publishing, 20 Bloomsbury Street, London, WC1B 3QA

Chapters 1, 2, 3, 5, 9, 13, 14, 17 first published in *The Household of the Grail*
(ed. John Matthews) The Aquarian Press, Wellingborough, 1990.

Chapters 4, 6, 7, 8, 15 first published in *At the Table of the Grail* (ed. John
Matthews) Arkana, 1984, 1987.

Chapter 12 first published as appendix to *The Underworld Initiation* (R.J. Stewart)
Thorsons 1985.

Cover design by Echelon Design

Cover photograph, *Gundestrop Cauldron*
© National Museum of Denmark, Copenhagen

Designed by Echelon Design
Typeset by WestKey Limited, Falmouth, Cornwall

Printed and bound in Great Britain by NFF Production

British Library Cataloguing in Publication data available
Library of Congress Cataloguing in Publication data available

ISBN 1 84293 035 4

Website: www.watkinspublishing.com

DEDICATION:

To All Who Seek the Grail

Contents

Notes on Contributors

HANNAH CLOSS was born in London in 1905 and died in Bristol in 1953. She was educated at the Slade School and the University of Vienna and her publications include a brilliant trilogy of novels about the Albigensian Crusade, *High Are The Mountains, Deep Are The Valleys*, and *The Silent Tarn*, (reprinted by Vanguard Press, New York, 1978). Her highly original essays on the Grail and Catharism have so far remained neglected, the one included here being printed originally in 1948.

PRUDENCE JONES is a writer and commentator on the European Pagan tradition, which she came across while still an undergraduate at Cambridge. She has extensive experience in Pagan exoteric and esoteric worship and has written and contributed many books and articles on the subject. These include *A History of Pagan Europe* (with Nigel Pennick: Routledge 1995) and chapters in *Paganism Today* (Harvey et al.: Thorsons 1995) and *Nature Religion Today* (Pearson et al.: Edinburgh UP 1998). *Goddesses and Gods of Europe* (with Nigel Pennick) and *The Three-Faced Goddess* are currently in preparation.

GARETH KNIGHT is well known as an esoteric writer. He has spent a lifetime rediscovering and teaching the principles of magic as a spiritual discipline and method of self realisation. He sees it as an aid to personal religious and imaginative experience that is of particular value in modern secular society. He commenced his occult training in Dion Fortune's Society of the Inner Light in 1953 and has made a special study of her Arthurian work, which has led him in later life to undertake an Honours Degree in French the better to study Chrétien de Troyes and Malory's original Arthurian sources. He has been a regular contributor to the *Inner Light* Journal for the past six years and is author of the much praised biography *Dion Fortune and the Inner Light* and *The Secret Tradition in Arthurian Legend* based upon Dion Fortune's work.

HELEN LUKE was born in England in 1904 and studied Italian literature at Oxford University and the psychology of C.G. Jung in London and Zurich. In 1949 she moved to Los Angeles where she practised as a counsellor, and later founded the Apple Farm Community, where she lived and taught until her death in 1998. Among her books are *Woman, Earth and Spirit* (Crossroads, 1981), *Dark Wood to White Rose: A Study of Meanings in Dante's Divine Comedy* (Dove Publications, 1975) and *The Inner Story* (Crossroads, 1982).

CAITLÍN MATTHEWS is internationally known as a teacher of the ancestral, shamanic and Celtic traditions. Her love of song, alchemy, poetry, performance and myth has led her to work across a wide range of spiritual traditions in ways that transcend time, place and language. She is the author of thirty-six books including *Mabon and the Mysteries of Britain*, *The Encyclopedia of Celtic Wisdom* and *Sophia, Goddess of Wisdom*. Her books have been translated into many languages. She is a co-founder of FIOS, the Foundation for Inspirational and Oracular Studies which is dedicated to the recognition of the oral and sacred arts and their integration into everyday life. Caitlín has a shamanic practice in Oxford, dedicated to the midwifery of the soul. For details of her courses, books and events see www.hallowquest.org.uk.

JOHN MATTHEWS has made a thirty-year study of the Grail legends and Celtic tradition. He has published more than 50 titles on this and related subjects. His most popular works are: *The Grail: Quest for Eternal Life* (1981), *The Celtic Shaman* (1996), and *The Winter Solstice* (1998) which won the Benjamin Franklin award for that year. He is an active member of the International Arthurian Society and recently edited a special issue of the journal *Arthuriana* on modern and post-modern Arthurian literature. Much in demand as a lecturer he travels widely to the USA and throughout Europe. He has made a number of guest appearances on TV shows for the Discovery and History channels. He recently published a book on the lives of the Celtic Saints: *Drinking from the Sacred Well* (1998) and an edition of Malory's fifteenth-century epic *Le Morte D'Arthur* (1999). For details of his courses, books and events see www.hallowquest.org.uk.

DIANA L. PAXSON first encountered the Grail legend while doing graduate work at the University of California in Berkeley. After receiving an M.A. in Comparative Literature, specializing in the Middle Ages, she went on to use what she had learned as a background for twenty novels and over seventy-five short stories, many of them set in the Roman through the Viking periods. They include *The White Raven*, a retelling of the story of Tristan and Iseult; the Wodan's Children trilogy, on the Siegfried legend; an Arthurian novel in four parts, *Hallowed Isle*; and *Priestess of Avalon*, a prequel to *Mists of Avalon* written in collaboration with her sister-in-law, Marion Zimmer Bradley. Ms. Paxson still lives in Berkeley, California.

GREG STAFFORD has been 'arthuring' since he was five years old. He has been practising shamanism for almost 10 years, and is president of the Cross Cultural Shamanism Network, the publisher of *Shaman's Drum* magazine. He is also a past president of Chaosium Inc. and the author of the experiential role-playing games *King Arthur Pendragon* and *Prince Valiant*. He teaches workshops in Experiential Arthurianism, mythology, and shamanism, and is a sweat lodge leader and vision quest leader. He lives in California.

ROBERT (R.J.) STEWART is a Scot, an author, and a composer. He has 36 books in publication, many translated worldwide, on mythology, magical arts, and music and consciousness. He has also composed, directed, and recorded music for feature films, television, and theatre productions. Currently living in the USA, R.J. Stewart also teaches workshops and seminars on various themes, and gives solo concerts. More information can be found at www.dreampower.com.

ELEMIRE ZOLLA, former Professor of American Literature at the University of Rome, was born in 1926 in Turin, Italy, to parents of Anglo-Alsatian origin. He is internationally known for his several longsellers on literary and social criticism and anthropology, including *The Eclipse of the Intellectual*, *The Writer and the Shaman*, *Archetypes*, *The Androgyne*, and more recently for his studies in Oriental metaphysics and alchemy. Editor of the quarterly journal *Conoscenza Religiosa* (1969–1981), columnist of *Il Corriere Della Sera* and since 2000 of *Il Sole 24 Ore*, Zolla has a unique place on the XXth century scene of East-West comparative religious and philosophic studies. Among his most recent books in Italian: *Uscite dal Mondo* (Adelphi 1992), *Le Tre Vie* (Adelphi 1995), *La Nube del Telaio. Ragione e Irrazionalite tra*

Oriente e Occidente (Mondadori 1996), *Il Dio dell'ebbrezza. Antologia dei Moderni Dionisiaci* (Einaudi 1998), *La Filosofia Perenne* (Mondadori 1999), *Catabasi e Anastasi, Discesa nell'Ade e Resurrezione* (Alberto Tallone 2001). With the same publisher in Alpignano (Turin), his monograph *Ioan Petru Culianu* 1950–1991 saw the light in 1994.

Introduction:
The Grail In All The Worlds

John Matthews

There are almost as many stories of the Grail as there are spiritual traditions. Classical Mystery School teaching, Celtic Druidic lore, medieval romance and legend, and oriental mysticism have all left their mark on the great body of material concerning the marvellous vessel and its actions both in the world and out of it.

None of this would be known to us today if it were not for the often unknown writers and story-tellers who helped fashion our under-standing as well as our knowledge of the Grail. The earliest authors, dealt with in Caitlín Matthews' essay, drew upon a fusion of Celtic and Christian myth – the place where Cauldron met Chalice. Their primal legacy has been taken up, shaped and reshaped by countless people ever since.

With the flowering of the Middle Ages came the first written texts: those of the great courtly poet Chrétien de Troyes, and Robert de Boron, of whom we know little more than his name and the works he left behind, which revolutionised the course of Grail history. Others, notably the fifteenth century 'knight prisoner', Sir Thomas Malory, broadened the stream of material with a degree of literary craftsmanship which have made their works live on.

In more recent times writers and practitioners from many fields of expertise have deepened the river-beds of the story to include the ideas of psychology (C.G. Jung), perennial philosophy (René Guénon and Julius Evola), ritual magic (Dion Fortune), poetry (Charles Williams and David Jones), and myth (Joseph Campbell). The way was opened for them by such inspired and pioneering scholars as Jessie Weston and Roger Sherman Loomis.

This collection is not intended to be read as a history of the Grail, although as many signposts as possible are given to the way the various strands interact. Rather, it concentrates on just a few high points, the works of outstanding individuals – known and unknown – who helped transform our understanding of the Grail, and on some of the many rich threads of wisdom, lore and history which have contributed to the vitality of the Grail myth as we know it today.

Each of these writers and traditions have added, in their own way, to our understanding of the Grail. Together they form a 'Household' made up of the lineal descendants of the Grail Family written about by more than one early authority. They carry forward into our own time the vitality of a tradition which places the Grail at the centre of Western culture and thought. Their words are filled with a light which comes from the vessel itself.

But this vast complex of Grail texts, stories and beliefs can be daunting for any reader, sometimes seeming as great a challenge as those met by the seekers themselves. To help overcome this, a brief summary of the basic history of the Grail is offered here, though it merely scratches the surface of this vast subject, which comprises so many themes and interpretations.

*   *   *   *   *

Some traditions hold that the Grail originated as a jewel – an emerald from the crown of the Light Bringer – Lucifer, the Angel of the Morning – which fell from heaven during the war between the angels. Others believe that Seth, the child of Adam and Eve, returned to the Garden of Eden, where he was given the Grail as a sign to all men that God had not forgotten them. But the first appearance of the word 'Grail' is in the context of Christ's crucifixion. At this time Joseph of Arimathea came into possession of the Cup of the Last Supper, and used it to catch a few drops of blood and sweat from the body of the Messiah – from which point it became a hallowed object. Thence it was borne into the West by Joseph and his band of followers; the first Company of the Grail, who arrived at Glastonbury in Somerset, where they founded a church dedicated to the Mother of Christ and enshrining the holy cup.

We next hear of the Grail in Arthur's time, when the first great Quest is recorded. It was then seen as inhabiting a castle, variously named as

Muntsalvasche or Carbonek, which lay in a place not wholly of this world, to which the Knights who swore to seek the Grail must journey, undergoing many perils and trials along the way. It is this quest or series of quests which forms the central history of the Grail. Thus we learn how it appeared at King Arthur's city of Camelot in a ray of brilliant light, and how all the company there were fed with the food and drink of their choice – a symbol of the spiritual food to be obtained from the Grail. In another text it is described as having five shapes or changes of shape which contain an inexplicable mystery. All seek it, some for good, others for evil purposes. It is found only by the good and the true. Three knights: Galahad, Perceval, and Bors, and one woman, Dindrane, are named: They alone of Arthur's followers find their way to the castle and the mysterious Fisher King, wounded through the thighs and unable to be healed until a ritual question – usually 'Whom does the Grail serve?' or sometimes, 'Who is it that serves the Grail?' is asked and answered. At which both the King, and the country he rules – until that moment a desert, blasted land – are restored.

The three knights, along with the Grail, depart by ship for Sarras, the Holy City in the East, where the final celebration of the mysteries of the Grail take place, and Galahad, the purest of the three, expires in an odour of sanctity. Dindrane dies also, and is buried at his side. Perceval returns to the Grail castle to become its new King, and Bors journeys to Camelot to tell of the miracles of the Quest.

*   *   *   *   *

Such is the story in its barest outline. There are many other versions and countless adventures of those who seek it; but the essence remains the same. The message of the Grail does not change, either then or now, as we will hope to show in these pages.

At the end of the thirteenth-century text known as *Perlesvaus*, when the miraculous vessel has passed away to appear no more in the world, and the knight Perceval has departed for lands unknown, the Castle of the Grail is left untenanted and becomes ruinous. Many wondered what there was about the place that made it somehow special, but the truth faded from memory and it became known only as the haunt of ghosts and memories. No one dared to go there except for two Welsh knights, who were, as the story tells us, very young and high spirited, and they swore that they would go, and full of excitement they entered the castle. They stayed there for a long while. And when they left they lived as hermits, wearing hair shirts and wandering through the forests, eating only roots; it was a hard life, but it pleased them greatly, and when people asked them why they were living thus, they would only reply: 'Go where we went, and you will know why.'[1]

To those who had not sat at the Table of the Grail there must have been a sense of bewilderment, even scorn, for a group of people willing to perch inside such a dilapidated ruin as the Grail castle seemed to be, but who seemed so transformed by what they saw. For those who follow the Grail in our own time there is often the same sense of achievement, the same enthusiasm as that felt by the two Welsh knights; but like them, the experience is hard to describe. Many will fall back on obscure imagery and parable, others will simply suggest that other seekers should 'go where we went, and you will know why'.

For the Grail did not suddenly become inaccessible to those who came after; any more than the castle shifted to some hidden location which can be discovered by means of a map reference. The country of the Grail is everywhere around us, and there are many signposts along the way. The Grail Company, formed of all those legion of seekers who have persisted in the Quest down the ages, is here among us, in the world. Its members are just as likely to be ordinary individuals as intensely mystical personalities from some high-powered esoteric order. The country of the Grail has stretched to encompass cities and indeed countries far beyond Britain, and the Grail table is nowadays grown vast – pilgrims arrive from every quarter to seek a place there.

There are as many possible paths to the Grail as there are roads to Rome, and every one of them is valid. Arthur may well have been a Christian king, though this is by no means certain, but he remained aware that his realm held other beliefs and traditions which could help strengthen the common purpose of the Round Table. When we sit at the Table of the Grail, or enter the castle of the Fisher King, who is Arthur's spiritual representative within Britain, we are similarly aware that around us are seated many who are not native to this land.

*   *   *   *   *

From their experience came new ideas, strengthening the purpose of all who begin the Quest with their initiative and active participation. It begins to dawn upon us that there is a freemasonry among those on the

Quest, just as there is among those who pursue the mystical path in all traditions. The Grail myths offer a common language, a mode of consciousness, almost a secret sign which can be read and recognised by all who are similarly engaged on the Quest.

We must not make the mistake of seeing the Grail as just a charming medieval legend, any more than as a relic to be sought by treasure hunters. You will indeed find many descriptions of the Grail in this book: as chalice or stone, dish or womb; as a cup from which each individual life receives nourishment, or as a witness to the beliefs of immemorial traditions. For some it is only one of many vessels; for others it has no real existence at all but serves rather as a numinous idea that shapes itself at will to the needs of the individual. To still others it is part of an ongoing process of transformation: an alchemical dream of the soul on its quest for human evolution or oneness with God.

Yet much as these views differ, they are at one in their belief in the companionship of Grail, perceiving it as a gateway to the interior life, the inner journey we must all travel to its end, beset by danger and doubt, fear and loss, strengthened by triumph and love, light and goodness.

You may learn much from these pages, yet if you learn nothing more than to recognise the Grail within your own being, you will have discovered a truth that will never desert you, one that will shine forth on the path before you and show you a way to self-realisation. No one who sets forth on the Grail Quest remains unchanged, and no one who reads this book with an open mind and heart will fail to see the patterns that form and dissolve again with each new definition, with each succeeding evaluation of the matter of the Grail. Echoes will be heard, perhaps distant at first, but growing clearer with each reading, until finally the Grail's message to each of us will resonate clearly through the chambers of the soul.

These essays are all written by people dedicated to the Inner Journey, seen from many different points along the way. Maybe as you read you will begin to recognise ideas long since learned and forgotten. This may be your way into the landscape of the Grail. Once there, you can only return with new insights into your own state of being, truths that will make life seem larger and more fulfilling than ever before; for on this journey, you are seeking absolutes.

*   *   *   *   *

It is nearly two decades since I first put together the first of two collections of essays: *At the Table of the Grail* (Routledge & Kegan Paul, 1984) followed by *The Household of the Grail* (Thorsons, 1990). The present volume is drawn in part from these, with the addition of several new essays written for various conferences and collections. 'The Rose and the Grail' was delivered at the extraordinary conference on the Rosicrucian Enlightenment, held at Cesky Krumlov in the Czech Republic in 1995; and 'David Jones and the Arthuriad' was delivered at the Temenos Academy in London in 1998. Caitlín Matthews' essay 'The Rosicrucian Vault & the Quest for the Grail' first appeared, under a slightly different title, as an appendix to *The Underworld Initiation* by R.J. Stewart. (Thorsons, 1985). On looking back at these writings, both my own and those of the group of people who contributed to the original volumes and who readily gave permission for their work to be reprinted in this new edition, I see that we were, indeed, a kind of Household of the Grail, each of whom, in their own way were, and of course still are, seeking a great truth. I am very glad to be able to bring these writings to a new audience, who like us may wish to 'go where we went', on our own journeys into the country of the Grail.

John Matthews
Oxford, 2002

1 *The High Book of the Holy Grail*, trans. N. Bryant, Brewer/Rowman & Littlefield, 1978, pp. 264–5.

PART ONE:

THE FIRST STORY TELLERS

The Voices of the Wells Celtic Oral Themes in Grail Literature

Caitlín Matthews

The beginnings of the Grail myths lie fairly and squarely in Celtic tradition, predating the more familiar Christian sources by several centuries. Most of these lie in oral rather than written traditions, and express the wisdom and knowledge of a legion of forgotten story-tellers and poets who, nonetheless, should be remembered for having kept the stories of the Grail alive during the dark days following the departure of the hero Arthur from the pages of history. In the essay which follows here Caitlín Matthews charts the course of these elusive, and often fragmentary scraps of lore and establishes their reappearance in later, Medieval texts, where they shine forth like rough-cut gems amid the highly polished pages of Arthurian literature and legend.

The Blessing of the Wandering Voice

In the dark green forests of the north-west seaboard of Europe, somewhere between the worlds of Imperial and Holy Rome, a story was forged. It was blent of precious ores hoarded since the world was begun, hammered into shape by the tongues of tribal and wandering story-tellers and delivered into the hands of Continental romancers, who wielded it to great effect. Whenever I open the pages of any medieval Grail romance, I am always hearing the distant hammering of those nameless story-tellers in their forge of song.

Our inability to name or identify specific story-tellers in the evasive network of oral tradition is frustrating, though hardly surprising. Though we know little enough about the early European romancers, we do at least have their names and can locate with some accuracy both their patrons and fields of influence. The feudal and regnal systems of medieval Europe give us a known framework into which these early writers fit with reasonable ease. Of the nameless story-tellers who brought the Grail legends in their earliest forms, we are less certain, though not from lack of evidence so much as from our inability to assimilate the nature of the oral tradition itself and the society in which it operated.

Our contemporary vaunting of the written word is partly at fault, for we have been educated to believe that books represent the prime instrument of civilization. Pre-literate peoples are not lacking in enriching culture, historical records or considerable bodies of traditional lore. The memory of an average pre-literate person is several times more developed than that of a literate person. Pre-literate societies inevitably boast a specific class of people specializing in the art of memory, and who frequently combine shamanic skills as part of their training.

The specialist in Celtic countries was the bard or *fili* whose 12-year training empowered him to memorize and tell over 350 stories, each of which might take several nights in the telling. In addition to this mind-stretching oral library, the bard was skilled in complex poetic forms, able at will to compose in any given metre and scansion, poems of praise or reproof whose magical effects made him a man to both fear and revere.[1] Celtic society fully supported such bards for very good reasons; they were the living memory of the tribe, of laws, precedents, genealogies and the wisdom of the ancestors. Such men were as far removed from the modern Arts Council supported poet as it is possible to imagine, for the Celtic bard was essential to the ordering of life, being mystically attuned to the processes of the Otherworld by virtue of his training.

Becoming the living memory of his people brought the bard the Otherworld. This was likewise the realm of the gods and other spiritual beings. With such knowledge in his head, the bard was attuned to the workings of the Otherworld whence his poetic and musical powers were likewise thought to derive.

The mystical *baraka* – the transmission of spiritual blessing – which happens in the presence of such attuned people is something which literary critics rarely deign to speak of. The indefinable translation of being which occurs when one sits in the presence of such artists is of course widely sought after in the field of media and general entertainment, where people will pay thousands of pounds to be present at a performance of their favourite opera singer, ballet dancer or actress. The barriers of perception are down and the heart is open to receive the full force of 'art'.

But what is this 'art'? Is it not nearer in nature to the *darshan* experienced in the presence of holy people? This is the real immediacy of the oral tradition, in which complex images and symbolisms are imparted by the combination of voice and body in a way which cannot be identically repeated because it is not merely performance but the shamanic sharing of vision.[2]

We may instance the manner in which spiritual teachings are imparted in Tibetan Buddhism, whereby even the audition of a spiritual text brings merit to the hearer, and where specific empowering initiations are imparted by a spiritual teacher to a pupil by means of oral exposition.

The oral tradition needs its living memories, the poets and story-tellers, but it also needs listeners in whose minds and hearts the symbols and images of the story are recreated. To this extent, pre-literate societies win out over ours, for the modern literate person is almost entirely symbolically illiterate or symbolically impoverished.

In this manner, bards supported themselves by noble patronage for many generations. But the structure of Celtic society suffered innumerable knocks. In Britain, the Roman colonization, followed by Saxon and Norman invasion, brought the Celtic framework toppling down. In Ireland, bards remained in full activity until the Norman colonization in the twelfth century, after which the long historical round of invasion and cultural repression brought the exponents of the living Celtic memory to virtual vagrancy.[3] However, such great learning, the fruits of memory, did not merely disappear; it was caught up, recognizably harmonious with existent native traditions in Europe, particularly Brittany, and grafted onto the Matter of Britain.

The oral tradition of the Celtic people has been an enduring one. Even up until the last century, traditional *seanchais* were telling folk-stories which still bore the traces of the proto-Grail legend within them.[4] It is now, sadly, a dying tradition. What centuries of oral memory have preserved, television and state education have eroded. The struggle of one such traditional Irish story-teller, Sean O Conaill, to retain his memory's store is recorded in *Celtic Heritage*:

> Lest he should lose command over the tales he loved, he used to repeat them aloud when he thought no one was near, using the gesticulations and the emphasis, and all the tricks of narration, as if he were once again the centre of a fireside storytelling. His son, Pats, told me that he had seen his father thus engaged, telling his tales to an unresponsive stone wall, while herding the grazing cattle. On returning from market, as he walked slowly up the hills behind his old grey mare, he could be heard declaiming his tales to the back of the cart.[5]

This is a far cry from the kind of rapt attention which Sean O Conaill's forebears enjoyed:

> The fair company gave ear to the Lay of Alys, sweetly sung by a minstrel from Ireland, to the music of his rote. When his story was ended, forthwith he commenced another, and related the Lay of Orpheus; *none being so bold as to disturb the singer, or to let his mind wander from the song.*[6] (My italics.)

This passage comes from Marie de France's *Lay of the Thorn*, written in the mid-twelfth century, probably somewhere in England at the court of Henry II. Apart from the internal evidence that the said minstrel was performing from memory and was thus part of the enduring oral tradition, this story suggests a cultural interface with which we are perhaps unfamiliar.

The Middle Ages are often thought of as hidebound, culturally insular and intellectually naïve. This proves to be far from the case, for though the land-bound peasant was a virtual slave of the land, there was considerable movement of people and ideas from region to region. Clerics, craftsmen and courts were as well-travelled as the average modern tourist, describing a well-trodden route between abbey, cathedral and European city. The expansionist dynasties of medieval Europe, particularly that of the Plantagenets, began to connect regions as far distant as Ireland and Provence, so that it would have been quite possible for an Irish minstrel to be present at an English or even French court and be understood in the *lingua franca* of the time – Anglo – or Norman-French.[7]

The *lai*, so familiar from French romance, has another origin entirely. The word *lay* itself derives from the Irish word for song, *laoidh*. When the Irish wish to express that a person has no evidence whatever to support his case, they use the expression *ní laoidh ná litir* – he has 'neither song nor letter' – which may indicate the original force of the spoken word, considered to be of equal value as the written word. Yet the *lai* was almost entirely imported from Ireland into France via Brittany.

There is little doubt that the key Celtic nation in the transmission of the proto-Grail stories was Brittany. Armorica had already started to be colonized by Britons in the troubled times even before the Roman withdrawal from Britain. The troops of Magnus Maximus had already been given grants of land there some years previously. Brittany, or Little Britain, as it became, was one of the chief repositories for stories about King Arthur. The memory of the exiled is generally strong, and so it was with the Bretons who preserved the core of the Matter of Britain so ardently that, after becoming proficient in French, they transmitted Arthurian tales into French romance.

In many ways, the Norman Invasion of 1066 was, for some Bretons, a strange homecoming or kind of reconquest, for many of William of Normandy's knights were Breton and they doubtless brought with them their household, including story-tellers. Once the Norman dynasty was established in Britain, tales of Arthur began to percolate back to Brittany and France.

The name of but one oral story-teller remains: Master Bleheris, variously referred to by the romancers as Blihos, Bliheris, Blihis, Bledhericus or Bledri. Medieval manuscripts are littered with what might be called 'literary coathooks', – supposed learned sources, fabricated 'old books' and legendary story-tellers which give the writer his literary justification. Master Bleheris may well prove to be one such coathook, though there is a sufficiently large amount of evidence to posit otherwise.

The second continuator of Chrétien de Troyes' *Conte del Graal* speaks of his literacy authority as a certain Bleheris 'who was born and reared in Wales ... and told it to the Count of Poitiers, who loved the story, and held it more than any other firmly in memory'.[8] Many attempts have been made to date this character by establishing just which Count of Poitiers was intended. It has been proved that the earliest French references to Tristan occur in the works of Cercamon and Bernard de Ventadour, both attached to the court of Poitiers in the 1150s.[9] This evidence may lead us to suppose that Bleheris did visit the court at Poitiers or briefly enjoyed the patronage of the Count and that he had a command of Norman-French.

Gerald of Wales in his *Description of Wales* likewise refers to a 'Bledri, the well-known story-teller, who lived a little before our time'.[10] Since Gerald was writing in 1188, we may conclude that Bleheris or Bledri flourished some time in the early 1100s.

But Master Bleheris turns up again, this time as a protagonist in *L'Elucidation*, an early thirteenth-century prequel to the *Conte del Graal* (though in fact written about 40 years after Chrétien's book). In this illuminating text, wherein we are told an alternative story about the origins of the wasteland, the Round Table Knights fight a group of knights found wandering in the forest, guarding certain maidens. They capture one of the company, Blihos Bliheris, who yields himself to Arthur: 'but right good stories he knew, such as that none could ever be aweary of hearkening to his words'. He relates the history of his company, telling how they are destined to wander the world until the finding of the Courts of Joy.[11]

L'Elucidation begins interestingly:

> Here worshipfully beginneth a Romance of the most delightsome story that may be, to wit, the story of the Grail, the secret whereof may no man tell in prose nor rhyme, for such a thing might the story turn out to be before it were all told that every man might be grieved thereof albeit he had in nowise misdone. Wherefore it is that the wise man leaveth it aside and doth simply pass on beyond, for, and Master Blihis lie not, the secret should no man tell.[12]

Truly this ill-named text, rather than shedding illumination upon the inner meaning of the Grail, merely strives, to obscure it even further. While Bleheris' appearance in *L'Elucidation* is obviously a literary device to lend the authenticity of a proven story-teller, we must ask, what status Bleheris held during the preceding twelfth century to be accorded such a key appearance here. For Blihos tells the Round Table Knights about the adventures which those who seek the Grail may find, and therefore initiates the quest.

Perhaps the answer lies in Blihos' own words:

> (we) all shall journey in common, and the damsels in likewise that wander at large through this country by forest and field behoveth it thus to fare until such time as God shall give them to find the Court from whence shall come the joy whereby the land shall again be made bright.[13]

The knights and damsels in whose company Blihos wanders are the descendants of the Otherworldly Damsels of the Wells who once used to serve all travellers with the food they most desired, in the manner of Irish *beansidhes*, the women of the Faery Host. King Amangons, in an age long before Arthur's, raped one of the damsels and stole her golden cup. His followers likewise raped the other damsels, until they no longer served at the wells. The text tells us that in the land of Britain 'they lost the voices of the wells and the damsels that were therein'.

Although there are other mystical analogues to this text, which I have discussed elsewhere,[14] it would seem that here we discover the true Household of the Grail. The story-tellers such as Blihos are the wandering 'voices of the wells', for they tell the story of the Grail's secret – neither in prose nor verse, as the text says, but in their own lives. They are the true memory of the Grail, these wanderers, telling no-one its secrets but implanting the seeds of the quest in the hearts of their hearers.

This is the function of the oral tradition: that the speaker should impart the story's *baraka*, the spiritual transmission of power, to the hearer who should become empowered by the story. As long as the traditional form is preserved, the *baraka* cannot be diffused, but lies dormant even in the mind of an ignorant story-teller. It needs only one hearer attuned to the story to realize the empowerment of the Grail legends anew for that transmission to become activated.

Bleheris is perhaps one of many such story-tellers who stand between the transition from oral to literary tradition. He is one of the very last story-tellers personally to enthuse his hearers in this way.

There are numerous witnesses to the fact that this *baraka* was passed to auditors of the Matter of Britain during the Middle Ages. Peter of Blois speaks of how *histriones*, by which he means wandering players, moved people to tears by their retellings of Arthur, Tristan and Gawain. St Ailred of Rievaulx, no less, reproaches himself, remembering how, as a novice, he could work himself up into considerable emotion over stories about Arthur, but could hardly shed a tear when reading the scriptures.[15]

The exponents of the oral tradition are, perhaps mercifully, beyond the reach of literary biographers who would psychoanalyse their lives and motives to come to definitive criticisms of their *oeuvre*. In attempting to discover the original or proto-Grail story, we can only be aware of underlying Celtic themes, not of authorly motives. The oral tradition is remarkably conservative, since successful transmission of tradition depends on accurate memory. This is why the transcriptions of Celtic stories from Ireland and Wales in the Middle Ages can be regarded as authentically ancient for, while they may only have been written down in the thirteenth and fourteenth centuries, the story-teller behind the transcriber was in receipt of a lineage of oral transmission which was unbroken. If variations creep in, it is usually at this point; the transcriber has less scruples about tampering with the story than the story-teller.

Thus, even within the complex *entrelacements* of medieval literary Grail texts, we may discern echoes of the forge of song in the images of Grail, quest and hero, in the descriptions of the Otherwordly Grail Castle, Faery opponents and supernatural wonders. How these ancient attributes of oral tradition voyaged to the shores of literary tradition is an interesting speculation.

The Matter of Britain was the chief vessel in which the Grail legends came to French shores. Within its hold, a host of stories, ideas and influences came to shelter, further enriching the Arthurian tradition beyond the wildest dreams of the first tellers.

The Saving Story

Every tradition has its own salvific or saving story. Psychoanalysis has discovered this and works on discovering and applying the indwelling saving story to its clients. Religion consciously operates along the lines of a sacred story to live by. The entire TV soap industry attempts to provide the same service, though with considerably less success. Story-tellers have always known about the sustaining quality of the story, none more so than the guardians of Grail story. The Grail is at once a potent symbol of transformation, a catalyst or touchstone of the emerging cultural blend of the Middle Ages; it is also the mythic corollary of timeless spiritual aspiration.

The fertile waters of the oral tradition are the medium of mystical concepts. 'We see by means of water,' says Wolfram von Eschenbach in Chapter 16 of his *Parzival*.[16] And it is only by crossing the waters which lie between us and the Otherworldly realms of the Grail Castle, by allowing the Grail story to work so upon our hearts that our eyes shed the cleansing tears which bring illumination to our inner sight, that we perceive the Holy Vessel.

We are driven to ask: What kind of spiritual empowerment or validation lies behind the Grail? How was it perceived by those who listened to the stories? Was the Grail originally central to native spirituality? There is clearly more to the story than a collection of Celtic cauldrons, transmogrified into celestial vessels. There is obviously more to the story than a straight parallel of the Christian redemption myth.[17]

The spiritual centre of Celtic society is the earthly paradise of the Otherworld, sometimes depicted as the Blessed Isle of the West, to which people sail never to return. It is a place of perpetual joy, where life wells up eternally. It is a place of empowerment, where the ancestral memories are accessible.

In the ancient Irish story of *Cormac's Adventures in the Otherworld,* Cormac mac Airt is miraculously transported to a marvellous fortress made of bronze beams, with wattles of silver and a thatch of bird's wings.

> Then he saw in the enclosure a shining fountain, with five streams flowing out of it, and the hosts in turn drinking the water. Nine hazels of Buan grew over the well. The purple hazels dropped their nuts into the fountain and sent their husks floating down the streams. Now the sound of the falling of those streams was more melodious than any music that men sing.[18]

He is later told by Manannan, the god of the Otherworld that he has seen the Fountain of Knowledge, and that the five streams are the five senses through which knowledge is obtained. Whoever does not drink the fountain or the streams will never have knowledge. And he says, 'The *folk of many arts* are those who drink them both.' He refers to the *aos daoine* – the gifted people, the poets and visionaries, who interpret the Otherworld to the created world. And it is such folk who are moved to find the Grail and bring its healing waters to the world through the medium of the story.

This story takes us directly into the Celtic Otherworld whose reality is timeless, accessible now as then by means of our imaginal involvement with the things eternal. The Celtic Otherworld is full of beauty, the primal pleasures of the earthly paradise. Here everything is complete, whole and perfect.

This wonderful image of the fountain which flows from the Otherworld into our own imaginal realms shows us the spiritual power of the talismanic symbol to bridge the worlds.

The Grail itself is such a symbol. But in the Celtic world it is one among many. The concept of the Hallows – the holy empowering objects of spiritual and earthly sovereignty – encompasses several such talismans.[19]

The cauldron sought by Arthur in the ninth-century British poem *Preiddeu Annwn* is but one among many Hallows which are found in British and Arthurian tradition.[20] The Thirteen Treasures of Britain, supposedly guarded now by Merlin in his Otherworldly observatory, form part of our native tradition.[21] The Irish preserve a similar tradition of treasures, which are kept in the Crane-Bag of Manannan mac Lir.[22]

The Tuatha de Danaan, the ancient gods of Ireland, brought with them four such symbols from the four mysterious cities from which they derived their strength. Since the Danaans themselves appear as gods within Irish tradition, we must struggle imaginatively to picture the kind of realms from which they bring symbols of even greater power:

the Sword of Nuada from Findias given by Uscias;
the Spear of Lugh from Gorias given by Esras;
the Cauldron of the Dagda from Murias, given by Semias;
the Lia Fail from Falias, given by Morfessa.[23]

Each of these great symbols has its intrinsic virtue: the sword deals certain death to whomever it wounds; the spear brings victory to whomever bears it; the cauldron satisfies all who eat of it; while the Lia Fail screams under a rightful king. Each of these Celtic Hallows has its equivalent in the Grail legends, where the sword is that carried by the Grail-winner. (Galahad pulls such a sword from a floating stone where other knights have failed, in likeness of Arthur's exploit with Excalibur.[24]) The spear's analogue is found in the spear which causes the Dolorous Stroke by which the Fisher king and the Land are simultaneously devastated.[25] The cauldron's bounty is transmuted into the abundant blessing of the Grail itself; while the Lia Fail, the stone of kingly inauguration, becomes the Siège Perilous – the seat at the Round Table which is strictly reserved for the destined Grail-winner and in which Perceval sits in presumptious and untimely haste.[26]

What other analogues of the Grail do we find in Celtic tradition? We cannot detail every cauldron or vessel from British and Irish tradition, for they are too numerous. But we can look at the properties of a few.

The cauldron of Ceridwen was to have brewed a draft of wisdom intended for her son, Afagddu (Darkness). However, Gwion Bach, set to stir the cauldron, accidentally splashed some of the fluid on his fingers and, thrusting them into his mouth, received enlightenment. After a long totemic chase, he was reborn of Ceridwen's womb as Taliesin, the great poet. She cast him on the waters in a basket and he was discovered in a salmon weir.[27]

The image of the salmon is paramount in Celtic tradition. It is a beast of everlastingness and of greatest wisdom, and it figures in many myths as the oldest animal who remembers things from the beginning of time. The salmon which swims in Conla's Well eats the hazel-nuts of knowledge. In another tale it is told how Fionn mac Cumhail helped catch and cook this very salmon for his Druidic master but, as in the story of Taliesin, Fionn alone was the recipient of the wisdom intended for another.[28] Both Taliesin and Fionn are initiates of wisdom who share the omniscience of the salmon.

The cauldron of Bran is, on the other hand, a vessel of rebirth. In the tragic British tale of Branwen, Daughter of Llyr, we read how the cauldron originally came from Ireland and that it had a singular property. Dead warriors who were put into it could be revived. However, they were subsequently unable to speak, for it is only the initiate who sees the Otherworld and can speak of it – but then only in the riddling tongue of poets which only other initiates can comprehend.[29] From Bran's terrible journey to Ireland to rescue his sister, Branwen, only seven return. Bran, mortally wounded, instructs his followers to cut off his head and bury it under the White Mount (the site of the present Tower of London). On route, they sojourn in an Otherworldly hall, forever feasting and enjoying the conversation of Bran, whose head regales his followers so brilliantly that they fail to notice the passage of time until one opens a forbidden door and remembrance of mortality falls upon them. As one who entertained his company for 87 years, Bran the Blessed can perhaps be lauded as the patron of all story-tellers.

The brilliant ninth-century poem *Preiddeu Annwn* (or *The Spoils of Annwn*) contains one of the earliest textual references to Arthur.[30] It incidentally provides us with his association with the prototype of the Grail – the cauldron. The cauldron for which Arthur goes in search in the *Preiddeu Annwn* is owned by Diwrnach. It boils a brew fit only for heroes; it will not boil the meat of a coward. This vessel is related to the Celtic tradition of the hero's portion – the cut of meat reserved for the most worthy warrior of the tribe. Arthur descends into the Underworld

of Annwn on his ship Prydwen on an *immram* (wondrous voyage) of
the great peril. As on Bran's journey to Ireland, only seven return to
speak of their adventures; Taliesin, the great poet, is significantly
present on both Arthur's and Bran's journey to make report. Arthur is
here shown to be the earliest Grail-winner, a long way in advance of
Peredur (Perceval) or Galahad, whose stories are not recorded until the
twelfth and fourteenth centuries.

So then, the cauldrons of Celtic tradition have one of the following
properties:

> they give rebirth;
> they bring initiation into wisdom;
> they give plenty.

The idea of nourishment, of fertility, whether of land or of spirit, is at
the heart of the Grail story.

These three qualities are retained by the Celtic cauldron's Christian
analogue, the Grail, but before we pass on, let us note that we stand
here at the heart of Celtic spirituality. The Celtic proto-story of the
cauldron, like that of the Grail, is about finding wisdom in the
uncreated world, in ways that have an effect on the created world itself.
The waters of life which well up, whether from Otherworldly springs or
magical cauldrons, are only achieved by those who are most worthy –
by the gifted people who have made wisdom their study, or by those
innocents who already have their steps set upon the path unknowingly.
They drink from these vessels and are conveyed to another dimension;
they enter into communion with the Otherworld. This is the ultimate
Celtic spiritual vision.

This sense of Otherworldly communion is seldom absent from the
medieval Grail legends. Faery women, white stags, lonely hermits of
great wisdom – all derived from the Celtic Otherworld tradition –
throng the medieval stories. If we strip away the Christian accretions
which make the Grail the Cup of the Last Supper and the Grail hero
a second Christ, we are left with a hero in search of an Otherworldly
treasure which will empower, in different combinations, himself, his
king or his land.

If we look at the medieval Christian manifestations of the Grail we
find that it has the following properties:

it gives the food most desired;
it restores the Wasteland and the Wounded King;
it empowers its finder with the spiritual gnosis.

These exact qualities are identical to the effects of the Celtic cauldrons, which gave plenteous nourishment, rebirth and wisdom. Like the Celtic vessels, the Christian Grail is only achieved by the most worthy: those who have pursued wisdom with great and urgent simplicity.

Between the earliest of our literary sources (the ninth-century poem about Arthur's raid on Annwn) and the achieved Grail stories of the Middle Ages, there is a significant and quite mysterious gap; for between these two traditions we pass from the pagan Celtic Otherworld to an apocryphal Christian alter native to the gospels. By what means does this transformation come about?

We are so used to looking at the Grail legends from the point of view of a Christian allegory that we are perhaps blinded to the cohesive nature of the oral tradition which incorporated both the old and the new into its vision. The Otherworld still held sway in the imaginations and hearts of many well on into the Christian era. It takes a considerably long time for old tribal and ancestral beliefs to become totally super-seded by the new – a fact which St Gregory the Great exhorted his missionaries to Britain to be aware of lest 'by scraping off the rust from the vessel they shatter it'.[31] Although we think of missionaries as zealots eager to purge old beliefs, in practice things were more organically integrated. The old customs of well-dressing, the sacred festivals of pagan deities and the elemental spirits of the land were gradually incor-porated into the local usages of Christianity.

The founding of Christianity upon certain elements within the Druidic tradition is one which has been perpetually remarked upon. Certainly the manner in which Christianity was rapidly assimilated suggests that the ground was fertile. However, it is not possible to assimilate fully any new spiritual tradition in one generation; it takes very many for spiritual consciousness to operate with the new symbols, characters and images. The first-century Christian apologist, St Clement of Alexandria, in order to acquaint an Hellenic audience with the Christian message, metaphorically described Christ as Odysseus strapped to the mast of the barque of the Church to avoid the cries of Scylla and Charybdis.[32] Likewise, the *Dream of the Rood* speaks of Christ as the young hero who stripped himself to mount the tree, like Odin, a concept familiar to Saxon listeners.[33]

There is no doubt that, at one level, the Grail legends typify the syncretic links between traditions which enabled Britons to accept the gospels more readily though this was not the sole purpose of the Grail tradition. The Grail legends were not at first conceived of as Christian documents or alternative mystical parables. They were told as part of the Matter of Britain – the Arthurian Legends – part of an ongoing and vast cycle of stories which it was a story-teller's duty to recite to his patron. The romancers certainly knew a salvific story when they came across one and certain analogies were obviously drawn. We are looking at the unconscious construction of an apocryphal Christian tradition into which certain native British strands are woven. People were more readily moved by the stories of their king and his heroes undergoing purgative quests amid the ancestral forests of home then they were to hear about the alien ramblings of foreign saints.

We should bear in mind that, though Europe was nominally Christian by the Middle Ages, the consciousness of the people had older mythic archetypes embedded within them, for, in the hearts and minds of the people, it was the old characters who held sway. In this way Arthur passed from military commander – whether as Romano-British *Dux Britanniarum* or as proto-Celtic war-leader – into a semi-deified state, becoming the sleeping Lord, the land's protector for all time. People likewise looked to the sustaining myths and stories of their ancestors; it was a skilful story-teller who knew how to weave the old gods and heroes into saints and martyrs of Christian tradition. This long looking over the shoulder to the eaves of the Otherworld was productive when it came to the retelling of the sacred vessel which heals, and gives life and empowerment to the chosen tribal representative.

From many of the Celtic pagan elements, and from an assured story-telling tradition, the first fires of the literary Grail were kindled. In the finely wrought pages of the medieval texts, some primal features of Celtic tradition emerge, giving tantalizing glimpses of themes and stories once commonly circulating but now voiceless. If we look at some of the medieval Grail texts, we frequently discern the vigorous voice of the Celtic story-teller.

The organic enfolding of Grail literature was primarily dictated by the audience which, during the early Middle Ages, was still largely a pre-literate one, used to hearing oral stories, not literary ones. But the audience was no longer a native one: the travelling story-tellers must have quite consciously adapted some parts of their telling for courtly audiences, just as Chrétien de Troyes continually admits to doing in the retelling of his romances. The raw material which the Grail writers worked from included a British story concerning the hero, Peredur, who achieves fame by his prodigious deeds in the service of King Arthur; he was later woven more intimately into the prevailing Christian tapestry. Peredur (and the proto-heroes before him) is shown to be akin to the Celtic archetype of the *Amadan Mor,* the Great Fool, a character whose quest is still central to the Gaelic folk tradition.[34]

Peredur is the earliest British literary Grail story. It is a story which had been exported from Britain, translated into French and reimported into Britain, where it was retranslated into Welsh and where it may or may not have been interwoven once more with extant oral sources.[35] It follows a similar shape to that of Chrétien's *Conte del Graal,* but *Peredur* betrays a far more pagan origin, and makes no association between the Grail and vessel of the Crucifixion. Indeed, it has been proved that *Peredur* contains elements of a far older tradition, incorporating such Celtic elements as the spear which drips blood, the head in the dish (which serves as the holy vessel in this story) and the hero's search for the empowerment of the Goddess of the Land, Lady Sovereignty.

I have written extensively elsewhere about this powerful figure who stands at the epicentre not only of the Grail legends but also of the Matter of Britain.[36] Within a society which saw a devolution of both women and female archetypes, it is not surprising that the strong female characters of Celtic tradition should have been diluted and diffused into more and more minor characters within the Grail legend. The Grail knights are frequently faced with challenges in which they must defend a defenceless woman or restore her to her rightful place. In these multi-plications of wronged virgins, mourning widows and dispossessed wives, we can yet discern the features of the Goddess and her represen-tatives. This mighty figure was one of the great deities of the Celtic peoples who continually looked back to her as the ancestress of their tribe, the preserver of memory and the mother of all people.

The nature of the Celtic clan system is discernible within the subtext of the Grail legends. Both the *Elucidation* and Wolfram's *Parzival* allude to a tradition of Grail guardianship which includes a combative military knighthood or warrior-caste with a complementary priestesshood of women – a royal and holy family which is comprehended in the medieval pun of San Greal/Sang Real (Holy Grail, Holy Blood). Wolfram's Grail is a Stone which has been brought to earth to remain in the guardianship of a Grail lineage (perhaps an analogue of the inaugural stones of a Celtic kingship?). Behind both texts there is a tradition of a sacerdotal caste or royal clan, figured forth as warrior-heroes and empowering priestesses, in whom the blood of memory flows. These potent figures are the mythic analogues of the story-tellers themselves on whose tongues the immortality of the saving story was assured.

The clan was the prime unit of Celtic solidarity. From its extended familial network would have been drawn the *tanaiste*, the candidate king who was appointed as regent before the demise of the king. Royalty, royal-connection, responsibility for the land and its peoples is a major theme running throughout the Grail legends. Similarly, the numerous empowering women who are guardians of the Grail have their root in the primeval matrilineal frameworks of pre-Christian Europe, where the royal woman was the priestess of her tribe, the inter-mediary between the people and the gods.[37]

Of course, one of the major factors underlying the Grail legends is the Wounded King, behind whom we can trace the very roots of Celtic kingship. A blemished man might not hold office since the king must physically embody the health and well-being of the land. A wounded king was demoted and his *tanaiste* appointed during the remainder of his life. This factor is plainly borne out in the Grail hero's champion-ship, for though Perceval finds the Grail, and heals the Wounded King, he usually replaces him as the new Grail guardian.

The Wasteland motif is a universal one which has particular promi-nence in Celtic tradition. The wounds of the Fisher King are really reflections of the enchanted land which is doomed to sterility, through which the healing waters have yet to flow. The Grail hero is called 'the Freer of the Waters', a ritual title which might well have its warrant in Celtic tradition. The hero who goes to the world's end to gain the waters of life is still very much part of Gaelic story-telling.[38]

The Wasteland of the Grail legends is closely paralleled in Celtic tra-dition by the enchantments of the land. This theme reveals that the land has been overlooked by an Otherworldly agency, as it is within the stories of *Manawyddan, Son of Llyr* and *Lludd and Llefelys*, in the *Mabinogion*.[39] In both instances, Manawyddan and Lludd, as wise rulers, must use their skilful wisdom to overcome or subvert these powers. Within *Peredur*, we see the hero battling with several *gormesaid* or plagues – monsters, giants and black wildmen – which he must over-come in order or become a 'Freer of the Waters'.

Peredur shows us also a very Celtic instance of the warrior-woman where Peredur is professionally instructed in the use of arms by the Nine Witches of Gloucester, who act as his foster-mothers in arms. Similarly, Cuchullin is instructed by the warrior-woman Scathach, in the Ulster Cycle.[40]

The Grail romances can also be seen as continuations to the *immrama* – the wondrous voyages to the Otherworld undertaken by Maelduine, Bran mac Febal and St Brendan.[41] All find Otherwordly treasure, wonders and challenges to overcome. The *immram* returns in *The Quest of the Holy Grail* of the Vulgate Cycle where Galahad, Bors and Perceval take the Ship of Solomon to the Otherworldly city of Sarras, there to participate in the mysteries of the Grail.[42] Similarly, in *Perlesvaus*, Perceval goes to a mysterious island, the Island of Ageless Elders, where a band of elderly but youthful sages sit in converse as ancient as that of Bran the Blessed and his company in the timeless bliss of the Otherworld.[43]

In the course of literary transmission, the home of the original Grail story is often visited by the new romance, and so it proves in the *Didot Perceval*, where it is revealed that the Grail Castle is established in Ireland:

> The Fisher King dwells in the island in one of the most beautiful places in the world.[44]

Elements of *Perlesvaus,* perhaps the most Christianized of the Grail texts, reveal a preoccupation with central Celtic themes: with the triple aspect of the Goddess of Sovereignty, the enchantments of the land and the blessed Otherworld.

The further into the Middle Ages we go, the more Christianized the Grail becomes. The writings of Robert de Boron give the Grail its full Christian antecedents with the story of Joseph of Arimathea's guardship of the Grail and his journey to Europe.[45] Until de Boron's *Joseph d'Arimathie*, the Grail story was firmly rooted solely in the Matter of Britain. De Boron's prequel connects the Matter of Britain to a specifically Christian tradition which provides Perceval and later Galahad with saintly ancestors, for Joseph founds a lineage of Grail guardians from whom the Grail-winners spring.

De Boron was quick to pick up on clues from Gnostic and apocryphal scriptural sources concerning Joseph's familiarity with the secrets of Christ. For Joseph is held in prison by Vespasian and fed by the Grail at the same time as receiving guardianship of the vessel and its secrets. And so the story of his coming to Britain and founding a lineage is tacked on to the existing story to form a kind of biblical prequel to the native story. These legends have themselves become inseparable from the ongoing folklore of the Matter of Britain in common consciousness.

When we reach the story of *Perlesvaus*, which is one of the crowning glories of the Grail legends, we find that Perceval has become analogous to Christ himself – a kind of superhero and saviour combined. He is reverently referred to throughout as 'the Good Knight'. This is a long way from his origins as a foolish young Welshman who can mistake knights for angels and catch deer with his bare hands. In this wonderful story the Grail quest becomes a mixture of redemptive pilgrimage and Otherworldly journey. The Matter of Britain has also been incorporated into the myths of Glastonbury in a new way. As the end of *Perlesvaus* relates:

> the Latin text from which this story was set in the vernacular was taken from the Isle of Avalon, from a holy religious house which stands at the edge of the Land of Adventure: there lie King Arthur and the queen, by the testimony of the worthy religious men who dwell there.[46]

Perlesvaus and *The Quest for the Holy Grail* both draw on this blended tradition of Celtic hero turned Christian saviour. But these are late texts, and tastes had changed. Perceval, the original and only Grail-winner, now becomes part of a composite questing company in which, with Bors, he plays second fiddle to Galahad. Malory's *Le Morte d'Arthur* and, more recently, Tennyson's *Idylls of the King* similarly promoted Galahad as the Grail-winner supreme, so that the earlier traditions have become overlaid and forgotten. The Celtic *Amadan Mor* with his innocent ignorance has been replaced by a faultless, Christly hero.

So we are left with an incredible strata of material which now includes native British myth, apocryphal Christian traditions, and the Arthurian legend. This brew is as potent as anything found in the cauldron of Ceridwen. Like any good soup the Grail legends have a basic stock and lots of mixed ingredients. The result is a salvific or redemptive story which has all the nourishment of native spirituality combined with the exotic spice of the Christian legend. The course of the Grail legends fulfils the criteria outlined in the Passover Haggadah, where the story of the Exodus from Egypt, the salvic Jewish myth, is rehearsed for the benefit of the whole company; 'the story must be given life and meaning'.[47]

The Grail legends form, in effect, a native apocryphal gospel in which the native hero stands in the place of Christ. He fulfils the same redemptive role as that of Christ, becoming the One who Frees the Waters. For the waters of life are understood to be chained until the Grail is found and manifest again.

The Otherworldly Celtic story transmutes to its Christian analogue with scarcely an alteration in the original motivation of the hero who is destined to gain the cauldron. He is still one who has an aptitude or predisposition for Otherworldly communion. The cauldron-heroes and Grail-Knights become bridges from this world to the other, allowing the healing influence of the empowering vessel to percolate between the worlds, just as the waters of Conla's Well bring wisdom into our world.

And if we look closely at the composition of the medieval Grail stories, we find that each is concerned with a spiritual obstruction – the waters of life are not reaching the land and its people. By the action of one man and his communion with the Grail, the Wasteland is healed, the Wounded King is made whole and the people once more enjoy spiritual bounty.

The timeless qualities of Grail and cauldron transcend the apparent barriers between Celtic and Christian stories. Both traditions are fundamentally telling the same story, seeking the same spiritual communion. The characters and events may change, but the story never changes. It merely finds new variations, each adapted by the writers, dreamers and visionaries of every generation – the 'gifted people' who hold open doors between the worlds.

It is they who go down to the roots of the world to find the waters of life and bring spiritual nourishment to those who hunger and thirst. That is the task of those Grail-seekers who are also the Walkers-between-the-Worlds.

In the story of 'Branwen Daughter of Llyr', Bran the Blessed, the titanic king of Britain, comes to Ireland to rescue his sister, but his troops cannot pass over the river which obstructs them and which has no bridge. His men come to ask his counsel. He says: 'He who will be chief let him be a bridge.' And he lies down across the river, hurdles are laid over him and his troops pass over his body to the other side.

We have no space to investigate the heroic and sacral manner of Bran's actions but his saying applies to all who go on the quest for the Grail. For they become bridges between the worlds just as Perceval penetrates the dangers of the darkness of Annwn, just as Christ descends into the realms of Sheol in order to overcome death for all time.

For the Grail Knights do not fulfil some pious but personally beneficial action in finding the Grail; they are in the process of becoming channels through which the waters of life may irrigate our world. Having found the Grail, however, they have entered another, holy, dimension. They cannot remain part of the world but are destined to be living bridges to the Otherworld, to Paradise.

Thus, if we look at the evidence of the Grail texts, we find that Galahad, though he seems to die on looking in the Grail in the mystical city of Sarras, is assumed to another state of life. Perceval returns to the world, but remains withdrawn from it as the new Grail guardian, as a kind of Hermit King. In the Celtic stories, Arthur and Bran both enter the Otherworld to find the power of the cauldron. They do not suffer death but remain the undying guardians of the inner realms. Christ dies on the cross but passes to the realms of Sheol to liberate the people of the past; he is resurrected with a promise of life for all ages to come.

The deathless waters flow down through time, ever waiting for new Grail-seekers to find the channels which may open in any generation.

Each generation has its own story-tellers, its band of eager auditors who seek the empowerment of the Grail for their time. Its appearances may differ, but its effect is always the same – spiritual regeneration. It is that most precious of all spiritual treasures, whatever our tradition, our sense of inner belonging. Whatever story causes our blood to quicken, our senses to be revitalized, our hearts or he gladdened *is* our path to the Grail. By aligning with the salvific story we are enabled to embark on our own quest for the waters of life.

The Grail romancers did not lose the secret of the story. They rewove and heightened the tradition, so that the ancient echoes of the 'carpenters of song' sounded once more in melodious harmony:

> And Bron the old placed the vessel in Perceval's keeping between his hands, and from the vessel there came a melody and a secret so precious that it seemed to them that they might be in Paradise with the angels.[48]

And so the story comes full circle, for so does the Celtic Otherworldly well of nine hazels dispense its secrets through the paradisal beauty of its song. From the intertwining of two traditions, the Grail emerges as the most powerful music of the spirit – the overspilling fountain caught by any with open hands for service by any with receptive, loving hearts to remake creation in the likeness of our spiritual home.

We do not know the names of those story-tellers and poets who moved over the face of Europe, promoting the ancient gnosis of the Grail. They are as brilliant as they are nameless. Yet why should we remember the story-teller? It is sufficient that we should remember the story – and what a story, a story whose power was so strong that neither time nor change of faith could condemn it to forgetfulness.

The Grail legends have been remembered because they are not just ancient stories but living myths which feed the spirit. Eternally current, they flow from the nameless sources of the dark forests of Britain and Ireland into the wider confluence of other rivers where the medieval romancers fitted them ready for sea. For the crystal *curragh* of Manannan, erstwhile god of the Blessed Isles, is the same as the Ship of Solomon in which Perceval, Bors and Galahad sail. It bears us to shores and dimensions beyond our beleaguered coastlines to the country of the Grail.

We may be sure that there the original story-tellers sit with those named romancers in the glorious entertainment of the Grail, forever telling and retelling, continuing and amending its never-ending story of wonder.

Notes and References

1 A.&B. Rees, *Celtic Heritage* (London: Thames & Hudson, 1961).
2 F.M. Cornford, *Principium Sapientiae* (Cambridge Univ. Press, 1952, Chap. VI).
3 Daniel Corkery, *The Hidden Ireland* (Dublin: Gill & Macmillan, 1967).
4 J. Curtin *Hero Tales of Ireland* (London: Macmillan, 1894).
5 Rees, p. 211.
6 Marie de France, *Lays*, trans. E. Mason (London: Dent, n.d).
7 The standard of Irish education remained high even after the restrictions and proscriptions upon the language. Irish sailors often spoke Spanish and Arabic in their maritime dealings with the south-western seaboard of Europe and the Mediterranean, while ploughboys and shepherds spoke a Latin and Greek often superior to their English employers in the last

century, having been taught by the descendants of the bards in proscribed hedge-schools. Though there is a tendency for early Arthurian texts to appear in Latin, presumably so transcribed by the only literate people – the clerics – the preferred language of Arthurian texts in the Middle Ages became the vernacular, simply because the audience spoke it.

8 Chrétien de Troyes, *Arthurian Romances* (London: Dent, 1987).

9 R.S. Loomis *Wales and the Arthurian Tradition* (London: Folcroft Library Editions, 1977, p. 193).

10 Gerald of Wales, A *Journey Through Wales,* trans. L. Thorpe (Harmondsworth: Penguin, 1978, p. 252.)

11 Evans, S., *In Quest of the Holy Grail* (London: Dent, 1898).

12 Ibid., p. 99.

13 Ibid., p. 105.

14 C. Matthews, *Arthur and the Sovereignty of Britain: King and Goddess in the Mabinogion* (London: Arkana, 1989).

15 R.S. Loomis, *Arthurian Tradition and Chrétien de Troyes* (New York: Columbia Univ. Press, 1949, p. 17).

16 Wolfram von Eschenbach, *Parzival,* trans. A. Hatto (Harmondsworth: Penguin, 1988).

17 I use the word 'myth' with respect, denoting 'a powerful salvific story grounded in ancestral memory'.

18 T.P. Cross & C.H. Slover, *Ancient Irish Tales,* (Dublin: Figgis, 1936, pp. 504–5).

19 A fuller exposition of the Hallows can be found in *The Arthurian Tarot: a Hallowquest* (Wellingborough: Aquarian Press, 1990).

20 Loomis (1977), op. cit., p. 131.

21 *Trioedd Ynys Prydein,* ed. R. Bromwich (Cardiff: Univ. of Wales Press, 1961 p. 241).

22 P.B. Ellis *A Dictionary of Irish Mythology* (London: Constable, 1987).

23 Cross, op. cit., p. 11.

24 Sir Thomas Malory, *Le Morte d'Arthur* (New York: University Books, 1961, Book 13, Chap. 3).

25 Ibid., Book 2, Chap. 15.

26 *Didot Perceval,* trans. D. Skeels (Seattle: Univ. of Washington, 1966, p. 13).

27 *The Mabinogion,* trans. Lady C. Guest (London: Ballantyne Press).

28 D. ó Hógáin, *Fionn Mac Cumhail* (Dublin: Gill & Macmillan, 1988).

29 *Mabinogion,* op. cit.

30 C. Matthews, *Mabon and the Mysteries of Britain* (London: Arkana, 1987, p. 107ff.).

31 Rule of St Benedict, n.d.

32 *Clement of Alexandria,* trans. G.W. Butterworth (London: Heinemann, 1968, p. 253).

33 C.W. Kennedy, *Early English Christian Poetry* (London: Hollis & Carter, 1952).

34 R.S. Loomis, *The Development of Arthurian Romance* (New York: Norton & Co, 1963).

35 *The Mabinogion,* op. cit.

36 C. Matthews *Arthur* and *the Sovereignty of Britain,* op. cit.

37 Ibid., p. 14.

38 Ibid., pp. 187–97.

39 *The Mabinogion,* op. cit.

40 Cross, op. cit., p. 162ff.

41 Lady A. Gregory, *The Voyages of St Brendan the Navigator* (Gerrard's Cross: Colin Smythe, 1973).

42 *The Quest of the Holy Grail,* trans. P. Matarasso (Harmondsworth: Penguin, 1969).

43 *The High Book of the Grail,* trans. N. Bryant (Cambridge: D.S. Brewer, 1978).

44 *Didot Perceval,* op. cit., p. 6.

45 Robert de Boron in *Medieval Narratives,* trans. M. Schlauch (New York: Gordian Press, 1969).

46 *High Book of the Grail,* op. cit., p. 265.

47 *A Passover Haggadah,* ed. H. Bronstein (Harmondsworth: Penguin, 1974, p. 32).

48 *Didot Perceval,* op. cit., p. 68.

~ 2 ~

Chrétien de Troyes and The Cauldron of Story

Diana L. Paxson

Chrétien de Troyes wrote his Contes del Graal in approximately 1208. It is the first written account of the Grail we possess. Chrétien wrote for a sophisticated audience who liked a good story with plenty of action, some love-interest and perhaps a pinch of religion. In other words, he was writing very much what we would nowadays call a novel. But Chrétien's work is not a novel. It is a poem. And, although it possesses all the qualities listed above, it is not typical of its time. Also, it was left unfinished, and thereby began one of the most extraordinary trails devised by the imagination of man.

Four other authors tried to continue where Chrétien had left off, with varying degrees of success. But the way remained open, and it still is.

Diana Paxson looks at the Contes del Graal with the eyes of a story-teller in her own right, and finds new things within it. Her essay shows us something we may have forgotten about Chrétien – that he wrote about 'something that must be experienced, not heard'. What Chrétien gives us still is just that – an experience that is not easily forgotten, the first, in all probability, of many, on what may well become an ongoing, personal search.

I want to tell you a story, '… the best tale ever told in any royal court.'[1] That is what Chrétien de Troyes, writing at the end of the twelfth century, called Le Conte del Graal, and he had good reason to know.

It is the story of a boy brought up (like most of us) in ignorance of his true heritage who one day sees something wonderful and goes after it. He has many adventures along the way, although none of his deeds turns out quite as he expected, for each achievement only serves to show him that there is more to learn. Finally he encounters something so remarkable that he does not even have the words to ask what it means, and so it is withdrawn from him, and he spends the rest of his life trying to find it again.

This, broadly outlined, is the story of Perceval. It could also be the story of many of the academics who have spent their lives trying to discover the meaning of the Grail. As Jean Frappier, perhaps the leading scholar on Chrétien de Troyes, has said, 'Today *The Story of the Grail* has become an adventure especially for erudite critics anxious to explain the origins of the mysterious and intriguing legend. Their own quest is strewn with enigmas, pitfalls, and temptations ...'[2]

Perhaps, like Perceval, they do not know what questions to ask. Or perhaps the answer is something that must be experienced, not heard. The genius of Chrétien de Troyes lay in his ability to construct a story which would allow his audience to experience the quest along with Perceval. This is the difference between sub-creation and scholarship.

What did Chrétien do? How did he do it? And most important of all, what does that accomplishment mean?

Interestingly enough, these three questions correspond roughly to Chrétien's own analysis of the major elements involved in creating a story. Not only did his Arthurian tales give definitive form to a new genre, the *roman*, he developed a critical language with which to describe it. In the prologue to his *Lancelot* (v.26) Chrétien states that a story must contain both matière – 'matter' (as in the Matter of Britain), or source material, and *sen* – 'sense', a meaning or theme. At the begin-ning of *Erec et Enide* (v.14) he says that a story requires *bele conjointure* – an effective joining of story elements into a coherent narrative.

If I bring any particular expertise to the consideration of this story, it is because I am a writer of much the same kind of tales, as well as being a long-time seeker of the Grail. As an author I find analysis of the creative process in other writers fascinating. It seems to me that by looking at the *Conte del Graal* from the point of view of a writer; by using Chrétien's own critical concepts as a framework for the examination of his creation, we may all not only arrive at a better (or at least a different) understanding of his achievement but also gain a new insight into its meaning.

Chrétien's *matière* was the Matter of Britain, the complex of motifs and characters which were precipitated around the figure of King Arthur. Although Celtic in origin, the Arthurian mythos included elements from a variety of sources; some of those which are considered most typical (and thereby, by extension, labelled 'Celtic') were introduced in their surviving form by Chrétien de Troyes. By *matière*, I believe that Chrétien means the kind of source material that fills what J.R.R. Tolkien, in his essay 'On Fairy Stories', calls 'the Cauldron of Story'. It should be no surprise that it is the author whose impact on modern Fantasy has been comparable in magnitude to Chrétien's influence on the literature of his own time who has analysed the writer's use of sources in this way.

> The Cauldron of Story has always been boiling, and to it have continually been added new bits, dainty and undainty …
>
> It seems fairly plain that Arthur, once historical (but perhaps as such not of great importance), was also put into the Pot. There he was boiled for a long time, together with many other older figures and devices, of mythology and Faerie, and even some other stray bones of history …
>
> But if we speak of Cauldron, we must not wholly forget the Cooks. There are many things in the Cauldron, but the Cooks do not dip in the ladle quite blindly. Their selection is important.[3]

Chrétien de Troyes was an expert Cook. How much of his material he invented may be disputed, but certainly he was the first to combine all of the elements of the Grail legend in such a way as to capture the imagination of his audience and not only to fix the quest for the Grail firmly within the Arthurian canon but to develop it into a major theme of Western literature which could be treated independently.

The question of Chrétien's sources seems to exercise a powerful fascination for the academic mind. It is certainly true that the medieval respect for *auctoritas* was a powerful inducement for a writer to conceal his originality (perhaps for the same reasons that many who wish to convey spiritual teachings today ascribe them to Ascended Masters, Wiccan grandmothers, or Native American shamans). And it is also true, as Tolkien points out, that no matter how far back one traces a tale there has to be an inventor *somewhere*. But it seems to me that we should at least consider believing what the poet himself has to say about the origins of his material.

In the introduction to the *Conte del Graal* (v.67) Chrétien states that his tale came from a book given him by the count (Philip of Blois). In the prologue to *Erec et Enide*, he introduces his story –

… d'Erec, le fil Lac, li contes,
que devant rois et devant contes
depecier et corronpre suelent

cil qui de conter vivre vuelent.
Des or comançerai l'estoire
qui toz jors mes iert an mimoire
tant con durra crestiantez;
de ce s'est Crestiens vantez.[4]

(... of Erec, son of Lac, the tale which before kings and before counts, those who wish to live by tale-telling have only torn apart and corrupted. Now I will begin the history which I have had in mind, so that it will last as long as Christianity, this is Chrétien's boast.)

Our poet is certainly not over-modest. In his introduction to the *Lancelot* he speaks feelingly of the *peine* and the *entencion* (the hard work and intense concentration) which is his own original contribution to the tale. If he had invented the *matière* of his tales he might even have admitted it. The tale-tellers he refers to seem to have been the Breton *conteurs* which are also mentioned by Marie de France, by Wace, and by Thomas. Among the scholars, the general opinion is that the migration of Breton bards into French courtly circles would have been quite sufficient to have given Chrétien access to a considerable body of traditional material. For a detailed examination of Celtic motifs in the work of Chrétien de Troyes, see the work of Roger Sherman Loomis in *The Grail: From Celtic Myth to Christian Symbol*, and elsewhere.

Scholars discussing Chrétien's sources often ask why, if an earlier version of the Grail story existed, it has not survived. One possibility is that it was not written down. In pre-Christian Ireland, the highly-trained *filidh* who had memorized the ancient poetic repertory and the sophisticated rules that governed its composition scorned the bards who invented and performed their own material. But when the old culture that had supported the *filidh* was destroyed only the bards, and their heirs, the story-tellers, remained. The Breton story-tellers were in even worse case; hedge-poets who struggled to communicate an ancient tradition in a foreign tongue. The results must have been much like '... the absurd English songs composed by some of the Irish peasant bards who knew English only imperfectly'[5] referred to by Kathleen Hoagland in her note on 'Castlehyde' in *100 Years of Irish Poetry*.

There is some evidence that the name of Perceval was already associated with a visit to the Grail Castle. In a poem by Regaut de Barbezieux, written before 1160, we find –

Just as Perceval, when he was alive,
was lost in wonderment at the sight,
so that he could never ask
what purpose the lance and grail served,
so I, likewise, mielhs de Domna,
for I forget all when I gaze on you.[6]

Chrétien certainly knew his hero's name before he wrote the Conte. He includes Perceval in his catalogue of Arthur's knights in *Erec et Enide*, and mentions him as a knight of great reknown in *Cligés*. Perhaps the reason that Chrétien's immediate source for his story did not survive was simply that if it *was* written down it was very bad! No wonder if Chrétien, whose effortless skill in French poetry led men to acknowledge him the master throughout the next century, thought he could improve upon his original!

Although the scholars speculating about Chrétien's sources express their interest more elegantly, they are asking essentially the same question that has at one time or another exasperated most writers of my acquaintance: 'Where do you get your ideas?' The question itself arises from a basic misunderstanding of the creative process. Ideas are everywhere; they come from a phrase in something one is reading, a comment made by a friend, sometimes one even seems to pluck them from the air. As in science, the same insights may come simultaneously to two writers who have had no contact at all. The problem is not where to find ideas but rather, sometimes, how to beat them off. The working writer goes through life like a hunter, noting every track or broken branch that indicated the presence of game. But he does not follow every trail. Every writer I know has enough story ideas in mind to last several lifetimes. The problem is to select those that will appeal to one's audience and that one can handle well.

The operative question in looking at a piece of literature should not be where the writer got his ideas but what he did with them once they were acquired. There are very few really new ideas around; the more deeply a story affects the human psyche the more likely it is to have been told before. Even when two writers do get the same idea at the same time, or work from the same source material, their results are very different (compare the story of Arthur as told by T.H. White and Marion Zimmer Bradley!) I believe that combining the elements effectively is what Chrétien means by *bele conjointure*.

Single story elements, like unmated human beings, have no progeny. It is only when they interact with others that a new story begins to grow. Whether or not Chrétien invented his story elements, he did select and interweave them – and therein lies his true originality. He seems to have been the kind of writer who approached his work with the intellect as well as with the emotions. His style is sophisticated; even at his most evocative, his effects are always completely under control. Despite the romantic image of the artist as some kind of wild man writhing in the throes of creation, literary production is often a rather cold-blooded affair. As Tolkien points out:

> Fantasy is a natural human activity. It certainly does not destroy or even insult Reason; and it does not either blunt the appetite for, nor obscure the perception of, scientific verity. On the contrary. The keener and the clearer is the reason, the better fantasy will it make.[7]

The genius of Chrétien was to turn the clear light of French reason upon the misty wonders of Celtic legend. When the critic does so, he is likely to make them disappear, but the artist illuminates them in the light of human experience. We cannot have any sure knowledge of Chrétien's creative process, but I know the kinds of questions that I (being the kind of sub-creator who likes to understand process as well as engage in it) ask myself in planning a new work; Chrétien's comments on his art suggest that he may have been this kind of thinker too.

Chrétien began with a selection of elements derived from the *matière*: the unknown youth who seeks his fortune at the court of a great king; the education of the hero; the damsel in distress; the visit to the fortress in the Otherworld; the wasteland and the wounded king ... I have given these motifs in the order in which the poet used them – in retrospect, it seems inevitable – but his first question must have been how to arrange them most effectively, followed closely by some decision regarding the perspective or narrative point of view.

Most of the young heroes who emerge from the wilderness make mistakes before they are integrated into civilized society, but surely none of them acts with quite so blithe a lack of social sensitivity as Perceval. From the first moments of the story, he is sublimely oblivious to the consequences of his actions and, like Odie in the Garfield cartoons, he leaves a trail of destruction behind him. I cannot think of another writer apart from John Erskine (*Galahad, Enough of his Life to*

Explain his Reputation) who dares to suggest that the Grail story might at times be funny. In the immortal words which Anna Russell applied to another epic hero, Perceval is 'very strong, very handsome, very brave ... very stupid!'[8] He is the 'innocent fool', and the action is presented from his naïve point of view. The audience has no choice but to identify with him. It is only after laughing at Perceval's mishaps that the reader begins to realize that, in proceeding through the story along with him, he or she is sharing in the fool's experience.

Perceval is, above all, profoundly unaware. He is at once completely self-centred and completely unselfconscious. He is not an allegory but rather an example of the spiritual state in which most people live their lives. A variant manuscript tradition includes some lines following v. 342 in which it becomes clear that at the beginning of the story Perceval does not even know his own name. His encounter with the knights is his first exposure to a larger world; his reactions show that he understands both their responses to his questions and his mother's counsels only in the most superficial way. He leaves her fainting at the gate and gallops away to seek adventure without any suspicion of the impact of his actions.

His encounter with the lady in the tent is only the first of a series of incidents in which his literal-minded interpretation of advice gets him into trouble and, like his abandonment of his mother, it will have serious consequences. Now that the poet has established Perceval's character, his next task is to give the story a broader context. Therefore he brings his bumptious hero to the paragon of all earthly courts, King Arthur's castle at Carduel. However mythic its beginnings, in the context of the story, the court represents the civilized world, an idealized version of the royal courts that Chrétien knew. Against this glittering background, Perceval stands out in striking comic relief. However, in his next encounter his lack of either empathy or imagination stands him in good stead. His fight with the Red Knight is one of the great humorous scenes in medieval literature, and he is able to defeat his opponent partly because it never occurs to him that he could fail. He is the Fool who stands with one foot poised above the precipice, the *puer aeternus* who transcends mortality.

By this time, the reader assumes that he understands what is going on, and has settled down to enjoy a nice comedy. But one of Chrétien's major strengths is his ability to delineate subtle changes in character, and with the next sequence, Perceval's knightly education by

Gornemant, the poet begins to transform him. Structurally, this episode provides some needed exposition of the process by which Perceval becomes the perfect knight. Perceval may be a 'natural', but the poet does not require us to suspend our disbelief beyond reason by having him overcome all opposition with no training at all. The poet, having gotten his audience thoroughly interested in his protagonist during the earlier episodes, can afford to slow down the action long enough to explain how Perceval's prowess acquires enough polish to get him through the rest of the story.

The second essential piece of exposition provided by this episode is Gornemant's fateful advice to Perceval to stop asking so many questions.

> *'Oui trop parole, it se mesfait',*
> *Por che, biax amis, vos chastoi*
> *De trop parler.* (vv. 1654–56)

('Who speaks too much does himself an ill deed', therefore, fair friend, keep yourself from talking too much.)

It is at this point, when Gornemant's teaching has begun to make Perceval self-aware, that he realizes for the first time that he should not have left his mother so abruptly. The motive that impels him away from his teacher's castle and eventually leads him to the Grail is the first impulse of concern for another. This, not the showier episode at Arthur's court, is the moment in which Perceval begins to change.

The result of this development becomes apparent in the sequence that follows. Having begun to think of others, Perceval is becoming capable of love. His next stop is the castle of Belrepaire, whose young mistress, Blancheflor, is being besieged by a villainous fellow who wants both the lady and her land. It is at this point that we remember that until now Chrétien was renowned as a teller of love stories. His previous surviving works focus on the romantic problems of hero and heroine, not solely for the sake of entertainment but as a means of exploring the relationship between love and life. Unlike the usual love story, which ends when the hero gets the girl, Chrétien's stories tend to focus on what happens after the wedding. Perceval wins Blancheflor without difficulty, although the marriage is delayed. The purpose of this episode is not to involve our hero in romantic entanglements but to further mature him by teaching him more about love.

Some scholars seem to be fixated on the question of Perceval's chastity. In some of the later Grail romances, the purity of the hero is indeed a major factor – but not, I think, in this one. Chrétien avoids both the churchly preoccupation with fleshly lust as sin and the defiant passion of the poet of courtly love. Whether his couples make love before marriage or wait, what matters is not the durability of their virginity but of their commitment.

By the end of the Belrepaire episode, Perceval is not only determined to do his filial duty to his mother but he has pledged himself to return to Blancheflor. The *Conte del Graal* differs from Chrétien's other romances in that the love story is only a means to further the main plot line. However, it is typical of Chrétien that the incidents that prepare Perceval to encounter the Sacred affirm rather than deny his ties to the world.

Here, I think we must pass from admiration of Chrétien's skills and sources as a writer to a consideration of his *sen* – the meaning of which his story was intended to convey. Without an underlying purpose, a medieval romance, like many contemporary fantasy novels, is only a collection of adventures. In the immortal words of Harold Shea, 'Travelling through Faerie is just one damn encounter after another'.[9] Chrétien rises above his contemporaries because his work is always 'about' the development of character. In each of his *romans* he shows believable people learning how to cope with real human problems, and sometimes something more.

Perhaps the key to what that something more in the *Conte del Graal* might be may be found in the introduction, in which Chrétien praises his patron above all for the virtue of *carité*, the Latin *caritas*, which is love (v.43). However many notable questions Philip of Blois may have had, I think that the poet's choice of this particular virtue for praise serves as an indication of his intention.

As a writer, Chrétien's main concern was with the many faces of love. In *Erec et Enide*, in *Yvain* and in *Cligés*, he showed the stages by which love matures; in *Lancelot*, he portrayed the mysticism of a martyr of love. Having covered human love so exhaustively, it is perhaps not surprising that he should have eventually attempted to tell a story which pointed toward union with the Divine – without rejecting humanity. The twelfth century may have been the only time during the Middle Ages when this was possible. A major concern of the times was the nature and practice of love, both carnal and spiritual. This interest culminated in the doctrine of *fin amor* in the court, and in the cloister it produced the mysticism of Bernard of Clairvaux. In succeeding centuries the clouds darkened, and later quests for the Grail are characterized by a desperation lacking in the serene narrative of Chrétien.

According to the Abbot of Clairvaux, the love of God begins with the soul's love of itself for its own sake, proceeds to the love of God for the self's sake, the love of God for God's sake, and finally the love of the self for God's sake alone. Its goal is the mystical union, which requires an apprenticeship having the stages of humility gained through a consciousness of sin, the development of charity, spiritual vision, and finally union.[10] The story of the Grail is not a Cistercian allegory, but Bernard's theology of love may well have influenced Chrétien's characterization of Perceval, which is not only a subtle piece of psychological analysis but a study of the evolution of spiritual consciousness.

At the beginning of the story Perceval deserts his mother – a sin against charity. In Bernard's terms, at the beginning of the tale he loves himself for his self's sake. Like a small child, he cannot even imagine that his actions might hurt another. By the time he leaves Blancheflor, he has begun to act altruistically. Without rejecting *Eros*, the poet moves beyond it to explore the meaning of *Caritas*.

What is remarkable is that the sequence of events through which Chrétien conveys his meaning is not Christian in any obvious sense but rather an experience that transcends the conventions of religion as it was commonly understood in his day, and still is in ours. After he has left Belrepaire, Perceval's wanderings lead him to the Castle of the Fisher King and the Grail.

In the *matière* of Celtic legend, Chrétien found a source of archetypal riches which challenged his sophistication and skill. It is when he dips most deeply into this part of the cauldron that he is at his most evocative and profound. The fountain of Barenton in Broceliande where Yvain wakes the storm, the sword-bridge which Lancelot must cross in order to reach Guinevere, and the Procession of the Grail in the Castle of the Fisher King belong to another order of reality than the passages of love and war which are the stock in trade of romance.

Valiantly, the poet tries to civilize his wonders – he is a Mozart, rather than a Wagner, in his orchestration and harmonies. Still, when Perceval comes to the swift flowing river where the *Roi Pecheur* is fishing, a deeper note sounds through the music of Chrétien's sprightly couplets, and we realize that we are moving from the fields we know (however legendary) to the borders of the Otherworld. The shift would have been even more apparent to the *roman*'s original audience. To the modern reader, the court of King Arthur and that of the Fisher King are equally fantastic, but the medieval audience would have found the former an idealized version of royal courts, as the glittering lifestyle of the soap operas is a fantasy of the lives of the rich and famous today.

The Fisher King's directions lead Perceval into an even deeper wilderness, and it is at the moment when he is despairing of ever finding his way, that –

> *Lors vit pres de lui en un val*
> *Le chief d'une tar qui parut.* (vv. 3050–51)

(Then he saw near him in a valley the top of a tower which appeared.)

Whether he lives in the twelfth century or the twentieth, the reader who sees the Castle of the Grail manifesting in the wilderness before him recognizes, like Dorothy upon catching her first sight of Oz, that he is not in Kansas any more. If only Perceval had been so perceptive!

He is welcomed into a great square hall more like King Cormac's hall at Tara as traditionally described in Irish literature than any French castle of the time. He is given a marvelous sword, which for him alone is '*voëe at destinee*', (vowed and destined) (v. 3168). And then –

> *Uns vallés d'une chambre vint,*
> *Qui une blanche lance tint*
> *Empoignie par le mileu,*
> *Si passa par entre le feu*
> *Et cels qui el lit se seoient.*
> *Et tot cil de laiens veoient*
> *le lance blanche et le fer blanc,*
> *S'issoit une goute de sanc*
> *Del fer de la lance en somet,*
> *Et jusqu'a la main au vallet*
> *Coloit cele goute vermeille ...*
> *Atant dui autre vallet vindrent,*
> *Qui candeliers en lor mains tindrent ...*
> *Un graal entre ses deus mains*
> *Une damoisele tenoit ...*
> *Atot le graal qu'ele tint,*
> *Une si grans clartez i vint*
> *Qu'ausi perdirent les chandoiles*

Lor clarté come les estoiles
Font quant solaus lieve ou la lune.
Aprés celi en revint une
Qui tint un tailleoir d'argant.
Li graaus, qui aloit devant,
De fin or esmeré estoit;
Prescieuses pierres avoit ...
Tout ensi com passa la lance ...
Et d'une chambre en autre entrerent.
Et li vallés les vit passer,
Ne n'osa mie demander
Del graal cui len en servoit ... (vv. 3191–3244)

(A youth from a chamber came who grasped a white lance by the middle; he passed between the fire and those who were on the couch. And all those who were within saw the white lance and the white steel, from which issued a drop of blood; from the tip of the iron lance down to the hand of the youth rolled this vermilion drop ... Then two other youths came who bore candelabra in their hands ... so great a radiance from it came that the candles lost their light as the stars lose theirs when rises the moon. After her came one who held a platter of silver. The Grail, which had gone before, was of fine, pure gold; precious stones it had ... In this way it passed, like the lance ... and from one room entered another. And the youth [Perceval] saw them pass, *and did not dare to ask who was served by the Grail*.)

This episode is one of the major battlefields of Arthurian scholarship. Roger Sherman Loomis has analyzed the Celtic analogues to its various elements in exhaustive detail. Other scholars have viewed the Grail Procession as a reflection of any one of a number of kinds of Christianity or Judaism, or as the last glimmer of a pagan fertility rite. In later versions of the story the Grail is said to give each one whatever he likes best to eat and drink; even in Chrétien's version, it seems to offer each scholar whatever meaning he or she would most like to find! But as Ursula K. Le Guin points out, 'Any creation, primary or secondary, with any vitality to it, can "really" be a dozen mutually exclusive things at once, before breakfast.'[11]

This polymorphic symbolism is indeed the trademark of Faerie. Perhaps the reason that the story has proved so enduring is that those elements that its author drew from the Cauldron are ancient indeed. The last spicing before Chrétien dipped in his spoon may have been Celtic, but I think that the essence of the Grail episode may well belong to that level which feeds the mythologies of many lands.

We have no reason to doubt that Chrétien de Troyes was a good son of the Church. Certainly the hermit who advises Perceval at the end of the story is orthodox in his counsels. But the Grail procession itself is like no known Christian ceremony. The combination of the Castle, the Procession and the Unasked Question may have come from Count Philip's mysterious book, but it was Chrétien who decided how to present them. In later versions of the story, the Grail is firmly identified as the Chalice of the Last Supper, and appears either as a vision or in a ceremony reminiscent of the Mass – but not so in Chrétien's present-ation. Eventually we (with Perceval) will be told that the Grail holds a Christian Mass wafer, but the episode in which it appears has not even a veneer of Christianity. Why should a Christian poet portray this holy thing in such a strange way?

The same question might be asked of some of the great fantasists of modern times. Why did J.J.R. Tolkien, a devout Roman Catholic, invent an entire mythology of Middle Earth with its own pantheon? Why did C.S. Lewis, famed as an apologist for the Anglican communion, set his version of the Christian story in a secondary world inhabited by creatures out of classical and medieval mythology? Why do so many contemporary writers of fantasy, whether they be good Christians or no kind of Christian at all, invent worlds whose mythologies and religions are peopled by old gods with new names, worlds which shimmer with a magic as marvelous as ever illuminated any Breton bard's tale?

C.S. Lewis provides a possible explanation when he discusses his reasons for writing about Narnia. He is careful to point out that in his case it was always the image that came first, bubbling uncontrollably from the depths of the Author's unconscious and demanding to be made into a tale. It was only afterward that the Man in him would apply his critical judgement to decide whether he ought to write the story, and what it might mean. To use a popular model of consciousness, for a successful act of sub-creation both the left and right must work together.

I thought I saw how stories of this kind could steal past a certain inhibition which had paralysed much of my own religion in childhood. Why did one find it so hard to feel as one was told one ought to feel about God or about the sufferings of Christ? ... But suppose that by casting all these things into an imaginary world, by stripping them of all their stained-glass and Sunday School associations, one could make them for the first time appear in their real potency? Could one not thus steal past those watchful dragons? ... That was the Man's motive, but of course he could have done nothing if the Author had not been on the boil first.[12]

The brilliant, allusive world of the fairy-tale affected Lewis in a way which he perceived as being related to his response to religion. By turning to the world of myth for his *matière*, as well as for his form, he was able to write a story which could communicate a Truth beyond sectarian theology.

Faerie lies between the worlds, and what is between the worlds transcends the world we know. When we enter the realm of myth and magic we leave behind the internal censor, who demands that things be real, and thus we are enabled to experience a deeper level of Reality. The archetypal motifs which appear in the Grail episode bypass the conscious mind in order to convey a truth which might be rejected if presented objectively, or ignored through apparent familiarity. Is this a Christian truth? Perhaps – or perhaps the Christian story, speaking the language of history, is communicating in another way a Truth that lies beyond all languages. Like Perceval, we may not understand what the Grail is or what it is for, but as the eyes see that blaze of light that outshines all others, the spirit recognizes that something numinous is here.

To write a story which will speak to its audience in this way, the author must walk like a shaman between the worlds, at once transcending consciousness to respond directly to the myth and shaping it with conscious judgement and skill. This is the genius of all great fantasists. Certainly it was an ability possessed in full measure by Chrétien de Troyes.

'What is fantasy?' asks Ursula K. Le Guin, and answers –

> ... as art, not spontaneous play, its affinity is not with day-dream, but with dream. It is a different approach to reality, an alternative technique for apprehending and coping with existence. It is not antirational, but pararational; not realistic, but surrealistic, super-realistic, a heightening of reality ... It employs archetypes, which, as Jung warned us, are dangerous things ... Fantasy is nearer to poetry, to mysticism, and to insanity than naturalistic fiction is. It is a real wilderness, and those who go there should not feel too safe. And their guides, the writers of fantasy, should take their responsibilities seriously.[13]

Chrétien thrilled to the horns of Elfland, thence came his power, but like Lewis he accepted the responsibility of the Man as well as the inspiration of the Author. When he wrote about romantic love, the honeymoon was only the beginning; his main concern was with the problem of making love work while living in the world. It is not too surprising that when he wrote about an experience whose impact was profoundly mystical that moment of illumination should be only the beginning.

It is symptomatic of Perceval's spiritual state that when he comes to the Grail Castle he is still paralyzed by a literal understanding of his teacher's counsels, and thus is unable to ask the question that would have healed the Fisher King and his land. The problem is not unusual. History is full of individuals who have kept the law of their religion while losing the spirit! But immediately after his unceremonious ejection from the castle, Perceval meets his cousin, who informs him in no uncertain terms just what he did wrong. It is at this moment that he for the first time becomes aware of his own name. Even though he failed the test, he has passed through an initiation. He learns also that his inability to ask about the Grail is the result of the same sin – or condition of character – that caused him to leave his mother to die. In the language of Bernard of Clairvaux, although not quite in the same order, Perceval has achieved vision (albeit momentarily) and consciousness of sin, and is beginning to develop the *caritas* that is the prerequisite to union.

'What is there left for me to seek?' he asks (v. 3622). He must wander for many years before he finds out.

His life has been changed, but he does not know what to do with it. It is only after his wanderings have finally brought him back to the court of Arthur, where he rights some old wrongs, that the Loathly Lady appears to upbraid him and amplify his cousin's explanations. Whether she is the other face of the Grail Maiden or an externalization of his own guilty conscience, her words restore his sense of purpose. He swears that he will neither stay two nights in one place nor refuse any challenge.

Tant que il del graal savra
Cui l'en sert, et qu'il avra
La lance qui saine trovee
Et que la Veritez provee
Li ert dite por qu'ele saine. (vv. 4735–39.)

(Until he knew whom the Grail served, and had found the bleeding lance, and proven the truth of why it bled.)

But though he is pledged to seek the mystery, Perceval is not destined to withdraw from the world. His task is to understand what he has experienced so that he can use that knowledge. His spiritual path is knighthood, and marriage with Blancheflor. Even before he wrote the *Conte*, Chrétien was a heretic in the theology of courtly love; except for the *Lancelot*, his works display a conviction that love is manifested most fully in marriage, or at least in equal commitment. Among Chrétien's successors, the idea that Perceval must marry in order to fulfil his destiny as the sacred king was developed by Wolfram von Eschenbach, while the later tradition of the *Queste del Saint Graal* and Malory replaced Perceval with the virginal Galahad. The German version is probably the most consistent with Chrétien's intentions.

Even when Perceval's wanderings lead him at last to the hermit who proves to be his maternal uncle as well as his mentor, the advice he is given is on how to live a holy life in a secular setting. One of the distinguishing characteristics of the *Conte* is this awareness that the world of the spirit is no distant paradise but a realm that interpenetrates our own, and that the sacred is part of the life of the world.

Perceval has had a glimpse of that radiant splendor which is one of the most commonly reported characteristics of mystical experience; as his uncle informs him, he has seen a thing whose purpose is to mediate union with the Divine. After five years of directionless wandering he is recalled to awareness and is able to perceive the connection between his failure at the Grail Castle and what has happened to him since then. Perceval has forgotten God, been silent before the Grail, and left his mother to die – he has not obeyed the call, he has not recognized the vision, and he has failed in love. He is one of those who –

> For all their effort have not attained the vision ... They have received the authentic light, all their soul has gleamed as they have drawn near; but they come with a load on their shoulders which holds them back from the place of Vision.[14]

One of the primary characteristics of the mystic illumination is the experience of supernal love. Chrétien's mystics, whether their religion be that of divine or earthly passion, must practise their faith in the world. That world is an idealized medieval landscape illuminated by the light of the Otherworld, in which, although the divine archetypes that speak directly to the spirit appear and disappear, *caritas* and piety are continually required. Throughout the story, it is Perceval's spiritual development that determines his ability to benefit from the gifts he is given, and the stages in his progress are marked by changes in his ability to care about others. As the visions of mystics from many times and faiths point to a single reality, so the quest for illumination is in essence the same. The way to the light is love.

The *Conte del Graal* was left unfinished. Although it includes further adventures of Gawain which are outside the scope of this discussion, the story of Perceval ends with the scene in which he is instructed by his hermit uncle. This truncated conclusion is even more frustrating for a writer than it is for the average reader. The frustration was obviously too much for Chrétien's successors for, in the generation that followed, Gerbert de Montreuil and others produced endless and only marginally successful continuations of the tale. Like Perceval they wander, but without Chrétien's clear vision they found it impossible to bring the story to a conclusion. That task was left to later writers, who returned to the beginning and assigned their own meanings to the tale.

To leave the story unfinished is unsatisfying, but it is perhaps more realistic – to very few is it given to attain more than a glimpse of the Grail. We are like Perceval in our ignorance when we begin, and we follow his path through the wilderness, only gradually coming to understand what it is we are looking for and learning how to recognize what we see. The Grail appears to each seeker in a different guise, and each author who tells the tale must dip into the Cauldron of Story anew.

To ask '*What* is the Grail?' leads the scholar astray. The question which must be asked is that of the writer whose artistry draws meaning from his *matière*. 'What is the Grail for?'

Notes and References

All French quotations from the *Conte du Graal* in the essay are from the edition of William Roach, (Paris: Librarie Minard, 1959).

1 Chrétien de Troyes, *Perceval, or the Story of the Grail*, trans. Ruth Harwood Cline (Athens, Georgia: Univ. of Georgia Press, 1985 vv. 63–4).

2 Jean Frappier, *Chrétien de Troyes, the Man and his Work*, trans. Raymond J. Cormier (Athens Ohio: Ohio Univ. Press, 1982, p. 151).

3 J.R.R. Tolkien, 'On Fairy Stories', *The Tolkien Reader* (New York: Ballantine, 1966, pp. 27, 29, 30).

4 Chrétien de Troyes, *Erec et Énide* (Paris: Librairie Honore Champion, 1963, v. 19–26).

5 Kathleen Hoagland (ed.), *100 Years of Irish Poetry* (New York: Grosset & Dunlap, 1962, p. 254).

6 Quoted in Rita Lejeune, 'The Troubadours', in Roger Sherman Loomis (ed.), *Arthurian Literature in the Middle Ages* (Oxford University Press, 1959, p. 396–7).

7 J.R.R. Tolkien, op. cit., p. 54.

8 Anna Russell, 'The Ring of the Nibelungs (An Analysis)' (The Anna Russell Album, Columbia Records, 1972).

9 L. Sprague de Camp and Fletcher Pratt, *The Incomplete Enchanter* (New York: Pyramid Books, 1962, p. 140).

10 Etienne Gilson, *The Mystical Theology of St Bernard*, A.H.C. Downes (trans.) (London: Sheed and Ward, 1940, pp. 98–9).

11 Ursula K. Le Guin, 'Dreams Must Explain Themselves', in Robert H. Boyer & Kenneth J. Zahorski (eds.), *Fantasists on Fantasy* (New York: Avon Books, 1984, p. 191).

12 C.S. Lewis, 'Sometimes Fairy Stories May Say Best What's to be Said', Ibid, p. 117.

13 Ursula K. Le Guin, 'From Elfland to Poughkeepsie', Ibid., p. 196.

14 Plotinus, *The Enneads*, vi. 9, quoted in Evelyn Underhill, *Mysticism* (New York: Meridian Books, 1955, p. 207).

Robert de Boron:
Architect of Tradition

John Matthews

Of all the medieval authors who added significantly to our conception of the Grail, Robert de Boron is unique. He stands between the earliest, oral traditions and the later literary heritage, drawing upon varied sources to create an individual synthesis which was to shape the future of the Grail ever after. We know little about him, but we can judge from the nature of his existing works that he was devout, serious, and widely read. He was also a very poor stylist, whose clumsy sentences fail to hide the luminous nature of his vision. But above all he saw that the Grail was much more than just a symbol. It had a concrete reality which made those who served it into a family – that very family who form the Household of the Grail.

The Story

In the early part of the thirteenth century there appeared a work some-times called *Le Roman d'Estoire du Graal*, sometimes *Joseph d'Arimathie*[1] by someone calling himself Messires (or Meistres) Robert de Boron. The story it told was an extraordinary one, part romance, part adventure story, part theological tract. With elements drawn from Celtic myth, Arthurian literature and Christian apocrypha, it changed for ever the matter of the Grail, then just beginning its extraordinary rise in popular consciousness with the *Conte del Graal* of Chrétien de Troyes.[2]

The story may be summarized as follows.

Beginning with a prologue summarizing the history of creation from the Fall to the Crucifixion, the text goes on to describe how the vessel in which Christ celebrated the first Eucharist at the Last Supper came to be given first to Pilate and then to Joseph of Arimathea who, during the deposition from the Cross, caught some of the blood of the Messiah within it. After this Joseph is imprisoned by the Jews and at this time is visited by the risen Christ who entrusts him with the 'Secrets of the Saviour' concerning the Grail and its uses.

Joseph remains in prison for many years, forgotten by the outside world but sustained by the Grail. The Roman Emperor Vespasian contracts leprosy and is miraculously cured by the Veil of Veronica. Determined to find out more about Christianity, the Emperor journeys to Jerusalem and there discovers Joseph, still alive, and sets him free. Joseph, together with his sister Enygeus and her husband Brons or Hebron, and a small following of Christians leave Judea and journey into other lands. There they dwell for a long time until some of the company commit the sin of lechery so that their crops fail and they all suffer from starvation. Requesting help from the Holy Spirit, Joseph is commanded to build a table in memory of that at which Christ celebrated the Last Supper. Brons is then told to go forth and catch a single fish, which is then laid upon the table opposite to the Grail. The company are then summoned to eat and only those who have remained pure and true to their beliefs are able to sit there, the rest being somehow prevented. All who sit at the table are fed from the one fish, for which cause Brons is ever after known as the Rich Fisherman. And all sitting there 'perceived a sweetness which was the completion of the desire of their hearts'.[3]

One place at the table is left empty, in token of Judas the betrayer, and when one of the outcast company, a man named Moyses, tries to sit there he is swallowed up by the earth. The voice of the Holy Spirit declares that the seat will remain empty until the grandson of Brons comes to sit in it.

Time passes and Bron fathers 12 sons, all of whom marry except for one, Alain, who declares his intention of remaining celibate. By this sign Joseph knows that he is to be the destined father of the one who will become the Grail's later guardian, and takes him in and begins to train him in the ways of the Grail. Eventually the Holy Spirit tells him that it is time for various of the company to depart for the West, preaching the gospel. The first to depart is Petrus, who is to journey to 'the Vale of

Avalon' to await the coming of Alain's son. Next Brons departs, having learned the 'Secrets of the Grail' from Joseph. He journeys to Ireland (according to the *Didot Perceval*), there also to await his grandson. Thus will the meaning of the Trinity be fulfilled.

Joseph remains behind, happily prepared for death. Messire Robert de Boron promises to tell what happened next, where Alain went, what befell him and what son he had and who mothered it, and what also happened to Petrus and Moyses, who was swallowed up. All these things he will recount if he can discover them in a book.

Who was Robert de Boron?

Who was the man who told this strange, mystical tale? Robert de Boron is an elusive figure who has been variously described as a Burgundian, a Swiss and an Anglo Norman, with the status of knight or clerk. He himself tells us little. In a much-quoted passage from *Joseph d'Arimathie* he describes himself as *Meistres Robers dist de Bouron*, (Master Robert of Boron), suggesting that he was a clerk, possibly in holy orders, as indeed the nature of his writings would also bear out. However, in a later part of the same text he appears as *Messires* (Master or Sir) Robert, which is to say a knight. Which of these are we to believe?

Elsewhere in *Joseph* Robert speaks of his authorship and patronage in these terms:

> *A ce tens que je la [l'estoire dou Graal] retreis,*
> *O mon Seigneur Gautier en peis,*
> *Qui de Mont Belyal estoit,*
> *Unques retreite este n'avait.*

> When I told [the History of the Grail]
> In time of peace to my Lord Gautier,
> Who was of Mont Belyal,
> It had never been told before. (My trans.)

This Gautier has been identified as Gautier de Montbeliard, Lord of Montfaucon, who went on the Fourth Crusade in 1202 and never returned. Nearby is the village of Boron, which we may presume to be either Robert's birthplace or the place where he settled and where he wrote his cycle of romances about the Grail. It is also generally presumed that Robert was in the service of Gautier and that he wrote his trilogy (or possibly tetralogy)[4] of poems for him, or at his behest, some time between 1191 and 1210, the year in which Gautier died. The words 'in time of peace' have been taken as a suggestion that the works were completed *before* Gautier set out on crusade, implying that Robert completed them in approximately 10 years.

Other clues to Robert's identity are the number of Burgundian dialect words in the poems, which seem to confirm Boron as his place of origin. There is also mention in an Essex charter of a certain Robert de Burun, who is described as granting land in Hertfordshire, England, to a monastery in Picardy. While this connection is properly regarded as doubtful[5] it is interesting for the implied connection with southern England. Robert seems to have been familiar enough with this part of the country to identify the place to which Petrus journeys as Avalon, then widely believed to be identified with the town of Glastonbury in Somerset. This also incidentally provides a possible *terminus ad quem* to the dating of the *Joseph*, since the 'discovery' of Arthur's body at Glastonbury and its subsequent identification with Avalon took place in 1191.

Apart from the *Joseph*, which is the only one of Robert's poems to have survived more or less intact, he is known to have written a *Merlin*,[6] of which only 405 lines now survive, and a *Perceval* of which nothing more is known. The possibility of a fourth book, a version of the *Mort Artu*, has been put forward recently[7] and more than one commentator has suggested that Robert may also be the author (or immediate source for) the so-called *Didot Perceval*.[8]

The complexity of manuscript traditions relating to Robert are outside the field of this present essay. However, certain points relating to his use of source material need to be examined for the light they throw on Robert's contribution to the history of the Grail.

Sources

It is not known whether Robert's presumed patron Gautier provided the *matière* (matter) of his works, as Count Philip of Flanders is supposed to have done for Chrétien de Troyes (see Paxson). But though Robert certainly derived parts of his material from the writings of the more famous poet of Champagne, it is clear that he also had access to a very different set of materials.

His own statement regarding sources comes in vv. 932–6 of *Joseph d'Arimathie*, where he refers to

Se je le grant livre n'avoie
Ou les estroires sunt escrites
Par les granz clers feites et dites.
La sunt li grant secre escrit
Qu'en numme Ie Graal et dit.

('The great book in which are the histories told by the grand clerks; there the mighty secrets are written which are named and called the Grail.' Trans. Charles Williams)[9]

These words have given much trouble to interpreters, who have been puzzled by the 'mighty secrets' which are the Grail. Richard O'Gorman suggests that a reading of the prose version of the *Joseph* which bears an alternative reading referring to the books as the place wherein 'the secret which is held concerning the sacraments of the Grail'.[10]

This certainly makes more sense at one level, though it must be said that the idea of the Grail being a body of secret tradition is not in itself nonsensical; indeed, it is more often the *content*, or the very *idea* of the vessel which is important rather than the vessel itself.

Nevertheless, this passage does raise a problem. On the one hand Robert states quite equivocally that he is the first person to tell the story of the Grail, and though this may be seen as a piece of typical medieval self-aggrandisement, it is somewhat in conflict with the reference to a *grant livre* or 'great book'.

Richard O'Gorman again comes to our rescue here. Examining the prose redaction he finds that in the famous passage quoted above Robert is probably referring to his own work, newly completed, in the hands of the reader; in the earlier passage he is in all probability referring to a book or books from which he obtained 'his rather conventional Eucharistic symbolism which he transforms into the secrets of the Grail'.[11]

This 'rather conventional symbolism' can be traced to two main sources: the *Gemma Animae* of Honorius of Autun[12] and the *Versus de Mysterio Missae* by Bishop Hildebert of Tours.[13]

In the first we find:

Dicente sacerdote, 'Per omnia saecula saeculorum,' diaconus venit, calicem coram eo sustollit, cum favone partem ejus cooperit in altari reponit et cum

corporali cooperit, praeferens Joseph ab Arimathie, qui corpus Christi deposuit, faciem ejus sudario cooperuit, in monumento deposuit, lapide cooperuit ... Hic oblata et calix cum corporali coopitur, quod sindonem mundam significat, in quam Joseph corpus Christi involvebat. Calix hic, sepulcrum; patena, lapidem designat, qui sepulchrum clauserat.

(As the Priest, said, 'For ever and for ever,' a deacon came, and, uplifting the chalice, laid it down upon the altar, covering it with a *corporal*, as Joseph of Arimathea did, when he took down the body of Christ, covering Him with a shroud, and placed the body in his own tomb, and closed it with a stone ... Here the offering and the chalice, with its corporal, signify the shroud in which Joseph wrapped the body of Christ, while the chalice signifies the tomb, and the paten the stone which covered the tomb. Trans. Caitlín Matthews).

The connection with Honorius is interesting since there is a link between this popular theologian and southern Britain, with which Robert may also have had connections. It is possible that he encountered Honorius' writings while on a journey to Britain, perhaps at the behest of his master, but it is unlikely that we can ever know this for certain. The fact that Honorius talks of the 'rite of Joseph of Arimathea' is certainly suggestive, though no other trace of such a rite exists.

Apart from these sources Robert almost certainly drew upon the *Gesta Pilate* and the *Evangelium Nicodemi*[14] as well as, to a lesser extent, such apocryphal works as *Vindicta Salvatoris* and *Curia Sanitatis Tiberii*.[15] In each of these we find details of the part played by Joseph of Arimathea in the events of the Crucifixion, Deposition, and Resurrection, very much as relayed by Robert – though they do not, of course, refer to the Grail or to Joseph's guardianship of it.

The *Acts of Pilate* tells the following story.

After the Crucifixion 'a certain man named Joseph, being a counsellor, of the city of Arimathea, who also himself looked for the Kingdom of God, this man went to Pilate and begged the body of Jesus. And he took it down and wrapped it in a linen cloth and laid it in a hewn sepulchre wherein was never man yet laid.'[16]

The Jews were so angered by these actions that they seized Joseph and imprisoned him in a house with no window and placed guards on the door. But when they returned two days later they found Joseph gone, and he was later discovered to be safely returned to his home, though the doors remained closed and sealed in the house where he had been imprisoned. Joseph is therefore summoned by the elders and an explanation demanded. He tells how:

> As at midnight I stood and preyed the house wherein ye had shut me up was taken up by the four corners, and I saw as it were a flashing of light in mine eyes, and being filled with fear I fell to the earth. And one took me by the hand and removed me from the place whereon I had fallen; and moisture of water was shed on me from my head unto my feet, and an odour of ointment came about my nostrils. And he wiped my face and kissed me and said unto me: Fear not, Joseph: open thine eyes and see who it is that speeketh with thee. (Ibid.)

The speaker is Christ, who takes Joseph out of the house where he was imprisoned to his own home and then departs. There is no mention here of the 'secrets of the Grail', which we must ascribe to Robert's own hand in lieu of any other source. Other details, Vespasian's miraculous cure and his releasing of Joseph from the tower years rather than days after his imprisonment, derive from the *Vindicta Sanitatis* and the *Curia Sanitatis Tiberii*, already mentioned above.

Celtic Tales

Other influences, however, are to be detected within the matter of Robert's tale, which derive from a very different source. It has long been recognized that a considerable amount of material relating to the Grail derives from Celtic myth – in particular the various stories relating to Cauldrons of Rebirth, which are recognizable prototypes for the later Christian Grail. Caitlín Matthews has already dealt with this material in some detail, and we need only touch here upon one text and one character – *Branwen Ferch Llyr* from the collection of early tales known as *The Mabinogion*,[17] and the figure of Bran the Blessed, the semi-divine king of Britain and the guardian of the sacred land after his death.

Bran has long been recognized as a prototype of the suffering Grail king who appears first in Chrétien and thereafter in most of the texts which follow.[18] Like the Wounded King, Bran suffers from an unhealing wound, remains in suspended life for a number of years, and entertains a company of followers with his bounty. He is also the possessor of a magical cauldron which gives back life to dead warriors placed within it. Add to this the fact that one of the key figures in Robert's poem is called

Brons (sometimes Hebron), suggesting a conflation of two figures, the Celtic Bran and one of the guardians of the Ark of the Covenant named Hebron, son of Kolath, in the Biblical Book of Numbers, and we have a fairly conclusive case for the Celtic influence.

If, as has been suggested by several commentators,[19] Robert either wrote or was directly influential in the composition of the prose *Didot Perceval*, this would further support the idea of extensive borrowing from Celtic sources. The *Didot* contains more Celtic themes than any of the texts normally associated with Robert, as a brief summary will show.

The Holy Spirit informs Alain that he must take his son Perceval to the court of King Arthur, and that after winning great honour he will go to Ireland, where he will visit the court of his grandfather, Brons, and cure him of a painful wound. But Alain dies before he can take the youth to court and when Perceval arrives alone he does indeed win honour in the tournament, but then foolishly sits in the Siège Perilous, which cracks beneath him and gives forth a great roar and a cloud of black smoke. A great voice announces that because of Perceval's temerity his grandfather will not be cured, nor will the stone seat be joined together again, nor will the 'enchantments' be lifted from Britain – until a knight comes who will ask what the Grail is and whom it serves.

Swearing never to remain more than one night anywhere until he has found the court of the Rich Fisher, Perceval sets out and has a number of adventures, including the overcoming of a proud lady in the Chess-board Castle where a magical set of pieces plays against him, the pursuit and capture of a white stag, a combat at a ford with Urbain (Owain) who is guarded by a flock of black birds who are really women in enchanted form, a vision of two children in a tree, an encounter with a shadowy figure of Merlin, who prophesies his destiny to arrive at the Castle of the Rich Fisher and achieve the quest.

Arriving at last at his destination Perceval sees the king fishing from the boat, watches the Procession of the Grail, but fails to ask the question. Outcast, he is reproached by a sorrowful damsel and then wanders for seven years until he happens on the cell of his hermit uncle and learns what he must do. Now he again approaches the Grail Castle, asks the Question and heals the Wounded King, who then gives the Grail into his keeping after teaching him its secrets. The Siège Perilous then reunites and Merlin announces the end of the quest and retires to have his master Blaise write all this down.

There then follows a section which is really the substance of the *Mort Artu*, following the usual direction of that story, including Arthur's success against the armies of Rome, his hasty return to Britain on learning of Mordred's treachery, the last great battle and Arthur's withdrawal to Avalon.

It will be seen that there are several points of overlap between this story and that of the *Joseph*, though it is not exactly a sequel. Episodes such as the quest for the white stag, Urban and the flock of black birds, the children in the tree, and Merlin's appearance as a shadow, and the character of Blaise and the episode of the Chess-board Castle all derive from Celtic sources.

Elements which specifically tie the *Didot* to those works definitely attributable to Robert are that of the Siège Perilous, which cracks and roars as it does in *Joseph*, and the continuing intervention and instruction received from the voice of the Holy Spirit, which in both texts acts as a kind of invisible counsellor to Joseph and his descendants.

The *Didot* itself lacks colour and characterization such as are found so abundantly in Chrétien. In an attempt to compress the quest for the Grail and the death of Arthur, along with something of the history of Merlin, into a brief space (the *Didot* is only 90 pages long in the modern edition), the author or compiler has lost much. This clumsiness of presentation has also been seen as a possible link with Robert's work, which is generally characterized by its poor quality of language, its often muddled thinking and careless construction. However, as Richard O'Gorman has shown, a comparison of the prose redaction, made only a short time after Robert had completed his work, indicates that the manuscript containing *Joseph*, the beginning of the *Merlin*, and a version of the *Didot Perceval* is itself corrupt, and that the prose redactor had access to a better copy which contained few if any of the clumsy transitions and constructions found in the existing manuscript.

Many of the contradictions found within the *Joseph* are in fact easily explained either by reference to the Prose version or by a careful reading of the original. We have seen already that the apparent discrepancy between the two statements regarding Robert's sources does not really exist. The same goes for the matter of Brons' son Alain, who in one part of the manuscript is described as electing to remain celibate – as in fact stating that he would as soon be flayed alive than marry – while later he sires a son, is easily explained by consideration of the text. There we find that of Brons' 15 children only Alain refuses to marry, and that this sets him apart in such a way that Joseph recognizes him as his father's successor. He is then given into the keeping of Joseph, who undertakes to train him in the ways of the Grail and eventually, when the time is right, to impart the 'Secrets of the Saviour' to him. Once he is in possession of these facts, and has furthermore become the Grail's new guardian, what more natural than that he should father a son to succeed him, *now that the time is right?*

New Architecture

All of this brings us to consider the way in which Robert used his sources. We have seen that he drew upon Christian apocryphal texts, as well as oral tales then circulating in Europe. Apart from these obvious materials there are subtler influences. He is clearly influenced by Chrétien, in that he brings the Grail to Britain, and makes it a provider of sustenance – though in Robert it contains the Holy Blood of the Saviour while Chrétien's Grail is said to hold a wafer and possibly a fish. Both poets refer to the Rich Fisherman, though in Chrétien the reason for the name is that the Wounded King fishes for amusement because he is too infirm to do more, while in Robert's text he acquires the title when he emulates Christ in feeding the Company of the Grail with a single fish. On the other hand Robert does not mention the Lance, which has a central place in Chrétien's narrative.

These points of similarity and variance may simply arise from the different source material available to the two authors. Robert seems to have spent much of his time searching actively for new material. It is clear that he meant to return to the stories of Petrus, Brons and Moyses 'if he could find them written in a book', an indication that he was not inventing the material at all but following a trail of his own devising after the elusive Grail, thus making him, satisfyingly, a Grail quester himself!

The change in the narrative between the section dealing with the history of the Crucifixion and its aftermath and the latter portion which deals with the adventures of the Grail Family may well mark a point of departure in Robert's work, It is almost as though having reached a certain point, and having heard perhaps of Chrétien's success, Robert strove to unite the two themes by the invention, or elaboration, of additional themes.[20]

One such theme in particular seems to have been Robert's own invention. If so, it was a happy one, which united the earlier and later material in a way which offered much food for elaboration. I refer to the three tables, the first of which is the one at which Christ celebrates the first eucharist, the second constructed at the behest of Joseph of Arimathea *in likeness of the first*, and the third, made at Merlin's command by Uther Pendragon and later conferred upon Arthur as the Round Table of romance, in imitation of the two earlier tables.

By establishing these three physical links between the cosmic events of the Crucifixion and the mythic world of Arthurian Britain, Robert also established a connection which allowed for the Arthurian Grail Quest to develop as it did. It is even possible that it would never have manifested there had not Robert de Boron made this connection. For in so doing he soldered for ever the Matter of Britain with Christian legendry, and enabled the Celtic myths to enter the world of the Grail.

An example of the way in which these intricate matters are worked into the texture of the story is the statement which refers to the meaning of the Blessed Trinity being fulfilled by the three who will hold the Grail – Brons, Alain and Perceval, who must therefore represent the Father, the Son and the Holy Spirit. The third and final emanation of the Godhead is therefore Perceval, who contains the essence of the two earlier guardians. Earlier, three of Joseph's original company go forth from the rest: Petrus to Avaron (Avalon), Alain to the far West (Ireland in the *Didot Perceval*) and Brons also to the West, perhaps somewhere in the south-west of Britain, maybe Cornwall with its strong traditions of Joseph and his family.

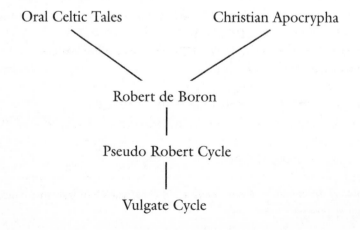

Oral Celtic Tales   Christian Apocrypha

Robert de Boron

Pseudo Robert Cycle

Vulgate Cycle

Looking again at the sources of Robert's work, and his place in the development of Grail literature, we see just how central is his place in the formation of the literary heritage.

Thus from Robert's work came the so-called Pseudo Robert Cycle,[21] which in turn gave rise to what must rank as the greatest and most evolved of all Arthuriads, the Vulgate Cycle.[22]

From this flowed many other important works of the mythus, including Malory's great interpretation (so called rather than a translation because of its individuality) *Le Morte d'Arthur* (see Greg Stafford's essay). Robert de Boron's version of the Grail text makes him a most valuable and important member of the Household of the Grail; one who expanded the already existing and emerging material in a way that made it wholly new and individual. He it was who stamped it for ever with the seal of Christianity, who shaped its potential for all times, and who provided matter on which many further versions could be based.

Notes and References

1 *Le Roman de l'Estoire dou Graal*, ed. W.A. Nitze (Paris: Champion, 1927). All quotations from this text unless otherwise stated.

2 Chrétien de Troyes, *Arthurian Romances*, trans. D.D.R. Owen (London: Dent, 1987).

3 *Medieval Narrative*, trans. Margaret Schlauch (New York: Gordian Press, 1969).

4 R. O'Gorman, 'The Prose versions of Robert de Boron's *Joseph d'Arimathie*', *Romance Philology*, 23 (1970), pp. 449–61.

5 Ibid. See also: W.A. Nitze 'Messire Robert de Boron: Enquiry and Summary', *Speculum*, 28 (1953), pp. 279–96.

6 Included in W.A. Nitze (ed), *Le Roman de l'Estoire dou Graal*.

7 O'Gorman.

8 Dell Skeels, *The Romance of Perceval in Prose* (Seattle and London: Univ. of Washington Press, 1966).

9 Charles Williams, *Arthurian Torso*, edited by C.S. Lewis (Oxford Univ. Press, 1948).

10 O'Gorman.

11 Ibid.

12 Helen Adolf, *Visio Pacis: Holy City & Grail* (Pennsylvania State Univ. Press, 1960).

13 Ibid.
14 M.R. James, (ed), *The Apocryphal New Testament* (Oxford Univ. Press, 1924).
15 O'Gorman.
16 M.R. James.
17 *The Mabinogion*, trans. Jeffrey Gantz (Harmondsworth: Penguin, 1976).
18 Helaine Newstead, *Bran the Blessed in Arthurian Romance* (New York: Columbia Univ. Press, 1939).
19 Pierre le Gentil 'The Work of Robert De Boron and the Didot Perceval', in *Arthurian Literature in the Middle Ages*, edited by R.S. Loomis (Oxford Univ. Press, 1959).
   W.A. Nitze, *Speculum* (1953).
   R.S. Loomis, *The Grail: from Celtic Myth to Christian Symbol* (New York: Columbia Univ. Press, 1963).
20 Linda M. Gowans, 'New Perspectives on the Didot Perceval', in *Arthurian Literature VII* (Cambridge: D.S. Brewer, 1987).
21 Fanni Bogdanow, *The Romance of the Grail* (Manchester Univ. Press, 1966).
22 H.O. Sommer, *The Vulgate Version of the Arthurian Romances*, 7 vols. Washington: The Carnegie Institution, 1909–1916.

~ 4 ~

The Meeting of the Waters

Hannah Closs

Theories about the origin of the Grail tradition exist in such numbers as to cause bewilderment rather than illumination: one of the most frequent bones of contention being the derivation of Grail lore from either Eastern or Western sources, one or other being championed by individual writers. What has seldom been attempted is an approach which seeks to reconcile the two, pointing to a dual origin, or even a unified urge which sprang into being in various parts of the world at the same time. Yet from this unified point of origin comes the harmonizing influence of the Grail itself, reminding us that out of the reconciliation of opposites comes rest, and the recognition of the true self. The simple power of the Grail images demonstrates how this may be achieved. To meditate on the symbols of the Grail is to activate them. Once activated, they become signposts in our own quest, pointing towards a personal point of harmony and reconciliation.

I

Few though the images of the Grail may be, their richness conjures up an infinite world – whether it be the green valleys of Usk or the dim forests of Broceliande – a world in which we may expect to encounter, at any turn of the path, the magic fountain of Owain's adventure, or catch between the trees a glimpse of Guigemer pursuing the fateful hart. Endless is the quest through the perilous wood. Dare we hope that, faint and doubting, we may reach at last, where the thicket lightens, the cell of Trevrizent, though the clouds still shroud the horizon that promised sight of the Grail?

The quest is still unfulfilled – even for scholars. Amongst those who have contributed most to the elucidation of problems relating to the

Grail was the late Jessie Weston, to whom T.S. Eliot acknowledges a profound debt in the notes to his *Waste Land*. In the book he particularly quotes, *From Ritual to Romance*,[1] as in other of her works, she set herself the task of proving the actual existence of a definite Grail Mystery. It was her belief that an ancient fertility cult still discernible in folk ceremonies the world over, but having an esoteric spiritual meaning traceable in Hellenistic-Oriental mystery religions ultimately sublimated to a Christian gnosis, was transported by the foreign legionaries to the furthest bounds of the Roman Empire. Finding a congenial soil in the realm of Drudical lore, it was adopted by the Britons, though sooner or later its practice, on account of the violation of one of the 'Grail' maidens, was relegated to the secrecy of the mountain fastnesses.

As in the East, this search for the ultimate Secrets of Life involved initiation and a test on different planes of existence. The text which Jessie Weston considers to reflect the earliest existing version of the Grail story[2] gives the description of such an actual test. The hero or rather the would-be initiate (he fails on the higher plane) is Gawain. Gradually, however, what was originally the account of an actual happening was converted through the influence of Christian relics (Glastonbury and Fescamp) into a romance of which Perceval, whom she considers as a folk-tale character, originally unconnected with the Grail, becomes the hero. With Chrétien de Troyes and Wolfram von Eschenbach, the ritual myth, according to her, becomes purely literary.

In tilting against the adherents of the purely Celtic school, Jessie Weston rightly warns us that visits to the Otherworld are not always derivations from Celtic fairy lore. (See also Ch. 15) Nevertheless, obsessed with the fertility aspect suggested by the dead king on the bier, the waste land, the sexual symbolism of lance and spear, she has hardly done justice to the divergence of certain versions from her accepted scheme. Their dismissal to a realm of literary fantasy and confusion remains unsatisfying. Is there really not a fundamental connection, for instance, between the seemingly conflicting versions which see the Grail now as a vessel, now as a precious stone, and a deeper reason for the 'introduction' of Perceval? Jessie Weston refused, as she herself admits, to be sidetracked down a bypath that can but lead into mists of a Celtic twilight. It is possible that we shall have to venture into a realm of far deeper shadows to achieve the quest and explain the perpetual re-occurrence of images that seem to combine two distinct patterns, which, in spite of local and periodic divergencies ultimately reveal an underlying affinity. Then we shall learn too that the repetition of such symbols may not depend only on conscious borrowings and factual transmission but on a repeated upwelling from the unconscious of a forgotten heritage, whether in the individual or in the group.

What follow are but a few suggestions in that direction. For the purpose of our own inquiry it will be necessary to consult not only literature but the products of fine and applied art. Ideally, of course, such a study would have to embrace also the province of music.

One of the chief recurrent images of Celtic myth and legend appears to be that of a visit to or from the Otherworld. It is significant that the landscape thus conjured up so often bears the same or similar features which, though they appear in different combinations and not always all together, enjoy one basic peculiarity – that of a realm somehow detached from this present world. It may be described as at most times, or to all but a chosen few, invisible. It may be visibly cut off by ocean, river and lake, by mountain rock or by mist, or hidden within the mountain itself. Sometimes it can only be entered by the overcoming of a test or through the sustaining of a mortal wound. But always it is cut off by some barrier from the world of daily existence. Thus Tristan and Guigemer, wounded beyond hope of healing are borne in a rudderless or fairy boat across unknown seas; thus in the lay of Ivonek, the lady following in the track of her elfin lover's blood has to venture into the very bowels of the mountain to reach the fairy world on the other side. Owain has to perform the magic rite at the well and over-come its consequences. The castle of the Grail itself lies in a mountain fastness, beyond the ocean, on the bank of an impassable river, or by a mysterious lake. It is impossible in this short space to enter into all the variations, even of the Grail landscape. Enough to point out that from concepts as widely divergent as the barbaric raid to secure the magic cauldron in the *Harrowing of Annwn* in which the magic land is conceived now as an island fortress, now as a dim subterranean land, lighted by lamps, now as hell, to the Christianized mysticism of the *Perlesvaus*, the image is retained. It occurs most clearly in a reference in the *Book of Taliesin*:[3]

> *Perfect is my seat in Kaer Siddi*
> *Nor plague nor age harms him who dwells therein.*
> *Manawyd and Pryderi know it.*
> *Three utterances around the fire will he sing before it.*
> *And around its corners are oceans currents*

And the fruitful [wonder-working] spring is above it
Sweeter than wine the drink in it.

The resemblance to *Perlesvaus* is striking:

La nef a tant coru e par jor e par nuit, issue com a Deu plot, que il virent un
chastel en une isle de mer ... Il esgarde desouz un molt bel arbre ... e voit la plus
bele fontaine ...

[The youth had hardly journeyed a day and a night, coming as God had
planned, when he saw a castle set upon an island in the sea ... He drew rein
beneath a most beautiful tree ... and saw a most lovely fountain ...]

We must consider now whether this land of youth, this magic realm of
plenty or spiritual bliss is after all so essentially Celtic.

If we turn to the field of art, we shall discover in Asiatic art countless
examples, often in symbolic or conventionalized form, of mountainous
peaks embraced by heaving waters. To this theme we shall return
presently. For the moment let us limit ourselves to the representation,
on so-called Byzantine reliefs, of a spring or a fountain entwined with
foliage amongst whose fruits and tendrils perch birds, or from whose
waters beast and bird may drink. Or again we have, as on a Sassanian
metal dish, the tree itself flanked by two antelopes. At their feet is water
that in many cases gushes from the tree's roots.

We are obviously confronted with the tree or fountain of Life. It
is due to the research of the late Joseph Strzygowski and Heinrich
Glück[4] that we have been able to get a clear picture of the perpetuation
of the Iranian Paradise, the Otherworld landscape which early
Christendom borrowed (and adapted to its own purpose) from
Mazdaism – that ancient religion in which nature expressed itself in
symbols. It may long before have travelled with Celtic migrations to
the West. Its roots lie buried deep in the Indo-European tradition. Is it
surprising that the imagery is continually reborn in medieval legend
both in West and East?

Franz Kampers,[5] in tracing the story of the Grail to Oriental myth
and Arab legends surrounding the fabled figure of Solomon, points to
numerous references and elaborate descriptions of the tree of life in the
Garden of Paradise so frequently associated with stories of the Eastern
Kingdom of Prester John. The tree which appears now heavy with
luscious fruits, now sparkling with jewels, is even described as

illuminated. As such it has strayed into the legend of the Grail itself, for instance, into a curious anecdote in Gautier de Doulens's *Continuation of the Grail*, where we hear how Perceval comes to a tree in which he sees a child who gives him no answer to his question concerning the Fisher King. Later he sees a tree illumined with candles which changes to a chapel. Kampers goes on to say:

> Both trees are probably identical. The given explanation, that the child climbed up and down the tree because it wanted to show Perceval how vast is the world, was scarcely needed to prove that we have here lit on the sun tree ... whose boughs spread over the whole world.

The identification is proved by a passage in Robert de Boron's version in which Perceval again meets with a similar tree with two children at the crossing of the ways – or from which issue forth the four streams of Paradise. But the imagery seems to lead us further back. I could not but be struck by the strange resemblance that the incident bears to a legend from the *Bhāgavata Purāna*[6] in which the hermit Markandeya beheld on a peak of the earth a young fig-tree bright with fruit and leaves.

> On a branch thereof that looked to the North-East he saw a babe lying in the hollow of a leaf, consuming the gloom with his own radiance ... Then the child drew a breath and Markandeya like a gnat passed into his body. And he beheld lying therein the universe in its fullness ... As he gazed upon the universe, the child's breath cast him out ... and he fell into the ocean of the dissolving world.

That the Paradise in which the Tree stands is often thought to be situated on the cosmic 'Mountain of the World' is proved by legend and art alike. Indian myth may have seemed remote enough and by many it may be considered a still farther cry to Buddhist Japan. Yet it is precisely here that we find several striking visual expressions of the Mountain, which, curiously enough, may throw some light on the Grail. For the moment we will consider only the Tamamushi shrine in the Horijushi monastery at Nara, on one side of which is depicted a most fantastic representation of the mystic mountain Meru. Encircled by coiling dragons which revolve it at its base, and rising in four tiers like a branching conifer, the mountain shoots into the heavens where, between two discs evidently representing sun and moon, fly winged creatures and genii mounted on the backs of birds. Beneath the lowest of the tiers or rocky continents, from each of which sprout shrubs and pavilions, appears a small temple in which the Buddha sits enthroned between two attendants or Bodhisatthvas.

On either side of this subterranean temple stands a bird with sweeping plumage – perhaps a phoenix – surrounded by a flickering line. Surely the ancient Aryan image of the revolving universe has here been translated into the language of Buddhism. But if we recall the prototype-Vishnu's own mountain Meru around which sun and moon revolve, may we not also be reminded of Celtic lore – of Malduin's revolving island and the fortress of the solar hero Curoi; above all of the turning castles in *diu Krone*[7] and *Perlesvaus*, whilst in the Grail Temple described with such fantastic elaboration by Albrecht von Scharfenberg in the *Jüngere Titurel*, the dome was covered with blue sapphire and strewn with gleaming carbuncles, amidst which appeared the sun and moon, moved on their course by a hidden mechanism. (See Ch. 6, p. 104) But we are reminded no less of the magic column in Orgeluse's enchanted castle in Wolfram's *Parzival* which he himself maintains was brought by Klingsor from India – Feirefiz's land.

It is significant that the legend of Prester John once more provides a similar image. The turning palace and chapel which in the latter crown the terrace structure like the firmament are hence not absolutely dependent on Babylonian astrological monuments. As in the case of Arthur's Round Table, which, according to F. Kampers,[8] also revolved, Arab and Babylonian cosmogony and Semitic legend centring on the fabled treasure of Solomon may well have played a part in the development of the Grail romance, but the more we become conversant with the evolution of northern and Iranian art, the clearer will become the hidden Indo-European root, and possibly *roots even deeper* from which that imagery has sprung. It was perhaps no mere stroke of artistic ingenuity that made Scharfenberg conceive his Grail Temple as a circular and radiating building.[9]

The influence of Templar architecture may have played its part, but even so we are led back to the centralized form of the Armenian churches and thence to the Iranian Fire Temple. How this latter was conceived standing in the midst of the holy garden or Paradise may very likely be seen in the ornamentation of Sassanian dishes.[10] It is possible that the very concept of encircling the ritualistic procession around the venerated symbol ultimately derives from a primal stage in man's religious consciousness, whilst it has been suggested that this rotating movement in Aryan ritual, added to references in the Veda to the thirty days dawn, points to the arctic origin of the northern peoples in the interglacial period.[11] (But it should be made clear that the term northern is here used without political perversion and not merely in regard to Indo-European tribes. Actually it embraces also the 'Amer-Asiatic' and 'Atlantic' races who may have migrated southward before them. Hence certain 'northern' tendencies, for instance, in the art and culture of Egypt.)

In the far north where the sun does not rise high in the heavens but actually wanders *round* the earth[12] and is, moreover, for six months wrapped in darkness, dawn is not a daily phenomenon, but denotes the advent of a whole season. There the sun's rising may well be a source of physical and spiritual rebirth. Perhaps some such unconscious memory is really reflected in the *Veda* where we read:

> She, the daughter of the sky, has appeared after, the young maiden in white robes ... She follows the course of the Dawns that have passed away, the first of the endless dawns to come ... rise up. Living life has come to us. The dark has passed away. The light comes. She has abandoned the path for the sun to go. We have come where men prolong their life.[13]

Incidentally, it may be noted that the old English goddess of Spring, Eostre, has been identified by some with the Aryan goddess of the dawn.

Be that as it may, it is certain that long after any migration southward and the change to a diurnal phenomenon, the image of the rising sun persisted with such intensity that it was taken over from Iran by Christianity itself. 'At the flaming of the dawn, when the gates of heaven are thrown wide ... the Saviour rises out of the far East, the fount and habitation of Light.'

The sun, therefore, the Light, the Radiance, may well have been conceived as the fount of Life itself.

At first such ideas may have been visualized only in abstract symbolism. In the course of time, however, the process of anthropomorphization takes place. The sun becomes a deity, Surya, Mitra, Vishnu. But the primal concepts linger on. The light, the sun, is now a tangible object of a raid, a heroic feat, whether it be Indra's theft of the food-providing broth-pot or the expedition of Arthur and his warriors to Annwn, to the land of youth, to secure the pearl-rimmed cauldron which also possesses amongst other properties the reputation of being a vessel of plenty. Thus in the Veda we read how Indra transpierced the Gandharva in the limitless skies to provide nurture for his worshippers. 'Out of the mountains he shot, held fast the ready-cooked broth. Indra let loose the unfailing shaft.'

The springs of the Celtic land of youth abound, as we saw at the beginning of this essay, in wine and mead. In the Vedic Sun-realm we likewise find not only milk and broth but mead. The last, however, is often identified with the Soma – the draught of the immortals. 'On the highest step of Vishnu lies the fount of mead. May I attain to this dear place, where men, devoted to the Gods, regale [inebriate] themselves; they the boon-companions of the wide-stepper.'

This 'third stride' of Vishnu – so often reiterated in the Veda – has given rise to much speculation. It is more than likely that the three strides refer rather to cosmic regions than to the time of day. The following Vedic hymn may offer suggestions. (Indu, incidentally, is a frequent epithet for Soma.)

> Where light is perpetual, in that realm where the sun is placed, to that immortal world bring me, Pavamana; flow, Indu for Indra.
>
> Where Vivasvat's son is king, where the inner chamber of the sun [is] where the eternal waters [are], there make me immortal; flow, Indu for Indra.
>
> Where in the third heaven, the third sphere, the sun wanders at will, where the regions are filled with light, there make me immortal; flow, Indu for Indra.
>
> Where yearning and desire [are satisfied] there where the region of the sun [is], where delight and sustenance are found, there make me immortal; flow, Indu for Indra.
>
> Where joy and pleasure dwell, and mirth and happiness, where the wishes of the wisher are fulfilled, there make me immortal; flow, Indu for Indra.

We are certainly in the 'land of youth' but we may also call to mind Wolfram von Eschenbach's description of the Grail as *'der Wunsch von Paradis, … Erden Wunsches uberval'* ('the wish for Paradise … which excels all earthly excellence').

The Soma has often been related to the Moon (apart from which there seems no Moon-worship in the Veda). But we have already read of the Soma in Vishnu the Sun God's highest step and the imagery here clearly points to the *sun's inner realm*. Thus Vishnu's highest step seems best to apply to the immortal realm of light – is in fact a land of the immortal dead.[14] This is borne out by the fact that the Soma is guarded by the Gandharvas, those strange creatures who can adopt bird or animal form, and who have at the same time been identified with the host of the spirits of the dead.

II

Step by step, the affinities between ancient Indo-European concepts and the Grail spring into sharper focus. The land of immortality where every wish finds fulfilment, where the Gandharvas (one recalls the 'bird' father of Ivonek and note particularly in this case Lohengrin) are in charge of the holy vessel – the sun, but perhaps also the moon (even as two vessels often appear in the Grail legend itself).

But the lance too finds its place, for Indra, who loots both sun and Soma, is described as wielding not only the thunderbolt and the arrow but also the spear. He is accompanied by the Maruts, a swift-footed host of youths in gleaming armour who are often interpreted as the storm winds, but also like the Gandharvas[15] as the spirits of the dead.

It is natural that Jessie Weston refers to them with gusto as helpers of Indra who, freeing the waters, brought fertility on the land. In their traditional dance (represented in ritual mime by the priests) she sees indeed a germ of the folklore sword-dance and even prototypes of the Knighthood of the Grail. Certainly the rain-making capacity of Indra must have been of primary importance to the dwellers of the plains and it may be justifiable to build up, step by step, a theory of the Grail romance which centres on the Waste Land, though that aspect does not seem to exhaust the problem. As she herself admitted, in some versions of the Grail legend the theme of the Waste Land has lost its point, or, as in Wolfram von Eschenbach's *Parzival*, plays practically no part at all. But in the latter case, there appears, it is true, what may be the remnant of an original substitute. First, as she herself states, the very nature of Amfortas's wound, whose sexual symbolism Wolfram in no way euphemizes, suggests a fertility motif which supports her theory. At the same time another point in Wolfram's description, and one that has caused great perplexity to scholars, namely, the treatment of the wound, may perhaps cast a yet clearer light on the subject.

The agony of Amfortas's wound was rendered most unendurable through frost. Now it appears that no less an authority than Hillebrandt held that at the time when the Vedic peoples inhabited a colder region,

Indra must have been a Sun-God who *melted the frost* on the approach of Spring. Hence the strange idea of laying the spear (Indra's weapon) on Amfortas's wound to alleviate the agony attains some sort of sense, as the residue of ancient beliefs mingled with medieval alchemy and folk customs, a fact borne out by the allegations of Suhtschek (to whose theories we shall be referring later) to the effect that a similar ritual is practised by the natives of Sistan today in treating the plague.

Another image that has given rise to much speculation is that of the Fisher King. Admitting the possible influence of Babylonian, Semitic, Christian and Hellenistic legend, it seems that striking affinities may nevertheless be drawn between the Grail Fisher and Indo-Aryan and Buddhist imagery. The golden fish is, for instance, a symbol of the first avatar (incarnation) of Vishnu. Transferred to the Mahayana Buddhism of Tibet, the fish, being golden, is regarded as symbolizing the preciousness of Samsaric beings who are to be freed from ignorance; immersed in the ocean of Samsara they are drawn by the Fisherman to the Light of Liberation. It was, however, once again through one of the treasures of Buddhist Japan[16] that a deeper significance was revealed to me. Here, drifting on the ocean which, like some vast lake girt by rocky tree-clad continents, surrounds the central boss figuring the mountain Meru, we find the actual figure of the Fisherman himself. As in the imagery of the Grail, the Otherworld landscape and the Fisherman appear united.

We have, then, an ever recurrent group of images surrounding the central idea of the *life-giving Light*; the sun-vessel (cauldron or pot), and the weapon used in its recovery; the secret landscape with cosmic mountain and tree where the light withdraws and where is likewise the fount of immortality. Desire and yearning for a happier or higher state of existence necessitate a quest for that secret realm easily associated with the immortal dead. The imagery lingers on in Nonno's description of the Argonauts in which a bowl (the heavens or heavens with the sun) hovers over the illuminated tree on the cosmic mountain. Sometimes the sun-vessel is actually a boat.

Doubtless the fertility, the sex aspect, forms an integral part but may one not also perhaps divine from the first a latent hankering for the transcendental which is borne out by the tendency of 'northern' art (from the Celtic West to the Asiatic East) towards abstraction, infinity and a symbolic conception of landscape? Already in a silver bowl from Maikop, Kurgan, South Russia[17] dating from between the third and second millenniums B.C. we have an instance of beasts moving in the ritualistic circumambulatory manner we have noted, in a symbolic landscape of mountain, tree and water. Perhaps such conceptions are really likely to be rooted in the nature of peoples who spent half their year in darkness, though not in the extreme cold that characterizes the Polar regions since the second Ice Age. When climatic conditions and other factors urged them in repeated migrations to drift southward, such ideas may gradually have found expression in vegetable and animal form (though still abstract or symbolic) the process of personification becoming ever stronger as they intermingled with races who, unlike themselves, held anthropomorphic ideals in religion and art. But behind the consequent evolution of systematized religions and the practice of varying fertility cults, the yearning for the light remains – the imagery persists – now, as in Indo-Aryan or Celtic myth, in the rape of the sun-vessel and the quest for a paradisal 'land of youth'; now, after an assimilation of Syro-Phoenician mysteries and identification with sexual symbolism and the dying God, in an ultimately embraced Christianity. Thus expressed as a Mystery of the Holy Grail it could even invoke Christian relics through identification of Cup and Spear with the instruments of the Passion.

It cannot, however, be denied that Wolfram's Grail differs from the latter imagery. His Grail is a precious stone – a radiant jewel. But is the jewel not also a solar emblem? We meet with it on the tree of Life – the illuminated Sun-tree. We find it in the three jewels of Vishnu's helmet and above all in the Buddhist *padma mani* – the jewel in the heart of the lotus which is itself of solar origin. It too leads to a gnosis and to liberation. It appears to be the Indo-Iranian concept. But it suggests perhaps, too, that the essence of the Grail is to be found in more than original fertility aspect; that the latter, though an integral part of the mystery, is subordinate to the concept of the radiance, the Light. But how was it that a German knight at the commencement of the thirteenth century should have chosen the Iranian in place of the usual Western form?

Friedrich von Suhtschek[18] challenged the whole academic tradition of Western literary history when he maintained the Arthurian cycle to be of Iranian origin and Wolfram's *Parzival* and Gawain's romance a free translation from the Persian. His view is extreme. Is it not more likely (as it has indeed been the purpose of this essay to prove) that there may well be various developments of a Grail concept deriving, part consciously part unconsciously, from a long forgotten source? The poet responds to every vital influence from outside, apprehends an analogy, grasps without knowing it the archetypal image. In Wolfram's case, however, there may be reason to suppose a greater degree of contact with the Eastern stream. Connections with the East, through the Crusades, the Arabs and even long before them were far stronger than most of us suspect.

There may not have been, as Suhtschek would insist, an actual 'Parzivalnama'. Enough perhaps that there certainly existed not only the curiously similar Manichaean tale of the 'Pearl' – the story of a quest and an initiation on the part of a fatherless and poorly clad youth – but that there were sufficient tales of Iranian chivalry to fire the imagination of a European knight. None the less the affinities are so remarkable that it almost seems as though Wolfram were describing the setting of such a Manichaean citadel as Kuh (Mount)-i-Sal-Chwadeha (his Muntsalvasche seems a perfect echo of the name) on the lake of Hamun in Sistan, whilst Gawain's adventure in Klingsor's magic castle gives the most astoundingly accurate picture of the Buddhist monasteries of Kabulistan and above all the palace in Kapisa, with its fantastic throne on wheels (the rolling bed), gigantic stupa and all. Particularly important for us is that this very corner of the globe, the borders of Persia and Afghanistan, was the melting-pot not only of various religions but also of influences in art, and that it is in Iran that we find, as already noted, the perpetuation of Mazdaian concepts of that Holy or Secret Landscape which afforded a starting-point for our inquiry. In Iran, indeed, that Paradise, through the grace of God's spirits – the radiance of the Chwarna – is made manifest on earth. Thus in the Awesta it is written of the Chwarna:

> It appears now as bird, now as a creature swimming or diving, as a ram or in the form of some other beast or it passes over into the milk of a cow. Chwarna causes the streams to gush from the springs, plants to sprout from the earth, winds to blow the clouds, men to be born; it guides the moon and stars on their path.[19]

Nature becomes a symbol, continually reborn through the spiritual fount of all life – 'for ever spending, never spent'. But the crux of the whole matter in regard to Wolfram's Grail is that, like the Manichaean Jewel, it possesses the qualities of the Chwarna itself. Moreover, upon that Manichaean stone alights a dove, to set upon it the Hanma Seed, just as Wolfram's dove brings a sacramental wafer to the Grail. It is on Good Friday (significantly on the advent of Spring – the northern sun's rebirth) that the power of the Grail or the Manichaean stone is thus renewed. Wolfram's Grail likewise possesses the qualities of the Buddhist *cintamani* – the wish jewel – Wolfram's '*Wunsch von Paradis*' ('Wish for paradise'). There are Buddhist paintings of the divine maiden bearing the joy-spending jewel. She might well be an Asiatic sister to Wolfram's Repanse de Schoye. It is significant that the latter married, in the end, the paragon of Eastern chivalry – Feirefiz.

Above all the Manichaean jewel or Pearl is the symbol of compassion. In Wolfram's version, does not the very significance of Parzival's initial failure lie in the fact that he does not ask 'King, what ails thee?' It takes him years to redeem that youthful lack of understanding, and signifi-cantly – though he is able to regain eligibility to the Grail kingship only through bitter experience, through inner growth and self-realization – understanding must ultimately come through the guru – the hermit Trevrizent. How important a part is assigned to the hermit's teaching in Wolfram's version! I would here quote an analogy with a passage I discovered quite independently of any Grail research in a book on Tibetan Yoga. 'This accepted conviction or truth hath not been arrived at merely by the processes of deduction and induction, but essentially because of the Guru's teachings which have made one to see the Price-less Gem lying unnoticed within one's reach.'[20] What is it that the Guru teaches Parzival? The need of '*demut*', i.e., humility, and self-recognition – '*Datta*' (give), '*Dayadhvam*' (sympathize), '*Damyata*' (control) – the doctrine of Eliot's *Waste Land*.

It is precisely that quality which the great emperor in the Alexander romance lacked, and which there too was symbolized in a stone sent from Paradise – the landscape with which we are by now so familiar: 'Go and say to Alexander that it is in vain he seeks Paradise; his efforts will be perfectly fruitless for the way of Paradise is the way of humility, a way of which he knows nothing.'

Influences from the East were doubtless transmitted through the Arabs and the Crusades, but the direct key to Wolfram's Grail probably lies in the riddle surrounding the much-disputed Kyot, whom Wolfram claims as his source. The very existence of this mysterious personage has been denied by many who would see in him only a mask for Wolfram's originality and, according to medieval standards, unforgivable adult-eration of the source. But is not the true test of creative imagination the vitality and poetic power with which he has obviously rendered both story and symbolism so that even if its source be Eastern it has become with him a fervent expression of the ideals of Western chivalry?[21] Who was Kyot? An Armenian, as Suhtschek suggests? Or, as Wolfram himself maintains, a Provençal – a terrain that can certainly embrace Languedoc? Surely it is more than likely that there, in the land of the Albigenses, a territory imbued with Manichaean beliefs and Arab-Sufi influences from across the Pyrenees, legends would find not only access but the most fruitful soil in which to develop, not only as literature but possibly even as a cult. If Jessie Weston is right in believing that an Attis-Mithras Grail cult flourished in Roman Britain, then a Manichaean mystery, originally deriving as we have seen from similar sources, may still more easily have found a home in the citadels and vast fortified grottos of the Ariège.

The Cathar citadel Montségur has been regarded by Otto Rahn[22] as the Castle of the Grail. However, any cult centring on the castle of Montségur must have been subsequent rather than antecedent to Kyot's story, for we know that it was only in the years immediately preceding the threatened Albigensian Crusade that the ancient ruin was refortified as a Cathar citadel. If it was conceived as a Grail Castle it was most likely as the expression of a wish-fantasy in which grim necessity and fashionable aesthetic snobbery mingled with the craving of a hyper-civilized people for spiritual rebirth. But the intermingling of ambition, of human frailty and passion does not cancel the power of the spirit's yearning. The quest remains. Still the Grail-bearer of Montségur haunts the imagination of the Pyrenean peasants – in the shape of Esclarmonde, a synthesis perhaps of the two Esclarmondes, one of whom – the great Cathar abbess – dedicated Montségur to the Cathar faith whilst the other died as a martyr at the stake.

Is it mere chance that the legendary Esclarmonde did not die, but was actually transported to the mountains of Asia? She makes one think, moreover, of one of those reincarnations of Repanse de Schoye's spirit as conceived by a modern German poet, Albrecht von Schaeffer in his own poem on the Grail.[23]

Die is Titurels, des Alten, Tochter;
Tragerin des Grales, lebt in ewiger
Jugend durch den Duft in dem Gemache
bis die Tochter eines neuen Konigs

ihr die Burde abnimmt und die Wurde
stirbt am Ende schmerzlos; wird geboren
augenblicks an audrer Erdenstelle;
heisst Beate oder auch Renate[24]
lebt mit Menschenlos; zu lieben leiden
ohne Wissen eingedenk der Heimat
und des Einhorns und des reinen Dienstes
kensch wie keine; endlich stirbt sie
ganzlich.

It is old Titurel's daughter,
Carrier of the Grail, who lives in eternal youth
By the fragrance of the apartment,
Until the daughter of a new king
Takes on the burden and the dignity.
She dies in the end, painlessly, is reborn
Instantly in another part of the earth,
And is called Beate or Renate,
Living by the lot of mortals: to love, to suffer
Without knowledge, yet mindful of her home
And the unicorn, and pure service
Chaste as none: In the end she is totally extinguished.

There are, nevertheless, numerous points of analogy between Montségur Manichaeanism[25] and Wolfram's Grail, amongst them the discovery in the Pyrenean citadel of earthenware doves. The dove as we have seen was closely connected with both Wolfram's Grail and the Manichaean pearl. It was, moreover, the badge of Wolfram's Templiesen – the name he gave to his knighthood of the Grail. This warrior caste, by the way, which stands in seeming opposition to Cathar pacificism, almost recalls the ideas on militarism expressed in the *Bhagavat-gita*. There is, moreover, the question of the Manisola – the secret feast of the Cathars – which still awaits further elucidation. Was it perhaps a mystic meal such as Jessie Weston associated with her Attis-Mithras cults? In any case it would involve an inquiry into the festivals of the dim past – the Aryan feasts of the dead. So once again the circle would close, leading back to the Land of Light, the realm of youth, of departed spirits.

We should also have to inquire into the report that the skeletons of the Cathars have been found arranged in a radiating circle, which suggests analogies not only with the circumambulatory and radiating formal arrangements in art referred to so often above, but also with the

Tantric designs in which Jung has discovered the magic power of the archetype. Indeed, it is perhaps ultimately only through the study of the ever-recurring Grail images that we shall understand the extraordinary creative power of a symbolism that has continued to have a hold over us for thousands of years, and which, if rightly comprehended, might lead us to a recognition of the hidden unity between East and West.[26]

For the way of the Grail is the way of self-recognition, of acceptance of the Shadow. In the dualism of the world of appearances, the darkness apprehended perhaps by primitive northern man in the nightly, or half-yearly, disappearance of the sun, cannot be denied, but it can be transcended. The path, whether it lead through the death-simulating gloom of a Celtic-Hellenistic mystery ritual; through occult alchemical searchings for the divine essence sleeping in the heart of matter (an aspect presented by Flegetanis in Wolfram's poem) or along the purifying paths of a Manichaean gnosis, has ultimately the same goal – the liberation from darkness into a realm of light, of higher consciousness, where the radiance of the spirit is no longer obscured but burns more eternally even than the never-dying sun of the cosmic heavens or the mystic jewel crowning the mountain of the world; where man breaking the bounds of all otherness enters at last into the holy landscape to recognize his true self in the likeness of God.

A deeper elucidation of the story of the Grail might indeed help in bringing about an understanding of that unity between East and West which Wolfram von Eschenbach and many of his contemporaries apprehended and which he embodied so fervently in a figure from India's *Westereiche* – Parzival's half-brother, Feirefiz. Had their spirit not been obscured in the centuries that followed, the world might never have been led to its present pass.

Notes

1 Doubleday Anchor Books, New York, 1957.
2 Wauchier in his continuation of *Perceval*, she maintains is here drawing from a version anterior to Chrétien's.
3 R.S. Loomis 'The Spoils of Annwn', in *Proceedings of the Modern Language Society of America*, December 1941.
4 Joseph Strzygowski, *Spuren indogermanischen Glaubens in der bildenden Kunst*; Heinrich Glück, *Die Christliche Kunst des Ostens* (Berlin: Cassirer, 1923). Both books contain numerous examples of the 'Paradise' symbols.

5 Franz Kampers, *Das Lichtland der Seelen und der Heilige Gral* (Cologne, 1916).

6 Strzygowski, op. cit., plate 127. Quoted by L.D. Barnett in *The Heart of India* (London: Murray, 1924), pp. 65f.

7 A curious compilation of Arthurian and Grail romances by the thirteenth-century German poet Heinrich von dem Turlin of which Gawain is the hero.

8 Kampers, op. cit.

9 Strzygowski, op. cit., plates 205–7 reproduce S. Boisseree's architectural reconstructions.

10 Ibid., plate 19.

11 B.C. Tilak, *The Arctic Home of the Vedas* (Poona, 1903); Biedenkamp, *Der Nordpol als Volkerheimat* (Jena, 1906).

12 Strzygowski believes that the ambulatory and semi-radiating form of the fully developed Gothic apse may be attributed to the unconscious persistence of those original concepts.

13 E. Thomas, *Translations from Vedic Hymns* (London: Murray, 1923).

14 It may be noted here that in Heinrich von dem Turlin's *diu Krone* the Castle of the Grail is described as the realm of the dead.

15 Leopold von Schroeder, *Die Wurzeln der Sage vom heiligen Gral* (Vienna, 1910).

16 A bronze mirror from the treasure of Shosoui in the Todajdshi monastery at Nara illustrated in J. Strzygowski, *Dürer und der nordische Schicksalshain* (Heidelberg, 1937), plate 47.

17 *Spuren indogermanischen Glaubens in der bildenden Kunst*, plates 11 and 123.

18 Wolfram von Eschenbach's *Reimbearbeitung des Parzivalnama, Klio* no. 25; and his *Parzivalnamanbersetzung, Forschung und Fortschritte*, 10.

19 Strzygowski in collaboration with Heinrich Glück, Stella Kramrisch and Emmy Wellerz, *Asien's Miniaturenmalerei* (Klagenfurt, 1933).

20 W.Y. Evans, *Tibetan Yoga*, Wentz (London: Oxford University Press, 1927).

21 A heartfelt appreciation of Wolfram as a poet is to be found in Margaret Richey's *The Story of Parzival and the Grail* (Oxford: Blackwell, 1935).

22 Otto Rahn, *Kreuzzug gagen den Gral* (Freiburg, 1933).

23 Albrecht Schaeffer, *Parzival* (Leipzig, 1922).

24 The heroine in A. Schaeffer's novel *Helianth* (Leipzig: Insel Verlag, 1922), who is brought into relationship with Akhenaten, the heretic pharaoh of Egypt.

25 Samuel Singer has pointed to Manichaean heretical influence in regard to
   Wolfram's 'neutral angels' in *Wolfram und der Gral: Neue Parzival
   Studien* (Berlin: Herbert Lang, 1939). Whilst Rolf Schroder in *Die
   Parzivalfrage* (Munich: 1928), considers the Manichaean problem at
   length.
26 Celtic concepts related to an ideal Byzantium are reflected in the poems of
   Charles Williams, *Taliessin Through Logres* and *The Region of the Summer
   Stars* (Cambridge: D.S. Brewer, 1982).

~ 5 ~

Sir Thomas Malory

Greg Stafford

Sir Thomas Malory (whichever contender one chooses) lived in an age when Chivalry was almost over. The institution of knighthood would continue for many years; tournaments would be fought on the green meadows of England and France – but Chivalry itself, what Thomas Malory called the 'High Order', could not survive the changing social and moral attitudes of the medieval world. Malory, therefore, entered into a world where nostalgia for the past already existed. His great book, perhaps the greatest single book on the Arthurian legends yet written, is a threnody for those lost times.

His version of the Grail myth, scaled down from the earlier, theologically weighted-down Vulgate Cycle, has a power and clarity rare in medieval authors. As Greg Stafford notes, Malory was not much interested in spiritual matters, but his vision was all-embracing; he had room for the Grail as well as for Arthur, Guinevere and Lancelot.

Greg Stafford's highly personal essay constitutes a love story as much as an examination of myth-making. He loves Malory's work and brings a remarkable sense of vision to play upon him. He shows very clearly why Sir Thomas is in the forefront of the Household of the Grail. He forms a living bridge between the originators and the continuators, shaping the earlier materials in a fashion that made them acceptable to both the audiences of Malory's time and those who came long after.

Sir Thomas Malory stands along the long literary trail of the Holy Grail like one of the mysterious guides a questing knight is likely to meet on a lonely road in the midst of a dark forest. He is really the first of the modern Companions of the Grail. He appears, at first, to be only a simple knight who can tell a great story. On closer inspection we seem to find a great gap between the story of the High Order of Chivalry and the man who did such a job of telling it.

Knights were my special way into the story. Back in the days of Dick, Jane and Spot literature, I traded all my indians and cavalry for other kids' knights, and assembled the neighbourhood's *hugest* knight army. Why I had this pre-literate fascination cannot be answered: it is a mystery. What I can tell you is that it led me to the realm of personal mythology. I think that anyone who has read this far would benefit from making a personal mythology.

To make a myth of your own it is sometimes useful to be irrational first. I suggest, for this essay, that you pretend you have a special perception which most people don't have: arthuring. It is a new use of your sixth sense, beyond seeing, smelling, tasting, touching, and hearing. Arthuring allows you to perceive some things which other people cannot fathom, because they don't have the sense. It also allows you to see some things in a new way.

When I was a kid I read Malory. I was in 5th grade, about 12 years old. Or, to be honest, I tried to read Malory. The language, lack of paragraphing, and sentence structure were too alien for me to understand fully. But in my perusal I was fascinated to discover a whole bunch of stories other than those in Bullfinch, and determined to figure it out somehow.

Like all the senses, your arthuring has to be practiced, used, and trained to get better. When you were an infant your eyes showed only light and dark, and blurry images, like my sense of knights. Then it became real perceptive sight, like my sense of arthur. Later it may become a full-blown case of mythification.

One of the first things your arthuring sense tells you is that there are several basic story themes. You might call them the King Story, Knightly Adventure Story, Love Story, Grail Story, and so on. With further arthuring you will eventually learn that there are the Merlin, Tristram, Arthur, Lancelot, and Grail cycles which contributed to the mythos, and that the Love Story might be, in your arthuring, the True Love of Lancelot and Guinevere and the Illicit Love of Tristram and Iseult.

Sir Thomas knew how to arthurize. He had to in order to rework his source material into his *Works*. In fact, he was a genius at it, and recorded a sense of King Arthur which speaks of us, modern people over 500 years later.

This version is important to us. From it come almost all the images and stories in modern Arthurian understanding. You must leave the mainstream to find a version other than a Malory-derived version. Tennyson's poems were inspired by Malory's text. T.H. White's *Once and Future King*, the single most useful book for introducing people to the legend uses Malory as its starting place. The musical and movie *Camelot* and the movie *Excalibur* both derive from Malory's work.

Malory's work has acted as a bridge between the Middle Ages and the modern age. His works do not depict the medieval attitudes which are found in the literature that he worked from, but instead provide us with a view which we can understand today. Our task, as myth makers, is to integrate the story and adapt it to our needs and understanding.

Part of the process of arthurizing is to let the story tell us what it has to say rather than just reading into it. This is an openly subjective input. It is a simple fact that certain parts of the story make us *feel* funny, or maybe just uncomfortable. Arthurization involves remembering those feelings, and in various ways getting into communication with them. Communication means receiving and giving information, and since most people are unfamiliar with communicating with ideas it is very hard at first. In fact, it is impossible to understand some of the processes, even after it is experienced several times.

I will arthurize first the story of the Holy Grail, and then the legend of Sir Thomas himself, our erstwhile Companion of the Grail. I cannot guarantee that you will understand this stuff. Especially my personal story, which this inevitably is.

But I think that anyone who has now come *this* far has at least a rudimentary sense of arthuring, and can use it to look at my version of the story. Remember how the knights come upon an obstacle and, if they fail, return home and relate it so that someone else can try to go farther. Those who follow up usually take a trail which is similar, but not the same. If you can arthurize my path, find the truth and falsehood and the personal from the universal, maybe you will go a step further than I went, or take a better path.

The Works

We need to look at least briefly at the rest of the works which Sir Thomas penned to gain some perspective on his interpretation of the Grail Quest, which was only one of eight books which he wrote. Although he had to constrain himself to remain within some limit of the stories, Sir Thomas was a vigorous reinterpreter, not an author who supported outdated sentiments.

We will concentrate upon what appears in print, and we will also look at the new material which Sir Thomas added to his sources. These will give us a clear idea of the points which he wished to emphasize. The changes occur mainly in his view of the Good King, the High Order of Knighthood, his views of Love, and his retelling of the Grail quest.

The eight books of Malory's Works are:

1 *The Tale of King Arthur*
2 *The Noble Tale of King Arthur and Emperor Lucius*
3 *The Noble Tale of Sir Launcelot du Lac*
4 *The Tale of Sir Gareth*
5 *The Book of Sir Tristram de Lyones*
6 *The Tale of the Sankgreal*
7 *The Book of Sir Launcelot and Queen Guinevere*
8 *The Most Piteous Tale of the Morte Arthur*

The first two books center upon King Arthur. They emphasize the role of the Good King and the benefits to be gained thereby. Tom rewrote his sources to make King Arthur's campaign against the Romans similar to the conquests of King Henry V, a near-legendary warlord who was the last strong king of England and who died when Tom was a young child.

These books introduce the great knights of the later stories: Launcelot, Gawain, Kay, and the rest, but is primarily about the Good King. Arthur is shown to be the fount of authority and leadership. He is not without fault, and he is not a great paragon of kindness. He is, when need he, ruthless and cruel to his enemies. yet he is also the origin of all the traditions which make men good. Arthur is a heroic warrior himself, and his personal activities inspire his knights to good acts and great deeds.

One of the striking features which appears in several of the tales which Malory chose to tell has to do with forgiveness. Most of the great heroes of the legend commit at least one grave error, yet mend their ways and rise to greater heights. King Arthur grievously committed the sin of Herod and destroyed the innocents born on 1 May, hoping thereby to destroy Mordred. Yet Arthur went on to become the ideal ruler, protector of all who were weak and helpless. Sir Gawain, on his first quest, recklessly slew a woman even though she was begging for mercy, yet he went on to become the great defender of all women. Sir Launcelot committed the greatest error of all by breaking trust with King Arthur and committing adultery with the Queen, yet in the end Launcelot found sainthood – he even rose immediately to heaven upon his death.

The next three books elucidate the tales of famous knights, recounting a series of adventures which illustrate the virtues of High Order of Knighthood. They center on Sir Launcelot, Sir Gareth and Sir Tristram. The basic format for adventure is for the knights to go out into the world to encounter whatever adventure they meet. Most affairs are fights against robber barons, outlaws, long-standing family foes, and occasional monsters. Personal virtue as well as martial prowess carry the day. If lovers, they dedicate their work to their lady.

These form the central set of examples for Sir Thomas' highest ideal: the High Order of Chivalry. This practice can change the ordinary knight into a gentleman, and more importantly, make its practitioners 'the sternest knights to their foes'. This is a practical guide to knighthood. Good breeding, gentleness, and loyalty contribute to the knight's battle prowess.

One of the things Malory did was to ground the lofty ideals of earlier works. Chivalry is not an abstract moral code, but a set of practical practices. Sir Thomas expresses an earnestness of belief in knighthood as a fellowship controlled by the heroic example of a strong king. He expresses no apologies or shame in the brutality of the task.

Tom's rewrite changed the emphasis of love in the story too. It was no longer the *fine amor* portrayed in the Vulgate Cycle. *Fine amor* was the formalized passion which indentured a lover to his lady, and ennobled the suffering as part of the process. The situation always struck me as a terrible form of love. It is too much like the dependency relationship, rather than love, which so many of us have discovered ourselves to be trapped in. Tom altered the understanding of what love was so that a knight is ennobled not by suffering, but by constancy. Constancy will provide stability to his life. In any altercation or misfortune, true love can help the lover through.

Sir Launcelot was already the knight in Malory's sources. In his version sympathy is increased for the knight. Through selected editing Tom shows us the type of love that is the highest form of existence. He added some significant passages. My favorite is the one where he compares love to the seasons (Caxton's XX, 1). Love is not some sort of rarified bliss but is a thing of this world. Elsewhere he praises the constant love which is not like love in his day which 'blows now hot, now cold'.

The next book is the one which concerns us here: *The Tale of the Sankgreal*. Details on it are given below.

The last two books depict the downfall of the Arthurian realm. They are grievously pessimistic, and both cold and cynical in their interplay of politics and personality. They portray the failure of great ideals when personal goals are at stake.

Tom rewrote an older French text called the Vulgate Cycle. We need to rewrite his story for ourselves. We can discover the potential range of our deviation from his text by comparing some of the changes which Tom wrought in his original.

Myths hold something which is universal, but they are also inevitably products of their time. They are mirrors for the ideals of the age in which they were created, and are always skewed by the author's point of view. Myth is liquid, contrasted with dogma, which is solid, inflexible, and immobile; it can be reshaped without changing its essence.

Thus we would expect Tom to make some changes to a story written 250 years earlier when Europe was undergoing a great social and cultural renaissance in affairs of church, state, art, and culture. The author of the Vulgate Cycle was a cleric and highly placed courtier for King Henry II, founder of the Plantagenet dynasty. Likewise, we must expect to make some changes to the story for ourselves as well.

The Vulgate Cycle was written in a style called *entrelacement*, or 'interlacing'. In this method a story, say about Sir Launcelot, is begun, but abruptly stopped before its conclusion. Then the plot with Sir Gawain starts and is similarly stopped, and then the Perceval story is begun. Then we return to the Launcelot story for a while, the plot around Sir Bors is started and stopped, Gawain and Launcelot join together for a while, Launcelot goes again and spins off a tale about Sir Lionel, Perceval goes on a bit, Gawain and Lionel go on for a while together, Launcelot and Galahad go on, then Gawain, then Perceval, then maybe Bors and Lionel, and so on and so on, creating many threads of stories, characters, and settings which weave back and forth to create the vast tapestry of Arthurian adventure.

Such a style was admirably suited for the audiences of the time. The books were made to be read aloud to the largely uneducated members of a court who had long winter hours to be entertained. It is easy for us to hear the wind howling outside a dark, drafty castle, and then to imagine the half-drunk knights listening intently as Sir Gawain goes about the countryside bashing heads and seducing maidens; then turning to joke as the giggling young girls sit up when their favorite Sir Launcelot enters the scene for a while; and then the idealistic younger sons paying close attention when Perceval comes into the picture. All the Round Table knights get some story time, and the story goes on and on over the long winter nights.

Thomas made a modern version of the story. He changed the method of story-telling from the French interlacing by unthreading several of the major, more interesting plot lines and stringing them into narratives. This type of lineal thinking, a natural outgrowth of Western thought, was already rooted in his age. Tom lived at the start of the age of print – his publisher was the first printer to use Gutenberg's invention of movable type in England. The way that he thought: along single story lines rather than tapestried weave, was very modern. The mass-produced books were also very modern. So were the ways that he thought about chivalry, love, the Good King, and the Holy Grail.

The stories preceding the Grail tales establish the boundaries of Arthurian civilization and culture. They provided a realm of ideals which were rarely practiced by the knights of the fifteenth century. Yet they were ideals, and recognized as being superior to plain brutality and bloodshed.

From this background we can peer closer at details of Sir Thomas's Grail Quest.

The Tale of The Sankreal

The title originally continued … Briefly Drawn out of French, which is a True Tale Chronicled for One of The Truest and One of The Holiest that is in This World.

Miracles begin the Grail adventure. Prophecies abound: Launcelot is decried as no longer the best of knights; an unknown name appears on the Siège Perilous, one of the Round Table chairs which has destroyed every knight who sat on it. A sword, stuck through a stone and floating on water, appears and cannot be pulled from its place. At the feast a handsome young knight appears, dressed in red clothes and armor, but without sword or shield. The Grail itself makes an appearance, giving each person the food which they most desire. The entire body of knighthood swears to search for the Holy Grail.

The knights depart together, leaving behind an unhappy king and queen. Eventually the knights separate and, though their trails cross and recross, each knight maintains an essentially solitary quest to find the Grail.

During this story everything which has been formerly held dear by the knights of the Round Table is cast down. Moral behaviour in the world of the Grail quest is reversed so that chivalrous acts of honor and martial vigor, the very stuff of the High Order, are condemned. Only spiritual virtues such as humility and chastity open the doors to the Big Adventure. The Grail quest is an anti-romance because of the way it inverts ideals of love, and exalts chastity as the highest of all ideals.

The tales illustrate how different types of knight relate to the spiritual quest. Three knights succeed, and other Round Table favorites illustrate the consequences of leading an ordinary, non-spiritual life.

Most of the questing knights are practical and worldly, and fall prey to their own vices. They practice the gentle ways of court and the violent ways of knighthood, but fail in the realm of the sacred. They naturally bring great harm to their fellows.

Sir Gawain is foremost among these knights. He was the first to swear to seek the Grail, but he is also among the most unfit to compete. Gawain is recognized as being courteous, chivalrous, friendly, and generous, but so imbedded in the mundane world that he cannot recognize the spiritual nature of his quest. Even when he gets explanations, Gawain makes excuses why spirituality will not work for him. Unable to discover any spectacular adventures he returns to Camelot, but only after accidentally killing several other questers, and inadvertently violating the Round Table oath against fighting other members of the fellowship.

Launcelot follows a path different from Gawain. The former Greatest Knight in the World is shown to have considerable moral fortitude, but his sinful liaison with Guinevere prevents him from participating directly in the Grail Mass. The love which was a noble philosophy and practice before is instead a weight which cannot be borne to the presence of the Grail.

All is not lost, and the Malorian attention to forgiveness comes again to the fore. Launcelot is dragged through the marsh of guilt and desire finally to renounce his worldly ways. His path is that of redemption through penance. No humiliation is too great for Launcelot to endure. Subsequently he is allowed to view a Mass of the Grail. Unfortunately, the old man presiding holds aloft the Grail and falters. Launcelot rushes to help him, crosses a line which he was told not to cross, and – pow! – he's out of the Grail quest.

Sir Bors was the least pure of the three successful questers, having once been tricked into a woman's lustful embrace. Bors is a knowledgeable knight whose intellect is continually challenged with moral dilemmas. For instance, on the quest he was once confronted with a choice: should he rescue his blood brother, Lionel, or a fair maiden who was being kidnapped. He chose the latter, and was tricked into thinking his brother was subsequently killed. Shortly after he found his brother alive, but Lionel fell into a fratricidal frenzy because he was so enraged at the decision, and Bors was saved only by the intervention of God.

Percival, who had been the lone hero of all tales preceding the Vulgate Cycle, maintains the simplicity which he exhibited in earlier tales. In fact, it is exaggerated to the point that Percival is stupid. He cannot recognize a miracle when he experiences one, and he shows he cannot even recognize evil when it manifests as the sexually alluring temptress. Percival succeeds through absolute total abandonment to his faith, a virtue which prompts his intuition enough to be saved by apparent accidents.

Sir Galahad is the third successful Grail quester. It is his appearance, in red armor without sword or shield, which initiates the Grail quest. As grandson of the Fisher King he is the fulfiller of many prophecies, and the ways of adventure open before him. He is more than saintly, being Christ-like in his perfection. Like Christ, Galahad is not entirely devoid of humanity. He reveals some of his human traits during meetings with his father and other knights, and over the grievous concern he shows when he kills his first enemies.

However, the allegory is so pertinent that it is impossible to ignore. Intentionally, of course, by the design of the author. In many cases the allegory intensifies the meaning of the story, and makes it more enjoyable. Sir Launcelot, for instance, mirrors the role of Adam as the Perfect Man who has been led astray by that greatest of sins, unchastity. Galahad, the son of Launcelot, is the Second Adam who has come to redeem humanity.

The Vulgate author added many other parts to the Grail story. To the thirteenth-century audience, the Grail quest was entertainment, but also a guide to spiritual life for the members of court. In case the audience might misunderstand a point the author had monks regularly appear to explain what is going on. These wise men are invariably clothed in white robes, the habit of a Cistercian monk.

The Cistercian brotherhood was active at the time and had not yet been polluted by worldly ways to stint on their vows of poverty, obedience, and chastity. These monks reveal the secret wisdom of the Grail quest in explicit terms where each lists the hierarchy of virtues. The path to spirituality is said to he through the practice of virginity, humility, patience, justice, and charity. These are the same as the vows taken by monks.

We ought not to be surprised to discover that these monkish vows are exalted in the tales. As we said, it was written by a monk. Those knights whose efforts proved their purity achieved the impossible because they were like knights and like monks. The Vulgate Cycle was written during the time of the great monkish orders of knighthood, the Templars and Hospitalers, which provided a model.

The monks also explain the secrets of the Holy Grail. These are revealed to be curiously in line with the dogma then being proselytized by the Cistercians. The quest illustrates that the Holy Grail is Divine Grace, a force which is necessary to allow us inherently evil human beings to find God. Divine Grace can be gained through the sacrament of the Eucharist, or Holy Communion, whose miraculous complexity is shown in the tale.

One of Tom's major changes, for the better, was significantly to shorten almost all of the explanations made by Cistercian hermits who are found after every mysterious event in the Vulgate Cycle. Thus we are not subjected to their pedestrian explanations. This has the wonderful effect of returning some of the ambiguity and mystery to the tale for us.

The quest draws towards its close. Sir Galahad, the most rarified and perfect of the questers, gets a close encounter of the First Kind and goes right to heaven, taking the Grail with him and away from us sinners. Percival fades out, rather anticlimactically, a year later. Sir Bors finally returns to Camelot, tells the tale, and hands out some final artifacts.

Sir Thomas, preparing the way for us today, questioned whether the effort was worth it. The monumental and inhuman effort required by the successful Grail questers result in nothing of value for the world, and any personal gains are totally selfish. The healing of the Fisher King and the realm are significantly downplayed. Sir Galahad, as if too ephemeral and fragile, departs the world in some sort of Dantesque beatitude. Percival just wimps out. Only Bors returns.

This last is significant: only Bors returns. Joseph Campbell has pointed out how the critical segment of the Heroic Journey is the Return phase when the quester goes back home with whatever boon he has uncovered to share with his people. Without a Return the quest is unfinished. Bors, who is the least holy of the questers to the monks in the earlier Vulgate version, becomes, for us, the most significant success among the knights who participated in the Grail quest.

Malory's Grail quest also alters the part of Sir Launcelot, especially in his reaction to the whole affair. Launcelot is returned to his station as the Greatest Knight of the World after Galahad fails to return from his holy encounters. And Launcelot is content with the limited success which he achieved. Launcelot is not fooled by visions of immaterial realms, but finds satisfaction in his good deeds, constant love, and fulfillment in the ideals of his High Order. Launcelot may not fulfill the Best Ideals (as determined by a church whose hypocritical corruption was monumental), but he was content with Good.

Malory reorganized the hierarchy of knighthood from that in the earlier version. The Vulgate Cycle had honored the monklike spiritual knight first, then the chivalrous one, and finally the lover. Sir Thomas, a man of this world, not a dreamer in another, saw the lover as highest, the chivalric as central, and the spiritual knight as the least important.

In short, Thomas preferred life, in this world, over religious excess. He preferred the constancy of love, even with all its dangers, over the abstract and unreal Grail. He did not shun or fear the emotional and physical passions which terrorized the prissy clerical author of the Vulgate Grail Cycle. He did not degrade life, or the desire for life.

The Author

All that is certainly known about the author of *Le Morte d'Arthur* is taken from his own works: that he was a poor knight prisoner when he wrote the books, and that he finished in the ninth year of the reign of King Edward IV (1470).

Human curiosity is insatiable, and scholars have been driven to discover more about this genius. Using existing records from the

Middle Ages, they have turned up four possible candidates. The most likely are: a Welsh knight; a knight from Huntingdonshire, of Papworth St Agnes; a knight from Yorkshire; and, a mercenary and outlaw knight from Warwickshire, holder of the manor at Newbold Revel.

Maybe none of these are correct. It is quite possible that the Sir Thomas Malory who wrote the manuscript has escaped the paper records which have survived the 500 years since they were compiled. It is, however, unlikely, and so we must choose one of these.

I do not find the choice difficult. Even if all other factors were equal I am drawn towards one of these candidates. Most authorities agree, on scholarly research, and I also find it emotionally satisfying, to choose the best-known candidate as our hero author.

Thus the author of *Le Morte d'Arthur* is Sir Thomas Malory of Newbold Revel. More is known about him than any other knight of his time and place. Much of it is embarrassing at best, unspeakable at the worst.

He was born sometime around 1415 in Warwickshire, in the Midlands of England. The year 1415 was when the English archers achieved their third great victory over the French knights, slaughtering them at the Battle of Agincourt. Henry V, the hero-king descendant of Henry II, began the penultimate phase of the Hundred Years War with the reconquest of France. Although this was a monumental English victory it was another great nail in the coffin of chivalry, for the knights did not take the day with their glorious mounted charge. Instead they dismounted, and peasants armed with bows brought victory that day.

When Thomas was a child, probably seven years or so, the heroic King Henry V died, and was succeeded by an infant son, later King Henry VI. Regents were appointed to oversee his childhood. Two major factions, called the Yorkists and Lancastrians, struggled to control the regency during Henry's childhood. Later the adult king was recognized to be mentally incompetent, and so the power struggle continued for years. Troubles simmered between the factions during the concluding years of the Hundred Years War, then later exploded into civil war. The 30-year civil war became known as the Wars of the Roses. However, the Hundred Years War still had a few years left to run while the factions accumulated grievances against each other.

In 1429, when young Thomas was of age to begin his squiring, Joan of Arc led her first victories in France, and the French began to reconquer their lands. Contemporaries thought something was very wrong with the world when that occurred. Not only was England being defeated, but all of knighthood took another great wound when it was a mystically-oriented woman who led the French war of liberation. She was betrayed by her countrymen and the English convicted her of witchcraft and burned her to death in 1431. But the damage had been done.

Sometime about 1434 Malory inherited his modest holding and was knighted. We do not know what his arms were. At that time the French had increased the pace of their reconquest. Young Sir Thomas went to France and fought, as was the custom, for pay and plunder. His presence did not significantly slow the French, and castle after castle fell to their cannon.

Newly-knighted Sir Thomas must have held few illusions of what he had inherited. He was an impoverished member of a privileged, but morally bankrupt, social class, raised in the time-honored tradition of killing men, but now ineffectual at it. The best weapon of the knight, the armored charge, had become more and more useless. The once-proud tradition of the fighting chivalry was gone. It had been replaced by titled men wearing terribly expensive regalia and going to luxurious tournaments which were becoming more of a pageant than a martial exercise. The cost of the accouterments was beyond the means of most knights, including Sir Thomas. Thus the showiest part of knighthood mimicked the Arthurian glory with empty pomp, and left the majority of its members out in the cold.

The only alternative to the expensive empty pomp was for a knight to serve as a paid mercenary in a brutal war of siege and plunder. Many did. Thus France proved to be a training ground for disaffected young men, and taught them how to make war. This was useful to politicians during the following years of civil disorder.

After some service Sir Thomas returned to England and began a criminal career. Well, let us be objective here: he began an *alleged* criminal career. He was never brought to trial for the accusations, and never found guilty. So if you believe that some sort of *legal ruling* determines criminality, you can rest assured that Thomas Malory was innocent.

Maybe it is useful to be objective about the courts during this time of history, too. After all, the legal system was viewed as one of several ways to get revenge, and the medieval noblemen were nearly as litigious as twentieth-century Californians. An accusation was often made without legitimate reason, Releases were often political, so a release does not mean innocence, just that the man was released. In the same light, prosecution may or may not mean guilt of the accused crime. Perhaps the guilty party was actually guilty of disagreeing with the stronger party about mill rights, or where to herd his oxen.

If subjective morality is your guide then Sir Thomas was again innocent of anything which landed him in prison. He did nothing unusual for his time. He was only one of many knights who was busy at armed robbery, rustling, plundering abbeys, rape, multiple arrests, and multiple daring escapes from prison.

Despite these possible excuses, our man Thomas has such a solid jail record that it convinces me that he was certainly an outlaw, even in the disintegrating order of his own world. A misfit. Not a total misfit, however. He was certainly successful at what he did do, illegal though much of it was. And he wrote his *Works*.

The year 1443 was a busy one for our author. Sir Thomas was married, and his trail of legal papers began. The first writ for his arrest says he committed robbery, but nothing came of it. Two years later he was elected as one of two knights of the shire, and served in Parliament. At least his shiremen trusted him, making the writ questionable. It is precisely this sort of empty, unfulfilled accusation which brings so much question into the legal records of the time.

Malory, a knight of Warwickshire, was a Yorkist. He followed the lead of John Mowbray, Duke of Norfolk, from whom Malory held his land, and of Richard Neville, Earl of Warwick, who was a key figure among the Yorkists and came to be called 'Kingmaker'.

In the fall of 1449 the dispute heated up. Several Lancastrian noblemen were attacked. One ambush was against Humphrey Stafford, Duke of Buckingham, who was one of the richest and most influential men in England. The attack was led by Sir Thomas Malory of Newbold Revel, and included most of the male population of his small holding. Unlike some of the other attacks in England this one failed to kill its victim. Shortly afterwards a writ was issued for Sir Thomas's arrest.

For almost two years Sir Thomas remained free, and went upon a monumental criminal spree. Most of his activity was directed against his neighbors. Offenses include robbery and extortion.

At this time our author also committed the crime most heinous in our eyes: breaking into a house to rob, and then raping Miss Joan Smyth there. He did this not just once, but is charged with committing the same crime eight weeks later. It is possible that this rape is only the old sense of the word, meaning she was carried off with some force or violence. Analysis of the precise terms, however, makes it clear that here rape meant just what it means today, and included sexual intercourse.

More writs were issued for his arrest, but he still eluded capture. He committed more violent offences: cattle and sheep rustling, entering and plundering a manor, and finally plundering the nearby Axholme Abbey, the first but not last of these institutions to feel his wrath,

Plundering possessions of the Church proved his undoing and another writ for his arrest was issued, this one sponsored by the Archbishop of Canterbury himself. Sir Thomas learned of its issuance, and before it could be enforced he and his men went on a rampage to exact revenge in advance. They broke into a game and hunting park owned partly by the Archbishop and destroyed much of it, even carrying off six does. The writ of arrest cites damage at the ridiculous value of £500! At last, however, he was captured by men of the Duke of Buckingham, and imprisoned.

Sir Thomas was unrestrainable. He broke out two nights after being captured, swam the moat, and rejoined his band of men who were hiding nearby. Without hesitation the gang broke into another monastery, Combe Abbey, robbed the monks, and caused great destruction. Not yet content, Tom and even more men repeated the action at the same abbey the next day, taking in triple the loot of the first day.

Sometime before 1452 Sir Thomas was apprehended and sent again to prison. He was detained only a short time, either escaping or being released, but rearrested a year later. This time severe penalties were placed on the warden if Thomas escaped again. The Church was making its charges against him stick.

In 1453 the Hundred Years War ended. All of France except Calais was back under French rule. The English had suffered a significant defeat, despite their much-praised archery. Their king was off his rocker. The noblemen, unchecked and divided into factions, turned upon each other in the Wars of the Roses.

In 1454 Malory was released, bailed out by other men of John Mowbray, Duke of Norfolk. This duke was Malory's own liege lord, and a leader of the Yorkists. The politicians needed the muscle of a loyal, experienced soldier.

Thomas immediately went to work, aiding first in an armed robbery and a great horse-stealing spree. After three months he was arrested again (his fourth capture), effected another violent armed escape (his second), but a few months later was caught again. And once again, a great fine was placed on the head of his jailer if Sir Thomas escaped, ensuring his continued imprisonment. This time his captor was the Marshal of England, a very powerful lord.

In 1456 Thomas presented a fake pardon to the courts, but it was recognized as bogus and he went back to jail. He then borrowed money, bribed a guard, and escaped. But he was unable to pay back the debt, and what the king's men could not do, Malory's bondsman quickly did: he was captured and put into debtor's prison.

He was removed to the Tower of London, a stronger prison, probably because his Yorkist patrons had begun to move towards open warfare. Malory's imprisoners had interest in detaining Yorkist soldiers. So Sir Thomas was in the Tower of London when the Yorkists gained a great victory at the Battle of St. Albans. Despite the success of Malory's friends, he was denied a pardon and removed to Marshalsea Prison.

In 1457 Sir Thomas was temporarily released again. His two months of freedom were uneventful, or at least legal enough to leave no paper trail, and he peaceably turned himself back in.

In 1459 Sir Thomas was released yet again. As had occurred many years earlier, his sponsors were the Duke of Norfolk, his liege, and the Earl of Warwick, Richard Neville the 'Kingmaker'. The politicians once again needed a tried and true soldier.

On 10 July 1460 Thomas fought at the Battle of Northampton. The Yorkists crushed their foes and the Duke of Buckingham, whom Thomas had ambushed eleven years earlier, was killed. The victors persuaded their candidate to accept the crown, and England got its King Edward IV in 1461.

After this military service Sir Thomas went peacefully back to prison. He was among those pardoned by the new king in 1462. He, and presumably many others recently freed, was with King Edward at the sieges of Bamburgh and Alnwick that winter.

He seems to have gone straight for a while, and appears in several documents as a witness to legal proceedings. In 1466 a grandson of Sir Thomas was born, and his son died.

About this time the 'Kingmaker' had a falling out with King Edward. Warwick, so long a champion of the Yorkist cause, turned against the man he had made king. Sir Thomas, true to the High Order, remained loyal to Warwick, who had helped him, and so he became an enemy of the king. Sir Thomas, who was around 50 years old by now, stirred up enough trouble to be captured by the king and imprisoned again sometime around 1467. He was in prison in 1468 and 1470, when he was among those specifically excluded in four General Pardons issued by King Edward.

During this period he wrote the majority of his stories. In 1470, at about the age of 55, as witnessed by his own hand, 'in the ninth year of the reign of King Edward IV', Sir Thomas Malory finished his last work, *The Most Piteous Tale of the Morte Arthur Saunz Guerdon.*

On 9 October 1470, King Henry VI was temporarily restored to the throne and Sir Thomas was pardoned. He did not go far from his latest prison. His final days were full of talk of another upcoming battle, and he may have felt a final desire to join his leaders in the fight. He did not.

The last document pertaining to Sir Thomas records his death on Thursday, 14 March 1471, and his subsequent burial at the sumptuous Greyfriar's Chapel in London.

The Middle Ages were ending. A month after Malory's death also saw the defeat of Malory's powerful protector, Warwick the 'Kingmaker', in the Battle of Barnet. The Wars of the Roses continued without either our great author's presence, or that of his powerful patron.

In 1485, 14 years after the death of Sir Thomas Malory, Caxton published his *Works* as *Le Morte d'Arthur.* That same year the Battle of Bosworth Field ended the Wars of the Roses. The mighty Plantagenet line, started by King Henry II 329 years earlier, ended. The Tudor dynasty began its Renaissance history. The Modern Age began its inexorable grind towards today.

Conclusion

Malory's work is especially pertinent to us because we can easily understand its modern form and extrapolate from it. We, like Sir Thomas, must take the legend and remold it to access the great secrets which it holds for us.

The democratization process which helped to end the Middle Ages interrupted general interest in the Arthurian romances. King Arthur was too much associated with an embarrassing past when a corrupt noble class exploited the masses. The rising middle class staked out more economic and political territory in their rise to social power. The class of luxuried, spoiled noblemen disappeared into the souvenir chest of history. Eventually the process toppled even the desire for *any* king, and fathered our own democratic political institutions.

No more is there a small body of rich folks to listen to idealized tales read aloud over long winter nights. Instead there is a populous middle class whose lowest members are better off than any medieval king.

No more do we have special people who know all the stories and can interpret them to us as they wish. Instead we have individuals who have access to a hundred different stories, and who are responsible for choosing our own favorites.

No longer are we able to leave leadership to those individuals who want it. We are the best-informed, potentially most-empowered people to walk the earth.

History has granted us great gifts, like medicine and democracy, but it has also stolen from us. What it has stolen are our myths, which are the very food of our souls. Now something inside of us weeps with hunger, and the myths move like memories of old banquets which we heard about in our youth, but of which we remember no details. The process which brought us medicine and democracy has also given us nuclear destruction and personal isolation. We are caught in conflicting currents of blessing and curse.

Some things have not changed. We still like a good story. We still wonder, in dark moments of depression, at the meaning of death. We still respond to joy, love, anger, jealousy, and loyalty. The fight/flight reflex still works. These things cannot be quantified in concrete terms, but they exist, and have to be addressed some way or another.

Mythology is the language to define these things which cannot be pinned down. It is not rational, and must sometimes just be experienced to understand at all. Some myths, like those of King Arthur or the Holy Grail, excite us beyond all reasoning. These are the places to start our personal mythification.

These stories are like sketch maps for us. Their deepest truths, hidden from casual perusal, are the same for many of us. The details will always vary. However, any familiarity in strange territory is welcome, and I have found comfort in Malory's tales.

It is no wonder that we feel so strongly for Sir Thomas's story: his times were a lot like ours. An age ends: in his case the Middle Ages, and in ours, the Age of Waste. Except that we can look back on his time to see what happened, and we do not know what is going on now with us.

Society is in turmoil: for Tom the heretofore unknown middle class was being reborn, though he could not tell what it was; and for us something is going on, though we cannot yet recognize it.

Spirituality is in reassessment: shortly after Malory died the Church ran out of heretics to burn and the Inquisition Bull of Innocent VIII loosed the Spanish Inquisition, when thousands of innocent people (mostly women) were burned by fanatical and sadistic misogynists in the name of God and Church. Shortly afterwards Henry VIII crushed the Catholic Church in England. Something is stirring among us now, and we do not know what it will become.

Violence abounds: Thomas contributed mightily to the murder and mayhem of his age, which was widespread enough without him. Random mayhem, street crime, and government policies keep violence active in everyone's life today as if it was just down the street.

Confusion reigns because we have no center, and we have not yet learned how to cope with that. Sir Thomas certainly felt the lack of a strong king to serve, yet loyally served his lesser lord until the end. His noble concept of chivalry as 'a fellowship controlled by the authority and example of a great king' (Vinaver, p. xxxiv) lacked a king. We have no king today, nor anyone who qualifies as a real leader who we can respect. We want King Arthur back, and if we cannot get him back in our mythology we open the way for a bogus king, the tyrant, to come to us in the political world.

King Arthur is said to come back to his people in time of need. Make what you will of literal truth, but he has in fact returned to his people during times of great trouble. (We will skip speculation about the pre-historic Sleeping God of Britain and talk only of this short trail of written references.) The sixth-century warlord certainly came during a time of crisis. The twelfth through thirteenth century started the post-Dark Ages renaissance. The fifteenth century, when Malory wrote, was the time of the Wars of the Roses, the start of the Renaissance and of modern times. Tennyson wrote his hopeful idealizations in the early twentieth century, like a mask over the cracking imperial edifice. And now, in books, and among individuals, it grows.

Arthur is coming back. Maybe he is here. Where? Among us, in you and me, in the same way that the rest of the King Arthur stuff is inside of us. Maybe he isn't in you, but he is in me and a whole bunch of other people! The dispersion of the royal power has made us all kings, and we must take responsibility for our own segment of the world. Find that King through arthuring!

What does my arthuring of the story of Sir Thomas Malory tell me? Well, I like the guy. I don't think he really raped Miss Smyth, not the same way *twice* (even though he has a fascinating penchant for repeating his deeds). I think Thomas loved Miss Smyth to the end of his days, and never once regretted ambushing the Duke of Buckingham to impress her, even if she did forget that constancy part of their love after he was imprisoned. 'It wasn't like that in the old days!'

And I like the fact that Thomas smashed up several monasteries. I am not inordinately violent, but I'd really like to tear down a church some time. The hypocrisy and lies of the Roman Catholic Church did my mother's little boy some serious harm back in those Dick and Jane days. I've learned not to complain since it helped make me what I am today, but the search has led me to also admit that, yes, I would like to trash a church. I don't plan to, thanks to my arthurizing. When I read about Sir Thomas's destruction I remembered when I was very young and watched St Joseph's church burn down, and how happy I felt about it, down there not far inside the attendant guilt. I'm really glad that Tom smashed them, in fact.

In fact, I *really* like the outlaw knight. Yes, he pushed things to extremes more than once. But he fulfilled his personal vows of loyalty and duty to his liege, and must have been pretty good at it since he was several times ransomed specifically to fight. ('Hey Neville, we got a fight coming up. Go bail out that guy who does in churches so well.') He was certainly not an ordinary character, and everyone has trouble realizing how this knight, who was like a rampaging Punk Biker of his time, was also the writer of the greatest work of Old English prose. That is because they have not met enough Punk Bikers, and because they just don't realize that everyone is a myth-maker today. And let us not forget to forgive.

I think Tom was a little bit crazy, like I am a little bit crazy, and like some of you are. One rime liner someone, maybe it was Sir Thomas, who said it was not only all right to be a bit crazy today, but it is also *good for me.* So I will continue to be crazy a bit, but I will also take the lesson from Sir Thomas and not go quite so far out.

Finally, I find solace in the fact that many years of research have brought me to conclusions similar to Tom's. I do not find the imbalance imposed by chastity to be suitable for our age and our future. The rarified, detached spirituality of Christianity is unsuitable for our future, when we will require a balance between the physical and spiritual, as well as between all opposites.

Literary arthuring has dragged me through the Vulgate and other versions, and my personal investigation has stuck me out in the desert without food. I know what suffering is, and I know some things for my future. I know the Wasteland, and I have seen people from the Grail Castle. And I do not want to be like Galahad, or Launcelot, or Thomas for that matter. But all of them have shown me lessons on being myself, and I am better for that.

The penultimate thing that Sir Thomas asks for in his last book is to pray for his soul after he is dead. If you do that sort of thing, try to remember Sir Thomas next time.

PART TWO:

THE SECRET TRADITION

~ 6 ~

Temples of The Grail

John Matthews

The way to the Grail lies within: this much is made clear by the nature of the Quest, in its imagery of the divine search for what is best in humanity. In this scenario the body, which has always been recognised mystically as an impediment to the realization of spiritual freedom, becomes a testing ground, where the good and bad aspects of the individual do battle, the one seeking to know God, the other running from Him. The Temple, of which the body is an image, performs a similar function, in the Grail story more especially so, where it reflects the duality at the heart of all matter, and the desire of humanity to conquer its divided self by stretching up to meet the descending love of creation.

I

When Sir Lancelot, in Thomas Malory's *Le Morte D'Arthur*, comes at last, after many adventures, to the Chapel of the Grail, an unearthly voice warns him not to enter. Hesitating outside the door, he nonetheless looks within, and sees:

> ... a table of silver, and the Holy Vessel, covered with red samite, and many angels about it ... and before the Holy Vessel ... a good man clothed as a priest. And it seemed he was at the sacring of the mass.[1]

Watching the events that follow, Lancelot sees the celebrant holding aloft the image of a man, as though he would make an offering at the altar. And, when it seems as though he would fall from the effort, Lancelot enters the chamber out of a pure desire to help. But he is struck down by fiery breath, and blinded by the light which flows from the Grail. For Lancelot does not know the way into the presence of the Grail.

That way is a hard one, for it consists of entering the Temple of the Grail, which is so designed that it serves as an initiation test for all who wish to share in the mysteries. Lancelot's experience is echoed by many who set out unprepared, and who end by being blinded by what they cannot understand. Properly followed, however, the way towards the home of the Grail can offer a means of knowing, of understanding the light. Many temples have fallen in ruins, but it is said that the true Temple is never destroyed. We would do well to keep this in mind as we examine some of the images assumed by that imperishable temple throughout its long history, hoping that we may thus learn something of our own part in the continuing mysteries of the Grail.

II

The earliest traditions relating to temple-building depict them as liminal space, as dwelling places for God; where the Creator, invited to enter his house, may choose to communicate with his creation. The earth upon which the temple stands is thereby sacred earth either through its being placed at that spot, or by a hallowing touch of the divine which calls forth the building as a marker for those in search of the sacred experience. Thus it becomes a *temenos*, a place set apart, where an invisible border shows that here is sacred space, to enter which means to enter the sphere of the divine, the reflection of the heavenly on earth.

For this reason the forms most often incorporated into the design of the temple are those of the circle and the square, symbolic represen-tations of heaven and earth, so that many consist of squared stones set up in circles (the Megalithic temples), or rectangular buildings supported by rounded pillars (Hellenic and Egyptian temples). These can also be seen as archetypal images of the masculine and feminine, so that the circle of the heavens and the square of earth unite in a single image.

This may be expressed graphically by a symbol known as the *vesica piscis*, two overlapping circles (Figure 1) which illustrate the link between God and his creation which takes place in the temple, whether directly or through the agency of priests and seers. Plotinus understood this perfectly when he wrote (using a slightly different analogy), that the human is drawn to the divine 'like two concentric circles: they are only one when they coincide and only two when they are separated.'[2]

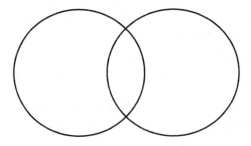

Figure 1

It is a state of *spiritual* separation that causes the failure of Lancelot and those like him, who seek the Grail for diverse reasons; and it is for this reason that the Grail temple exists, to show the way back to a state of unity with the divine impulse of creation.

It is for this reason also that we first read of the appearance of the Grail as an aftermath to the story of the Fall. It is said that the Grail was entrusted to Adam at the beginning of time, but that after the Fall it remained behind, since it was too holy an object to be taken into the world. But there is a tradition which says that Seth, a child of Adam and Eve whom the Gnostics revered as a hidden Master, made the journey back to the gate of Eden in search of the Sacred Vessel. There, he was permitted to enter, and remained for forty days, at the end of which the Grail was given into his keeping, to serve both as a reminder of what had been lost, and as a sign of hope and redemption to come – though this remained unrecognised until the time of Christ, when the symbol of the Grail as Chalice became established in Christian belief.

What is most especially important here, as the Vulgate Grail Cycle says, is, 'that those who possessed the Grail after [Seth] ... were by this very fact, able to establish a Spiritual centre destined to replace the lost Paradise, and to serve as an image of it.'[3] It is this image that is represented by the temple of the Grail, as a place where God and his creation can meet and converse as once they had in Paradise.

In this way the temple can be seen to represent a cosmic evolutionary diagram. It is as though the temple builders, by inviting God to descend into the *temenos*, were asking not only to be guided along the path towards the unity of perfection, but also anticipating that God would actually evolve through contact with them. For, God is spirit and humanity matter and the two cannot evolve separately – they are indeed linked like two interlocking circles, which are only complete when superimposed precisely one upon the other – at which they become one. Thus all temples and churches were intended as physical glyphs to be read by both mankind and their gods, as a mirror reflecting back images of the temporal and divine upon each other.

This imagery is continued in the iconography of the Virgin Mary, who becomes a human temple and a vessel for the divine, and whose reply to the Angel of the Annunciation in the painted imagery of the icongographers, is represented in reversed, mirror writing. This is done so that her words may be read by the angelic power above her, while Mary herself is sometimes referred to as 'a mirror of the greatness of God'.

Thus the earliest temples we know – the stones which gave Megalithic man his name – were erected in circles: set up on power points in the ground, so that they served as living extentions of the earth Herself – the Mother holding out her arms towards the Moon, the Sun and the Stars. These huge astrological observatories were built as much for the gods as for mankind – not just to honour them but to invite them to participate in the ritual living out of life in and around them. Or to quote Plotinus again.

> … those ancient sages who sought to secure the presence of divine beings by the erection of shrines … showed insight into the nature of the All [perceiving that] though the Soul is everywhere its presence will be secured all the more readily when an appropriate receptacle is elaborated … serving like a mirror to catch an image of it.[4]

In its most complete and complex form, this cosmic mirror for the reflection of God becomes also an initiator into the divine mystery of creation, the most perfect object of the Quest. As such it may be expressed by the eternally fixed but changing pattern of the maze, and it is no accident that the architects of the Gothic cathedrals such as Chartres, in an endeavour to encode the mystery of the temple into the design of the great medieval churches of Europe, chose to include this form so often on both floors and walls.[5]

The temple of the Grail was a logical outcome of this, and it is not surprising to find how closely it conforms, throughout its many representations, to the traditional archetype.

III

The imagery of the Grail Temple is consistent. It is usually at the top of a mountain, which is in turn surrounded either by impenetrable forest or deep water. Access, if any, is by way of a perilously narrow, sharply edged bridge, which became known as the Sword Bridge. To make entrance even harder, the whole temple, or the castle which contained it, would often revolve rapidly, making it almost impossible to gain entry by normal means. Once within, more perils awaited, and for those few who succeeded in reaching the centre, where lay the Chapel of the Grail, the experience could, as in Lancelot's case, be both chastening and parlous. Nor was the castle without its human guardians; at an early stage in the mythos a family of Kings, supported by a specially chosen body of knights, appeared to serve and protect the sacred vessel.

The most completely developed description of the medieval Grail Temple is to be found in the Middle High German poem *Der Jüngere Titurel* (c.1270) attributed to Albrecht von Scharfenberg. Here the lineage of the Grail Kings is traced back to Solomon – a detail which, as we shall see, is of some importance – but the setting is firmly medieval in its details. According to Albrecht, Titurel, the grandfather of the famous Grail knight Parsifal, was fifty when an angel appeared to him and announced that the rest of his life was to be dedicated to the service of the sacred vessel. Accordingly he was led into a wild forest from which arose the Mountain of Salvation, *Muntsalvasche*,[6] where he found workers gathered from all over the world, who were to help him to build a castle and temple for the Grail – which at that time floated houseless in the air above the site, supported by heavenly hands.

So Titurel set to work and levelled the top of the mountain, which he found to be of onyx and which, when polished, 'shone like the moon'. Soon after he found the ground plan of the building mysteriously engraved on this fabulous surface.

The completion of the temple took some thirty years, during which time the Grail provided not only the substance from which it was built, but also food to sustain the workmen. Already the Grail is seen as a provider – a function which it continues to perform. But more rarely, and importantly for our argument, it is here seen as contributing *directly* in the construction of its own temple, making one a part of the other, the design non-human in origin, the execution attributed to the hands of man.

At this point in the poem Albrecht devotes one hundred and twelve lines to a description of the temple so specific in detail as to leave one in little doubt that he is describing a real building.[7]

The temple is high and circular, surmounted by a great cupola. Around this are twenty-two chapels arranged in the form of an octagon; and over every pair of these is an octagonal bell-tower surmounted by a cross of white crystal and an eagle of gold. These towers encircle the main dome, which is fashioned from red gold and enamelled in blue.

Three entrances lead inside: one in the North, one in the West, a third in the South from which flow three rivers (thus indicating a debt to the image of Paradise with its rivers and gates whereby they flow out). The interior is rich beyond compare, decorated with intricate carvings of trees and birds; while beneath a crystal floor swim artificial fish, propelled by hidden pipes of air fuelled by bellows and windmills. Within each of the chapels is an altar of sapphire, curtained with green samite,[8] and all the windows are of beryl and crystal, decorated with other precious stones.

In the Dome itself a clockwork sun and moon move across a blue enamelled sky in which stars are picked out in carbuncles. Beneath it, at the very centre of the temple, is a model of the whole structure in miniature, set with the rarest jewels, and within this is kept the Grail, itself a microcosmic image of the whole universe of creation.

It is clear that what is being described in Albrecht's poem is a type of Earthly Paradise. Details such as the three rivers, as well as the overall layout of the building, frozen and perfect in its jewelled splendour of artificial birds and fishes, all support this conclusion. The first home of the Grail is being rebuilt in medieval terms, but it remains a copy, a simulacrum of the true temple whose reality it merely mirrors.

But the image described in the poem is not limited either to mythical, or indeed literary, manifestation. It is possible to trace the origin of Albrecht's temple to an actual site, though this did not come to light until the 1930s, when the Orientalist Arthur Upham Pope lead an expedition to the site of the ancient Sassanian (Persian) temple known as the Takht-i-Taqdis, or Throne of Arches, in what is now Iran.

Attention had already been drawn by earlier scholars[9] to the literary evidence suggesting a link between the semi-legendary Takht and the Grail Temple, but it was not until Pope published his findings that it became known that the reality of the Takht closely approximated the description of Albrecht's thirteenth-century poem.

The site contained evidence of a great central dome surrounded by twenty-two side chapels (or arches) as well as other architectural details similar to those described in the *Jüngere Titurel*. Even Albrecht's mountain of onyx was accounted for by the presence of mineral deposits around the base of the site. These, when dried out by the sun, closely resembled the semi-precious stone.

Pope's excavations also confirmed that the Takht had once contained a complete observatory, with golden astronomical tables which could be changed with the seasons. A star map was contained within the great dome; and to facilitate matters even further the entire structure was set on rollers above a hidden pit, where horses worked day and night to turn it through the four quarters, so that at every season it would be in correct alignment with the heavens. Literary evidence from Persian writings such as the *Shah-Nama* further supported the details of the site, and made clear the nature of the rites which had been celebrated there. These were of a seasonal and vegetational kind, and, when performed by the priestly rulers of ancient Persia, ensured the fertility of the land and the very continuation of its people's life. Pope commented that the beauty and splendour of the Takht 'would focus, it was felt, the sympathetic attention and participation of the heavenly powers'[10] – so that once again we have an expression of the desire for the direct entrance of God into a man-made temple – a temple which furthermore revolved, as did both the Grail Temple and, according to some versions, the walls of the Earthly Paradise – without which it cannot be said to be complete.

IV

Many of the attributes discussed so far bring to mind an even more famous temple – that of Solomon in Jerusalem, the story of which is indissolubly linked with the history of the Knights Templar and with the history of the Ark of the Covenant, which is itself an image that shares many of its attributes with the Grail. It is also the story of a chosen race and their communications with their God.

Built to house the Presence of God (the Shekinah) the Solomonic temple was the concretization of an idea which began with the revelation of Moses, who created the first Tabernacle to contain the Ark and later extended it into the great image of the temple itself. From within this holy house God spoke 'from above the mercy seat, from between the two cherubim that are upon the Ark of the Covenant'.[11] But the Tabernacle was never intended as a permanent home, and it was left to Solomon to complete the fashioning of a final resting place for the Ark at Jerusalem.

Even this remained merely a pattern for the Heavenly Temple, the Throne of God, the Temple Not Built By Human Hands: it possessed also a secondary, spiritual life, made from stones crystallised from the river Jobel which flowed out of Eden. Here there is a sense of an image behind an image; while the link between the heavenly and earthly dimensions of the temple is part of the Edenic mystery, and therefore of the Grail – which in turn performs the same function as the Ark as a place for the meeting and mingling of God's essence with that of his Creation.

This can be taken a step further by reference to Jewish Qabbalistic tradition, where the earthly temple is said to possess 'two overlapping aspects: one heavenly and one divine'.[12] Moses, who received the plan of the temple in much the same way as Titurel in Albrecht's poem, is enabled to witness the mystery performed in the divine dimension, where the high priest is the Archangel Michael. Beyond this is a still higher and more secret sanctuary, where the 'high priest' is 'divine light' itself.[13]

The mysteries of the Grail, which undergo a division into mind, heart, and spirit, echo the formation of the Solomonic sanctuary into the Temples of Earth and Heaven and the Temple of Light. In Jerusalem worshippers entering the outer court of the temple were said to have reached Eden; beyond this, in the Holy of Holies, the dwelling place of the Ark or the Chapel of the Grail, are the mysteries of the heavenly world, where the concerns of mind and body are left behind and those of the sanctified heart begin. Of those who went in search of the Grail, few except Galahad went beyond this point, and those who did were assumed into Heaven. It is as though, looking out of a window, the eye was lead beyond a glimpse of the immediate world, to gaze up into the heavens, and on looking there was suddenly able to see beyond, through all the dark gulfs of space to the Throne of God itself, there to be lost in light.

Lancelot was struck down and blinded by that light, for which he was unprepared. Only his son Galahad was allowed to look directly into the heart of the Grail, and then only at the direct invitation of God – an answer and a reversal of the continuing invitation of mankind to God to enter the temple built in his honour.

Of the several non-biblical accounts of the Solomonic temple which exist, that of the Islamic historian Ibn Khaldun is one of the most interesting, for in it he states that the vaults below the temple, which are still generally believed to have been the stables for Solomon's horses, were nothing of the kind; they were built to form a vacuum between the earth and the building itself, so that malign influences might not enter it from below.[14]

There is a suggestion of dualism in the opposing of the dark forces of the earth against those of the sky, and this is borne out by what we know of the construction of Greek and Roman temples, where the *adytum* stretching *below* the earth was of equal or perhaps greater importance to the building above ground, and which served as a meeting place for the subterranean gods and their worshippers.

By medieval times, when the original site of the Solomonic temple had become a Muslim shrine, the chamber mentioned by Ibn Khaldun had become known as a place of entrance and exit for the spirits of the dead, while of the original structure nothing now remained above ground. The Crusaders however, continued to refer to it as the *Templum Dominum*, (Temple of God) and it became sacred to the three major religions of the time. For the Jews it was the site of Solomon's Altar of the Holocausts, while to the Muslims, as the place from which the Prophet had ascended to heaven, it came for a time to rival Makkah (Mecca), and was attributed with the property of 'hovering' above the earth. Thus the geographer Idrisi referred to it in 1154 as 'the stone which rose and fell' (*lapis lapsus exilians*), which interestingly recalls Wolfram von Eschenbach's description, in his thirteenth-century poem *Parzival*, of the Grail itself as *lapis exilis* (stone of exile), sometimes interpreted as 'the stone which fell from heaven'.

It seems that here we have a paradigm for the whole history of the Grail and of the temple built to house it. The Grail, originating in Paradise, can also be said to have 'fallen' by being brought into this world by Seth. Through its use by Christ to perform the first Eucharist, it is hallowed, and the world, like the lost Eden, redeemed, so that it too 'rises'. Equally, the stones used in the building of the temple, and the design for its construction, as described by Albrecht, can be seen to have 'fallen from heaven'.

The Solomonic temple was to give rise to several imitations in the history of the Western world, one of which at least concerns us in our examination of the temple of the Grail. It became common practice among the Crusader knights to chip off fragments of the rock upon which the Temple had once stood. These they would take home as talismans of their visit to the Holy Land. One such man, a French knight named Arnoul the Elder, brought back one such piece to his home at Ardres in 1177, along with a fragment of the Spear of Antioch and some of the Manna of Heaven (though how he obtained the latter is not related). According to the Latin *Chronicle* of Lamber d'Ardres, Arnoul then proceeded to have a castle built to house these holy relics.

It was of curious design, containing rooms within rooms, winding staircases which led nowhere, and 'loggias' or cloisters (a feature of Chrétien's Grail castle) and 'an oratory or chapel made like a Solomonic Temple'.[15] According to Lambert it was here that Arnoul laid to rest the objects he had brought with him, and it is interesting to note that these objects coincide precisely with the 'Hallows' of the Grail. The spear had long been identified with that which had pierced the side of Christ, and as such had become one of the features of the Grail temple. Manna, the Holy Food of Heaven, is the substance which the Grail provides, either physically or in spiritual form. The stone from Jerusalem was part of the 'stone which rose and fell' and thus recalled the Grail stone described by Wolfram von Eschenbach. So that we have, assembled in a temple or castle constructed to resemble the Solomonic temple, all the elements of the Grail Hallows originating from the Holy Land.

Nor do the links with Solomon and his Temple to the greater glory of God end here. Two important facts remain to be considered. The first concerns the Ark of the Covenant, which may be seen as the Grail of its age, and concerning which a well-founded tradition of the Ethiopian church maintains that it was removed from Jerusalem before the destruction of the Temple by Menelik, a child of Solomon and Sheba. It is still kept in the cathedral at Aksum in modern day Ethiopia, and has remained a central part of sacred practice within the Ethiopian Church. Known as the *Tabot* (from the Arabic *tabut 'al 'ahdi*, Ark of the Covenant) it is carried in procession at the festival of Epiphany, to the accompaniment of singing, dancing and feasting, which recalls the time when 'David and all the house of Israel brought up the Ark of the Lord with shouting and with the sound of the trumpet.[16] Replicas of the *Tabot* are kept in every church in Ethiopia, and where these are large enough to possess a Holy of Holies, this representation of the Ark is kept within, as it was of old in the Temple of Solomon at Jerusalem.

Is it possible that we have here one of the contributing factors of the Grail story? It has been pointed out[17] that stories concerning a quest for a sacred object, undertaken by the fatherless son of a queen, may well have reached the West, where they became the basis for another story of a fatherless child (Parzival) who goes upon such a quest. Add to this the nature of the Ark itself, along with the fact that apart from the *Kebra Nagast*, in which this story is told in full, the only other known source is Arabic, suggests that the semi-mythical Flegetanis, to whom Wolfram attributes the ultimate source of his poem, and who was also of Arabic origin, may have been the disseminator of this narrative. Flegetanis/Wolfram speaks of the Grail as being brought to earth by a troop of angels where 'a Christian progeny bred to a pure life had the duty of keeping it'[18], Similarly, the *Kebra Nagast* tells how Menelik, the child of Solomon and Sheba, bringing the Ark out of Israel to reside in a specially protected *temenos* in Ethiopia.

Two further thoughts may be added. We have heard how Lancelot fared when he entered the chapel of the Grail to help the 'man dressed like a priest' who was serving at the Mass. Even though his intention is good, he is not permitted to touch or to look upon the mystery. So, too, in the story of the Ark's journey from Gebaa, described in the Biblical *Book of Kings*, when it had reached the threshing floor of Nachon, the oxen pulling the cart on which the Ark rode, began to kick and struggle and 'tilted the Ark to one side; whereupon Oza put out his hand and caught hold of it. Rash deed of his, that provoked the divine anger; the Lord smote him, and he died there beside the Ark.'[19]

In a Medieval Grail poem attributed to Robert de Boron, we find the story of Sarracynte, wife of Evelake of Sarras, whose mother had for a time shared the guardianship of the Grail, in the shape of a host, and kept it in a box, which is specifically described as an ark.[20] She at least was allowed to touch it without harm, but such cases are rare in the mythos. Generally the mystery is too great to be looked upon or touched by one who is unprepared. A visit to the Temple of the Grail must come first, and its perils overcome, before the revelation of the mystery can take place.

V

We have already noted that one of the most frequently occurring forms in temple design is that of the circle and the square. These may be seen, in part at least, to reflect a polarisation of the masculine and feminine imagery which lies at the heart of the Grail myths. This mystery is borne out by two seemingly unconnected things: a design incorporated into the great cities of Classical Rome, and an adventure of the knight Sir Gawain at the Grail Castle.

The plan upon which all Roman cities were based, like that of Titurel's Grail Temple, was supposed to have been divinely inspired, revealed to Romulus in a dream. It really consists of two separate designs, which together make up the total image of the city. These two designs incorporate the circle and the square; like the four square walls of the Earthly paradise, Rome is built on the principle of the rectangle.

The *urbs quadrata* is divided across and across by the *cardo* and the *decumanus*. The *cardo* corresponds to the axile tree of the universe, around which the heavens revolve, and is therefore a type of the same artificial, astrologically inspired plan as that of the Takht and the Grail Temple. The *decumanus* (from *decem*, 'ten') forms the shape of an equal armed cross when it intersects the *cardo*. Within this complex were situated the temples dedicated to the sky gods, the masculine pantheon inherited from the Greeks; while adjacent to the *urbs* or living quarters of the city, stood the citadel of the Palatine Hill, a circular form known as the *mundus*. This was the home of the dark gods of the underworld, and of the older worship of the Earth Mother, the Dark Goddess who held the secrets of birth and death in her hands. In token of this, the centre of the *mundus* contained a hole which went down into the earth, covered by a stone called the *lapis manalis*, which was only raised three times a year for the entrance and egress of dead souls, following the pattern established by the Greek temples and followed later by the Solomonic builders.

Here the hidden place at the centre is represented by the ancient Mother worship, existing within the place where male deities were honoured. The representation is reflected by the physical organisation of the city in the forms of circle and square.

In another dimension of the Grail Temple, known as the Castle of Wonders, we find another kind of adventure, that of Gawain and the magic chessboard. Gawain, the sun-hero whose strength grows greater towards midday and subsides towards evening, enters the feminine realm of the circular castle, where he finds a square chessboard set out with pieces which move of their own accord at the will of either opponent. Gawain proceeds to play a game against an unseen adversary – and loses. Angrily he tries to throw the board and the pieces out of the window of the castle into the moat, and it is at this moment that a woman rises from the water to prevent him. She is identified by her raiment, which is either red or black, spangled with stars, as an aspect of the Goddess, and after at first rebuking Gawain for his anger and thoughtlessness, she becomes his ally and tutor, reappearing later in a different guise as his guide on the Grail quest.

It does not take much stretching of the imagination to see that here we have a restatement of the masculine and feminine elements associated with the temple. Gawain enters a circular (feminine) *temenos* and finds within it a square (masculine) chessboard, which is none the less chequered in black and white, a reconciliation of the previously opposing figures. When he tries to dispense with the board, he is prevented from so doing by an agent of the Goddess who, in subsequently helping him, teaches the necessity of establishing a balance between the masculine and feminine sides of his nature.

This imagery is borne out by a further story from the Grail mythos, which brings us back to the themes of both the Solomonic temple and the Ark of the Covenant.

In Malory and elsewhere there are numerous references to the Ship of Solomon, the mysterious vessel which carries the Questing knights or even the Grail itself, to and from the everyday world into the timeless, dimensionless place of the sacred. In fact, however, it does more than this, being in some ways not unlike a kind of mystical time machine, programmed to bear the message of the Grail through the ages, from the time of Solomon to the time of Arthur.

It was built, not by Solomon himself, but by his wife, who is called Sybyll in the medieval *Golden Legend*, and may be identified with

Bilquis, the Queen of Sheba. She, according to another Grail tradition, gave a vessel of gold to Solomon as a wedding gift – a cup which later became enshrined in the cathedral of Valencia as a type of the Grail.[21]

According to the story related in the thirteenth-century *Queste del Saint Graal*, certain objects were placed within the ship, which was then set adrift, unmanned, to sail through time as well as space to the era of the Grail quest. These objects were: Solomon's Crown, the Sword of King David, a great bed supposedly made from the Rood Tree, and three branches from the Edenic Tree of Knowledge, one of red, one of white, and one of green, which were arranged to form a triangle above the bed from which a canopy could be suspended.

We should not be surprised to find images of paradise contained in the Solomonic ship – for the vessel is clearly an image of the Temple, this time afloat on the sea of time – its destination the country of the Grail. But perhaps the most important detail is that it contains wood from the tree which supposedly grew from a branch taken out of Eden by Adam and Eve, and planted in the earth. From this tree, it was widely believed in the Middle Ages, the cross of the crucifixion was constructed, and part of it was used to make the Ark of the Covenant. The presence of this wood within the floating temple of Solomon's ship makes for some fascinating speculation. The ship, as has been said, was built at the behest of Solomon's wife. It thus becomes doubly an expression of a feminine archetype, often regarded as a vessel, and sometimes shown iconographically as an actual ship.[22] It becomes an emblematic prototype of all the traditional imagery of the human vessel, the womb of the earth and the womb of woman; Mary as the living Grail who carries the Light of the World within her, and the blood which will at length be spilled into the Cup which will in turn become the Grail. Within this female temple are placed the images of kingship: sword and crown; together with the three branches from the Tree of Knowledge, coloured in red, white and green, the colours of the alchemical process. Read in this way the myth becomes clear: it can be seen as an expression of the masculine contained within the feminine – of the square within the circle, images of the Grail Temple in all its aspects.

During the same account of the *Quest*, the Grail knights voyage together for a brief time in the mysterious vessel. When the healing of the Wounded King is achieved, the final act of Galahad and his companions is to carry the sacred vessel to Sarras, the Holy City which is itself an image of paradise on earth. They do so in the floating Temple of Solomon, and in token of his Christ-like role Galahad lies down on the great bed which had been made from the wood of the Cross. Symbolically, he is undergoing a species of crucifixion, and in doing so brings about the completion of the Grail work for that age.

After Galahad's death, however, we may believe that the ship returned to these shores, bearing the Grail hither again, to await the coming of the next Quester, and of the time when it would be redeemed again, and help thereby to redeem the time in which this far off event occurred – our own time perhaps.

But the image of the temple as vessel, and of the Grail as a human vessel, brings us to the most fundamental aspect of the Grail Temple – or indeed of the temple everywhere – the Temple in man. This notion has been a common one since earliest times. In the *Chandogya Upanishad* it is held that:

> In the centre of the Castle of Brahma, our own body, there is a small shrine, in the form of a lotus flower, and within can be found a small space. We should find who dwells there and want to know him … for the whole universe is in him and he dwells within our heart.[23]

Or, as one might say: In the centre of the Castle of the Grail, our own body, there is a shrine, and within it is to be found the Grail of the heart. We should indeed seek to know and understand that inhabitant. It is the fragment of the divine contained within each one of us – like the sparks of unfallen creation which the Gnostics saw entrapped within the flesh of the human envelope. This light shines within each one, and the true quest of the Grail consists in bringing that light to the surface, nourishing and feeding it until its radiance suffuses the world.

'*Chaque homme porte à jamais l'age du son temple*', 'each man is the same age as his own temple', wrote the traditionalist philosopher Henri Corbin, adding that the completion of the temple on *Muntsalvasche* was a kind of second birth for Titurel who, after this, we next see four hundred years old but perfectly preserved. The Temple of the Grail is really a divine clearing house for the souls of those who go in search of it – a kind of adjunct to paradise, with glass walls that reflect the true nature of the seeker (like the floor of Solomon's Temple) and demand that he *recognise himself*.

The image of man *is* the image of the Temple, as writers as disparate as Corbin, Schwaller de Lubicz, Frederic Bligh Bond and Keith Crichlow have all noted. Man must make himself into a temple in order

to be inhabited by God. *This* is the object of all the tests, the Sword
Bridge and the turning door, the Perilous Bed and the blinding light of
the Grail. The concept begins with the Egypt of the pharaohs, if not
earlier, in the caves of mankind's first dwelling; and it continues
through Platonic and Neoplatonic schools of thought. To them the
temple was microcosmically an expression of the beauty and unity of
creation, seen as a sphere. Expressed thus, it was reflected in the soul,
and became indeed, 'a bridge for the remembrance or contemplation of
the wholeness of creation',[24] words which could be as well applied to the
Grail or the divine enclave of which it is a part.

This is the origin of the temple of light (the *haykat al-nur*), the
macrocosmic temple which lies at the heart of Islamic mysticism, of
which the Sufi mystic Ibn al-Arabi says: 'O ancient temple, there hath
risen for you a light that gleams in our hearts,'[25] the commentary to
which, states: 'the gnostic's heart, which contains the reality of the
truth', is the temple.

Here we are back again in the world of the Solomonic Grail temple,
the image of which, transformed and altered, together with that of the
Earthly Paradise, were enclosed in the world of the Arthurian Grail
mythos. And that world becomes transformed in turn, back into the
Edenic world of primal innocence, the original home of the sacred
vessel, possession of which 'represents the preservation of the primordial tradition in a particular, spiritual centre'.[26] The centre of which is
the heart.

Ibn al-Arabi wrote[27] that the last true man would be born of the line
of Seth. Do we not have in this statement a clue to the destiny of the
Grail bearer who will come among us at the time of the next 'sacring' of
the divine vessel? All the Grail knights were followers of Seth – who was
the first to go in quest of it – and their adventures are transparent glyphs
of the human endeavour to experience the divine. Most of us, if we
found our way into the temple unprepared, would probably suffer the
fate of Lancelot. But the Grail Temple exists to show us that the way
is worth attempting, that the centre can be reached, if we are only
attentive enough to the message it holds for us.

But what happens when we do finally reach the centre? If we look at
what we have learned so far about the image of the temple on earth and
in the heavens, we may begin to arrive at an answer.

All the temples are incomplete. They can only be made whole by the
direct participation of God, who must stretch down to meet and accept

the rising prayers of his creation. So with the Grail, it too must be hallowed, made complete, as by the touch which makes blood of wine and flesh from bread. The Grail is made whole only when it is full, and it is not for nothing that the shape most often assumed by it is that of the chalice. If we see this as two triangles, one above the other, meeting at the apex point to form a nexus, we can see that it is an image of this divine meeting of upper and lower, temporal and divine. The same event occurs in the sanctuary of the temple, and is best expressed, as we saw earlier, by the figure of the *vesica piscis*, the two overlapping, interlocked circles which can represent God and mankind, and in the centre of which, outside time or space, the opposites are joined; the male and female, dark and light imagery we have been examining and which are represented, in the Grail story, by the chessboard castle.

We can see also that, in the human temple, this is expressed by the need of each individual to reach upwards and to be met halfway. We are all Grails to some degree, lesser or greater; but we are empty vessels until we offer ourselves to be filled by the light.

It is perhaps time that we looked finally at some of the imagery which has built up throughout this study. Indeed, there comes a point at which unsupported words can no longer make sense of the complex of ideas presented. In the simple image with which we began, that of the *vesica piscis*, we have most of the story. The centre of the design with the outer edges of the two circles taken away (Fig. 2) makes the shape of the Grail. Turned upon its side, it is still the same, except that now it represents the image of the Grail as Temple, the building above, the adytum below, or as they may be seen: the God/Goddess with, between

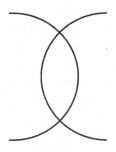

Figure 2

them at the meeting point of time and place, the figure of mankind. And, in the *temenos* between, the reconciliation of opposites, the perfection of sacred space, sained by the touch of the divine which interpenetrates the temporal at the point of human experience. So that this experience can be shown as an exchange, to which we can contribute equally with God as was suggested earlier, the image of the temple is at once a glyph of creation and of the evolution of the gods.

The images of the ship and the chessboard castle, the *urbs quadrata* and *mundus* of the Roman world, are also harmonised within this single point of interaction. The object of Gawain's visit to the Castle of the Grail was to be humbled and made to recognise the chequered pattern of all life, which is black and white, male and female in proportion. The importance of the containing vessel cannot be overemphasised. The lower part of the Grail is of this world, penetrating time and space at once, its upper part is already in the paradisial state of beyond-time and beyond-space. At the centre is the Temple, the sacred space at the heart of the circle, lies the adytum which stretches below the earth but is open to the sky. Thus the ancient temples were the simplest and most direct means of contact with the divine, as today the most simple and direct method is the building and establishment of an inner temple, a temple of the heart.

Dealing with the response in mankind to the voice of God, the Word, the Gnostic *Authoritative Teaching* says: 'the senseless man hears the call, but he is ignorant of the place to which he has been called. And he did not ask ... "where is the temple into which I should go and worship my hope".'[28] This could hardly be clearer. In the quest of the Grail, the failure to ask an important question is the cause of the failure of many knights who arrive at the castle. It is Lancelot's failure, and it is the failure of all who do not listen to the Voice of the Light.

Qabbalistic teaching has it that 'the temple has been destroyed, but not the path of purification, illumination, and union that lay concealed in it'.[29] For when the perfected soul of mankind 'rises like incense from the golden altar of the heart and passes through the most inward curtains of his being to the holy of holies within'[30] then the two cherubim who stand guard over the Ark of the Covenant (of the heart) 'are united in the presence of the One in Whom the soul recognises its eternal life and its own union with Him. Henceforward the soul is called the eternally "living" [*hayah*], the "one and only" [*yehidah*]',[31] the perfect. The Light has come like veritable tongues of fire upon all who reach the centre of the temple and find there the seat of God in the heart of His Creation.

This was the aim of the Grail knights, of the *Templiesen* of Wolfram von Eschenbach, of the priest-kings who built the Takht-i-Taqdis or the Capitoline temples of Rome. Before them it was the desire of the people who erected their stone circles to echo the dance of the cosmos – awaiting that moment when God would reach down and hallow their seeking with a touch. And so we wait now, who are modern Grail questers, for that touch that awakens the light within: as must all who seek to enter the Temple of the Mysteries.

Notes

1 Sir Thomas Malory, *Le Morte D'Arthur*, ed. John Matthews (London: Cassell, 2000) bk. 17, ch. 15.

2 Plotinus, *Enneads*, quoted in K. Crichlow, *Soul as Sphere and Androgyne* (Ipswich: Golgonooza Press, 1980), p. 23.

3 René Guenon, 'The Symbolism of the Graal', in *Tomorrow* (Winter 1965), vol. 13, no. 2.

4 Crichlow, op. cit., p. 23.

5 Louis Charpentier, *The Mysteries of Chartres Cathedral* (London: Research into Lost Knowledge Organization, R.I.L.K.O., 1972).

6 This later became confused with an actual site: Montségur, a stronghold of the Cathars in Southern France. From this grew a tradition that they were guardians of the Grail, a supposition which has yet to be firmly proved, though there is some evidence to support it. See John Matthews, *The Grail: Quest for Eternal Life* (London, Thames & Hudson, 1981).

7 Albrecht von Scharfenberg, *Der Jüngere Titurel* (Augsberg: 1477).

8 Green is a colour much associated with the Grail. In some versions the vessel originates as an emerald from the crown of Lucifer, the angel of light, while in Islamic tradition, the Black Stone of the Ka'aba, recognizably an image of the Grail, is carried on a cloth of green *archmadi*.

9 In particular: Lars Ivar Ringbom, *Graltemple und Paradies* (Stockholm, 1951). For Pope's account, see 'Persia and the Holy Graal', *The Literary Review* (New Jersey), 1, 1957, pp. 51–71.

10 *Supra.*

11 Exodus 25:22.

12 *Zohar: Terumah 159a*, quoted by Lee Schayer, 'The Meaning of the Temple', in *Sword of Gnosis* (New York: Penguin Books, 1974). *supra*, p. 363.

13 *Supra*, p. 363.

14 Ibn Khaldun, *The Muqaddimah* (London: Routledge & Kegan Paul, 1958).

15 see 'The Arthurian Tradition in Lambert D'Ardres', by Urban. T. Holmes in *Speculum*, XXV, 1965, pp. 100–2.

16 2 Samuel 6:15.

17 Helen Adolf, 'Oriental Sources for Grail Romances', *Publications of the Modern Language Association*, LXII, 1947, pp. 306–23.

18 Wolfram von Eschenbach, *Parzival*, trans A. T. Hatto (Harmondsworth: Penguin Books, 1980), p. 232.

19 2 Kings 6; 6–8.

20 Robert de Boron, *Joseph D'Arimathea*, trans. H. Lovelich (London: Early English Text Society, 1874).

21 Estha Quinn, 'The Quest of Seth, Solomon's Ship and the Grail', *Traditio*, XXI, 1965, pp. 185–222. I am indebted to this article, which contains a full treatment of the Ship of Solomon.

22 See the picture of the Virgin as Vessel in Matthews *The Grail*, p. 86.

23 *The Unpanishads*, trans. Juan Mascaro (Harmondsworth: Penguin Books, 1965), 8:1.

24 Crichlow, op. cit.

25 Ibn al-Arabi, *The Tarjuman Al-Ashwaq* (Acra: Theosophical Publishing House, 1978).

26 Guenon, op. cit.

27 Ibn al-Arabi, *The Bezels of Wisdom*, trans. R.W.J. Austin (London: SPCK, 1980).

28 *The Nag Hammadi Library*, ed. & trans. James M. Robinson (Leiden: E. J. Brill, 1977), p. 282.

29 Quoted by Schayer, op. cit., pp. 364–5.

30 Ibid.

31 Ibid.

The Return of Dindrane

Helen Luke

It seems to have passed largely unnoticed that it is always the knight, the masculine representative of the Quest, who goes in search of the divine vessel – perhaps because it is a feminine symbol to begin with, but also because women do not need the quest, are already vessels of the Holy Blood, their archetype the Virgin, and are therefore Grail bearers rather than seekers. Each may give birth, therefore, to the new Grail Lord. It is to these 'whole women', the Grail priestesses, that we should turn for enlightenment, and in so doing discover that we have always known the Grail secret, merely failing to recognize it, as men fail to recognize the feminine element within themselves and women their symbolic masculinity. Out of this realization, as we have said before in this book, comes a new syzygy, an intermingling on all levels which presents us with a healing face of creation we have never seen before, but which is the true nature of the Grail.

C.G. Jung, writing of archetypes dormant in the unconscious, says that they are activated when one-sided attitudes prevalent at a particular time and place are in urgent need of a compensatory image. By the end of the first millennium of the Christian era the rejection of the body, of the feminine, of matter itself, had reached a peak. There were some who actually believed that the material world was a creation of the devil, and earlier there had even been an unsuccessful movement within Christianity denying that women had souls. In a letter written in 1953 Jung said that the twelfth and early thirteenth centuries saw '... the beginning of Latin alchemy and of the natural sciences and also of a feminine religious symbol, the Holy Grail.'[1]

The Grail itself is indeed a supreme symbol of the lost values; for without the vessel of the feminine all the 'ten thousand things' must exist in a state of unrelatedness to each other – a chaos without meaning. The Grail is the cup from which each individual life receives its essential food and drink: it is the chalice containing the mystery of blood and spirit: it is a maternal womb, the body of Mary herself. Without a vessel no transformation on any level can take place – no cooking of ingredients in a kitchen, no chemical experiments or alchemical search for 'gold', no *metanoia* in a human soul, no incarnation of the Word to dwell among us.

Almost another millennium has passed since the Grail legends rose from the unconscious, and their vitality has never faded. Again and again poets and story-tellers have breathed new life into them – have, indeed, re-created them. The need for the affirmation of the feminine has not lessened since the twelfth century and has become particularly insistent in our own technological age.

The many legends surrounding the Grail image are for the most part concerned with the adventures of the knights, of the men who seek to find its meaning in their own souls. But the liberation of woman and the fight to establish her equality with men in hitherto masculine fields of work and thought has meant that she too has great need of a much more conscious awareness of the symbols of her own deepest feminine roots. Many women today are even contemptuous of the nature of the feminine being – of that which contains and nurtures and is still, which responds to people and things without any will to use or manipulate them, which guards in silence the mystery of life. If women do not themselves take up the quest of the Grail within, it is certain that their new-found equality in the masculine sphere will lose its meaning and become another 'wasteland'. A great hope for the future lies in the fact that so many individual women are now entering upon that quest.

Charles Williams, who died in 1945, was in my view one of the great re-creators of the Grail myth in our century. His Arthurian poems are not easy to read – often so obscure that even C.S. Lewis, his friend, who wrote a commentary[2] on them, had occasionally to admit defeat, but the more often one returns to them the more vividly they speak to the imagination, particularly through the poet's profound insight into the fundamental nature of woman; and we are left with shining and unforgettable images.

I shall discuss two of these poems, 'Taliessin in the Rose Garden' (*The Region of the Summer Stars*, Oxford University Press, 1950) and 'The Last Voyage' (*Taliessin Through Logres*, Oxford University Press, 1938).

First, however, it is necessary to say something of the people from the legends who appear in these poems. Dindraine is Sir Percival's sister who appears briefly in the *Morte d'Arthur* of Sir Thomas Malory, though Malory does not name her. Williams called her sometimes Dindrane (from Welsh sources) and sometimes Blanchefleur (from the French poems). Taliessin does not appear in Malory. He was the great Welsh legendary bard and seer – the twice-born child who tasted of the cauldron of wisdom of the mother goddess, Ceridwen. Williams made him the central figure of many of his poems (as the king's poet at Arthur's court). Taliessin in Williams's story loves and is loved by Dindrane; it is a total commitment on all levels, but it is not consummated in the flesh since both have freely and consciously chosen celibate vocations.

Guinevere in the Rose Garden poem is, of course, Arthur's queen, through whose love for the king's friend, Lancelot, the fellowship of the Round Table was finally split and Arthur brought to his death. In the other poem, almost the last of the cycle, we meet Sir Galahad, Sir Perceval and Sir Bors. These are the three knights who, in Malory, achieved the Grail, and who took ship with it on its voyage to Sarras, the eternal place, where it was withdrawn from the war-torn kingdom of Logres. 'Logres' is the temporal kingdom of Britain; the forest of Broceliande is, in our language, the unconscious; Caucasia, for Williams, stands for the flesh and Carbonek for the spirit; Camelot is the temporal city.

There is one phrase that recurs in the poems whereby Williams defines the wholeness of such a woman as Dindrane. 'Flesh knows what spirit knows but spirit knows it knows.' It expresses the truth that the material and instinctual world remains innocent, at one with itself – every stone, plant, insect and animal fulfilling unconsciously its nature as it was created to be. But since consciousness dawned in man (as in the myth of the Fall) he has been split between the opposites, between light and dark, male and female, conscious and unconscious, good and evil – all in opposition to each other. The feminine was identified with flesh, the masculine with spirit, but the woman who is one-in-herself in full consciousness is the woman who 'knows she knows'. She has integrated the life of the spirit with the instinctive life of her flesh through the living in this world on all levels of the love which is the way of conscious return to the unity of all the opposites. The same integration, of course, applies to man, but he more usually must approach it from the opposite end of the spectrum.

As the poem 'Taliessin in the Rose Garden' opens, the king's poet is walking among the roses making poetry and he sees three women at the entry to the long garden path: Queen Guinevere talking to Dindrane and a maid doing garden work beyond. The sparkling red of the queen's great ruby ring and the glowing red of the roses unite in Taliessin's imagination with the red of falling blood and there follows a long meditation on the nature of woman.

Guinevere was a queen; on her was laid the great responsibility of carrying for her country the symbol of the feminine side of the holy marriage between Heaven and Earth, the symbol of humanity united to God, of the flesh infused by the spirit – giving birth in due time to the new king.

> Glorious over Logres, let the headship of the queen be seen, as Caucasia to Carbonek, as Logres to Sarras

But Guinevere had betrayed her vocation

> ... under her brow she looked for the King's friend Lancelot

Here at the outset Taliessin foresees that the Queen's betrayal of her feminine wholeness, her refusal to accept her great responsibility for the symbolic image which she carries as queen (the 'consummate earth of Logres' he calls her) will mean that the 'falling blood' which could have been the redemptive blood of sacrifice, will become the blood of war, bringing destruction of the kingdom when finally the king is forced into awareness by his own misbegotten son Mordred and makes war on his friend Lancelot to his own undoing. Thus any civilization is doomed when the 'queen' (the leading feminine principle, the dominant attitude in women) loses integrity of heart and succumbs to what someone has called 'love as a release of tension' in place of commitment to the relatedness of the true *eros*.

We may here ask why it is that through the ages adultery in a woman has been regarded as so much more terrible a thing than in a man. For centuries and in many places a woman was put to death if discovered in adultery. It is not enough to answer that the domination of men over women has been the sole cause of this attitude. There is also a profound psychological reason.

Nature is equally promiscuous, whether it be male or female, but since woman is so much closer to the unconscious than man she is far more likely to be swallowed by the instinctive life and so lose her humanity if she separates her body from her feeling values. Because the flesh is symbolically feminine man has projected on to woman his deep fear of the chaos and lack of order with which the growth of human consciousness is always threatened. This projection is mercifully waning and the extreme cruelties visited upon a promiscuous woman are a thing of the past. But an individual modern woman ignores at her peril the fact that very real damage may be done to her psyche if she gives her body indiscriminately without a commitment to relationship of heart and mind. Whether this commitment is lived through a life-long marriage or for one night only is not the point. Depth of feeling, not frequency is the vital thing. It is not a matter of conventional taboos or moral condemnation; it is a question of the fundamental difference between the masculine and feminine psyches.

I am not, of course, implying that a man is absolved from a similar feeling of commitment; far from it. No person of either sex can come to wholeness without full consciousness of the values of *eros* and willingness to accept the ties and the sacrifices which all true relatedness demands. Because, however, these values are the dominant principle for a woman, she is in much greater danger of disintegration if she betrays them than is a man, and the effects of her betrayal on the environment are deadly. It was Guinevere, not Lancelot, who bore the greater responsibility for the final disaster.

In the story of Lancelot and Elayne and of his begetting of the Grail hero upon her we can feel at once these distinctions. Lancelot was tricked into spending a night with Elayne, thinking that he was lying with Guinevere. It was therefore an inevitable fate and Lancelot remains morally innocent. It is inconceivable that Galahad, the High Prince, the whole man who 'achieved' the Grail, could have been born from a union of Guinevere and some great knight with whom she might have lain, unconscious of his identity. Symbolically that would be so false that we revolt at the very thought. Elayne, Galahad's mother, loved Lancelot that night and ever after with all her heart and soul as well as her body, even though she could never be with him again, and she accepted the pain of this knowledge. Our reason replies that so also did Guinevere love Lancelot – both he and she were equally guilty of betraying the king, her husband and his friend. Both of them were equally faithful on another level to their love for each other. Why then if Lancelot could father the Grail Prince could not Guinevere have been his mother? First, of course, because Guinevere, while accepting Lancelot, was at the same time pretending to be faithful to her husband – she had her cake and ate it. Her devotion was never whole, and she betrayed her symbolic feminine vocation as queen, as well as her personal husband. But still more important, it is an ultimate necessity for a woman that in the instinctual area she be *conscious of what she is doing* as was Elayne, if she is to give birth to the divine hero within – conscious, not in the rational analysing sense, but in the sense of awareness of her own feelings, and a responsible commitment of her body and heart together. If she were to be tricked in this area she would be less than woman – merely female (or possibly in these days an imitation man).

There is a trinity of women at the beginning of 'Taliessin in the Rose Garden', the three being a queen, a virgin soon to be a contemplative nun, and an ordinary working woman. In all women this trinity exists, lived or unlived, either positively or negatively. We may know and live the 'queen' through our sense of responsibility, not only for those around us but for all mankind. 'Through words and deeds the superior man moves heaven and earth – even if he abides in his room,' says Confucius. This is the royal quality – awareness of the symbolic power of everything we are. Or, for we are free to choose, we may identify with the queen and demand to be first all the time, to be served and protected and personally admired. The working woman is equally essential: to live in the present and do each task as it comes, tending the growing things, both of the earth and in the psyche. Without this we are no longer human; but, again, if the work we do, whether with hands or mind, absorbs our whole personalities, it becomes one of the most seemingly virtuous ways to evade reality. These two persons of the trinity are easily understood.

But what of the virgin? In our time it has become almost a shameful word. I was told the other day of a boy aged twelve who said to his mother, talking of a girl his own age, 'She's nothing but a virgin.' Asked what he meant by this, he replied, 'Oh, a virgin means a complete dud, boring and dull.'

A young woman who is still a virgin at twenty often has a miserable sense of inferiority on this account. A 'virgin' in common speech means a woman who has never had intercourse with a man, but in its more ancient and deeper meaning a virgin is a woman who, whether she has had intercourse or not, has no *need* to unite physically with a man in order to become whole, one-in-herself, for she has known intercourse with the god within. This has always been the symbolic meaning of the life of the nun. As the bride of Christ, she seeks the inner marriage of the human and the divine. It is easy, however, to see how the affirmation of a vocation to prayer and contemplation can sink into the negative repression of the sexual desires themselves. Chastity, which means purity of heart, has come all too frequently to mean a denial of the purity of instinct itself. No one can become 'virgin' in the true sense without going through the fire of instinctual emotion. This experience, however, does not necessarily include fruition on the physical level and the time has surely come not only for a resurrection of the true meaning of the word 'virgin' but for a return of respect for those whose inner truth may demand virginity in the ordinary physical sense.

Robert Grinnell, in his book *Alchemy in a Modern Woman*,[3] writing of a woman patient who suffered from frigidity, says that this problem in a woman may come from her high ideals in the realm of *eros*, together with a mistaken interpretation of them through a typical masculine over-valuation of physical sex. Grinnell adds that *eros* in a woman may be called a 'sort of feminine conscience' which takes her beyond the demands of the ego and lifts her out of her momentary desires. Thus the natural woman is transformed into the woman who 'knows she knows'.

Virginity and the quest for the holy marriage within are emerging from behind the walls of the cloisters, which through so many centuries have guarded that great symbol, and in our time, only individual women can give it new life. To one the god may come through her sexual fruition, to another through suffering its absence – and both are 'virgin' in the deep sense.

To return to the poem, Taliessin, musing on these things – the glowing ruby, the red rose, the falling blood – and on their meaning in woman, sees a great vision of the Zodiac. Each of the twelve houses, he says, is a door to the whole, 'All coalesced in each.' But Cain, by killing Abel, split the Zodiac at a blow and through the incoherence of the houses at war with themselves the blood flowed and the way of return 'climbed beside the timed and falling blood'. The shedding of blood can only be redeemed by the offering of blood. Then, as Taliessin looked on the stricken world, he heard

The women everywhere throughout it sob with the curse
and the altars of Christ everywhere offer the grails.

Well are women warned from serving the altar
who, by the nature of their creature, from Caucasia to Carbonek,
share with the Sacrifice the victimization of blood.

The woman's monthly shedding of blood is the outer sign and an inner symbol of her female capacity to give birth. Williams means, I believe, that the menstrual blood of woman is a continual reminder of the truth that after the Fall, after the split in creation, there can be no 'return', no healing of the split, without sacrifice, without the giving of blood. If the woman or the feminine in man does not 'bleed' there is no creation in this world. Therefore, he says that women 'share with the Sacrifice the victimization of blood'. The piercing of Christ's side was the wound in the heart of his feeling nature. (The liver was thought by the ancients to be the seat of the emotions and is on the right side.)

I do not know any other writer, theologian or psychologist who has given this very profound, yet very simple and, once seen, obvious explanation of the intuitive revulsion which many feel at the thought of a woman priest celebrating the Mass. If a truly mature woman, fully aware of her 'animus' (the masculine aspect of her unconscious) were to read services and preach sermons it would not offend. The Mass, however, is a *symbolic* rite, and no matter how developed her spirit may be a woman remains biologically female. Since her shedding of blood, says Williams, is in her flesh an equivalent of the blood of the victim, therefore, if *in her flesh* she offers the blood of Christ she usurps on the wrong level the function of the spirit. 'Flesh knows what spirit knows,' Williams goes on, 'but spirit knows it knows.' In this, of course, he is emphatically *not* saying that individual women cannot know they know; indeed he goes on to show this with great clarity. He is speaking only of her symbolic feminine role in a ritual, not of her individual being. A symbol is, of course, that which makes one the two levels of reality – spirit and matter, inner and outer truth.

There is usually a symbolic meaning hidden behind an old wives' tale. During the Second World War I lived in a small village in Berkshire where a local woman cooked for our family. I remember that she told me she never tried to make jams during the days of her menstrual period since it was well known to be useless; the jam or jelly simply would not set! In other words, no *transformation* could take place at these times – the separate ingredients, the fruit and sugar, could be mixed but could never transform into the third thing – that which is both and neither.

The relevance to the transformation of the bread and wine on that other level of the Mass is plain. Projected on to such things as the making of jam it is nonsensical in the light of our scientific knowledge, but the ancient symbolic truths which express the mysteries of being have always been preserved both in folklore and in the rituals of the great religions.

Though in the ancient world there were everywhere priestesses they were never, I believe, charged with killing the sacrificial animal or offering its blood. The tearing to pieces of victims by the women in the Dionysian rites was not a priestly act but a ritually contained release of instinctual frenzy. The priestesses served as links to the unconscious through their mediumistic power – the sibyls, for instance – they tended the sacred fire, as did the vestal virgins, fulfilling the great religious functions of woman; but they did not wield the knife of sacrifice or offer the blood. Rather it is their task to draw up the waters under the earth from the well of the unconscious that all may drink of the *aqua permanens*, as the alchemists called the water of life. It is the measure of the masculine one-sidedness of our culture that there have never been priestesses of this kind in institutional Christianity.

It would be useless for the church at this stage to attempt to introduce new rituals for priestesses. A true rite is born, not made, and if consciously contrived is merely sentimental. Nor does the answer lie in the current urge to admit women to the priest's role. Nevertheless, we cannot put the clock back in a mood of nostalgia. In most Protestant sects the communion service is not a symbolic transformation rite but a commemorative meal, so that there should be no objection whatever to women ministers. Only to the Catholic, Orthodox and Anglican rites do the words of Charles Williams apply. But the demand for women in the priesthood is perhaps one of the indicators that for growing numbers of people the symbolic life is slowly being pushed out of the collective institutions as such. In the coming age, as Jung frequently pointed out, the symbols must come to birth in the individual soul, in the man or woman who enters on the lonely quest for the Grail within, and this applies to church members as profoundly as to anyone else. It was always in the legends a quest that must be undertaken alone, but it is never achieved without the discovery of objective relatedness to others, as opposed to the all-too-easy unconscious 'mixing', or the 'togetherness' which submerges any true meeting between human beings.

As C.S. Lewis points out in his commentary on Williams's poems, the menstrual blood of women differs from the blood of animals in heat. For animals it is the only time at which they can conceive. In human beings it is the proof of the possibility of motherhood, as in nature, but there is a major difference in that conception can take place at any time. The beginning of the monthly flow at puberty is, moreover, a sign in the body of the psychic split – that is, of the 'Fall' which was the beginning of the conscious 'way of return' for Eve as for Adam. The innocent wholeness of childhood, of Eden, is over. At puberty the longing begins for completion by physical union with the other sex, a longing which continues (symbolically) until the 'stanching' at the menopause. In Plato's image the original human being is a sphere which, being cut in two, forever seeks to reunite with its other half. (See Ch. 6.)

At a later point in the poem Williams hints at the inner identity of the woman's menstrual blood, which tells her that she has not yet conceived, with the blood of the wounded Grail king, bleeding because he cannot bring to life the new consciousness of the Christ, the Self. In some beautiful lines Taliessin speaks of how woman may consciously give birth to the new keeper of the Grail, within herself, and so heal the wound in the psyche.

First, however, Williams speaks of the natural woman living instinctively the One way.

> Women's flesh lives the quest of the Grail
> in the change from Camelot to Carbonek and from Carbonek to Sarras,
> puberty to Carbonek, and the stanching, and Carbonek to death.
> Blessed is she who gives herself to the journey.

Camelot is the city of men, the life of this world, which is entered at puberty – the potentially creative blood begins to flow, and primitive woman already begins her vocation as wife and mother. She cleaves to her man and receives the seed, she gives birth in pain, she is the earth without which the creative seed is sterile. But when this flow of her blood is stanched at the menopause and she must let go of her desire to conceive and give birth to a physical child, then her lifelong experience of 'Camelot' can bring her to that instinctive wisdom which we still may find in old women of this simple kind who have given themselves to the journey – who accept the 'stanching', as they have accepted the pains and joys of motherhood. They come to Carbonek, the place where the 'holy' is glimpsed and from it go on in peace to the goal of death. By the generous, rich living of her feminine nature such a woman is whole, but without knowing that she knows.

Taliessin, making poetry in the Rose Garden, having sung of the quest of the Grail in the flesh of woman – of the blessedness of those who give themselves with the simple diffuse awareness of the natural woman to life's journey, goes on in the next stanza to sing of the blessedness of the conscious woman on this same journey.

> *The phosphor of Percivale's philosophical star*
> *shines down the roads of Logres and Broceliande;*
> *happy the woman who in the light of Percivale*
> *feels Galahad, the companion of Percivale, rise*
> *in her flesh, and her flesh bright in Carbonek with Christ,*
> *in the turn of her body, in the turn of her flesh, in the turn*
> *of the Heart that heals itself for the healing of others,*
> *the only Heart that healed itself without others, when*
> *our Lord recovered the Scorpion and restored the Zodiac.*
> *Blessed is she who can know the Dolorous Blow,*
> *healed in the flesh of Pelles, the flesh of woman;*

The philosophical star of Perceval – the image of the wisdom in the heavens, the light of man's soaring spirit – shines on the roads of this world and penetrates into Broceliande, the darkness of the feminine unconscious. Happy the woman, says Williams, who is flooded by this light of consciousness, and who then feels 'Galahad', the new whole man, stir to life within her. We are carried perhaps for an instant into the thought of a woman rising above the earth and *becoming* a sort of female Galahad, but the next line jerks us firmly back to the true blessedness of the new vision for woman. She feels Galahad rise in her flesh; the point is that she feels him *consciously* in the actuality of her feminine nature and so reaches full awareness of the truth of the heart, of the love that is both personal and rooted in the transpersonal life. Her spirit then reaches maturity and 'she knows that she knows'.

Only in the Heart of the Self is the split healed. The use of the word Heart here is vital in our context. As James Hillman has so compellingly shown in his essay on the feeling function, the desperate need of our time is for the discovery of *eros*, of feeling values. Emotional experiences for their own sake and theoretical truths we have in plenty, but true feeling which leads to the perception of the abiding values is still rare in our time. It is for individual, conscious women to lead the way.

How difficult it is for men, who are so dangerously exposed in this age to possession by the intellect, by technology, or by their inferior unintegrated femininity, to find the meaning of *eros* without this mediation of true women who do not only live these things instinctively, but 'know that they know'!

There is a letter written by Jung to Aniela Jaffe in 1947, which most beautifully illustrates the value to a great man of a feeling response by a woman who 'knows she knows'. It was written in answer to a letter from her in which she had evidently spoken of his essay on the Trinity. He writes:

> I thank you with all my heart for your response to my 'Trinity': I couldn't imagine a more beautiful one. It is a 'total' reaction, and it had a 'total' effect on me too. You have perfectly imaged what I imagined into my work. It again became clear to me from your letter how much one misses when one receives no response or a mere fragment, and what a joy it is to experience the opposite – a creative resonance which is at the same time like a revelation of the feminine being. It is as though a wine, which by dint of toil and sweat, worry and care has finally become mature and good, were being poured into a precious beaker. Without this receptacle and acceptance a man's work remains a delicate child, followed with doubting eyes and released into the world with inner anxiety. But when a soul opens to the work, it is as though a seed were lodged in good earth, or the gates of a city were closed in the evening so that it can enjoy surer repose.[4]

Reading these most beautiful words, how horrifying is the attitude of those many women who are so busy doing things and demanding their rights, personally or collectively, that they reject altogether that 'precious beaker', the Grail of the feminine being which receives the wine of the mystery so that in due time many may drink.

Let us now return to those strange words, 'Blessed is she who can know the Dolorous Blow/healed in the flesh of Pelles, the flesh of woman.' The so-called Dolorous Blow caused the wound in the thigh of the Grail King Pelles, and bled without healing until the coming of the new man, Galahad. The wounded state of the king was reflected in the sterility of the surrounding wasteland. What lies behind these images? C.S. Lewis, in his commentary, is silent. There is, of course, the obvious connection with what has gone before; the stanching at the menopause of the shedding of blood is a symbol of the making whole of wounded humanity in a natural woman, who, her task of rearing children over, turns towards death with a sense of joy and acceptance during those last years – acceptance which only comes to those who have given themselves freely to the experience of the dark as well as of the light. 'Blessed is she who gives herself to the journey,' says Taliessin. But the second blessing is different. 'Blessed is she who can know' – the meaning of these things.

It is significant that so many modern women suffer acute and painful problems at the menopause both physical and psychic and that it often drags on for years causing all sorts of disturbances. It is beautifully called 'the change of life', but how many women do in fact change their lives – change their attitudes, turn inward to find meanings and to prepare for death, and so enter consciously on the new phase of the journey, from 'Carbonek to Sarras'? Very few; the majority cling desperately to 'Camelot' because they have never fully given themselves to that phase of the journey, and so the energy released by the biological change, instead of flowering into a creative activity of the Logos within her, into an imaginative confrontation with the meaning of death, is eaten up by the unassimilated drives of the 'animus', the masculine component in her psyche which turns destructive instead of connecting her to the spirit within. The wound inflicted by the Dolorous Blow – that is, the split between spirit and flesh, is not healed in such women but bleeds more freely than ever in the psyche. So the wasteland spreads and the heart shrivels. We see all around us the plight of middle-aged women substituting ever-increasing outer activity for the inner life, or searching miserably for a man, any man, or his equivalent, to fill the void by preserving the illusion of youth.

'Blessed is she who can know the healing of the Dolorous Blow.' In such a woman the shedding of blood and its stanching both become conscious sacrifice and are filled with meaning. She is aware of the 'change of life' on every level and embraces it with her whole heart.

These words of Williams, 'Blessed is she who can know the Dolorous Blow! healed in the flesh of Pelles, the flesh of woman' surely derive from the strangest of all the legends in Malory's *Morte d'Arthur.* As the three knights Galahad, Perceval and Bors approach the end of their quest they are joined by Perceval's sister, who, as has been said, is not named by the earlier writer, but is called either Blanchefleur or Dindrane by Williams. Malory tells of how this 'noblewoman' led Sir Galahad to the 'ship of Solomon', which was later to carry the Grail and the three knights away from Logres to Sarras. Here they found Sir Perceval and Sir Bors waiting, and the lady, fulfilling her role of link to the unconscious, revealed to them the story of the ship, and of the sword which Sir Galahad found there. She was not recognized even by her brother Perceval until she revealed herself as a daughter of King Pellinore. Then all four set forth on the last phase of the quest.

As they journeyed they came to a castle from which armed knights emerged, who tried to seize the princess, Perceval's sister. There was a battle, but finally the travellers were induced to listen to the reason for the seizure. The lady of the castle was very sick and had long lain in a coma, and it had been foretold that she could only find healing through the blood of a princess of royal descent who was also a virgin; therefore every noblewoman who passed that way was seized upon in the hope that she would fulfil these conditions. When Perceval's sister heard this she said at once that she was both a princess and a virgin and offered freely to give her blood to the lady. 'Who will let my blood?' she said. One of the ladies-in-waiting stepped forward and made an incision in her arm and the blood gushed out into a bowl. So much blood did she lose that she knew she would die, and she spoke to the three knights bidding them not to bury her but to put her in a ship at the next harbour and set it adrift. 'And when you come to Sarras,' she said, 'you will find this ship with my body in it waiting for you, and there you shall bury me.'

And so she died, and the other lady rose from her sick bed and lived. The three knights obeyed her and leaving her body in the ship they came to Carbonek, the Grail city, and Galahad healed the wounded king. From thence they came to the sea and boarded the ship of Solomon, to which the Grail had removed itself; and without sail or oar they were borne over the sea to Sarras.

This legend is the basis of Williams's poem 'The Last Voyage'. In his own recreation of the story he significantly shows us the body of Dindrane, the woman, travelling in the same ship with the Grail and with the three knights – Galahad, the 'alchemical infant', the holy child; Perceval, the star of wisdom; Bors the ordinary practical human being. There is now a quaternity in this ship. All four are carried to the 'spiritual place' where, in the unconscious, two of the knights and the dead woman will remain with the Grail until the time of its rediscovery, while Bors alone returns at once to the world. The ages of growing emphasis on man and his works were ahead – the Renaissance, the Enlightenment, followed by the industrial revolution and our century of technological materialism. This is the great significance of Bors's solitary return, Galahad's intuition, Perceval's inner wisdom and the feminine values of Dindrane are all removed into the unconscious.

Bors is in Williams's poems the husband and father, the down-to-earth householder, the extrovert. The poet sees him as the guardian of the Grail vision during the coming centuries, but we have watched the gradual eclipse of the simple human values of Bors, in the sterility of intellect and technology divorced from feeling. Now surely the time is ripe for the emergence of the Grail from Sarras – for the resurrection of Dindrane.

Malory's story of Perceval's sister and of her shedding of blood for another and her close connection with the Grail is unique, as far as I know, in the versions of the legend. No one took much notice of it, it seems, until suddenly in Williams's poetry it moves into the centre of that last picture of the swiftly receding Grail.

> Before the helm the ascending-descending sun
> Lay in quadrilateral covers of a saffron pall
> over the bier and the pale body of Blanchefleur,
> mother of the nature of lovers, creature of exchange
> drained there of blood by the thighed wound,
> she died another's death, another lived her life.
> Where it was still to-night, in the last candles of Logres,
> a lady danced, to please the sight of her friends; her
> cheeks were stained from the arteries of Percivale's sister.
> Between them they trod the measure of heaven and earth,
> and the dead woman waited the turn and throe of the dance
> where, rafting and undershafting the quadruplicate sacrum,
> below the saffron pall, the joyous woe of Blanchefleur,
> the ship of Solomon (blessed be he) drove on.

To me these lines are some of the most powerful in the whole cycle of poems; they positively vibrate with meaning, if only we can bring to them a 'total response', in Jung's words.

In Williams's experience of the myth, springing from the hints in Malory, Dindrane is above all 'virgin', one-in-herself, the companion of the poet Taliessin, on all levels – body and heart, mind and spirit; she is the foster-mother of Galahad, the sister of Perceval – the feminine wisdom which is essential to his 'philosophical star'. But Logres, the collective culture of that era, was not ready for the 'new woman' who shines briefly through the story. Woman collectively would remain subject through many centuries to the dominant male, largely unconscious of that which her flesh always knows. Nevertheless the lady, 'mother of the nature of lovers, creature of exchange' had, before her disappearance with the Grail, given her life's blood so that an ordinary woman of this world might carry her life in her bloodstream and transmit it to the future. The sick woman had been in a coma – the 'flesh', the earth, had been too long despised in Christianity. The blood of Dindrane, the whole woman, gave her the possibility of renewal.

> *Where it was still to-night, in the last candles of Logres,*
> *a lady danced, to please the sight of her friends;*
> *her cheeks were stained from the arteries of Percivale's sister.*

This lady, dancing in the simple delights of human exchange, carried in her veins, unconsciously in the depths of her being, the life of the 'dead' woman whose 'exchanges' encompassed heaven and the whole world.

> *Between them they trod the measure of heaven and earth,*
> *and the dead woman waited the turn and throe of the dance.*

She, Dindrane, waited in the unconscious of women for the day when one here, one there, would awaken her from her sleep. She awaited 'the throe of the dance', and a throe means a pang of anguish, and more particularly a pang of childbirth. And the place where she lay in the poem was the ship of Solomon, Solomon whose image carries the meaning of the wise and understanding heart. She is held as in a womb, the fourth in the 'quadruplicate sacrum' of the Grail.

There is one other line which as yet we have not looked at, 'drained there of blood by the thighed wound'. By the use of the word 'thighed' Williams links the sacrifice of Dindrane to the wound of the maimed king, soon to be healed by Galahad. (It will be remembered he had also likened the menstrual blood of the natural woman to the blood of the Grail king in the Rose Garden poem.) The extraordinary interest of this passage lies in the fact that the actual wound of Perceval's sister was cut into her *arm*. The arm is a symbol of creative activity in this world; the thigh indicates male sexual power. The Grail King is wounded, his masculine strength is maimed so that he is unable to beget any new vision. The woman on the other hand is drained of blood from her arm, and her potentially active creativity sinks down again into the unconscious to await 'the throe of the dance' – those birth pangs which have come indeed to woman in the last 100 years. It is immediately after this shedding of Dindrane's blood that Galahad, her foster son, symbol of the whole man, heals the Grail King, but the great vision fails to become incarnate in the world precisely because the values of the whole woman could not yet be accepted. The Grail is withdrawn and with it Dindrane, the 'seeing' woman.

All this may be read as a symbolic statement of the situation in the middle years of this century – when the poet was writing – and also of the inner quest of every conscious woman, whether Williams was aware of this or not. If a woman's true creativity in the realm of Logos is wounded – if her 'arm' activity is used to manipulate instead of create, then man is emasculated. (It is not, of course, fundamentally a matter of cause and effect but of synchronicity.) If, however, her wound becomes sacrifice (the willing death for another which is the giving up of the animus-possessed demands of her ego) there will follow the rebirth. She returns in the 'throe' of the dance, in the true 'exchange' encompassing both earth and heaven, and with her she brings the long hidden Grail.

The human arm is that which distinguishes man from the animal and it symbolizes, as has been said, his relatedness to life. Dindrane gave blood from her arm and life to another. The dancing lady with the blood of Dindrane in her veins was the feminine counterpart of Bors, the husband and householder, who transmitted to his sons, as she to her daughters, the hidden intuition of the Grail, down through the centuries of growing humanism. With the dawning of the age of Aquarius, the age of seeing, which is contemplation, the age of the carrier of the water of life in a vessel, may we not see indeed the awakening of Dindrane, the woman consciously one-in-herself, no longer secluded from this world, but walking the streets of the City of God and mankind. So, in the words of Taliessin in the Rose Garden, she may 'bring to a flash of seeing the women in the world's base'.

Notes

1 C.W. Jung, *Collected Works*, vol. 18 (London: Routledge & Kegan Paul), p. 678.
2 C.S. Lewis, *Arthurian Torso* (Oxford University Press, 1948).
3 Spring Publications, Dallas, 1973, p. 52.
4 C.G. Jung, *Letters*, vol. I (Princeton University Press, 1971, 1973), p. 474.

~ 8 ~

Sophia:
Companion on the Quest

Caitlín Matthews

We are all involved on a personal quest, of which the Grail is an image, put there, as Caitlín Matthews tells us, 'to make us fall in love with an inner world'. For though the quest is indeed an interior one, it has to manifest in the outer world in order to satisfy our deepest needs, which are by extension the world's. We are all in exile from something: our homes, our childhood, love or God. The Grail shows us that we are also in exile from paradise, which is perhaps all these things, and that the Grail itself shares that state. This is made clear by the nature of the guide and companion who accompanies the Grail knights (and ourselves) on the quest, who shares our exile and seeks to return, through us, to the desired state. So that we see that we are as necessary to the guide as the guide is to us, a truth also applicable to the Grail. As we read: 'to drink from the Grail is to remember Paradise'. This is the experience sought for by all seekers; it should be our greatest source of inspiration.

The Grail quest is in many ways a paradigm of our own spiritual journey. It is a journey upon which we continually find and lose our way as we rediscover and forget what we have learned. The cyclic nature of life ensures that, whatever our achievements, we can never rest on our laurels: we cannot retain that moment of revelation. Whatever our path, this schema holds true. Whether we follow the well-beaten path that others have trod before us, or stride out into new regions of our own devising we meet the same defeats, make the same mistakes, follow the same wrong directions, whether through laziness, ignorance or despair. We embark upon our spiritual journey in a state of primal innocence, like Perceval, that most guileless of knights, when he leaves the

womb-like enclosure of the wood where his mother has hidden him
from life's realities. From the very first Perceval is hardly aware that he is
on a quest at all: mistaking armed knights for angels, he acts
unchivalrously to all and omits to ask the important Grail question
which will end the Wounded King's pain. But, just as no one who sets
out upon the spiritual journey is ever alone, neither is the Grail-seeker
left lonely. It is with the identity of one mysterious companion on
the quest that we shall be concerned in the course of this essay. She
accompanies both the Grail knight and the mystic, and she is rarely
absent from any spiritual tradition. In her localized appearance within
the Grail legends she is called the Hideous Damsel or Cundrie; mystically speaking, her stature is vast – her ultimate archetype being that of
Sophia, the Holy Wisdom of God. However we see her, the task of
Sophia is to stimulate awareness or remembrance of paradise; for she is,
par excellence, the symbolic personification of exile from paradise, as
well as showing us the way of return to our original state. Whether we
believe literally in the fall of the soul from grace or not, it is clear that,
most of the time, we are in a state of forgetfulness – we are divided from
our true nature. Sophia, in the person of the Hideous Damsel, fulfils
this function specifically for Perceval, and as her role is neglected within
the Vulgate cycle, where Galahad is shown as the Grail-winner, I shall be
using examples only from those texts which feature Perceval.

Let us meet the Hideous Damsel, then, at the point when Perceval
has omitted to ask the Grail question. Peredur (Welsh equivalent for
Perceval) is seated with three others in Arthur's court when there
enters:

> ... a black, curly haired woman, riding a yellow mule ... she had a rough,
> unlovable appearance: her face and hands were blacker than pitch, and yet it
> was her shape rather than her colour that was ugliest – high cheeks and a
> sagging face, a snub, wide-nostrilled nose, one eye speckled grey and
> protruding, the other jet black and sunken, long teeth yellow as broom, a
> stomach that swelled up over her breasts and above her chin. Her backbone
> was shaped like a crutch; her hips were wide in the bone, but her legs were
> narrow, except for her knobbly knees and feet.[1]

She then admonishes Peredur for not having asked the Grail question,
in this case why the spear ran with blood; for: 'Had you asked, the king
would have been made well and the kingdom made peaceful, but now
there will be battles and killing, knights lost and women widowed and

children orphaned, all because of you.'[2] Likewise in *Parzival*, where the Hideous Damsel appears as Cundrie the Sorceress. Her appearance is equally hideous, yet she is given an extra dimension of learning, she is termed the Grail Messenger for by her coming is the Grail quest both hastened and eventually achieved.

But who is this ugly hag, and what is she doing in a tale which is an allegory of transcendent spirituality? There are many who would deny her place within the Grail canon at all, for is she not a creature grimed with vile matter and, moreover, a woman? To answer these questions fully we shall have to investigate the origins of the Hideous Damsel and consider the nature of the Divine Feminine. It will be necessary to put aside the mental overlay of dualism which has crept into our appreciation of the spiritual journey and to remember a time when the divine could be as well expressed by female as well as male symbolism. The Grail story has its own female protagonists, as we will see, whose function is as important as that of the Grail knights: their origin lies deeply embedded in the Celtic consciousness and has a direct bearing on our own approach to the spiritual journey.

Standing in seeming opposition to the Hideous Damsel within the Grail story is the Grail Maiden, she who carries the vessel in the Grail procession. Her description ensures that we do not confuse this lady with the black Cundrie:

> Her face shed such refulgence that all imagined it was sunrise. This maiden was seen wearing brocade of Araby. Upon a green achmardi she bore ... The Gral ... She whom the Gral suffered to carry itself had the name of Repanse de Schoye. Such was the nature of the Gral that she who had the care of it was required to be of perfect chastity and to have renounced all things false.[3]

Both she and the Grail Messenger, Cundrie, serve the same end, yet how different is their appearance. The fact that these two figures are in the service of the Grail should give us some clue that they are the same archetype embodied in two guises. Yet this is not at all clear to anyone reading the texts. The nature of the Divine Feminine has been split into two camps: the pliant, acceptable image of sanctity and the threatening image of dark power.

The place of the feminine within the spiritual world and particularly within Christianity, has been ill-defined. The Church, having purged itself of its esoteric or mystical elements (or at least having relegated them to an 'official' position), developed the cult of the Virgin Mary as its only outlet for the feminine principle; stereotyped as the supreme mother, or as lifeless sanctities, the Virgin and the Holy Women, hardly presented fully developed examples of the Divine Feminine. The only 'dangerous' woman within the Christian corpus is the Magdalene, redeemed from earthly concupiscence as the penitent sinner: an archetype for all women to look up to. It was this heavy dualism which depressed the one supreme Goddess to the status of a female demon. As with the Divine Feminine, so with woman: woman was the gateway of the devil, the daughter of Eve through whom came the Fall. Our Hideous Damsel seems at first to partake of this dark image, yet she comes up through deeper levels than the Christian, from substrata which allowed the feminine to assume a fuller prominence than it did during the twelfth century, when the Grail legends were first recorded.

The Grail as vessel of grace is perhaps a familiar idea, but a specifically feminine symbol it is almost unknown due to the Christian overlay having obscured much of its mysterious origin. The Grail legend existed in one form or another before Christianity shaped its framework and utilized its symbolism. It is perhaps only the greatest symbols which can be so universally applied. Although it seems far from the Christian ethic of Grail as Chalice of the Last Supper, it was once the province of the Divine Feminine to guard knowledge or wisdom. There has been much dismay in some circles that the Grail Bearer should be so unliturgically female: no woman of the time would have been allowed to touch the holy vessels after all. But this argument can be scotched straight away if we look at the Celtic roots of the Grail and its guardian. The Grail and its contents, although subsumed as an apocryphal Christian legend, have no connection with the Cup of the Last Supper and the Redemptive blood at the *earliest* levels of the story: they are directly descended from the ancient and holy belief in sovereignty – the personification of the land whom the candidate king has to espouse.

The ancient rite of kings is deeply concerned with the marriage of the sovereign to the land. This idea has not been totally lost as we can understand if we look no further than the English coronation rite where the monarch is ceremonially wedded to the land with the 'wedding ring of England', at the presentation of the regalia. If we go even further back we may trace this custom to the time when the Goddess and matrilinear descent were the rule; then the king held the land by right of his female relatives. He would often have to undergo a symbolic marriage with a priestess who represented the Goddess for the purposes of the ritual.

In the Irish tale the *Baile in Scaíl*, *The Phantom's Prophecy*, Conn, the King of Tara, stumbles into a mysterious landscape in which he enters a house. He and his companions see there 'a young maiden in a glass chair with a gold crown on her head and a cloak with borders of gold round her. A bowl of silver with four golden corners before her, full of red beer. A cup of gold on the ground. A beaker or cup of gold at her lips.'[4] The maiden is the Sovereignty of Ireland and she gives the bowl of silver to Conn, for it is his descendants who will rule the land. She could well be mistaken for the Grail Bearer, the one who confers enlightenment upon the knightly candidate on the quest; yet she has another face, which is revealed to us in a second Irish tale, that of *Niall of the Nine Hostages*. Here, Niall and his four brothers are serving their weapon training and living off the land. They lose their way and need water. The first brother finds a well but it is guarded by an ugly old hag who will only allow him to drink if he will kiss her. They each go in turn and have the same difficulty: each one returns waterless. Then Niall approaches the hag: he not only kisses her, he embraces her. As he releases her he finds that she has changed into the most beautiful woman in the world. In answer to his question, she replies: 'I am Sovereignty, King of Tara; your descendants will rule over every clan.' And she bids him return to his brothers but to grant them no water until they have acknowledged his seniority over them.

This is a powerful story which tells us much about the early origins of the Grail itself and its guardian. Whether we read of the maiden with the silver cup in the *Baile in Scaíl*, or of the Welsh tale of Ceridwen's Cauldron of Inspiration, or of the hag who guards the well, we may be sure that we are witnessing the ancient Goddess archetype in action.

In the quest for kingship the Hideous Damsel, Sovereignty, cannot assume her proper form nor can the quest succeed, if her ugly form is rejected. The test seeks to discover the one who shows himself more concerned with the land than with the glories of kingship. But what are the implications here for the Grail knight? If we relate the quest for the Grail with the quest for sovereignty, we will see many things in a new light.

We may recall that the result of achieving the Grail is the healing of the Wounded King and the flowering of the Waste Land. From earliest times, especially in Celtic understanding, a maimed or wounded king

could not reign – he had to be a whole man. This is the theme of another
Irish story when Nuadu, King of the Tuatha de Danaan, loses his arm in
the Battle of Mag Tuired. Sovereignty is disputed and bestowed upon
another, even though Nuadu is provided with a silver arm in replacement. It is not until his arm is miraculously restored in the flesh that he is
allowed to resume the kingship. The implication with the Wounded
Grail King is that he is wounded in the genitals or, euphemistically,
through the thigh, so that he cannot be joined in union with the land as
Sovereignty – therefore the Land is laid waste. The Grail knight's quest,
then, is the healing of his king: a fate in which he shares for the whole
kingdom suffers. Sovereignty, then, is radically important to an understanding of the Grail legends: not only is the Grail Maiden a reflection of
a once-potent image of the Divine Feminine, but so too is the Grail Messenger, the Hideous Damsel. The two faces of Sovereignty re-emerge in
the Grail legend as two separate characters; they also may stand for the
Land which suffers and is laid waste – as black and unwanted as the
Hideous Damsel – and for the healing of the Land, whereby Sovereignty
can assume her former condition as the beautiful Grail Maiden.

If the pagan origins of the Grail legends have been over-stressed here,
it is only in an attempt to balance the over-emphasis elsewhere on the
Christian parallels which are often easier to perceive. The companion on
the quest, the Hideous/Beautiful Maiden, is not peculiar to the Grail
quest alone; nor is she solely the province of the pagan past. Before we
can see the Grail quest as a type of our spiritual journey, we must
examine the mystical tradition – Jewish, as well as Christian – where we
shall find our companion in other guises, as well as uncovering a secret
tradition which perpetuates the hidden wisdom of the ages.

*   *   *   *   *

'Exile chills my heart. May He who numbered the stars guide you in
helping us and lead us back to happiness'[5] says Arthur's mother in
Parzival. The sense of exile is strong upon us. In every culture there is
some legend of how humanity fell out of harmony with God. Among
Jews and Christians this legend is found in Genesis, where we follow the
Fall of Adam and Eve from paradise: it is an account, in mystical
language, of the rupture between God and humanity. Unfortunately,
mystical accounts have a way of being interpreted fundamentally, with a
view to historicity rather than as allegorical parallels. The Fall, read in
isolation, augurs ill for a people exiled from God. But within Christianity

the Redemption is a natural concomitant of the Fall which is known liturgically as *felix culpa*, the happy fault whereby Christ came to redeem the world; without the first Adam there would have been no second Adam (Christ) to help us. Logically, following from this, the *ave* of *Ave Maria* (Hail Mary) is a reversal of Eva's name, as Mary also redeems the fault of Eve, the Mother of all living. The Fall is our exile from paradise; we make a Waste Land of the Garden of Eden. The quest is our spiritual journey and the Grail is our return to our sovereign condition as kings and queens of creation. Whatever the orthodox account of the Fall, every culture seems to have developed its own apocryphal explanation of how a part of paradise dwelt among humanity in order to provide a chance of return. The Grail legend is the European response to this exile: but why wasn't the religion of the time deemed sufficiently efficacious?

In his *Flight of the Wild Gander*, Joseph Campbell asks why 'anyone in the Middle Ages should have thought it necessary to embark on such a lonely, dangerous enterprise (i.e. the Grail quest) when the Holy Mass, with Christ himself on the altar, was being celebrated, right next door, every day'.[6]

As we have already seen, the Grail itself does not necessarily derive from Christian origins, although it has been incorporated into its symbolism. The Grail quest incorporates dimensions which are implicit yet not doctrinally apparent within Christianity. It is a necessity for every soul to find its individual return from exile: a return which may pursue or avoid the usual channels of exoteric belief. The fact is that achieving the Grail was not just a parallel experience to that of receiving communion at Mass: it was far more than this. Partaking of communion can be the ultimate knowing – the union of Creator with created – but unless the communicant brings imaginative awareness to the sacrament, the inner and outer worlds run forever on parallel tracks, never to merge as one. The mystery of communion must be actualized in everyday life, not be relegated to some never-never land of spirituality. In its exoteric expression, Christianity fails to give any sense of personal responsibility for one's redemption. Few Christians think beyond the possibilities of free will which is the birthright of humanity alone. It was the exercise of free will which resulted in the Fall; yet why should free will not be exercised positively towards ending our exile?

This question has never been squarely faced within exoteric Christianity: faith, good works and the reception of the sacraments are proposed as the instruments of the Redemption. Mystically, there is an esoteric quorum within all religions which proposes an alternative and more personally responsible response. Christianity has relegated its esoteric tradition to a 'safe' expression of mysticism; it has purged itself of the Divine Feminine, of a mystery tradition, of anything smacking of private revelation. Yet, despite this, the Grail tradition lived on through an age which saw the destruction of both Cathars and Knights Templar, two different groups whose show of autonomy and grasp of mystical insight, among other things, antagonized the Church. The Grail has never been officially sanctioned by the Church, yet neither has it ever been denied. The Church even had its own Grail story. So popular were Arthurian tales at one time, the Grail legend was turned to good effect by the monks of Glastonbury who took Perceval the Fool and turned him into Perlesvaus: 'He who has lost the valley', recognizing him as a type of Christ, and making the Grail story one of scintillating Christian allegory. So the Grail legend worked on two levels: exoterically as a popular story, esoterically as an alternative path to God, a release from exile.

But what of other traditions? The Jewish conception of the Fall has a distinctly different emphasis. Here the sense of exile is stronger, the urge to return more immediate. In esoteric Judaism, specifically within the Qabala, we see the exile from God expressed in terms of a relationship. The Covenant that God makes with Israel is more like a marriage contract than a legal document. If we follow the esoteric symbolism of Qabala we find our companion once more: not as Hideous Damsel or Grail Maiden, although they share a common imagery, but as Shekinah. The Shekinah was said to reside with God from the beginning of creation; her appearance in the biblical books of wisdom and within Qabalistic texts such as the *Zohar* give us a clear picture of her function in the way of Return.

She appears in this account of the creation from the book of Proverbs:

> The Lord created me at the beginning of his work, the first of his acts of old. Ages ago I was set up, at the first, before the beginning of the earth ... When he established the heavens, I was there, ... when he marked out the foundations of the earth, then I was beside him, like a master workman; and I was daily his delight ...[7]

It is evident from this account that God and his Shekinah are joined together in a loving partnership. When Adam and Eve eat of the Tree and are cast out of paradise, the Shekinah decides to descend with them; if the unity of God and creation is broken then there can be no union between God and his Shekinah. She goes into voluntary exile with humanity, then; wherever she appears it is as the expression of God's compassion. Yet she is more than an abstract emanation from the Godhead. She inhabits the Ark of the Covenant, going before it in the desert as pillar of cloud by day and a pillar of flame by night: a visible presence of God's dwelling among the Israelites. The Ark, like the Grail, is a relic of great power: it is a piece of paradise. (We will remember that the Grail in *Parzival* is termed *lapsit exillis* or 'stone that fell from heaven'; it is said elsewhere to have been an emerald which fell from Lucifer's crown at the rebellion of the Fallen Angels.) The Shekinah herself is both a personification of that lost paradise as well as becoming associated with the exile from it. She accompanies Israel through the desert until the Ark is eventually housed within the Temple. The destruction of the Temple in 586BC strengthened the Jewish sense of exile on every level: the Ark was dispersed and its whereabouts became unknown. (But see Ch. 6) The Shekinah had no dwelling; henceforward she would live in the hearts of her people. By performing such acts which were pleasing to the Shekinah, the pious Jew hastened the return; works of evil saddened the Shekinah and prolonged the exile. For the Jews, the Ark takes on the significance of the Grail – the subject of an interior quest.

The Shekinah is, then, the female counterpart of God; Qabalistic texts go so far as to call her God's wife, for whom he is sundered by the Fall and the continuing sinfulness of humanity. The complexity of the Shekinah is appreciable only if we understand that her imagery stems from that of the Canaanite and Mesopotamian goddess Astarte, or Ishtar, who reigned in heaven supreme with her consort Baal, or Tammuz. Divinity was once expressed by the divine Lord and Lady who ruled as a partnership. The Shekinah is the symbolic descendant of this goddess as well as expressing the feminine nature of an otherwise very patriarchal deity. God's Shekinah was associated with the state of the Israelites themselves who were also the exiled and the promised of God. In the Lamentation of Jeremiah over the fall of Jerusalem we see the city personified as the Shekinah:

> How like a widow has she become, she that was great among the nations!
> She that was a princess among the cities has become a vassal.

> She weeps bitterly in the night, tears on her cheeks,
> among all her lovers she had none to comfort her. ...
> Judah has gone into exile because of affliction and hard servitude;
> she dwells now among the nations but finds no resting place ...
> From the daughter of Zion has departed all her majesty.[8]

This is a picture of the manifest Shekinah, the exiled majesty and wisdom of God; personification of a people who have lost their sovereignty. In the biblical books of wisdom, the Shekinah is also called Chokmah, or Wisdom: she who cries aloud in the streets, the one who guards the fountain of wisdom which, like the Grail, brings the soul to its right senses. Wisdom or the Shekinah is the hope of restoration; on the day when the exile is ended she is commanded to:

> Take off the garment of your sorrow and affliction, O Jerusalem, and put
> on for ever the beauty of the glory from God.
> Put on the robe of the righteousness from God;
> put on your head the diadem of the glory of the Everlasting.
> For God will show your splendour everywhere under heaven.[9]

Here the Shekinah as Wisdom is spoken of in her transcendent guise: the one who is no longer in exile but in union with God. For the most striking image of the Shekinah is that of wife, of beloved. The mystic has always dealt in sexual imagery to express his union or separation from the Divine. With the Shekinah the image is extended, by implication, to humanity which is seen as God's beloved. Pious Jewish couples made love on the eve of the Sabbath in imitation of God's union with the Shekinah. Qabalists employed extraordinary techniques of meditation for visualizing this divine union, striving to hasten the return to God.

The symbolism of the Shekinah did not just remain the province of Judaism: the post-exilic period (500BC onwards) saw the rise of Qabalistic mysticism and the great cross-fertilization of religious concepts within the Jewish, Hellenic and Christian worlds. Gnostic Christianity raised the figure of Wisdom, Sophia, to a position which almost rivalled that of Christ; within their apocryphal gospels they reworked the Shekinah's descent as Sophia's Fall, making her responsible for the creation of the world. Despite the incipient dualism of these texts we find again two faces of Sophia: the fallen Sophia, called Achamoth, who roams the world in sorrow and confusion, and Sophia herself, the transcendent queen of heaven whose union with the Logos (God's emanation or Word) marked the end of creation's exile.

Orthodox Western Christianity may have neglected its esoteric side, but the great mystical texts of the Bible still convey a sense of both Shekinah and Sophia to those mystics who are able to interpret them and comprehend their significance. In both Jewish and Gnostic texts we find the same account of the exile from God, the separation of lover and beloved; Shekinah and Sophia make their appearance among humanity as a way of return, taking on firstly the dark, exiled face as an identification with a lost people; lastly they both appear in their radiant and transcendent guise as saviours. This is most clear in *Parzival,* where the Hideous Damsel, Cundrie, rides to the Grail Castle, where the Wounded King still lies in agony; she goes dressed in a hood of black samite upon which is embroidered 'a flock of Turtle-doves finely wrought in Arabian gold in the style of the Gral-insignia'.[10] She accompanies Parzival to the castle in order that he may answer the Grail question correctly. At sight of her habit, the Grail knights cry: 'Our trouble is over! What we have been longing for ever since we were ensnared by sorrow is approaching us under the Sign of the Gral! ... Great happiness is on its way to us!'[11] Cundrie's black appearance may have deceived us into thinking her a malevolent witch concerned with obstructing the Grail quest, but we see from her apparel that the Hideous Damsel is sister to the Shekinah and to Sophia. The dove has always been the symbol of divine compassion. It was a bird sacred to the Goddess and it passed into the panoply of the Shekinah where it symbolized God's Holy Spirit. Within Christianity the Holy Spirit's doubtful gender has been obscured by its symbolization as a dove: the promise of ultimate redemption, the perfect indwelling of God. From the beginning of time where the Holy Spirit brooded over the waters at the Creation it is this image of hope which inspires those upon the spiritual journey to continue. However the Holy Spirit is theologically understood today, it stems from its origins as part of the Divine Feminine: the holy Motherhood of God. In this tangle of symbolism Christ has assumed the attributes of Wisdom; he is seen as the expression of God's Word (Logos) and God's Wisdom (Sophia) throughout the New Testament: 'In the beginning was the Word, and the Word was with God and the Word was God. He was in the beginning with God,'[12] just as Wisdom or the Shekinah is in Proverbs 8, Christ is the one 'in whom are hid all the treasures of wisdom and knowledge'.[13] But although there has been a transition of genders the symbolism has been perpetuated within esoteric Christian tradition. The Shekinah is primarily a figure of the Old Testament. The New Testament sees a restatement of both Sophianic and Messianic principles, the manifestations of God's power, investing both in the person of Christ. Christ is male, yet the feminine symbology is not neglected as the Messiah needs the means to manifest. 'The first Adam is moulded from the vile dust of the earth, the second comes forth from the precious womb of the Virgin.'[14] Mary fulfils the role of the second Eve, as well as embodying the principles of the Shekinah. For she is not just a receptacle or vehicle of incarnation for Christ, but she is also a representative of exiled humanity. Her flesh clothes the divinity of the manifest God, Christ. Human and divine meet in a mystical marriage which is birth, death and consummation all at once: this is the experience of communion. In transubstantiation, ordinary bread and wine are changed into the body and blood of Christ: in metaphysical terms, the body and blood of Christ are of Mary as his mother, yet they also represent the inspiriting divinity of the Messiah. It is not possible to think in terms of the feminine as matter, the male as spirit in this context, for a real union of the two has taken place. The spiritual realities are almost alchemical:

> ... the heavenly Spirit makes fertile the womb of the virginal font, by the secret admixture of his light, that it may bring forth as heavenly creatures, and bringing back to the likeness of their Creator, those whom their origin in earth's dust had produced as men of dust in miserable state.[15]

Both Sophia and Christ share the Messianic task; both share the exile among humanity, striving to make it remember its likeness to the Creator; both are the means of return from exile.

If we re-examine the Grail legend in this light, we will find startling parallels which are pertitient to our spiritual journey. In the common language of mysticism there is really no conflict between Judaism, Christianity, or any other religious path: these are but means to arrive at a cessation from exile. If the exoteric sides of religion have not been clear enough in their definitions, an esoteric response has always arisen within or parallel to that religion. Within the Grail legend symbolism, both cultural and religious, mingles in a spontaneous and immediate story.

We are in exile, or in a state of forgetfulness. We have lost our sovereignty, our state of union with the divine. Yet the companion of the quest is with us as a potentiality. Perceval is called 'the son of the widow'; an image in which we see ourselves reflected as children both of the exiled Sophia, and Christ, the son of Mary. The Waste Land is our state of exile: the place that is not paradise; it is the violated Jerusalem: whether as the Holy City fought over by Jews, Christians and Moslems, or as the exiled Sophia herself. The Grail is that piece of paradise which remains among us, hidden and transcendent, the cup of sovereignty, of wisdom: a draft from that cup is a remembrance of paradise, a union of soul with God. The Wounded King *is* the potential Grail Knight himself, a symbol of lost sovereignty; or he is Christ, the crucified King wounded with five wounds, whom each sin wounds afresh. Within the Grail legend we find a mystery tradition which embodies much that is common to the major religions. It is not difficult to see just why it evokes such a popular response wherever it is spoken of.

*   *   *   *   *

The awareness of our exile has been blunted in this age. Few people concertedly follow a mystical path which helps them recall the fact that they have a spiritual heritage. We live in a state of forgetfulness. Yet while the major religions seem to decline, there is a corresponding upsurge of interest in the spiritual quest. This often takes some very strange forms. In Steven Spielberg's film, *Raiders of the Lost Ark* (1980), we see the goal of the spiritual quest pursued as a physical object. Like the Grail, the Ark of the Covenant is hidden or withdrawn; its power is immanent, not apparent. In the film the Ark is sought by rival interests: on the one hand, evil seeks to use it for its own ends, on the other, the Ark is sought as an archaeological treasure. Neither side take into account what can happen if one seeks a spiritual principle as though it were an object. The Ark, like the Grail, is full of power; within the film, the force of the Shekinah reveals itself in such strength that evil is completely overcome on either side, and is replaced by a sense of responsibility. Although this film is a shadow of the real spiritual journey, its universal distribution may have helped awaken some sense of exile, of a yearning to rediscover what is truly our heritage. Stranger vehicles for the action of Sophia have been known. The confusion of an earthly for a heavenly treasure has dogged the history of religion. The heavenly Jerusalem cannot be established on earth; the Wounded King is not a real king, nor is the Grail a physical object. We understand this better if we see these symbols as belonging to the soul itself. The mystique of the Grail symbolism is set there to make us fall in love with an interior world; we must yearn with all our hearts to be there, to inhabit that world and work with these principles. If we apply the Grail principle spiritually, it follows that it will automatically have its reflection in the real world.

The Grail Maiden, the Shekinah or Sophia, is a personification of that holy object; she is the Grail or the Ark, the hidden treasure which symbolizes the union of the soul with the Divine. We find and lose this Grail continually. There is no means to come to spiritual union, to meet the shining glory of Sophia without we first embrace the Hideous Damsel who is the reality of ourselves. As individuals we cannot embark upon a quest to save the world, without first attending to our own condition. The bitter cup precedes the golden Grail. We are all lost, in exile, out of harmony with ourselves, unaware of the divine spark within us. We all yearn to recover our lost happiness; yet how shall we do this? First of all, by assuming a sense of responsibility towards ourselves: this is not selfishness but common sense. Only those who start the journey deserve to win the Grail; if we wait for everyone else to join our party we shall never begin. It does not matter if we make mistakes along the way. The Grail Messenger, the Hideous Damsel, will soon let us know: we must heed her as the inner voice, the Will of God. Her voice is harsh and its advice unwelcome; but only by knowing ourselves thoroughly will we be able to continue.

As the quest continues, the idea will begin to impinge upon us that we are not searching for a physical object: this is but a symbol of our yearning for union. As day succeeds day, the awful thought grows: there is no Grail, no blaze of glory, no merging into the infinite. Perhaps we will never see the reality of the Grail Maiden, we will be in exile for ever? There is no progress on this path; it is a false assumption that the further on we go the better we become. The path is about forgetting and remembering, and, therefore, ultimately about *awareness*. We need to ask the Grail question. The spiritual journey, our quest, is also its conclusion. We are all on this journey: all we have to do is make the decision to be aware of the fact. We begin to be aware of the suffering of others and their sense of exile from themselves; we begin to realize the compassion of Sophia, our hidden companion, as our own compassion.

Those who are on quest are like those who devote themselves to the Bodhisattva concept. In Buddhism, a Bodhisattva is one who vows never to re-enter Nirvana until 'the last blade of grass' enters first. It is an awesome concept. We begin our quest in seeming selfishness and continue in total unselfishness. We identify with the sign of hope – the exiled Sophia – becoming co-workers with her in seeking to hasten the union of all beings. God, the Divine, is not outside us but within us. While there can be no ultimate universal union yet, we can strive for remembrance of what we really are, unifying ourselves with the principle of quest which we live by. For the essence of the Grail quest is not to disappear into a never-never land of no return; our duty is to return bearing the gifts of the Grail within ourselves, that we might be a cup, a means of regeneration and remembrance to every living creature. We become the Grail that others might drink; for to find the Grail is to become it. Perceval, unlike Galahad, returns from his Grail quest, becoming the king of the Grail castle. The Wounded King finds his sovereignty once more and is healed. The Waste Land and, by implication, the Hideous Damsel, are restored to their former beauty. The Grail itself ceases to be an object and becomes a living reality. Sophia is restored to unity once again, returning from exile in union with the Grail winner.

The two faces of Sophia as Hideous Damsel and Grail Maiden have accompanied us on our quest, the one prompting, the other leading us on. We understand now that the return to paradise will not be bequeathed to us from on high; the reality lies in our hands. Our spiritual journey is after all the return from exile, the quest upon which Sophia accompanies us always.[16]

Notes

1 *Peredur*, in the *Mabinogion*, trans. Jeffrey Gantz (Harmondsworth: Penguin, 1976), p. 248.

2 Ibid.

3 Wolfram von Eschenbach, *Parzival*, trans. A.T. Hatto (Harmondsworth: Penguin, 1980), p. 125.

4 Arthur C.L. Brown, *The Origin of the Grail Legend* (Harvard University Press, 1943), p. 219.

5 *Parzival*, op. cit., p. 330.

6 Joseph Campbell, *Flight of the Wild Gander* (Indiana: Gateway Editions, 1951), p. 219.

7 Proverbs VIII: 22, 23, 27, 29, 30. R.S.V. Bible.

8 Lamentations I: 1–3, 6.

9 Baruch V: 1–3.

10 *Parzival*, op. cit., p. 386.

11 *Parzival*, op. cit., p. 393.

12 St John I: 1–2.

13 Colossians II: 3.

14 St Peter Chrysologus, Sermon 117, in *The Divine Office*, vol. 3 (London: Collins, 1974), p. 684.

15 Ibid., p. 685.

16 See Caitlín Mathews, *Sophia: Goddess of Wisdom, Bride of God* (Wheaton, IL: Quest Books, 2001).

~ 9 ~

The Grail: Quest as Initiation Jessie Weston and the Vegetation Theory

Prudence Jones

Of the writers discussed in this book only one truly deserves the ascription 'Grail scholar', and that is Jessie Laidley Weston (1850–1928). Others, such as C.G. Jung and Joseph Campbell, were learned in the extreme, but none devoted so much of their time to the explication of a single theme. 'Miss Weston' (as she was universally called by her peers) brought an entirely new spectrum to the study of the Grail in the twentieth century. Her scholarship is impeccable – despite occasional flights of fancy which she was never afraid to make, and she paved the way for a whole generation of investigators to come. Her books and articles, now at last being republished,[1] still make exciting and challenging reading, and she deserves to be remembered as someone who caused an entire generation – those who disagreed as well as agreed with her – to look again at the Grail, and to see new possibilities – possibilities which are still being followed up.

The Vegetation or Ritual Theory of the origin of the Grail is long overdue for consideration at the present time, when the pagan religions of Western Europe are being reborn in a new form for the twenty-first century.

The Ritual Theory claims that the Grail was originally conceived as the mysterious source and origin of life, both of physical life – the renewal of crops, of animal and human existence sought in the fertility rituals of Nature religions worldwide – and of spiritual life – the immortality of the soul, or our potential for union with the Divine, which is sought by the inner, esoteric practitioners of all religions, whether pagan, Christian, Buddhist, Moslem or any other. Because all religions share this search for personal knowledge of the source of spiritual life, the theory claims, it was possible in the twelfth century for a Celtic tale from the native pagan religion to be assimilated, in its mystical aspect, to the mystical practices of Christianity. Thus a magical tale about a folk-hero who renews the failing spirit of vegetation each year could give rise to a mystical tale about an initiate's hard-won knowledge of the source of both physical and spiritual renewal. This source, the Grail, could also be described as a Christian relic, both as the vessel of the earthly feast, the cup of the Last Supper, and as that of the Mystery of the Incarnation, the cup which had caught the blood of the incarnate God, the dying Christ.

The theory thus involves a definition of the Grail, which, in the earliest text we have, the *Perceval* of Chrétien de Troyes, is described only as an object 'wrought of fine gold and having many sorts of precious stones', whose brilliance outshines the candles just as the sun and the moon outshine the stars. It is 'a very holy thing' and it serves the Fisher King's father with a single Host. The description is tantalizingly vague, but it may well describe some kind of platter. Most people nowadays understand the Grail to be the cup of the Last Supper, the object of a disastrous quest by the Knights of the Round Table in Arthurian romance, something that is of uncertain practical value but no doubt highly spiritual for those of a mystical bent. This too is an over-concrete definition, for not only does the Grail appear in many forms, including a cup, a dish, a stone, etc., but it is not always of Christian provenance. After many years' study of the manuscripts and commentaries, Dr Jessie L. Weston, originator of the Ritual Theory, chose to define the Grail conceptually, rather than identifying it with any particular relic, as 'the mysterious source of physical and spiritual life.' This precise and yet broad definition allowed her to harmonize many conflicting features of the texts which have come down to us, to give them a coherent meaning, and also to propose a possible history of their development in the world not of concepts but of facts.

Jessie Laidlay Weston was born on 29 December 1850, and was educated at Brighton, Paris and Hildesheim. She also studied art at the Crystal Palace School. Her background was that of a scholar of medieval literature, but in her leisure hours she was keen on Wagner's operas. Their source legends, from Saxon poetry and Icelandic saga, were little known in England at the time, and at the Bayreuth Festival of

1890 she conceived the idea of rendering Wolfram von Eschenbach's
Parzival, the original of Wagner's Grail opera, into English. The verse
translation was published in 1894, followed by a retelling of the
Lohengrin story in ballad form, and then in 1896 came *Legends of the
Wagner Drama*. These renderings were for a popular readership, but
the following three studies of Arthurian romance, *The Legend of Sir
Gawain* (1897), *The Legend of Sir Lancelot du Lac* (1901), and the
two-part *Legend of Sir Perceval* (1906 and 1909) were textual analyses
of the origin and development of the story concerned. It was in these,
however, that the groundwork and first formulation of the Vegetation
Theory appeared.

Writing with all the tools of literary scholarship at her disposal,
including, from her background at the Sorbonne, the rigorous French
method of *explication de texte*, a far more detailed analysis of style and
argument than the English usually undertake, Dr Weston began trying
to solve some puzzles in the presentation of Sir Gawain in the Arthurian
romances. She eventually concluded that Gawain – Gwalchmai, the
Hawk of May – had originally been a Celtic solar hero, a mythical
figure, son of Lugh the light-bearer, and that his function had been to
restore the spring after winter's cold. Even after he developed into a
fully human figure, the first of Arthur's knights, Gawain always retained
his connection with the Otherworld, his Faerie mistress and his magic
horse and sword. As a character, he was particularly favoured by
medieval English ballad-writers, and although in the later, highly
ecclesiasticized Arthurian romances he appeared as a treacherous
libertine, eclipsed by Lancelot, Perceval and the others (no doubt
because he still represented the pre-Christian order of things), in the
early French and German stories he retained his original heroic status as
the bravest and most courteous of all the king's knights.[2]

Jessie Weston's research was the first systematic attempt to establish
the relative dates and origins of the multitude of Arthurian stories.
Previously, it had been assumed that since Chrétien's *Perceval* was the
oldest manuscript, it represented the oldest version of the story. By
careful analysis of the texts, Dr Weston showed that this was not the
case. On the contrary, it eventually appeared that the Gawain version,
attributed by Gautier to Bleheris, represented the earliest attainable
form of the story. Her discoveries about the Gawain texts surprised the
author as much as they surprised her readers. 'I had formed no definite
conclusion on the subject,' she wrote in the preface to *The Legend of Sir*

Gawain, 'the results, such as they are, have evolved themselves naturally and inevitably in the course of careful study and comparison of the different stories.' This combination of open-mindedness with utter clarity and ruthless adherence to the evidence characterizes all of Jessie Weston's work and even today makes it extremely exciting to read. At the time, it reduced some of her critics to incoherent frenzy.

Her next study, of Lancelot, again vindicated some unpopular theories. She demonstrated the late arrival on the Lancelot tales in the Arthurian canon, and suggested that his love affair with the queen was probably modeled on the already popular romance of Tristan and Iseult. Although he supplanted Gawain as the king's best knight, because of his adulterous relationship with the queen, Lancelot could not similarly replace Perceval as Grail winner in the popular but increasingly moralistic Grail cycle. As the Lancelot tales show signs of having been influenced by the Perceval tales, and vice versa, some rivalry between the two heroes would have been inevitable, and it was for that reason, our author suggested, that the sketchily-drawn figure of Galahad was introduced, a pure and holy Grail winner who would bring his father vicarious glory in this most compelling of quests. Many adherents of the Christian theory of origin were not happy to see Galahad relegated to the status of an afterthought, perfect example of the *genre* though he undoubtedly was.

Already, Jessie Weston's interest in the folk-tales of northern Europe evidenced in her Wagner studies, had allowed her to recognize the origin of the Arthurian tales in Celtic legend, at a time when many scholars still thought them to have been mere literary imitations of Chrétien. Dr Weston's main concern at this stage was to untangle the developmental threads of the whole Arthurian corpus. The Grail was not, in itself, a prime source of interest. But while writing the next volume in the series, the first part of her Perceval study (1906), her emphasis shifted decisively. Recognizing that Perceval was not in his origins a Grail-winner (the Anglo-Norman poem *Syr Percyvelle* making no mention of the Grail), and investigating other possibilities as to his origin, she realized that the original Grail-winner, the hero who appeared in the earliest versions of the story, those attributed to Bleheris or Blihis the Welshman (whom she later identified as a historical person-age), must have been none other than the Celtic solar hero, Gawain.

This theory caused controversy until her death in 1928 and beyond. 'In its origin, of which the *Gawain* stories are the survival, the Grail was purely Pagan,' she wrote at the end of the first volume of the *Perceval* studies.[3] This was of course heresy. The Grail was generally thought to have been the container for the Holy Blood, a cup or cruet, supposedly brought from Jerusalem to Glastonbury by Joseph of Arimathea or one of his descendants. In the more literary of the Arthurian romances it was treated as an object of high Christian mysticism, and its Pagan origins are loftily ignored by many of its commentators even today.

However, Jessie Weston argued, ordinary textual investigation revealed the earliest versions of the Grail stories to be those containing the Celtic elements of the magic stag hunt, the challenge by the Green Knight, the welding of the broken sword, etc., rather than any Christian element. Why then had a Christian interpretation been added to what would ordinarily have become an entertaining secular adventure? Why too had so many distinctly non-Christian elements been retained? Why was the Grail always kept in a castle, associated with a king, rather than in a temple, associated with a priest? Why did it miraculously and automatically provide people with the food and drink they most desired; and why did the successful hero's question about its nature miraculously restore the Wasteland or its king to health? Such features argued for the Grail's origin in a Pagan fertility religion rather than in Christian iconography. Why was the Grail always carried by a maiden rather than by a priest? This would have been sacrilege to medieval Christians.

Furthermore, the story called the *Elucidation* is utterly unilluminating from the standpoint of a Christian origin. Added as a prologue to the Mons MS of Chrétien's *Perceval*, it tells how once in the land of Logres, a King Amangons and his men raped the mysterious maidens of the hills, who had previously offered refreshment to all travellers. As a result, the court of the Rich Fisher disappeared from view and the Grail was seen no more. However, if we see the story as explaining how the priestesses of a Pagan fertility cult, responsible for the prosperity of the kingdom, were driven out of public life and their cult reduced to an underground existence, then the *Elucidation* is precisely what its name implies. Once more, this argues for a Celtic Pagan origin to what had already become a Christian tale. Now what was it about the original story that had made it susceptible of Christian development?

Jessie Weston's researches into the adventures of Gawain, Carados and Bran de Branlant in Chrétien's poem, stories which seemed to have been interpolated randomly into the Grail narrative, which described the winning of a magic castle and a lady associated with it, soon convinced her that here too were meaningful parts of the original narrative. These 'interpolations' were all modelled on the same archetypal theme, important enough in its own right to have retained an air of numinosity. Here at last was the Pagan forerunner of Perceval's Christian Grail adventure.

This was not some single folk-tale containing all the elements of Perceval's story. No such original had been found. It was rather 'the confused remembrance of a most ancient and widespread form of Nature worship ... which underlies many of the ancient Mysteries';[4] the cult of the dying and resurrected god, the spirit of vegetation and ultimately of prosperity, once known to Greeks as Adonis, but personified in what we now call Native religions throughout the world. The ailing Fisher King of the Grail romances was originally the vegetation god, the Lance which dripped blood, the symbol of his wounded virility, and the Cup, where this appeared, the corresponding female symbol. The hero who asked the question about the nature of these objects had won the sacred kingship not by valour alone, but by entering into conscious awareness of the instinctive process of renewal. He was thus entitled to supplant the King, or, by restoring the latter to conscious awareness of his role, to heal him.

This is, in essence, the Vegetation Theory. The Grail is a Life talisman, bringing fruitfulness to all who have the right relationship to it. The theory relies heavily, and explicitly, on the theories of Sir James Frazer in *The Golden Bough*, newly published at the time and which made sense of what had previously seemed to be barbaric and primitive superstitions the world over. The theory also highlights features of the native European religion, and Frazer's examples of modern Fertility Cult survivals, such as mumming plays and Easter celebrations, delighted folklorists all over Europe. (Jessie Weston had joined the Folklore Society in 1897.) The healing of the land, however, and the hero's winning of the divine Kingship, while no doubt giving rise to a compelling adventure story, are not in themselves enough to justify the legend's conversion into the more personal spirituality of Christian mysticism. It was this shift from the physical to the spiritual aspect of healing which now engaged Jessie Weston's attention.

In her 1906 paper to the Folklore Society, 'The Grail and the Rites of Adonis',[5] Dr Weston explained in detail how the Vegetation Theory accounted for otherwise inexplicable features in the texts, such as the weeping women in the Grail Castle, the greening of the land when the King is healed, the presence of doves in the ceremonies, and other features too numerous to mention here. The Grail ceremony itself would thus have been a standard ritual of the fertility cult, perhaps carried on secretly in some corner of the Christian kingdom – presumably Wales, from which the story's author, Bleheris, was said to come. The experience of the visiting knight, however, the Grail quester, was of the nature of a test, which he must pass in order to learn the nature of the marvels he had seen. Could it therefore have been an initiation?

Medieval scholars do not usually think in terms of initiation, and they certainly did not in the days before Jung gave a psychological gloss to esoteric ideas. But a footnote to the first *Perceval* volume[6] runs: 'Having lent the Volume of *Gawain-Grail* visits to one whom I did not then know to be connected with Occult views and practices,[7] it was returned to me with the remark, "This is the story of an Initiation told from the outside." ' Jessie Weston took her informant's evidence seriously. The Grail stories, so it seemed, described the experiences of one who had happened unawares on a ceremony for which he was unprepared, either through blundering in by accident, or else through replacing the rightful candidate, as when Gawain took the place of the knight who had been slain while under his protection.

Now an initiation presupposes a body of secret knowledge, which only prepared souls are able to witness without harm. In her Adonis paper, Jessie Weston cautiously assumes that the Grail rituals were secret simply because they were forbidden relics of the Old Ways surviving in a Christian land. In Volume 2 of the Perceval studies, however, she distinguishes between the outer, public practice of religion and its inner Mystery cult, containing teachings suitable only for a few. The annual ceremony of the restoration of greenery to the land by the coming of the Hawk of May, for example, was not important enough to occasion a link with the Mysteries of the new religion. However, the inner ceremony, the initiation into the secret not of physical but of spiritual life, could indeed have lent its setting and its symbols to the equivalent teachings of Christianity.

The means of transmission, though, was obscure. Granted that any modern initiate could recognize that the Grail romances made esoteric sense, granted that the Celtic background described in their more primitive versions was that of a fully Frazerian Nature religion, how was she to prove that an esoteric core of Celtic Pagan teaching ever existed, and even if it did, how could she show the original story-teller had actually understood it? We have no easily accessible record of the hypothetical Celtic Mystery teachings; there is no Celtic Plato, no Plotinus, no Apuleius with his story of initiation. In recent years, initiates and psychologists have been piecing together the scattered fragments of evidence, but in Jessie Weston's time, before Jung, before the Human Potential Movement with its workshops on breakthrough and transcendence, the task was almost impossible.

Nevertheless, the Ritual Theory stands as a hypothesis. The story of the finding of the Grail, having its origin in Celtic fertility religion, was thus told by Bledri the Welshman to his Norman allies in the early years of the twelfth century. As (what we would now call) an archetypally powerful story, it caught its hearers' imagination, was embellished as a romance by poets at the court, and was then reworked by a handful of other initiates who understood its significance, such as Robert de Boron and Wolfram's source, Kyot. The outer Pagan teaching about the source of physical life had been refined, in the hypothetical Mystery cult whose story Bledri transmitted, into an inner and universal teaching about the source of spiritual life. This source, the vessel of the Divine outpouring, was what the poets called the Grail. It was something which Christians could recognize, on the mystical level of the higher emotions, as easily as Pagans could, and it was something which could be equated with the chalice of the Eucharist as easily as with the magic feeding vessel of Celtic symbolism.

As well as providing an explanation for particular features of the Grail stories such as the weeping women, etc., Dr Weston was the first to mention in print that the four Grail Hallows were identical with the four Treasures of the Tuatha de Danaan, and with the four suits of the Tarot pack. Drawing on Classical and Hermetic sources as well as on her Western Mysteries informant, she was also specific about the nature of the initiation described. This was a twofold process. The Grail in its lower, animal aspect was the Cup, paired with the Spear, associated with the colours black and green, and ruled by the King of Castle Mortal. To pass beyond this mortal realm of impermanence and attain to the earthly Paradise, the red land of the 'rich Grail', the feeding vessel, ruled by the Maimed King, the spirit encased in flesh, the initiate had to brave the ordeal of the Chapel Perilous, the meeting with the Black Hand of Death. (This was the point at which Arthur's squire Chaus, in the

Perlesvaus, failed.) Having attained to the Castle of the Grail, and seen the wonders there, the initiate was next required to re-solder the Sword, symbol of conscious awareness, and/or to put the Question which signified his recognition or his desire for awareness of what this earthly richness signified. if he was able to do this, he had won to the 'Holy' Grail proper, the Grail on the highest level, invisible to mortal eyes, source of spiritual life and blessedness, whose kingdom was the white land ruled by the Fisher King.

Though we know little about Jessie Weston's personal life, it would seem that she was never an initiate. She criticized the sloppy scholarship of most 'occult' writing of the time as freely as she gave credit where it was due. Her loyalty to 'our faith', the Christian religion, remains unquestioned in all her writings. Yet clearly she understood the mystical realm of insight where all religions meet and can communicate their different approaches to the truth. The tone of commitment and enthusiasm in the passages referring to this realm would suggest that she knew it from personal experience.

The two volumes of the Perceval studies were followed by a little book for esotericists, *The Quest of the Holy Grail* (1913), which summarized her ideas to date for an audience which was willing to look for their inner coherence rather than simply for external evidence in support of them. The more academic business of editing and commenting on medieval poetry continued (see Bibliography), and she also contributed the section on Arthurian legend to the *Encyclopaedia Britannica*. By the second decade of the twentieth century, she was in her 60s, working as hard as ever, still based in Paris, still attending the Bayreuth Festival, and still fascinated by the universal Mystery embodied in the myth of the Holy Grail.

The search for proof of an esoteric pagan cult in Britain continued, in one of his volumes of Gnostic fragments, *Thrice-Greatest Hermes*, G.R.S. Mead had published an account of a Christianized Pagan Mystery cult in first-century Asia Minor. At last there was proof that in centuries long past at least the Christian Mysteries and the Pagan Mysteries had combined. An early Christian Gnostic sect, the Naassenes, had based their rituals on those of the Great Mother Cyhele and her dying and resurrected son, the vegetation god Attis. 'These Naassenes frequent what are called the Mysteries of the Great Mother,' thundered their third-century adversary, Bishop Hippolytus of Portus,[8] believing that they obtain the clearest view of the universal Mystery from the things done in them.' They had a lower initiation 'into the mysteries of the fleshy generation', and a higher initiation 'into which no impure man shall enter', to which the Christians added a third, that of Jesus: 'for we alone are Christians, accomplishing the Mystery at the third gate'. Such an outlook, while anathema to the orthodox of any faith, is in perfect accord with Dr Weston's own view in 1906: 'I do not think it matters in the least whether or not the Grail was originally Christian, if it was from the first the symbol of spiritual endeavour ... the symbol and witness to unseen realities, transcending this world of sense.'[9]

It is also surprisingly similar to the attitude which, she had argued, would have characterized the initiates who transformed the pagan story of the Grail into its later Christian form. Perhaps for this reason, although there is again no evidence that the cult was transmitted from Asia Minor to Britain, much less remained intact until the twelfth century, the Naassene document underpins the argument in her last book, *From Ritual to Romance* (1920). This book received wide popular acclaim. It summarizes her previous arguments, presents the evidence of the Naassenes, and so challenges the reader to deny that such a coherent development of religious thought, which had a document prototype from an earlier age, and which alone gave the fullest explanation of the conflicting features of the Grail romances, was the true background to the Mystery of the Grail.

From Ritual to Romance exercised a profound influence on the thought of the twentieth century. The poet T.S. Eliot took it as his theme for his 1922 poem *The Waste Land*, describing the barrenness and anomie of the early twentieth century. The Waste Land, where there is plenty of expediency but neither true love nor true purpose, has become a commonplace image of the century. 'What shall we do tomorrow? What shall we ever do?' ask the hopeless characters in his barren scenario. This is the land of existential futility, where the passions have no place and where every occurrence is arbitrary. In the years since the Nazi terror and Second World War, Europeans and Americans have perhaps integrated their passions better into the routine business of everyday life. The inner sickness, anomie, is no longer an urgent problem. The problem now is the outer manifestation of Europe's earlier hopelessness; the Waste Land is here in fact. Our ecological crisis can no longer be ignored, and in no uncertain sense we must rediscover the secret of the Grail in order to restore greenness to the earth.

How ironic that Jessie Weston should have left us with the image of a curse, the Waste Land, when the whole aim of her work was to point the way to its solution.

In 1923 she was awarded the D.Litt by the University of Wales for her services to Celtic literature, and on 29 September 1928 she died in London, having not quite finished what she considered would be her final volume on the Grail mystery. Her obituary in *The Times* spoke of her many friends world wide, and of the students to whom she had also devoted much of her tremendous energy and impartial commitment to the truth. Her books are now required reading for students of medieval literature, and the theme of the Waste Land has passed into modern literary studies through commentaries on Eliot.

But Jessie Weston's influence does not end there. The Ritual Theory has not been prominent in Grail studies recently, but the historical link left unforged, the demonstration of a Pagan Mystery cult in twelfth-century Europe, has been worked on from quite a different direction, by those who laid the framework of a religion for the New Age. Unlike her exact contemporary Jane Ellen Harrison, whose work she acknowledges warmly in *From Ritual to Romance*, Jessie Weston did not emphasize the female aspect of deity, so obvious in ancient Paganism and also, as she acknowledges herself, in the Grail cult. The Cup as a female symbol, the importance of Perceval's sister in the versions where he is unmarried, the female Grail bearer and the prototypes of all these figures in Irish legend and folktale, were all mentioned by Dr Weston, but not presumably seen as important. She describes both the Cup and the Spear as 'phallic symbols'; the female principle is as invisible in her commentaries as it was at the time in the culture at large.

The new versions of Paganism which have emerged in the twentieth century, based partly on the native folklore heritage, partly on classical models documented by such as Jane Ellen Harrison, and partly on new inspiration, have, however, taken the Goddess as a central figure. In her form as Earth Goddess, the Great Mother is a powerful symbol for those who are working to restore the ravages of technology and inspire a new philosophy which will no longer desecrate the earth. The feminine aspect of deity is currently more effective here than her masculine counterpart, the Green Man, Great Pan, Adonis – the Spirit of Vegetation in his many cultural guises.

So the outer philosophy of Paganism, which we would see but few would name as the practical work of the Grail in the world, the healing of the Wasteland, has reinvoked the ancient power of the Goddess. The Mystery core of Paganism, the secret world of initiation, is correspondingly unambiguous. The Goddess *is* the Grail, both the feminine principle symbolized by the Cup, and the mystical principle of fulfilment. Passages from Mead's Gnostic fragments, paraphrases of Jessie Weston and of the Cambridge Ritualists – Harrison, Murray, Cornford – dot the handwritten pages of modern witches' Books of Shadows. Someone, somewhere in the twentieth century, took up the unfinished research of Jessie Weston and her contemporaries and discovered the missing inner Mysteries of Paganism, no mere relic from the twelfth century, but already existing in potential as a framework for the spirituality of the twenty-first.

Notes and References

1 *The Romance of Perlesvaus*, ed. Janet Grayson (Holland, Michigan: Studies in Medievalism, 1988).
2 The full theory, summarized here, was not completed until the *Perceval* volumes; *Gawain* simply laid the groundwork.
3 p. 322.
4 *The Legend of Sir Perceval*, vol. 1, p. 330.
5 In *Folk-Lore* V, xviii, now reprinted in John Matthews *An Arthurian Reader* (Wellingborough: Aquarian Press, 1988).
6 p. 253.
7 This informant is generally thought to have been G.R.S. Mead, to whose volumes of Orphic and Gnostic fragments Dr Weston refers throughout the second volume of her Perceval studies. A footnote attributed to 'A.N.' (Alfred Nutt, the folklorist and Grail Commentator) on p. 314 of that volume describes the four treasures of the Tuatha de Danaan, and footnotes on pp. 78 and 79 of *From Ritual to Romance*, 2nd edn., credit A.E. Waite and W.B. Yeats respectively with information concerning the corresponding four suits of the Tarot minor arcana.
8 *From Ritual to Romance*, p. 157.
9 *The Legend of Sir Perceval*, vol. 1, p. 336.

Select Bibliography

Books by Jessie L. Weston

1894   (Tr.) *Parzival: A Knightly Epic*, Wolfram von Eschenbach, 2 vols. (London: David Nutt).

1896   *The Legends of the Wagner Drama* (London: David Nutt).

1896   (Tr.) *The Rose-Tree of Hildesheim, and other Poems* (London).

1897   *The Legend of Sir Gawain: Studies Upon its Original Scope and Significance* (London: David Nutt).

1899   *King Arthur and his Knights: A Survey of Arthurian Romance* (London).

1900   *The Soul of the Countess and Other Stories* (London).

1901   *The Legend of Sir Lancelot du Lac* (London: David Nutt).

1901   *The Romance Cycle of Charlemagne and his Peers.*

1905   *Sir Gawain and the Green Knight.*

1906, 1909 *The Legend of Sir Perceval*, 2 vols. (London: David Nutt). Reprinted 1988 as *The Romance of Perlesvaus*, ed. Janet Grayson (Holland, Michigan).

1907   *Sir Gawain and the Lady of Lys.*

1910   *A Hitherto Unconsidered Aspect of the Round Table.*

1911   (Tr.) *Old English Carols from the Hildesheim MS.* (London).

1912   *Romance, Vision and Satire: 14th Century English Alliterative Poems.*

1913   *The Quest of the Holy Grail* (London: Bell).

1914   (Ed.) *The Chief Middle English Poets* (London).

1920   *From Ritual to Romance* (Cambridge Univ. Press).

Articles by Jessie Weston

Arthurian entry in *Encyclopaedia Britannica*.

Same in *Cambridge History of English Literature*.

Articles in *Modern Quarterly for Language and Literature*, *Romania*, *Révue Celtique*, *Athenaeum*, *Modern Language Quarterly*, *The Quest*, and *Folk-Lore*, including 'The Grail and the Rites of Adonis' (1906), since reprinted in John Matthews, *An Arthurian Reader* (Wellingborough: Aquarian Press, 1988).

Her Predecessors

Sir J.G. Frazer, *The Golden Bough*, 2 vols, 1st edn. (London, 1890).

——, *Adonis, Attis, Osiris*, published as separate volume of 3rd, expanded, edition of *The Golden Bough* (London, 1907).

Leroux De Lincey, *Essai sur L'abbaye de Fescamp* (Rouen, 1840). Contains Fescamp *Saint-Sang* legend.

W. Mannhardt, *Antike Wald- und Feld-Kulte, aus nordeuropäischer Ueberlieferung erläutert*, 2nd edn. (Berlin, 1877).

Alfred Nutt, *Studies in the Legend of the Holy Grail* (London, 1989).

——, 'The Ayran Expulsion & Return Formula', in *Folklore Record*, vol. iv.

Gaston Paris (1881, 1883) 'Etudes sur les romans de la Table Ronde', in *Romania*, vols. x & xii.

——, *La Littérature Française an Moyen Age* (Paris, 1988).

K.J. Simrock, *Wolframs 'Parzival' übergesetzt*, with introduction (Stuttgart, 1842).

G. Waitz, *Die Fortsetzungen von Chrétiens 'Perceval le Gallois'* (Strasburg, 1890).

Her Contemporaries

Adolf Birch-Hirschfeld & H. Suchier, *Geschichte der Französischen Litteratur von den ältesten Zeiten bis zur Gegenwart* (Leipzig & Vienna, 1900).

F.M. Cornford, *The Origins of Attic Comedy* (London, 1914).

F. Cumont, *Les Religions Orientales dans le Paganisme Romain*, 2nd edn. (Paris, 1909).

——, *Textes et Monuments Figurés Relatifs aux Mystères de Mithra* (Brussels, 1894).

Jane Ellen Harrison, *Prolegomena to the Study of Greek Religion* (Cambridge, 1903).

——, *Themis, a Study' of the Social Origins of Greek Religion* (Cambridge, 1912).

S. Langdon, *Tammuz and Ishtar* (Oxford, 1914).

——, *Sumerian and Babylonian Psalms* (Paris, 1909).

G.R.S. Mead, *Fragments of a Faith Forgotten* (London, 1900).

——, *Thrice-Greatest Hermes* (London, 1906).

Sir G. Murray, *Four Stages of Greek Religion* (New York, 1912).

——, *Euripides and his Age* (London, 1913).

W.A. Nitze, 'The Fisher King in the Grail Romances', in *PMLA* (1909).

L. Von Schroeder, *Mysterium und Mimus im Rig-Veda* (Leipzig, 1908).

A.E. Waite, *The Hidden Church of the Holy Grail* (London, 1909).

Her Heirs

A.C.L. Brown, *The Origin of the Grail Legend* (Cambridge, Mass., 1943).

J.D. Bruce, *The Evolution of Arthurian Romance* (Göttingen, Baltimore, 1923).

[Antagonistic comments.]

T.S. Eliot, *The Waste Land* (London: Gollancz, 1922).

[Reprinted many times since.]

Prudence Jones, *The Path to the Centre: The Grail Initiations in Wicca* (London: Wiccan Publications, 1988).

Sir W. Ridgeway, *Dramas and Dramatic Dances of non-European Races in Special Reference to the Origins of Greek Tragedy* (London, 1915).

[Criticism from alternative anthropological theory.]

~ 10 ~

Charity of Light:
The Sacred Grail Kings

Elémire Zolla

Through the interplay of light and dark in the imagery of the Grail, and especially in the figure of the Sacred King, an historical opposition of Eastern and Western Christianity, Byzantium against Rome, is reflected. In Zoroastrian and Tibetan mysteries also this figure emerges as a type of all suffering humanity, and of that humanity's inner division which perhaps the Grail alone can cure. Drawing upon sources as various as Persian Mithraism and the writings of Dante, Elémire Zolla points to the clear indication that beyond these dualities, and perhaps within them, is to be found a harmony of opposites.

The parapet of the vast stairway leading onto the platform of Persepolis is carved in the shape of eagles' feathers. Beneath one's palm runs the smooth plumage of stone as one slowly climbs the steps, the roar of the hot desert wind in one's ears.

As I reached the first row of pillars, the tall shafts shooting skyward out of lotuses, there came above the wind an uproar of voices from what is known as the King's Council. I walked in through the huge doorway where King Darius the Great is sculpted under the parasol symbolising his glory, and there I met the remarkable man who knew the meaning of the Grail.

At his feet a Persian youth knelt feverishly taking notes, now and then gesticulating in approval or hoarsely shouting his admiration, overdoing it and enjoying it. He was now beseeching in a wailing voice: 'Slowly, slowly, my master! I mustn't lose one word of what you say!'

Towering above him stood a stout man in his shirtsleeves, a blue tie flapping against his face. He was waving a reproachful hand and resumed of a sudden his lusty bawling: 'Don't deny it! You actually did! You said that we Zoroastrians placed above King Darius Ahura Mazda the God of Light, representing him as an eagle! How dare you? Never, never have we represented God!'

'Never, never, never, you never did!'

'Then tell me, what is that eagle above the King, if It is not Ahura Mazda?'

The youth paged nervously through his notebook, found the passage and barked out: 'The eagle is the Emperor's Majesty, his guardian spirit become visible!'

There followed a pause.

I stepped forward, making a slight bow.

The youth sprang to his feet and rushed to pump my hand: 'Sir, it is now five full years that I am studying this site. I've even learnt a little Avestan. I believe I've read almost everything worth while about the Achemenians. But I was a blind man until I met him, my master, my guide, my leader. Since two o'clock this morning I've had the honour to be at his service.

'He has deigned to show me how Persepolis was built to catch the rays of this morning's rising sun. I saw, sir, the solstitial sun entering the Gate of Nations. In all Persepolis not a shadow is now cast. As my master said, every pillar becomes a ray, a finger of the sun. I saw the all-triumphant Sun move from yonder Gate towards yonder mountain in a perfectly straight line!'

'Line? Line? What do you mean by line?' howled the man. 'It is of the very path of righteousness that you are speaking, my lad!'

'Of course, sir! The path, of all places in the world, where at the solstice no room is left for the lord of shadows, Ahriman.'

'Angra Manyu!' thundered the man. 'And now, tell me. Why did we build Persepolis precisely here?'

The youth closed his eyes tight and rapturously recited: 'Along this latitude of the earth and at this moment of the year, no shadow darkened the reflection of the sun and of the moon as they were caught in the sacred pools.'

While the youth spoke. the man surprised my gaze on his Oxford tie, and immediately addressed me: 'Sir. my name is Sohrab Ardeshir Eruchshaw Jamshedji Sola Hakim, *medicinae baccalaureus, baccalaureus scientiae, philosophiae doctor Oxonensis*. But it is as a Parsee that I feel entitled to wear a tie inscribed *Dominus Illuminatio Mea*, a motto whose meanings only we may fathom. In fact only we comprehend the symbols which you people, I am bound to say, use unwittingly. But this stands to reason, since it is from us you derived them, and you have forgotten having done so. Please raise your eyes to our Emperor upon yonder pillar.

'Round him a ribbon forms a loop. Its two ends are tied together and fall dangling like two tassels.

'Do you not recognise the ribbon and seal whereby, without knowing what you are doing. you swear by the Sun that your documents are as true as our Emperor's majesty?

'Indeed, sir, I even suspect you might not understand what majesty is. It is not royalty. Your queen was a royal highness, but only after her coronation did she truly acquire majesty. At Westminster you drew down upon her a Holy Ghost which is actually a translation of *Khwareh*, our Celestial fire. You dressed her as a Parsee child at *Navjot* and you anointed her on her heart with sacred oil from an eagle-shaped ampulla. Eagle-shaped! Please raise your eyes once more to yonder pillar.

'She then donned the *sudreh*, the sindon worn by our children at their consecration. Finally she received her crown, the Sun edged with rays. Thus was the Golden Eagle of Majesty brought down upon her.'

He very slowly averted his-gaze from me, turning to face the youth whose attention had visibly wandered.

Persepolis is not only an astronomical observatory, my lad!' he cried.

'Oh no, sir! It is, as you taught me, a site for Initiations.'

Doctor Hakim very slowly pivoted back to face me: 'Hence the pools, which were used for the preliminary baptism of the king.'

'What does baptism mean?' queried the Persian youth.

'Baptism is a ceremony of purification by water which, competently performed, allows you to descry the descent of the eagle of Majesty in the case of a monarch, or of the dove of wisdom, in the case of a prophet, baptism's purpose being to enable one to perceive here and now the guardian spirit, which is otherwise met only at death. To the wicked it will appear as a loathsome hag, to the righteous as a lovely virgin of light.' He faced round again: 'Such was Dante's Beatrice. The idea of a journey to the worlds beyond derives from the *Denkart* which one of our Emperors wrote after having ritually partaken of *bhang*.

'But this need not concern us where we are now standing. Look around, please. Pray, would you call this a Council Room, as it is generally known? Of course not. This was a fire temple.

'But do you realise what a holy fire is? Can you imagine what a fire can become when subjected to ever-lowering mantrams down to eight octaves below? At this point it acquires a soul. It speaks, and prophesies.

'But hush! Has anybody among you people ever meditated upon fire?'

Through my mind, as if of its own accord, there flitted the name of a then living holy man.

Doctor Hakim questioningly uttered precisely that name, and quickly added that that holy man was often supernaturally contacted by a friend of his, a Muslim saint in Bombay. All this he seemed to brush aside as he started off on a new track: 'Sir, before Christ spoke, we knew him. In 7AD three planets seemed to coalesce into one star, and we understood that it meant that a ritual of gold, incense, and myrrh was relevant.

'Have you an idea of what I am speaking about?

'Incense is hot. It stands for the warm current which passes through our right nostril. Myrrh is cold. It stands for the cool current which passes through our left nostril. When the two breathes are supremely balanced and knit together, they circulate, like a golden wreath up here' – he slapped his forehead – 'What do you call what we have under here, in physiology? *Corona radiata*.

'Can you imagine what one becomes when thus inwardly crowned? One discerns in all things the light which is their essence, the spark which is their driving life-force.

'Real magi, who have developed their crown, are granted the vision of the compendium of all these sparks, *Khvareh*, Glory descending as a Cup of light.

'They look at the stars and read the writing of destiny. They see the light of the stars descending as a Cup upon a person chosen by destiny.

'The Glory of Kingship they see issue forth from the conjunction of Saturn, Jupiter and Mars in a single sign of the Zodiac, descending upon the chosen sovereign. This happened just before the birth of Kurush, and again just before he entered Babylon. It took place likewise before Darius' Coronation. That is what all these bas-relief beliefs are telling you. At the inauguration of Persepolis, Mercury was in conjunction with Jupiter and the Moon. Eagle, Scorpion and Lion shone above, whilst the Bull sank crushed by the lion. All around you see the Lion pouncing on the Bull, and Darius as Archer, Sagittarius, overcoming a being compounded of Eagle. Scorpion and Lion.

'Our wisdom was somehow transmitted to Abu Sina, so when he saw the conjunction of Saturn and Jupiter Capricorn he wrote his *qasida* foretelling the fall of Baghdad and the Egyptian victory over the Tartars. You may read the story in Al Biruni.'

'You say that the light of the stars of such conjunctions is perceived as descending in the form of a Cup?' I queried.

'We remember the names of the great kings and magi who saw it – Jamshid, Faridun, Kai Khosraw, Zarathustra the Golden, the Ageless, the Powerful One.'

I remembered my Avestic classes, when I was taught so tamely to read the name Zarathustra as Old Yellow Camel.

'Such heroes knew how to draw down the fire from above into a cup or a stone. When this is done, a retinue gathers. At Kang-dez, our Scriptures say, at the spiritual heart of the world, Kai Khosrow thus mustered the Order of Knights described in the *Shah Nameh*. On him had descended the Cup *Jam-e Khai Khosraw*.

'Seeing the Cup invests one with Glory. One becomes the manifestation of one's mandate. When this has been fulfilled, one does not die, but goes back into the space from which such mandates issue. Until they all wind up into their conclusion, the final coming of the *Saoshyant*.

'That is why the Cup is said to confer immortality. In its presence even the thoughts of evil men are cleansed, as shadows that flee the Sun. You may read our text as either 'cup of fire' or 'fire from the sun.'

'We know furthermore that the Cup could be solidified, hidden under the form of a black stone. This a true king and magus could energise with mantrams, turning it into a radiating ruby. This is what Zarathustra is represented as carrying in his hand – his smokeless fire.

'Rumi knew. He writes that the sun in its mysterious way quickens embryos in wombs, inserts sparks into steel, ripens fruits and, inside mountains, transmutes ores into gold, black stones into radiating rubies.

'The Cup is the ruby, the ruby is the Cup.'

The youth had grown excited and he cried impatiently. 'Master, you promised to take me to see where the fiery ruby was kept, at the original Ka'aba at Naqsh-i Rustam!'

'All right. But if we are to get there before noon, we have to rush,' bellowed Doctor Hakim.

I found myself at his heels, along with the Persian youth, leaping down the stairway of Persepolis, heading for Naqsh-i Rustam.

*   *   *   *   *

Alas, not long after our encounter, Doctor Hakim died, leaving me a few wonderful keepsakes of his knowledge. It sometimes happens, on receiving the gift of a few precious items of a set, that one by one the remaining pieces start falling into one's hands. They beckon from improbable shop windows in out-of-the-way places, one comes across them with collectors who volunteer an exchange, they turn up at auctions where nobody else bids for them.

Doctor Hakim's most intriguing hints concerned the Grail's alchemical aspect. It must have sometimes appeared as a transmutatory Cup or stone.

The commonest case of a vessel capable of indefinitely imparting a medicinal quality to its content without any ponderable loss, was that of vases made of antimony, which were said to turn any amount of water into strong medicine. Alchemists in Newton's time drew weighty consequences from the fact. In ancient times it had been fabled that British megaliths were similarly transmutatory. According to the twelfth-century *Historia Regum Britanniae* of Geoffrey of Monmouth, water which washed over them acquired special properties, and they served as alchemical bathing pools. They were therefore called mystical stones. If their projective quality was homeopathic their effectiveness must have been subject to the very strict conditions under which hyperdilutions work. Such must have been the case with the sheep market pool of Bethseda (John 5:2–4).

The nexus of projective vessels – alchemy – kingship and kingly immortality is posited by a crucial passage in *Ssuma Chhien* (it is quoted by Needham, *Science and Civilization in China*, V: 3, p.293, and by Jenny Davis and Roruko Nakaseki *The Tomb of Jofuku or Joshi*, in *Ambix* no 2, Dec. 1937, p.109 ff., in a somewhat different version).

The alchemist Li Shao-Chun, summoned by the Han Emperor in 133 BC is reported as saying: 'By making offerings to the oven' (a practice which is spoken of also in an Assyrian tablet) 'natural substances can be caused to change' – or, in an alternative offered by Needham: 'Natural phenomena can be caused to happen. Or in Davis and Nakaseki's version, 'one may learn about the various beings.' 'If one can cause substances to change', or: 'If one can call down the various beings – cinnabar can be transformed into gold. When such gold has been produced, it can be made into vessels for eating and drinking, the use of which will prolong one's life [...] and make one see the glorious Immortals'. The procedure is prototypically attributed to the Yellow Emperor. Practitioners did not die, but went into occultation.

Such talismans, which helped acquire the charisma of kingship, were the original regalia, and were containers for the essence of power.

Jurisprudence seems to assume the truth of the vibratory character of regalia even today in a case like that of the Hungarian crown. It is reminiscent of the shamanic crowns of Siberian and Korean monarchs, and it was legally construed to 'own' Magyar kingship. When it was smuggled out of the country and entrusted to the US House of Representatives, the Communist Government, rather than pay off the receiver by considering the piece a mere commodity chose to fight for the magic object as such.

In Ceylon the English spirited away Lord Buddha's tooth, which was a receptacle of Kandyan kingship, and restored it after royalist feelings, no longer sustained by its 'vibrations', had died out.

Kingship is a spiritual path. It implies more than mere rulership. It does not only consist in luck, victory and supremacy, which are however even today connected with a Cup at any sporting competition. A peculiar unconcern and ease are expected to run in a King's blood, *Sang real* – and were attributed to his affinity with the sun and with gold. But the king is not only the solar promoter of Justice, Peace and Good Harvest, he also belongs with the Moon of the Wild Hunt, of Warfare and of animal fertility. The throne of Korean Emperor was flanked by Sun and Moon.

In the horoscope of a king's Glory, Jupiter and Saturn, Grace and Severity, Heartiness and Iciness are conjoined. As their lights mix in the sky of a favourable horoscope, so on earth a king must gear their influences together. A beloved Provider and a fearsome Shearer is the Shepherd of men. The all-seeing and all-powerful sun-like monarch in admired by the same people who are ready to consider him an Irresponsible innocent whom ministers and councillors fatally keep in the dark.

The conflict of feelings which his presence evokes is called awe. The king is the sacrificer who must draw down the highest blessing on his people, but the choicest and most obvious blessed offering is himself.

> *What kind of god art thou, that suffer'st more*
> *Of mortal griefs than do thy worshippers?*
> *[...]*
> *O be quick great greatness.*
> *And bid thy ceremony give the cure*
> (Henry V, iv: 1, 261–263; 271–272).

To solve the dilemma kingship has often been split into a Sun King and a Darksome, grotesque substitute – a Winter Solstice Saturnine Lord of Misrule, or a Spring equinox, lunar Mock-King of Carnival, whose heavenly counterpart is Lucifer Morningstar, the trickster who pretends to light the world with his twinkle and is impaled for his cheek, or else exuberantly heralds in the Sun, only to be burnt in the bonfire of its rays.

Strabo tells (XI: 4:7) how the Albanians of the Caucasus got round the difficulty – in a manner which seems typical with most of the peoples likewise named, from the worshippers of Alba the White Goddess in Celtic lands, to the inhabitants of Nemi in the Alban hills.

'Sacred men' served at the shrine of the White Moon. Periodically one of them tranced off and roamed the forest prophesying in his frenzy – the model of all the White Goddess's Green, Wild Men. He was captured, brought back to the temple and there for one year kept in state as king, to be finally sacrificed to the Moon, by the thrust of a spear in his side.

A wound in the left side is what Elohim inflicted on a sleeping-tranced Adam, drawing hence Eve the Lunar Womb of life. In the Middle East the Goddess was Ishtar and her seasonal victim Tammuz or Adonis, the Lord. His wound was in the thigh also. Patterns of kingship vary, but the presence of a Medusa-like goddess is inherent in the king's necessary link with the moon.

Often a magical challenge is offered to the prospective king's daunt-less courage, purity of intent and magical resourcefulness by a Loathly Hag or a Saturnine-Lunar Temptress – lips red, locks free, skin as white as leprosy, Life-In-Death who thickens men's blood with cold, as the poet archetypically saw her. It is for the true king to turn her into the

White Bride of the Honey-Moon who will bestow on him her magic power over the land. He must not fear to lose his head to her.

In the Germanic world kingship was related to Woden, the master of *seidr*, rituals of which we know nothing except that they were called unmanly, and that the trickster Loki hinted at them, taunting fierce Woden about his masculinity. Victims to Woden were hung from trees in the holy grove at Uppsala, and stabbed with a spear.

Myth and theology considered the offerer, the offered and the receiver of the offering as one and Woden the proto-King was said to have sacrificed himself to himself, wounding himself with his own spear; after that he was able to master magic runes – which could be seized only by one 'howling' (*oeoir*) as in the spasms of death.

The king must feel that he is the Hunter – the Hunted Eagle or Lion – only 'ceremony' leading to this realisation 'gives the cure' for kingship.

A virtually complete coronation ceremony was devised in Babylon. S. Mayassis meticulously reconstructed it from the sparse documents in *Mystères et Initiations dans la Prehistoire et Protohistoire* (Athens 1961).

The king was purified with light – he keenly observed his stars with words – he uttered mantrams; with touches, with water – he received baptism perhaps in the pools of forgetfulness and steadfastness.

He then made his Confession of sins, starting from the worst of all, that of having been born. He was tonsured, and led into the temple where he was boxed on the ear – a kind of beheading, way of making him lose his head, and was obliged to kiss the earth – as in certain myths to kiss the Loathly Hag. Once he resumed his standing position, he was slapped in the face. He was now one of the poor, a humbled beggar, and as such faced a night of incubation, the imaginal harrowing of hell of planets, whence he arose to be anointed with 'celestial' oils kept in bulls' horns or golden vases. He now 'saw' the tree of life – to a dynast all one with his genealogical tree – alive in his blood. Above it spread the wings of the eagle of Empire.

There followed the holy meal of cakes 'full of divinity' and of wine, and the final hierogamy with the priestess into whom the Goddess had been drawn. The Psalms of the Bible seem to be asides to this ritual, from dejection to triumph.

One may try to reconstruct the inward transformation of which the pageant's timing was a projection. Portraiture proper, which is the art of reading into inwardness, at least of a mystical quality, ceased to be obvious in late Greek times. It was Alexander who relived the mystique of Babylonian and Iranian kingship, and through his campaigns he felt or sought to feel like Dionysus resurrected – beaming and swooning, wild and glorious, carried along by the effulgence of his stars – he was portrayed with a gaze that verges on suffering, such was the might of his inward elation, his head was slightly slanted as if he were listening to divine words, his curly locks were ruffled by the gust of inspiration, his full, swollen neck was that of *bolus hustericus*. Yet at the same time a divine poise loftens gracefully all his features – such in the result of a true coronation. It caused the crowned one to realise at the core of his being the coincidence of opposites and led him to identify with light.

Ancient initiations all stress the one teaching, that everything living is moved by light, which emanates from the sun and the stars. Seeds are buried sparks of celestial light which are striving to rise back to their origin, and in so doing open into leaves which absorb sunlight and distil it into life-giving sap. The Sun-Eagle and the Tree-of-Life are two in one. On sun-drenched trees animals feed, which they distil into blood which contains their soul, which through the eyes meets and rejoins the Sun, its Self.

Life is the Sun sinking for love into its grave and re-ascending out of love to its source. Every earthly magnetism is an episode in the striving of homesick light. Kingly initiation makes the king into light descending to the people's hearts and soaring in acclamation above them. The magic of monarchy does not work through tricks of reason, but by sheer, naked magnetism, it attracts eyes and hearts by offering a replica of the world. This is seen archetypally in the descriptions of the Grail Castle of Camelot. It was expressed in actual life at Babylon and in Thebes in Persepolis and hence in the *Domus Aurea* on the Oppian hill, finally in Byzantium which sought to incorporate also the glamour of Taqd-i-Suleiman, the new and greater Persepolis of the last Iranians.

The courtiers around the Sun-king mirror the celestial hosts. The palace rests on a cosmic layout. The royal garden shelters all plants and all animals (where Frederic II went, his zoo followed), the love of monarchy is a transposed love of nature.

The king identifies as an adept with light, feeling that he is giving life to everything and out of everything he draws feelings of exultation which are his own light, that he re-absorbs into himself. He thus no longer 'suffers of mortal griefs'. The likes of Henry V are actually cured by ceremony.

Mace and Seal make things real, the orb creates peace, the sceptre decrees what is and is not. The royal ointment helps a state of mind where this is obvious. Even the witches' and Grail-knights' art of herbal mashes was possibly below the perfection displayed in such balms by the priesthood. Some Medieval alchemical recipes for oils to rub into the crown of the head are preserved in the thirteenth-century treatise Compostella of Bonaventura d'Iseo (an Italian translation with the title *Antiche Vie dell'alchimia* appeared in Rome in 1973). Chelidon variously distilled and mixed with camphor, incense and myrrh and other ingredients are supposed to confer wisdom and memory. Ayurvedic ointments for the head such as *Maha Vatha Gaja Wardini* are today used to abate tension, oppression, blood-pressure while at the same time affording vigour and tonic.

*   *   *   *   *

The Christian story was adopted by the Roman Emperors because if they became the icons of King Jesus, his vicarious sacrifice provided them with all the necessary darksome suffering element of kingship. The Emperor of Babylon had to shed tears of good omen. Christian Roman Emperors remind one of Edward VI with his whipping boy.

Morningstar became Jesus at his mock-coronation, Saturn's grip was shown in the nails of the Cross. Good Friday was Saturn's darkness given away free.

Dante insists that for Christ's atonement to work, the sentence of death had to be unimpeachable, issued by the lawful God-appointed Imperial authority. The Emperor in his Glory mirrored Crucifixion – he offered its image in reverse. The archaic symmetry between the Hunting Monarch and his favourite victim, Lion, Eagle, Dragon or Deer was fully restored. The Wounded Christ perceived in a Medusa. Blood from Medusa's left side was life-giving. The Emperor is a Perseus, he and his quarry are two in one and one in two, as the Beast flying on the royal banner and decorating, the king's shield proclaims. The King wore the hide, decked himself with the feathers and antlers of his symmetrical selfhood.

The Sun-Emperor is two in one, as is the seed in the light, the food in the belly, the hunted in the hunter, in Jesus as in the Imperial Spear which pierced him and in the Cup that was not passed from him.

The kingly metaphysical realization of oneness expresses itself in kingly virtues. By these the king differed from other initiates into the metaphysics of light, whose lot was private knowledge and magic.

The Iranian talismans of kingship were transferred to the Byzantine store of Imperial magic. After Eraclius overcame Taqd-i-Suleiman, the new Persepolis, all its pageantry was absorbed. The Grail stories relayed an amalgamated Byzantine-Iranian doctrine of kingship. The blend had Scriptural support, in the episode of the Magi.

Dr. Hakim shed light on these manipulators of kingship, whose actual historical existence is immaterial, but whose meaning is crucial. They practised a ritual for the blending of *ida* and *pingala*. Without such an inner equalisation the kingly identification with light could hardly be achieved. Without it, regalia remain idle toys.

The legend tells that when the Magi saw the heavenly conjunction, they set forth to perform the ritual. On a child? This was the case in Tibet and Nepal, and a child (or, according to Dr. Hakim's calculations, a boy) may benefit by ritual even better than an adult. Innocents are shown accompanying seventeenth-century exorcists in Baroque pictures, and it was they that did the scrying in eighteenth-century occultist lodges.

A child cannot be taught a treatise on *ida* and *pingala* but it can well become familiar with the actual referents of the terms which the treatise jostles about in games of reason and learning.

The older magus was called Melchior, King of Light, and he carried the golden Cup. The middle-aged one's name was Balthazar, God's Protection, which can be rendered as Mandate of Heaven. He carried myrrh on a paten. To Dr. Hakim he was concerned with the activation and control of the cooling force, with mindfulness.

Third came Jasper, the youth. Jasper is green-hued quartz sprinkled with vermilion. Quartz is common in initiations. It is thought that by assimilating it, by identifying with its glitter, one may attain to identification with light as such. Dr. Hakim believed that the gift of incense stood for control of the right column of breath, the inward warming force. Incense is the symbol of sacrifice, while in India internal warmth and inward effort are both called *tapas*.

In Flanders during the Middle Ages a procession was staged for the Epiphany, the feast of lights. It was described by J. Duchene-Guillemin (*Die drei Weisen aus dem Morgenlande und die Anbletung der Zeit*, in *Antaios* VIII, 3; Sept. 1965).

In this Jasper was smeared with pig's blood, the principle of animal warmth. Balthazar carried a stick ending in a star – he stood for mindfulness of heaven's mandate. Melchior played a bagpipe made of pig's hide. Bagpipes symbolize transformation.

A Medieval charm for retrieving a lost horse, which might well have originated in some Guild of the Horseman's Word, identifies the Horse and the Word made flesh, and runs:

'Jasper holds you, Balthazar ties you, Melchior leads you.'

The three Magi answer to the riddle of the Sphynx, who, according to Pausanias, requested of travellers the pass-word of Theban kingship. Kingship is the unification of the three divisions of time; it means living up to the past by bearing the future in mind – thanks to what runs in one's blood. Jamshid's Cup showed, gathered into its concavity, all time and space.

*   *   *   *   *

The Magi however were intruders into Jewish magical territory, within which their ritual act implied that they considered Jesus the living Temple.

Moses had compounded an oil of incense, myrrh, and other spices, with which he anointed the golden covering of the tabernacle, the alter, the ark, and the golden vessels. Not only was the oil holy, and not only did it make holy what it was poured upon, but the anointed vessels were alchemically energized, and made holy whatever they carried, like those mentioned in Ssuma Chhien's passage.

Anointment severed from the commonalty, empowering for prophecy and compelling rites.

The imitation of Moses' oil and the anointment of a stranger even with an ersatz were punished with death. Moses also concocted a balm which caused YHWH 'to be present'.

The ritual of the Magi was akin to what is described in *Exodus: 30*. The Talmud does not add much thereto, the only technicality it discloses concerns the soaking of the herbs and the pouring of oil over the water so as to absorb their sheer quintessential aroma. Moses' concoctions were kept in a horn (Zacharias speaks of YHWH raising his horn of salvation, *Luke 1:69*).

The Talmud informs that the anointer traced a wreath of oil round the king's head and rubbed a little of it between the eyes – in due Yogic order – and 'the spirit of YHWH burst on him from that day' (*1 Sam.*

XVI:13). The Spirit of YHWH was also 'a rock', possibly the rock of the Temple which was considered the stone from which issued the primal ray of light, out of which everything is born. The present Israel is legally founded upon this rock.

By coronation the King was reborn, YHWH begetting him in the womb of dawn, at the origination of light. Melkitzedek, by whose delegate power the Jewish priesthood operated, is described as the collector of the purity of light in the Gnostic *Pistis Sophia*. Jewish kings lived in fear of someone being anointed in secret. They knew the ointment worked; Solomon, who set the model for kingship, was anointed twice. He practised additionally hierogamies with various priestly queens and established a close association with Hiram, possibly an alchemist (*1 Kings 7: 13–15*). He understood the language of animals as a magical Hunter, and settled megaliths like a Merlin (*Exodus R. 52.4*). Over his marriage bed lay a canopy of the constellations.

*   *   *   *   *

The new Christian dispensation in the spiritual history of kingship was started with the foundation of Byzantium.

Constantine forbade the casting of the Emperor's horoscope, putting an end to the Augustan tradition in the Roman art of enamels and ivory cameos depicting the Imperial nativity. A new mandate was now operating.

The version of the Roman See was that Constantine was a leper about to bathe in the blood of innocents, but who was cured instead by Baptism – the new Emperor was 'an ailing king' healed by Rome's Hallows and thereby in debt to her for ever.

The Byzantine version instead was that Constantine received a direct mandate from heaven, confirmed through the finding of the true cross, his all-powerful talisman.

The Byzantine formula was that he was Christ's icon and a ray of God's Wisdom. As Hunter and Warrior he carried a Spear. On Good Friday the adoration of his Spear took place in the Palace followed by the presentation of the golden table and of the golden vessels.

On the other hand he drank the Eucharist from the Cup as did the clergy, and, not from a spoon as did the laity. At Nativity the courtly ritual stressed that he was the Bringer of Light.

Spear, Cup, and Paten were the main liturgical instruments in the introductory and cosmogonical section of the Mass. Inside the secret part of the church, beyond the iconostasis, on the altar stood the cross, the tabernacle and a candelabrum. But the *proskomidia* – before-the-meal – ritual took place on a table to the left of the altar. It was performed on a piece of bread stamped with a quartered square inscribed 'Jesus Christ Overcomes'. Beside it stood three vials, containing wine, cold and warm water respectively.

The cosmogonic pantomime began with a thanksgiving for being exempted from the damnation of the Law. The square was carved out of the bread with a small Spear, placed on a paten, and declared to be the Sacrificial lamb. (The Emperor was by implication the Ram. At Easter shepherds leave for the mountains, and the little lambs which cannot make it are sacrificed, in order that the Ram be saved and live.)

The celebrant dug into the lamb's left side with the Spear, declaring that out of the wound immortality gushed forth. He then blessed with the spear the whole loaf, and poured wine and water into the Cup. Out of the bread he carved a triangle and placed it to the right, declaring it to be The Lady in the Golden Mantle.

Smaller triangles of bread he carved and placed on a line at the left to represent the Baptist and the saints. Finally he placed small triangles on two rows beneath the square, to represent the living and the dead. The world was served on the paten.

After blessing the incense, he recalled the apparition of the star and placed over the paten the *asterisk*, made of two crossed metal semicircles fastened together with a vice from which hung a star. Balthazar's gift was the mandate from heaven, the *asterisk*, Jasper's was victory, intimated by the inscription on the square of bread, Melchior's was the source of immortality – the spear's wound. The three tokens of kingship now hovered above the world.

The celebrant finally glorified God and veiled the *asterisk*. He begged for salvation while veiling the Cup. Finally, with a larger veil, called *aer*, representing the Spirit, he covered up everything.

*   *   *   *   *

All these liturgies, the peculiar palatial processions and the cosmogonic prelude to the Mass, were absent in the Roman West. Rome has slowly, methodically, unflinchingly cleared the West of all Byzantine traces. It was an herculean task, since Rome itself had been partially a Greek centre up to the ninth century. Afterwards, the various succeeding

Roman styles would seek to smother beneath their theatrical displays the mosaics, the icons, all traces of the Byzantine enemy.

The non-Roman liturgies of the West, all of Oriental origin, were slowly stamped out. The Lombard variety survived partially and only in Milan, the Spanish only in Toledo, of the Gallican all trace was lost, while the Celtic was supplanted in Irish monasteries all over Europe by the Benedictines and its inroads in England were meticulously mopped up.

The Roman See is a proof of the immense magic power of sheer persistence of imagination – by unflinchingly keeping in mind the Pontificate of the Augustan Empire, regardless of external circumstances, the popes lived to see it triumph.

Rome crowned Charlemagne Emperor of the West. Dante kept up the pro-Byzantine protest against its illegality 400 years after. In payment for the balm Charlemagne uprooted the Oriental liturgies by main force wherever needed, throughout his Europe.

The Byzantine presence had been strongest in Ireland. The peak of Greek metaphysics was reached with Scotus Erigena, whose books Rome later suppressed.

Rome offered *her* balm of kingship to the rulers who bowed to her Pontificate, but it rarely seemed to work. All the sovereigns who sought to live up to their kingly calling felt a lack in what Rome provided and smarted under the checks she imposed on them; Byzantium was the secret ideal example that kindled Ghibelline dreams.

The issue was quite old. St. Augustine's *City of God* had been a plea for the Church which was charged with having wrecked the magic of Empire. The charge was later voiced in Scandinavia. The blight hanging on the land was blamed on King Inge's conversion to Christianity and a volley of stones drove him out of the Swedish Thing.

The skald Einar Skalaglamm wrote a *drapa* about Hakon, a Norwegian jarl who did as Cnut's father would, going back on his baptism and rebuilding the old shrines, thus drawing down once more the gifts from 'the God of the Cup of Offering' – *heill* and *hamingia* (the Virgin of Light).

The Roman balm and ritual vesture of the ruler in priestly garb appeared fully satisfying however to the various Anglo-Saxon kings, who traded for Roman magic securities their descent from Woden, the self-spearing leader of the Wild Hunt and dispenser of rune-lore.

But a split between Rome and Anglo-Saxon royalty finally occurred. Rome backed the Norman invasion to stave off the possible consequence. What these could have possibly been might be guessed from the Anglo-Saxon refugees seeking asylum in Byzantium. Bede had based his annals on Byzantine indictions. Beowulf's attack on Grendel's cave was modelled on the liturgy of Baptism as a descent of Jesus-the-Warrior into the Jordan to vanquish Behemoth (Allen Cabaniss makes the point in *Liturgy and Literature*, University of Alabama 1970).

The Byzantine theory of kingship and the motif of Christ's five wounds as the Quincunx of Imperial victory inspired *The Dream of the Rood*, a description of the Byzantine Imperial talisman studded with five jewels, reminiscent of the square of bread in the *proskomidia*. The crucifixion was a warrior's feat – the late *Ancrene Riwle* depicted Jesus as a warrior jousting upon the Cross for his lady, the human soul.

Cynewulf's *Elene* is a re-telling of the central Byzantine legend of the finding of the True Cross, described as 'the Glory of Kings, the light of the righteous'. Appearing to the Emperor in his dream, it is said to promise to lead him to 'the Guardian of Souls, the Glory of Kings'. The Emperor's mother, Helen, determined to unearth the relic, is said to torture an esoteric Jew, urging on him: 'You cannot keep the thing hidden, you cannot conceal the secret powers.'

A late Anglo-Saxon adaptation of a Byzantine original, *Solomon and Saturn*, transforms the Lord's Prayer into a Warrior king's runic song culminating in *Ger*, the rune of plenty, and *Daeg* the rune of light. Aelfric called the Holy Host a rune, the author of Solomon and Saturn identified with a rune each single request in the Lord's Prayer, which is presented by Solomon as a song of victory (*gepalm-twigoda*) for a king of Caldea.

The guardian angel whose presence the prayer secures, helps the soul to grow and to seek 'the Measurer's Glory', ignoring the evil spirit which would obsess it with the bad thoughts (*misgemynd*) of evil men.

The rune *Daeg* 'comes with five-fold power', the magic of the Quincunx. A Middle English poem reveals the kind of meditation associated with the five wounds. The right hand issues loyalty and unity, the left hand righteousness and justice; from the heart flow the blood of love and the water of truth and pure thoughts, whilst the right foot signifies devotion and the left self-guidance.

The 'Coventry ring 'of the fifteenth century preserves the tradition of associating the wounds with Jasper, Melchior, Balthazar respectively, and the feet with Ananyzapta-Ananias who paid with his life for his lack of devotion, and Tetragrammaton, YHWH – the power, respectively, of the Church and of Empire (all these later, crucial documents on the method of meditation on the five wounds are gathered by Douglas Grey in *Notes & Queries*, Feb–May,1963).

As Rome unleashed William on Anglo-Saxon England, it sped another band of Normans through Byzantine Italy, helped them form a new kingdom, which was about to crush Byzantium, but finally failed to accomplish the job. The Crusades were launched, with Byzantium as their unavowed target until the Fourth Crusade was successfully diverted thither, and lo, finally whores were seated on the altar at St. Sophia, monasteries were burnt with their monks inside them.

Dauntless Byzantium recovered. Indefatigable Rome then hurled the newly mustered Angevine might against her rival. Back in England the Norman kings also ended finding themselves at odds with the Roman See.

Whatever the peculiar grievances, the underlying issue was that their material skills were not enough to cope with magic – this is summed up in the lines of T.S. Eliot's *Murder in the Cathedral*:

'But what is pleasure, kingly rule,
Or rule of men beneath a king.
With craft in corners, stealthy stratagem,
To general grasp of spiritual power?'

But the knights who killed Thomas Becket lie buried in El Aqsa, which was the Templar's church of Jerusalem. The Templars, at a given moment in history, started holding the balance between the two magical forces, kingly glamour and ecclesiastical authority. Becket's killers were pawns in the Templar game. The Arthurian Celtic mystique became usable.

One is tempted to read meaning into coincidences. Richard I stops over in Sicily, consults with Joaquin of Fiora whose prophecies could become magical weapons aimed at Rome, and the encounter takes place in the territory of the Templar preceptory on Mt. Etna, where king Arthur was said to bide his time.

*   *   *   *   *

About 1150 the Grail literature starts being spread. It deals with the very core of all the disputes between kings, bishops and grand masters. Was not kingship lacking in magical legitimacy in the West? And what was the role of Empire? Answers to questions which deal with magical power can only be given in terms of myth and ritual. The Grail romances centre round a liturgy and its hallows.

The powers behind their fortune, the prompters of the minstrels were Ghibelline minded. There is no need to control the law-making if you control the ballads, observed one of the American founding-fathers.

The twelfth-century *Historia Regum Britanniae* of Geoffrey of Monmouth is a first attempt to provide a non-ecclesiastical mythical, magical, imaginal foundation for English kingship. It was followed by Wace's *Brut*, openly patronised by Henry II.

The Grail romances proper start with Chrétien's *Perceval*. A dream emerges of knights whose ethics are more akin to the members of Iranian *futuwwas* than to those of the Christian peoples of the West. Their piety consists in seeking for a mystical interpretation of their exploits, from hermits whom they approach in the spirit of Ismailis or Sufis seeking spiritual uplift from their shaikhs. In Chrétien Jesus is called 'the prophet killed by the Jews'.

Perceval starts on his quest refusing to cross himself before presences which are presumed to be infernal. When he comes across a king-like figure he cries: 'Here I descry God himself'.

As the ethical background is Sufi, the spiritual path is that of kingship as such, which has become, however, a suffering spiritual lineage needing pure-hearted adepts uncompromised with the existing persuasions.

The king lies bleeding – a proof that Jesus' atoning passion is not working, that kingship has to take upon itself the burden of propitiation. A fisher king points the way.

On coats of arms a fish connotes silence and faith in God. The fisher king speaks not of his distress and has faith in the coming of a healer – he is a fisher of souls, who shows the path to initiation. The souls he is awaiting must be untainted, not drawn into the prevailing system of allegiances and beliefs.

The initiator proper is the ailing king himself. Kingly initiations are not open as a rule to candidates from outside a royal family – save in time of need. The Grail romances connote such a period, when a call is

issued to form an Order of initiates into the secrets of kingship, because
the ruling king is in dire straits. The romances create the favourable
atmosphere and the expedient jargon for recruitment. A distressed
dynasty makes known that it will share its secrets, that it is rebuilding
a retinue.

But the instinct of the old and the defeated is to ruthlessly use the
new adept in their plans of revenge. A sharp-witted initiate should kill
his initiator in time, as the Siegfried-Fafnir myth suggests.

The difficulty for the ailing king is that initiation is not something
that one can proffer. It has to be sought for. Only a formal request may
trigger the process of magical teaching – the question: 'What ails thee?'
Or better still, 'Whom does the Grail serve?'

All the ailing king can do is stage a dumb-show – the procession of
the Hallows. The message is as clear as Grail-light if the onlooker would
only observe, ponder, and connect.

A Cup, a Spear, a Paten, two Candelabra head for the door of a royal
chamber. Anyone at the time might know that these were the liturgical
instruments of the Byzantine *proskomidia*. It took more than seven
centuries for an historian to see the point – Konrad Burdach first
noticed the purloined letter of the Grail in his 1938 book *Der Gral*.

The procession of the Hallows enters the impenetrable chamber of
the King – the Byzantine clergy retires behind the iconostasis through
the Royal Door.

Certain later Grail romances show an additional touch. A Child
appears on the altar. This too is Greek liturgy. Forty days from their
birth, boys are taken up by the priest and placed upon the altar in
memory of Simeon who took up 'that holy thing' born of Mary
(Luke 1:35). The message could hardly be clearer. Only a Byzantine
ecclesiastical and ritual order could restore kingship to health.

Evidence of the liturgical issue at stake is given in the later
anti-Ghibelline Tannhauser cycle. The Arthurian Grail romances had
spoken about a mountain in which the adept of kingship – Arthur
himself – lives with Felicia, the Happy-one, a name reminiscent of that
of the Grail Queen 'Outflow of Joy'. Felicia is the daughter of Sybil,
pre-Christian Wisdom.

This motif in denounced as diabolical in the Tannhauser cycle. The
adept repents of his years with the Lady in the mountain, but his sin
will only be washed away by 'listening to the Pope's Mass in Rome'.
The political message coincided with the liturgical bent.

The Hallows of the Grail were silent vindications of the Byzantine system – in which the clergy was restricted to providing for the execution of ritual and for guidance on the mystical path. Active life came entirely within the kingly sphere. The manifesto of the Grail precedes Dante's by more than a century.

The ailing king reappears in the *Divine Comedy*. In the fourteenth canto of the *Inferno* the island of Crete is described as waste land which once was the thriving, golden-age realm of Saturn. In its mount Ida, Jupiter the god of kingship was born. Therefore the image of Empire stands there, within the mountain, halfway, significantly between Jerusalem and Rome. It is as Daniel imagined it, a Grand Old Man whose head is of gold but whose body is made of base metals. He looks to Rome 'as to his mirror'. Rome has betrayed the idea of Empire, so the Old Man is wobbling – his two feet are not on even, level ground.

The left leg is of iron and denotes Empire's mission, the hallowing of active life. (In the Quincunx of aforementioned English texts it would correspond to the foot of self-guidance in active life and to the sign of YHWH, the Lord of Hosts.)

The right leg is of clay, the life of contemplation and of the Church – corresponding to the foot of devotion, and to the sin of Ananias who would not part with his earthly belongings – according to Dante the main blemish of the Roman Church.

The Old Man is gashed from his chest to his loins and tears ooze out of the fissure, forming at his feet infernal rivers of seething blood. The healing will only take place when the Church is confined to her proper domain – as in Byzantium, when the Church's Cross is placed at the root of the Tree of Life, and the Eagle of Empire is on its crown.

To be 'saved', according to Dante, we must hope in the advent of the avenging Emperor; the blessings of contemplation are not fully redeeming if they do not culminate in Imperial hope.

Likewise sacramental life in not enough on the path of Grail knighthood. It is not even mentioned. In fact in the case of Perceval it is even ignored. The hope of restoring the Cup or Paten to their function is the way of knightly redemption.

In *Purgatory* IX, Dante dreams that the Eagle of Empire is leading souls to heaven, but that it does so only from the mountains of Troy, overlooking the Bosphorous.

*   *   *   *   *

After Chrétien's lovely romance there followed Grail books of a different kind, in which the central question is still that of ailing kingship but the answer is a specific scheme of alternative Christian ecclesiastical structure. The Grail is identified with the Cup of the Last Supper, in which Joseph of Arimathea caught the blood of Jesus' wounds.

Joseph becomes the trustee of Christ's kingship, and brings the privilege and the magic of Empire to Celtic England. The Cistercian movement which was to father the Templar Order gave rise to romances in which the Grail means simply a mystically full sacramental life, in which the real presence of Christ in the Host becomes an hallucinatory experience, of the kind which will be taught in later times by Ignatius of Loyola.

Galahad, the champion of chastity, becomes the true knight, and the problem of an ailing kingship seems to be solved by his hallucinatory participation in the Eucharist. His name may recall Elijah the Gileadite whose mission was to rebuke wayward kings and erring priests from the depths of mystical contemplation. The purely contemplative Order of the Carmel considered itself his ward.

These new Grail romances however insist on an esoteric transmission of kingship by means of an ark of Salvation carrying the bed of royal hierogamy and the sword – the ship built by Solomon following his queen's advice. The ship brings the Holy Empire to England and the story leading to Camelot unfolds. The Grail becomes identified with the Pentecostal fire which re-unifies languages and makes possible a Tower of Babel, which also Dante hoped for.

The final, German group of Grail romances culminates in the greatest of all, Wolfram von Eschenbach's *Parzival*, which coincides with the great Ghibelline moment of hope – the accession to the Empire of Henry VII. Dante hailed him 'silently' as he said in his Epistle, 'the lamb of God'.

Wolfram begins his poem by stating the gist of kingly initiation. The candidate is a magpie, piebald, black and white like the chessboard of the world. Kingship teaches him to accept and ignore the chequered world, to transcend the oppositions where all are trapped. Kingship implies pure resolve and steadfastness, thanks to the 'knowing of blessedness'.

Through uncertainty, hesitation, vacillation one becomes sheer darkness. By becoming as the fountainhead of life, the kingly one becomes all-resplendent.

Kingly men are under Saturn and have to endure that their Lady, their higher soul, chill them with a stony, icy gaze. At loathly Cundrie's sight a knight's heart stiffens – yet she urges on towards the Grail; at lovely Orgeluse's sight love is born, but her wickedness is such that the heart is gripped by the horror of it – and yet she may become the Bride.

In Dante and Petrarch the Lady who is the higher soul casts a stony gaze on her lover and dooms him to suffer. In *Paradiso* XXX this is so until all around pity distressed Dante, and he sighs and weeps until the ice that grips his heart is melted as in a new baptism. The shattering final question that Beatrice put was: Do you not know that in earthly paradise man must be happy?

If one truly hopes for Imperial redemption, by anticipation and trust one must already enjoy the earthly paradise which a true Empire would be, in which Saturn's curse would be lifted.

Wolfram intimates the same message. His ailing king suffers at the changes of the moon – and 'calls that his hunting day. But what he can catch with his painful wound, would not provision his home'. The Hunter aspect of kingship is thwarted – the king is pitifully enticing candidates by exhibiting his wound.

He fares even worse when Saturn combines with certain constellations and his wound festers and frosts. It becomes an inflammable glass. Words of pity then help him shed the necessary tears which renew his baptism.

The renewal of baptism is an Easter celebration which concludes Saturn's Good Friday triumphs. The Cup is the sepulchre; the promise of salvation lies in concealment and in pain during a Good Friday period of history.

Kingly adepts now live as in tombs – anonymously. The Templar Grail of Wolfram bears an inscription saying that if ever a knight of the Order become king it shall be on condition that he is not asked his name. Now only in deep secrecy may a kingly calling be fulfilled. On Easter night, at baptism, the Psalm is read (139): 'The night shineth as the day; the darkness and the light are like to thee'.

Wolfram intimates that when it becomes the object of meditation, the Grail which on Good Friday is the Sepulchre, turns into a stone – the stone of exile. From it a new spark will be struck, and it will set aflame the onlooker, burning him to ashes. From these his phoenix nature will be resurrected. The one message runs through all these metaphors and imaginations – only by delving into the doom of Saturn, only by drinking its poison and feeding on its horror as Avicenna recommends in his *Epistle of the Birds*, does one rise above all earthly traps set for kingly birds.

The Grail is now a black stone. But from this utter desolation a Zoroastrian hope is drawn at the Easter service, when the new fire is kindled and the prayer offered: 'God, who through your Son have brought to your believers the fire of your clarity, drawn from a stone, sanctify this new fire.'

In Wolfram's story the Zoroastrian motifs cluster around Feirefiz, the knight born of a black queen who bestowed kingship on her lovers. Her black head was encased in a ruby as in a red bubble. When her son Feirefiz is shown the Grail, he has eyes only for the lovely lady who carries it, Outflow of Joy. He is willing to be baptised if this will obtain her for him. A basin is accordingly brought, scooped out of a single shining ruby. He is baptised and the Grail becomes visible to him; on it however the new message, which prescribes for future kings, issuing of the order of Templar knights, strict occultation and anonymity. The son of Feirefiz and Outflow of Joy will become Prester John, the real king at last. With an emerald sceptre he will rule over Asia. The dazzling green light of this sceptre leads to a Buddha who seems to sum up all these teachings

As Wolfram's marvellous cryptic envoi ends the revelations of the Grail in the West, eastward from their Iranian homeland they were continued in Tibetan Tantra. Kingly initiation is one of the five paths in the Quincunx of cosmic Buddhas. Its presiding Buddha is Amoghasiddhi, the Unerringly Powerful. *A-mogha*, the unerring, is a Sanskrit kenning for 'spear ', and for the night. The unfailing Amoghasiddhi's mount is the eagle Garuda. The passion he tantrically deals with is envy, which moves the Titans. Amoghasiddhi, true to Tantra, does not suppress envy, he in fact fans it into its most vicious intensity, extracts out of it all its sheer, raw energy, which he skilfully deflects from its natural, paltry goals. Envy is a fierce involvement in the world of honours, distinctions, fame and glory. Its colour is the dull red of a smouldering fire. Amoghasiddhi obliterates from its sight the objects of its malice, casts over it the blue mantle of his night, and he appears in the resulting green, which corresponds to the costume of Gawain's initiator, the Green Knight, as it shines forth in the emerald splendour of Prester John's sceptre.

Amoghasiddhi, the spirit of kingship, grants the impeccable grasp of situations, the unswerving steadfastness and the ability to remove obstacles of the true monarch. His fundamental gift is that of all Buddhas – the realization of the equality of all things with the unity of being, but the specific result, with him, is an unselfish volition, an activity for the good of the all – the love (*materia*) and the compassion (*karuna*), of a sword-wielding lord adept at bewitchment. He is the midnight sun, which operates unseen and imperceptibly in nature. His spiritual influence is of the same order, it is active on the level of deep motivations. He is the rainy season. He makes the sign of fearlessness, the open hand raised level to the head, the thumb held across the palm. He grants victory over terrific visions.

As in Western Quincunxes of the Five Wounds, he is symbolized by the two feet. As with regal Jupiter his province is the air. On the vessel of the body he moves the rhythmic waves of the breath and of the blood; in the atmosphere he plays in the ever-changing currents of wind; in the political body he builds up the airy consistency of fame and belief, which are made up of a myriad slight rumours, alternately dissolving or compacting commonwealths. In yoga, Amoghasiddhi teaches concentration on the navel centre, where dauntless courage can be evoked, at the origination of all breaths. His specific ritual is *Chod*, 'Cutting off' (*Tibetan Yoga and Secret Doctrine*, ed. W.Y. Evan-Wentz [London, 1935], p. 340)

In the ritual one first gathers into the hub from which the five main spiritual paths extend – the Clear Light of Primordial Consciousness. Once centred there one evokes the Wrathful Goddess, as Loathful Hags are introduced in Grail romances, and the Cruel Queen of the Moon is brought into play in kingly initiations. She severs the practitioner's head and uses his skull for a cauldron in which she flings the various chunks she cuts off his body. The same scene is imagined in most shamanic initiations and Gawain has to endure it in an attenuated form at the hands of the Goddess' agent, in *Sir Gawain and the Green Knight*.

The adept's flesh and blood in the cauldron turn into the liquor of immortality, and with it a feast is offered to all beings, while the adept himself acquires a new rainbow resurrection body.

In Lamaism there also exists a rite of the Cup as distinct from the Cauldron, and it transcends the sphere of Amoghasiddhi, being the concern of all five Cosmic Buddhas. In the 'ritual of long life'

(L.A. Waddell, *Tibetan Lamaism*, London), the performer speaks this consecration over a bowl of rice wine.

> 'This Vase is filled with the immortal ambrosia which the
> Five Celestial Classes have blessed with the best life.
> May it be strong like an eagle and last for ever.
> May I be favoured with the gift of undying life,
> and all my wishes be realised.'

The Tibetan bowl is a version of the Golden Cup of the Hindu conferment of royal charisma which also is considered ideally placed at the centre of the five-fold compass, as the primal awareness of light. It is convertible in the jewel of meditation, which emanates a halo of flames and averts evil, grants wishes, bestows power.

*   *   *   *   *

Wolfram wrote his masterpiece when the world in which kings dared speak their name came to a close. They still reign, but anonymously.

The Grail belongs to a time when one dared to openly state the unbearable mysteries of power.

The sky was likened to a reversed cup and the king was he who held that cup in his hands, drinking of the light which filled it. He alone drank not the products of light, but light itself. He thus intimated that as light from the sky overcame darkness and yet emerged out of darkness, so he overcame wild beasts and human foes whose presence had called for him, a king, from amid the people.

In order to compact the people and for the sake of the king's glory, enemies must be created when needful. What makes them such is the king's word, as it is the sun's light that etches out darkness.

As light penetrates invisibly into the recesses of the earth, stirring life in seeds, so does the king's word sink into his subjects' hearts. For his word is like a double-edged sword cleaving, in souls, the royal domains of light – what he ordains from the powers of darkness – all that which he forbids, thus separating the subject's law-abiding will from his very nature, setting the two at odds with one another. This is the lot of the subject, of him who drinks not at the Cup of the Grail, in which kings read revelations of covenants, the whole of the law, just as the dervish reads love poems in the bubbles of the tavern boy's Cup.

The subject as such is a split creature. The king's word within him wages war on the shadows of his very being. Because there are not dark foods, sombre thoughts, bleak deeds, smutty parts of the body, black corners of the soul, but a king's word, which is law, makes them such, and in the *name* of the Sun, turns a kingly word into the tragedy of the subject's will.

The subject is he who dare not seek for the Grail and for its drink.

A subject's inward world is a black threatening forest, thither he dare not look for light which he only hopes to find in the outward world, lit up by the king's presence. There everything is black or white, as on the chess-board; which knights adopted for their coats of arms to signify that to them warfare was a game, a kingly sport. They were companions to the king rather than mere subjects.

To him whose inwardness has been made into a dungeon by the king's word, the king is everything. Only a king has light within. A subject can descry in his soul only murky, confusing reflections of kingly rays from without. His ear catches an inner voice which is nothing but the muddled echo of the king's mighty words.

The king, after compacting the people with the threat of an enemy and the need for his word, places on the people the final unifying seal of terror. He regularly shows then the heart of darkness, evokes the darkest of dark deeds – which can only be, given the king's word, the murder of the king. 'The king of mercy is slaughtered in the name of light by order of the king of justice' (or in the domains of the White Goddess, on behest of the queen of Lust).

The subject's shudder gives his acclamation of the king its proper, rich tone as he is told that the Grail of light is a Cup of royal blood.

All this will be as true as light, as long as there are the few kings who see light within, and the numberless subjects, who only see light without. But this Grail truth will be shown less and less, because subjects can no longer face being told the Grail truth – which is however the only form of wholesome intellectual charity conceivable, explaining honestly how things stand, how so very few find the light and whole of the law within them. Showing the Grail, telling the truth is *maitri* and *karuna*, love and charity of light. Why give what hardly anybody wants? Charity is unmotivated, a strange urge. Coomaraswamy explained how the Grail became Lord Buddha's begging bowl, and in the Hebrew *King Artus* Grail is translated *tamhin*, charity bowl. Charity of light.

The Grail and The Rose

John Matthews

Among the many strands which go into the weaving of the multi-cultural tapestry that is the story of the Grail, one stands out with particular clarity: the great nexus of Christian and Judaic myth, esotericism and prophetic mysticism which flowered under the title of Rosicrucianism. From the end of the Middle Ages to the later years of the Renaissance, a whole series of mysterious works grew out of a mystical awareness that spoke of great changes, both inner and outer, which were to change the course of human history forever. A number of these themes are reflected in the literature of Grail, which throughout its long history had again and again brought the concerns of the time into its sphere of influence. The following essay explores the symbolism which links the Grail myths to the mysteries of alchemy and the spiritual heritage of the Rose.

The Grail and the Rose: two streams of wisdom flowing side by side, sometimes entering the same channel and flowing together, sometimes separating again to lead into different enchanted byways of the soul.

To begin with the Grail. This is surely one of the supreme symbols of the Quest for absolutes – truth, wisdom, healing, union with the beyond – to come out of the Western Mystery Tradition. It begins obscurely, with the twelfth-century poem *Conte du Graal*[1] by the French poet Chrétien de Troyes, but in the hundred years from approximately 1200 to 1300 it became the most popular strand of all that collection of wonder-myths known collectively as the Matter of Britain – the cycle of Tales and poems centering around the figure of the great medieval image of King Arthur. Before this the origins of the Grail recede into the mists of Celtic myth and hero-tale, and earlier still into the beginnings of human myth-making, with the image of the *crater*, a mixing bowl of the gods from which the very stuff of creation was poured forth. In this it prefigures its later incarnation in the *vas spirituale*, the vessel in which the alchemists wrought their mysteries of the spirit.

But it is with the medieval, and specifically Christian incarnation of the Grail that we are concerned here – as the chalice in which some of the holy blood of Christ was caught, and which was used in the first great celebration of the Christian mysteries of the Eucharist. Here we already see aspects of the theme that will later find restatement in the mysteries of Alchemy and their subsequent importance to the Rosicrucian Enlightenment. From the beginning the Grail is a vessel which has contained some of the Divinity of God, the blood which is symbolised by the wine in Eucharistic symbolism. And it is the very embodiment of that transubstantiation in the mystery of the Eucharist.

In the intensity of the Christian interpretation it is also the womb of Mary, in which the Divine seed is transmuted into the body of the infant Christ. Thus Mary herself, in the medieval *Litany of Loretto* is praised as:

vas spirituale,
vas honorabile,
vas insigne devotionis ...

spiritual vessel,
vessel of honour,
singular vessel of devotion ...[2]

In effect, Mary becomes a *living* Grail, a vessel in which the blood and essence of Christ are both contained. The *Litany* makes this point even more powerfully when it calls the Virgin:

Cause of our joy
Ark of the Covenant
Tower of David
Tower of Ivory,
House of Gold,
Seat of Wisdom
Mirror of Justice,
Queen of Prophets,[3]

each of which reflects an aspect of the Grail. For it too was a vessel of the spirit and devotion, a cause of joy to those who came into its presence, an Ark of the New Covenant between God and Man. It is also associated with a house of Gold (the Temple of the Grail) with a Seat of Wisdom (the Siège Perilous in which only the one destined to achieve the mysteries of the Grail may sit) and with Prophecy, an aspect specifically attributed to it in the medieval German poem *Parzival* by Wolfram von Eschenbach.

In the full spectrum of medieval symbolism Mary is Queen of Heaven, as well as mirror, vessel, house of gold and star of the sea. Her supreme symbol is the Rose – Rose of the World, Rosa Alchemica, Queen of the Most Holy Rose Garden in which the Grail lies hidden – as Wolfram von Eschenbach puts it, the Grail is:

'The wondrous thing hidden in the flower-garden of the king where the elect of all nations are called.'[4]

The mysteries of Mary, represented in Catholic tradition by the Rosary, are arranged in multiples of five: five decades (or tens) repeated three times, a total of fifteen decades. Five was thus the number of Marian devotion; the rose was always depicted in symbolic representation with five petals; Christ was wounded five times, in the hands and feet and side; the Grail underwent five changes … 'the nature of which no one ought to speak' according to the thirteenth-century Grail-text known as the *Perlesvaus*.[5] The last of these changes is into the form of a child – a restatement of the divinity held by the vessel of the spirit. Finally, in the elaborate and extraordinary symbolism of Courtly Love – that medieval dream which placed women on a pedestal while making her the subject of adulterous passion – the Rose Garden was the place where the Beloved awaits the coming of the Lover, who must pluck the Rose in order to achieve his desire.

All of this can be interpreted in both mystical and Alchemical fashion. According to Catholic doctrine Mary is the Vessel in which the Divine Child is brought to term. In Alchemical symbolism the *vas mirabile* is the vessel in which the Mercurius, the burning Child brought forth by the spiritual wedding of the elements, finds manifestation. The coming together of the Lover and the Beloved is the same allegory of Divine Love extolled by Dante, who fully understood the symbolism of the Rose. In the *Paradiso* he makes the rose the final symbol of revelation and union with the divine, granted to him at the behest of Bernard of Clairvaux, who prays for the intercession of the Virgin. The symbolism is interchangeable here; it works as well for profane (Courtly Love) sacred (the Marian impulse) and alchemical (the birth of the Wondrous Child).

Thus the infinite is born into the finite, Christ becomes man, the spiritual transformations of the Grail and the alembic are shown to be the same. As St Ephraem wrote in the fourth century, invoking Christ:

> In the womb that bore you are Fire and Spirit,
> Fire and Spirit are in the river where you were baptised,
> Fire and Spirit are in our baptism too,
> And the Bread and Cup are Fire and Spirit.[6]

It is not surprising therefore if we find the Troubadours, who fuelled the Arthurian myths with their burning and joyful light, referring to Mary as 'the Grail of the World', and applying the term with equal validity to the Lady of the Rose Garden – where 'The beloved one is the heart's Grail, her lover will not be alone, for she is to him the highest Grail, which protects from every woe.'[7]

Much of this symbolism is Catholic and founded on Catholic doctrine, though it also embodies a recognition of the importance of the Divine Feminine at a time when the established church was exoterically opposed to this. Devotion to Mary, while never criticised, was considered as secondary to devotion to Christ. The Grail stories, it seems, were giving voice to an undercurrent of belief that harked back to pre-Christian times when devotion to the feminine principle – the Great Goddess – was either as important or more important than that to the God. The Grail's own pagan heritage focuses this in a number of ways – by the implicit femininity of its form – the Cup or Vessel – and in the story of Dindrane, the only female Grail quester of which we have knowledge. Sister to Perceval, one of the three knights who achieved the mystery of the Grail, Dindrane not only foresees the coming of the sacred vessel in a vision, but actually sets forth in search of it. Her death is a parable of the feminine mystery – and of the Grail and the Rose.

Joining the three knights on their Quest, Dindrane gives up her life to save another, giving her life-blood to heal a woman suffering from leprosy. The blood that is taken is symbolic of the monthly blood loss of all women, of the blood in the Grail, and of death of the Rose. Charles Williams, a modern Grail poet, puts it magnificently in the poem significantly entitled 'Taliesin in the Rose Garden'.

'Woman's flesh lives the quest of the Grail
in the change from Camelot to Carbonek and from Carbonek to Sarras,
puberty to Carbonek, and the stanching, and Carbonek to death.
Blessed is she who gives herself to the journey.[8]

Taliesin is the magical poet of Celtic tradition, and in these lines he draws together a knot of symbolism – of the Grail itself, of the suffering of the Wounded King, the Guardian of the sacred chalice whose wounds continue to bleed until he can find healing – something which can only be brought about by the successful accomplishment of the Grail quest itself.

The Jungian analyst Helen Luke wrote of these lines:

'Williams hints at the inner identity of the woman's menstrual blood, which tells her that she has not yet conceived, with the blood of the wounded Grail king, bleeding because he cannot bring to life the new consciousness of the Christ, the Self ... Taliesin speaks of how woman may consciously give birth to the new keeper of the Grail, within herself, and so heal the wound in the psyche.'[9]

Again the message is alchemical, and would have found a receptive chord among those who gave voice to the Rosicrucian Enlightenment. They, who emerged from the new Protestant order, which rebelled against the strictures of Roman Catholicism, gave birth also to a new myth which, borrowing from the older story of the Grail, gave form to a new Quest – for the mystery of Christian Rosencreutz and the Rosicrucian Vault. (See Caitlín Matthews Ch. 12)

At the end of the Arthurian era, in terms of literature and pursuit of the Quest, the Grail vanished for a time. As Adam MacLean has rightly noted:

'The Grail mystery returned underground, wrapped itself again in its esotericism and waited for another time to unfold its inner revelation. Such a point was reached after the Reformation, when the inner Grail mystery ... surfaced again in the Rosicrucian movement of the early seventeenth century. At this time ... the Rosicrucians tried to incarnate an esoteric Christianity within the Protestant movement ... in order to provide a much needed resolution of the polarities of Protestantism. Thus we should see the Rosicrucian movement as being inwardly related to the Grail mystery. The spiritual alchemy that was the esoteric foundation of Rosicrucianism can be seen as a development of the Grail impulse.'[10]

This is indeed the case, and in the symbolism of the Rosicrucian Wedding we see an unfolding of the original Grail story in a new form. As so often in the past, and again in recent times, an outwardly rigid spirituality is underpinned by an esoteric core. The Rosicrucian movement is just such an esoteric resonance, flowering within Protestantism just as the Grail myths flowered within the outwardly patriarchal form of Catholicism.

In *The Chymical Wedding of Christian Rosencreutz* – the primary work of the Rosicrucian Enlightenment – although the text is assumed to be about the symbolic marriage of the King and Queen, in fact the title is descriptive of the spiritual coming together of Christian Rosencreutz and the Lady Venus.[11]

If we turn the pages which lead up to Christian Rosencreutz's secret hierogomy, we glimpse the real Christian Rosencreutz who, though his hair is grey and he accounts himself as no longer young, shares the same innocent earnestness as Perceval in the Grail myths at the outset of the Quest. Here is one who would sell all that he has for the possession of the pearl of wisdom, and who suffers the rigours of his initiation into wisdom with the greatest humility and determination. His approach is ideal for a candidate towards initiation, unaware that, although he has been invited to a royal wedding, he himself is the groom. In the same way, Perceval sets out to find the Grail and is at once the guest in the castle where it is hidden, though he does not know this, and sets out on a quest that will take him full circle, back to this point of beginning.

Christian Rosencreutz and Perceval both suffer the lot of all men. They are thrust into incarnation, into the captivity of matter, where they are yoked to their fellows by the service they both offer to the Quest. We see this in the *Chymical Wedding* in Day One, where C.R. dreams that he emerges from his dungeon with the help of 'an ancient matron'.[12] He is wounded in such a manner that blood covers him from head to foot. He is released from the dungeon by the ancient matron and told that he should be proud of his wounds and 'keep them for my sake'. There are echoes here of the Christ-like Perceval and of the wounded Fisher King of the Grail.

C.R. arrays himself for the wedding with crossed red bands over his breast and four red roses in his hat. These roses proclaim his loyalty to the Goddess and show that for all its Protestant veneer, the *Chymical Wedding* is in fact an exposition of the mysteries of Venus, which can be traced back both to the practices of Pagan Europe and through the

Grail myth itself in the parallels between the Venusburg of German folk-lore and the Holy Mountain (Muntsalvasche) of Rosicrucian and Grail myths.

The roses themselves are a clear indication of the initiate's dedication to his task. As A. Bothwell Gosse says in his study of *The Rose Immortal*:

> The disciple, servant of the Rose and of the Cross, progressing along the narrow Path and passing through the narrow gateway of Initiation, keeps ever before his eyes the Goal, remote at first, but ever growing nearer. From the beginning he has been pledged to the finding of Unity, for Unity stands at the end of the Path.[13]

And that Path leads, inevitably, upwards, to the Mountain of Salvation, the place of Mystery, the site of the Grail Temple where the unutterable mysteries of unity with the Beloved are celebrated.

Suffering is a part of that path. Just as C.R. suffers in the *Chymical Wedding* so does Lancelot in the Grail Story. There, the great worldly knight comes to the doorway of the Chapel of the Grail and looks within. There he sees:

> ... a table of silver, and the Holy Vessel, covered with red samite, and many angels about it ... and before the Holy Vessel ... a good man clothed like a priest. And it seemed he was at the sacring of the Mass ...
> (Malory Bk. 17, ch. 15)[14]

Watching the events that unfold, Lancelot sees the celebrant holding aloft the image of a man, bleeding from hands and feet and side, as though he would make an offering at the altar. And, when it seems as though he would fall from the effort, Lancelot enters the chamber out of a simple desire to help. But he is struck down by a fiery breath, and blinded by the light that flows from the Grail. For Lancelot is a fallen man, and does not know his way into the presence of the Grail. C.R., looking upon the form of Lady Venus, is likewise blinded – by the Goddess's radiance.

Both of these events happen in a temple of the Mysteries, and it is in the account of two such temples, one devoted to the Grail and the other to the Rosicrucian Mysteries, that we find further analogies and links between the Grail and the Rose.

The earliest traditions relating to temple-building depict them as dwelling places of Deity, where the Creator, God or Goddess, invited to enter into his or her house, may choose to communicate with the created. The earth upon which the temple stands is thereby made holy – either through its being placed in that spot or by the hallowing which takes place through the touch of the divine, and which in a sense 'calls forth' the building as a marker for those in search of the sacred experience. It becomes, in effect, a *temenos*, a place set apart, where an invisible line shows that here Divinity lives, and that to enter this space means to enter the sphere of the divine, the reflection of heaven on earth. (See Matthews: *Temples of the Grail*, Ch. 6)

The imagery of the Grail Temple is consistent throughout the texts in which it appears. It is usually situated at the top of a mountain, which is in turn surrounded either by an impenetrable forest or deep water. Access, if any, is by way of a perilously narrow bridge. To make the entrance even harder, the whole temple, or the castle which contains it, may revolve rapidly, making it almost impossible to gain entry by normal means. Once within more perils awaited, and for those few who succeeded in reaching the centre, the heart of the Grail-Rose, the experience could, as in the case of Lancelot, be both parlous and chastening.

The most completely developed description of the medieval Grail Temple is to be found in the Middle High German poem *Der Jungere Titurel* (c. 1270) attributed to Albrecht von Scharfenberg.[15] Here the lineage of the Grail knights is traced back to Solomon. According to Alberecht, Titurel, the grandfather of the famous Grail knight Perceval, was fifty when an angel appeared to him and announced that the rest of his life was to be dedicated to the service of the Grail. Accordingly he was led to a wild forest from which sprang the Mountain of Salvation, where he found workers gathered from all over the world who were to help him build a castle and temple to house the sacred vessel.

So Titurel set to work and levelled the top of the mountain, which he found to be made of onyx. Soon after he found the ground plan of the temple mysteriously engraved on this fabulous surface. The completion of the temple took some thirty years, during which time the Grail provided not only the substance from which it was built, but also food to sustain the workmen. The Grail is thus seen to participate directly in the creation of its own temple, as perhaps the followers of C.R. did in the creation of the Vault. There, the uncorrupted body of C.R. lies in suspended animation, just as the body of the wounded Fisher King is preserved in the Grail Temple.

The allegory here is dense but perceivable. The image of the Temple as vessel, containing the holy matter of creation, relates to a fundamental aspect of both the Grail Temple and the Rosicrucian vault – the idea of the temple within, or, as we might say, the Grail as bodily vessel. This notion has been a common one since the earliest times. In the *Chandoga Upanishad* it is said that:

> In the center of the Castle of Brahma, our own body, there is a small shrine, in the form of a lotus flower, and within can be found a small space. We should find who dwells there and want to know him … for the whole universe is in him and he dwells within our heart. (8:1:1–2)

Or, as one might say: in the centre of the Castle of the Grail, or the Vault of C.R., which is our own body, there is a shrine, and within it is the Rose, the symbol of the Grail of the Heart. We should indeed seek to know and understand that inhabitant of ourselves. It is the fragment of the divine contained within each one of us, the light that shines within everyone. The true quest of the Grail consists in bringing this rosy light to the surface, nourishing and feeding it until its radiance can be seen by all.

But the way is hard, and the mountain steep, guarded by wild animals and powerful otherworldly opponents. In the Grail myths this takes the form of such challenging figures as The Black Maiden, sometimes called Kundry, who appears from time to time to urge the Grail knights on their way when they are beginning to fall by the wayside. However it is the mountain which remains the most fearsome and terrible trial.

In Rosicrucian terms we have the famous Rosicrucian allegory, *The Holy Mountain*, which has been attributed to Thomas Vaughan. Here we find the following description:

> There is a mountain situated in the midst of the earth or centre of the world, which is both small and great. It it soft, yet also above measure hard and stony. It is far off and near at hand, but by the providence of God, invisible. In it are hidden the most ample treasures, which the world is not able to value. This mountain – by envy of the devil, who always opposes the glory of God and the happiness of man – is compassed about with very cruel beasts and ravening birds – which make the way thither both difficult and dangerous.[16]

However, if you succeed in daring all these perils, in recognising that the mountain is not just a mountain and the treasure not just a treasure, you will find that:

> The most important thing [on the Mountain] and the most powerful, is a certain exalted Tincture, with which the world – if it served God and were worthy of such gifts – might be touched and turned into most pure gold. This Tincture ... will make you young when you are old, and you will perceive no disease in any part of your bodies. By means of this Tincture you will find pearls of an excellence which can not be imagined ...[17]

This is so like the function of the Grail it is hard not to believe that its author was directly influenced by the medieval texts – though it is more likely that both are an expression of a hunger for spiritual sustenance. However, if one turns to one of the most famous and esoterically based of the Grail texts – the *Parzival* of Wolfram von Eschenbach – we will see at once just how close the two streams are.

To begin with we find the following passage from Wolfram, which, when set alongside the above extract from *The Holy Mountain* displays remarkable similarities. The passage in question is where Wolfram describes the Grail and its effects:

> There never can be human so ill but that if he one day sees the stone [that is, the Grail] he cannot die within the week that follows ... and though he should see the stone for two hundred years [his appearance] will never change, save that his hair might perhaps turn gray.[18]

It important to know that here the sacred object is, uniquely, described as 'a stone of the purest kind ... called *lapsit exillas*'. This phrase has been taken to be a reference to the *lapis philiosophorum*, the Philosopher's Stone, the pursuit of which occupied the minds and energies of generations of medieval and Rosicrucian alchemists alike, and which symbolised the ultimate completion of the Great Work. If we consider alchemy here to mean a spiritual rather than chemical process we will see how apt the analogy is. The Grail transforms those who come into its presence. It preserves their bodies and extends their lives indefinitely. It feeds the hunger of the spirit which is present within every seeker. It is an alembic in which the transformation of base material into spiritual gold takes place – in other words it is an expression of the Great Work, of the resurrection, and of the flowering of the Rose and the Grail which takes place in both the medieval romances and the Rosicrucian allegories.

But there is yet another parallel between the story told by Wolfram and one of the most fundamental aspects of the Rosicrucian movement. In *Parzival* we read:

> As to those who are appointed to the Grail [that is, to be its guardians] hear how they are made known. Under the top edge of the Stone an inscription announces the name and lineage of the one summoned to make the glad journey ... Those who are now full-grown all came here as children. Happy the mother of any child destined to serve there! Rich and poor alike rejoice if a child of theirs is summoned and they are bidden to send it to that Company! Such children are fetched from many countries and forever are immune from the shame of sin and have a rich reward in Heaven.[19]

This is so much in the spirit of that other great Rosicrucian document the *Fama Fraternitatis*, in which we learn of the existence of a brotherhood selected and called by God to bear witness to the great mystery of C.R., and whose task is to remain hidden until the time when the world is ready for their message. Robert Fludd, in his defence of the Rosicrucian Brotherhood, makes the connection even clearer when he says:

> Here then you have that House or Palace of Wisdom erected on the Mount of Reason. It remains however, to learn who are those ... to whom this House is open. These most fortunate of men and their spiritual house are described by the Apostle in the following manner: 'To whom come, as unto a living stone ... [the] chosen of God ... [to whom] are built up a spiritual house, a holy priesthood, to offer up spiritual sacrifices, acceptable to God ... A chosen generation, a royal priesthood, an holy community, a ransomed people, that you should practice the virtues of him who has called you out of darkness into his royal light. For previously you were not a people, but now you are the people of God.[20]

This is certainly an echo of the 'Christian progeny bred to a pure life [who] have the duty of keeping [the Grail]' in Wolfram's poem. These are summoned to their task in the same way as the young knights in another Arthurian Grail text, the *Perlesvaus* who, long after the mysteries of the Grail are over in that age, hear rumours of the existence of the Castle of Wisdom and set forth in search of it:

> They were fair knights indeed, very young and high spirited and they swore they would go, and full of excitement they entered the castle. They stayed

there a long while, and when they left they lived as hermits, wearing
hair-shirts and wandering through the forests, eating only roots; it was a
hard life, but it pleased them greatly, and when people asked them why they
were living thus, they would only reply: 'Go where we went, and you will
know why.'[21]

This is the essential experience which those who seek the Grail have
been undergoing ever since. It is this which sends thousands to the little
town of Glastonbury in Somerset every year, where the Grail was
supposedly brought by Joseph of Arimathea – in search of the mystery
which has reached out far beyond the simple story written down in the
twelfth century by Chrétien de Troyes.

The alchemist Arnold of Vilanova said: 'Make a round circle and you
have the Philosopher's Stone.' The Grail, whether as a stone, a cup, a
container or that which is contained, remains at the centre of the circle,
like the Rose at the centre of the *Hortus Conclusus*, the mysterious Rose
Garden of the Beloved. But the centre is also the circumference, and all
quests lead to this place of hallowing. The knights in their wanderings,
like the disciples of C.R., attain the goal that would have remained
inaccessible had they gone purposely to the Grail castle by a direct route.
In surrendering themselves to chance they are enabled to make the way
to the heart of the Mystery – where some at least recognise the truth,
pluck the rose, or drink from the Cup of Truth.

A place long associated with the Grail is the castle of Karlstein, which
lies twelve miles outside Prague in the Czech Republic, on a wooded
hill near the river Beroun.[22] Karlstein was built between 1348 and 1365,
soon after the first flowering of Grail literature, by the German King
and Bohemian Emperor Charles IV, whose life and work prefigure
that of the later monarchs of Bohemia who fostered the work of the
Rosicrucian Enlightenment. Described by Rudolf Steiner as 'the last
initiate on the throne of the Emperors', Charles understood the
connection between the Rose and the Grail perhaps better than anyone
before or since. Karlstein was consciously built to reflect this.

The following description shows just how deeply the two themes of
the Grail and the Rose become one in this place. 'The adornment of
the walls in the various chapels to be found in the castle, with their
quantities of semi-precious stones and gold, the way in which the light
is diffused through these semi precious stones which – set in gilded lead
– take the place of window glass, lead one to conclude that Charles IV
knew about the [esoteric] powers of precious stones and gold. The

small chapel of St Catherine, for example, is a veritable gem. The entire walls, up to the ceiling, are inlaid with semi-precious stones such as amethyst, jasper, cornelian and agate, while the cross vaulting above has a blue background, adorned with roses, according to the Rosicrucian motif. According to tradition it was here that Charles IV withdrew every year from Good Friday to Easter Sunday in order to meditate in undisturbed privacy ...'[23]

This period is, of course, not only associated with the period of the Crucifixion and Resurrection of Christ, but also with the Grail mysteries which took place at the same time. This is reflected in the design of the Castle in a number of ways. Throughout the building are murals which reflect the shape of the Rosicrucian initiation – the releasing of the prisoner from his chains, the sowing of seed in darkness, its milling and baking – (all aspects of the alchemical process), the burial of the dead, the feast which reminds us of the Wedding Banquet in the *Chymical Wedding* – and finally, execution and dismemberment.

These images guide the seeker towards the great tower of the castle which is approached across a narrow bridge – the Sword Bridge of the Grail story. Within the tower is the Chapel of the Holy Cross, again decorated in semi-precious stones, beneath a roof representing the sun, moon and stars, interspersed with the motif of roses. The windows are formed of pure topaz, amethyst and almandine, through which the light enters in bands of glorious colour. The symbolism is clear: the initiate makes his way through life, learning, forgetting, re-learning, following the path of spiritual alchemy, until he is able to cross the perilous bridge and enter the chamber of the Mysteries. The parallels need hardly be spelled out. This *is* the chapel of the Grail, where the Rose also blooms.

Rudolf Steiner understood this precisely when he said of Karlstein:

> I was recently in a castle in Middle Europe in which there is a chapel and where one can find, symbolised, thoughts from the turning point of this new era. In the whole stairway are rather primitive paintings, but what can be found painted throughout this whole stairway – even if the paintings are primitive? – *The Chymical Wedding of Christian Rosenkrutz*! One walks through this *Chymical Wedding*, finally reaching the Chapel of the Grail.[24]

Here indeed the two themes with which we began, the Grail and the Rose, come together. To seek one is to seek the other. To follow one form of enlightenment is to find another. The Rose blossoms within and from the Grail – Rosicrucianism stems from the root of the Grail myths as a natural outgrowth of the spiritual search.

Notes

1 Chrétien de Troyes, *Conte du Graal*, Trans N. Bryant (D.S. Brewer, 1982).

2 John Matthews, *The Grail: Quest for the Eternal* (Thames & Hudson, 1981).

3 Ibid.

4 Wolfram von Eschenbach, *Parzival*, Trans A.T. Hatto (Penguin Books, 1981).

5 *Perlesvaus*, Trans N. Bryant (D.S. Brewer, 1975).

6 Matthews, *The Grail*.

7 Lizette A. Fisher, *The Mystic Vision in the Grail Legend and the Divine Comedy* (AMS Press, 1966).

8 Charles Williams, *Arthurian Poems*, ed. D.L. Dodds (Boydell & Brewer, 1994).

9 Helen Luke, 'The Return of Dindrane', Ch. 7.

10 Adam MacLean, 'Alchemical Transmutation in History and Symbolism', in *At the Table of the Grail*, ed. J. Matthews (Routledge & Kegan Paul, 1982).

11 Caitlín Matthews, *The Rosicrucian Vault as Sepulchre and Wedding Chamber*.

12 *The Chymical Wedding*, trans. E. Foxcroft.

13 A. Bothwell-Gosse, *The Rose Immortal* (J. Watkins, 1958).

14 Thomas Malory, *Le Morte d'Arthur*, ed. John Matthews (Orion Books, 2000); 'Sacring' is the consecration of the bread and wine of the Eucharist.

15 Albrecht von Scharfenberg, *Der Jungere Titurel*, ed. W. Wolfe (Berlin, 1983).

16: *A Christian Rosencreutz Anthology*, compiler and ed. Paul M. Allen (Blauvalt, N.Y.: Rudolf Steiner Publications, 1981).

17 Ibid.

18 *Parzival*, A.T. Hatto.

19 Ibid.

20 *A Christian Rosencreutz Anthology*.

21 *Perlesvaus*, N. Bryant.

22 See Carlo Pietzner's 'Introduction' to *A Christian Rosencreutz Anthology*.

23 Ita Wegman, 'On Castle Karlstein and its Rosicrucian Connections', in *A Christian Rosencreutz Anthology.*

24 *A Christian Rosencreutz Anthology*, p. 15.

The Rosicrucian Vault as Vessel of Transformation

Caitlín Matthews

The emblem of the rose flowering upon the equal-armed cross is one of the central images of the Western Esoteric Tradition. It represents, at a basal level, the 'pure work' of the initiate within the realm of the mundane world and may also stand for the achievement of the seeker whose dedication results in the manifestation of the Grail's healing. The myth of Christian Rosenkreutz and the 'invisible college' of initiates has many correlatives with the dense strata of the Grail legends, especially the more evolved medieval versions like Perlesvaus, with its oblique and alchemical emblems. Here, Caitlín Matthews draws out the golden thread of the Grail initiate from deepest ancestral levels through Gnosticism, esoteric Christianity and folk memory to form an endless knot. The vault in which Christian Rosenkreutz lies sleeping, like the secret castle of the Grail, is an initiatory chamber in which the initiate-seeker encounters the transformatory powers at first hand. Into this dense theatre of memory, we are led to discover scenes as emblematic and allusive as anything from the alchemical texts which inspired them.

1. In the House of the Holy Spirit

'*Ex Deo Nascimur, in Jesu Morimur, per Spiritum Sanctum reviviscimus*'
('From God we are born, in Christ we die, by the Holy Spirit we live again.')
– *Fama Fraternitatis*

In 1614 and 1615, two anonymous Rosicrucian manifestos appeared in Germany, the *Fama Fraternitatis* and *Confessio Fraternitatis*, relating the adventures of a seeker after wisdom called Christian Rosenkreutz. (Afterwards called C.R. here.) Born in 1378, C.R. is said to have founded a Brotherhood of Rosicrucians, dedicated to the enlightenment and reformation of the whole wide world. The *Fama* tells of C.R.'s wanderings in the Middle East and relates the extraordinary discovery of his tomb, a seven-sided vault which was illuminated by the inner sun. The tomb was no tomb but an altar, a touchstone for all, an inspiration to change all things.

Just as the Grail had once inspired seekers, so these documents resounded throughout Europe in the hearts of all seekers after wisdom, who were drawn to its strangely allusive promises: 'Although we might enrich the whole World, and endue them with Learning, and might release it from Innumerable Miseries, yet we shall never be manifested and made known unto any man, without the especial pleasure of God.'[1] The enrichment promised here was nothing less than the alleviation of misery and the spiritual enlightenment of seekers – a promise that Grail also fulfills. And, in the same way that the Grail caused many to leave their everyday lives and seek for its healing, so too, the Rosicrucian manifestos inspired many to live according to its tenets, agreeing to meet once a year in the House of the Holy Spirit, just as once Arthur's knights met once a year at the Round Table at Pentecost.

The Rosicrucian manifesto arose partially as a reaction to the Protestant Reformation which had pared the rich symbology of the Christian faith down to its simplest constituents. Beggared of a rich Catholic tradition, the Protestant authors of the manifestos turned to gnostically influenced alchemical traditions, incidentally breaking into a lode of early Christian, as well as pagan, symbolism, although this is not immediately apparent. Now, no mythology arises parthenogenically; it must be fertilized by existent bodies of symbology. The Rosicrucian impulse is no exception to this rule, drawing upon dense alchemical and magical emblems which speak in the encoded language of the initiate.

Let us look at the Rosicrucian Vault and follow the golden thread that leads into and through it, this continuous knot that has passed through the hands of seekers after wisdom in all times and places.

If we search for the sources of our knot we will be well rewarded, but this can only be achieved by the frustrating task of Penelope at her loom, unweaving her work endlessly until she stands with more threads than she has fingers to separate them. We stand to lose our thread here also unless we can distinguish the central strand around which the other threads are wound.

This central strand is that of Resurrection, particularly the Resurrection of Christ, an exposition of which concludes this essay. It may be argued by some that the Christian impulse has been rendered null and void in this century. I would say rather that a vast body of esoteric wisdom lies hidden, right under our noses, within the Christian tradition. It is partly neglected through over-familiarity and over-simplification of its holy mysteries, which nonetheless are as potent as earlier paradigms. The Rosicrucian experiment teaches us a lesson for our own time: that it is impossible to separate the twin slips of pagan and Christian stock which are too strongly grafted onto one another for any such separation.

In an era that venerated the divine publically and in all under-standings, the Rosicrucian manifestos do not strike us as overtly Christocentric: this is because Christian Rosenkreutz stands in the place of Christ. This is not a new observation, nor is it a device which is used solely within Rosicrucianism. It is employed throughout medieval literature, particularly of the more popular sort. Piers Plowman is but one example of the Everyman-Christ so dear to the hearts of the medieval peasantry. The more bourgeois appeal of the Grail legends has had a more lasting impact because they are grafted onto the national Matter of Britain. *Perlesvaus*, the most Christianized Grail story, shows Perlesvaus (Perceval) as a perfect type of Christ, undergoing his trials in a marvellous medievalized Celtic Otherworld. C.R.'s legend is in the same mould as that of Christ and Perceval, as we shall see.

This identification with the hero-initiate is crucially important for the practical, rather than the armchair, mystic: unless each of us can stand in the place of Christ (or Perceval or C.R.), the lessons of life cannot be assimilated, and we return to our Creator neither better nor worse off than when we entered incarnation. We must seek to transform our prima materia into the Hidden Stone through the process of Resurrection. It is not through any disrespect or hubris that this identification is made by the initiate, but rather as a craftsman takes only the most perfect model to fashion his own copy.

So this strong Christian strand lies at the core of our knot, but it is not the only thread we hold in our hands. There are deeper, earlier resonances which strike our ears faintly as though from the Hades-bound harp of Orpheus. The base note of the Rosicrucian chord is the Mother herself – the Goddess. Around her and her exemplars – Lady Venus, Dame Kind, Nature, Sophia – hinges the Great Work upon which C.R. is engaged. In the light of her presence, the Vault assumes some fantastic and unguessed-at shapes, which we will visit later.

Finally, there is the synthesis of these twin threads. When all the threads are reworked, the immense scale of the tapestry may be missed if we stand too close. This synthesis is the most speculative part of this essay; it can only be comprehended if the reader enters it himself. It is the loom of Creation and of Apocatastases.[2]

I have dealt only with those resonances – the places where the Vault 'touched-down' in its Tardis-like ambulation which are most relevant to the themes of Sepulchre and Wedding-Chamber. I have left to others the task of mathematical computation and the arcane Rosicrucian logarithms of the Vault's dimensions – these prove baffling to those esoteric innumerates such as myself. Mythological pot-holing and symbolic synthesis are my field. I cannot pretend to have explored the entirety of the Vault, nor indeed that honeycombed edifice, the Invisible Magical Mountain, which needs a longer-burning lamp than I can currently obtain.

'This Vault we parted in three parts,' writes the anonymous author of the *Fama Fraternitatis*, and I have followed his lead in this matter. Walls, floor and ceiling are all present, though the builder's materials in question may look little like bricks and mortar to the entered apprentice. The past master will, however, realize that the House of the Holy Spirit is built of dreams, symbols and aspirations.

2. The Hidden Stone

Visita Interiora Terrae, Rectificando, Inveniens Occultum Lapidem.
Visit the interior parts of the earth: by rectification thou shalt find the Hidden Stone
– Basil Valentinus

The whole world's happiness is based upon the discovery of the Hidden Stone and its rectification. It is known that it dwells in darkness, yet it gives forth light. Do we know what it really is? Like the Grail, the Hidden or Philosopher's Stone remains obscure in its origins. But, as the Grail quest is not confined to Arthurian knights, neither is the search for the Hidden Stone confined merely to alchemists. Both quests are paradigms of the Great Work; both are analogous to the Great Work undertaken by Christ in the Holy Sepulchre – the mystery of which we will discuss later.

How do the Hidden Stone and the mystery of the Resurrection relate to the Vault of C.R.? A full exegesis of this question must be arrived at by as winding a route as any which tracks the Holy Mountain of the Rosicrucian adept. Many points can only be touched upon, and some themes must be either anticipated or suspended before the full answer lies before us. It may help if we make some parallel examples from Christian, Grail and Rosicrucian sources. (See fig.1)

Textual Source	Christian	Grail Corpus	Rosicrucian
Representative figure:	Christ	Perceval/Galahad	Christian Rosenkreutz
Hidden Stone Motif:	Stone which was rejected	Stone which fell from heaven	Philosopher's Stone
Place of Confinement:	Sepulchre	Bed on Solomon's Ship	Vault
Method of Resurrection:	Bodily	Transfigured in Sarras	A body of knowledge is recovered
What is redeemed:	Creation	The Wasteland	Those in ignorance
Mode of being after Resurrection:	Saviour Grail	Grail King/ Guardian	Inner Master

Fig 1: Some analogies in the life of the Hero-Initiate

The course of the hero-initiate, be it Christ, Perceval or C.R., begins in obscurity, proceeds in the face of Promethean torments and difficulties, is subject to accusations of foolishness, and ends in a death which is only death to the world. At this point the course of the hero-initiate departs totally from the expected pattern. He flies 'out of the sorrowful, weary wheel [and] pursues with eager feet to the circle desired.'[3] Turning from the pattern of his own life, he stands ready to guide the pattern of others. The tomb of his life's ending is really the cradle of his life's beginning. What happens at the turning-point must be explored later.

Christ enters the tomb and is resurrected; Galahad goes aboard the Ship of Solomon,[4] and is transfigured in Sarras, the heavenly city; C.R. enters the Vault and a body of incorrupt teaching is discovered after 120 years. These analogies need not be strained after; they can be seen as variants of the Holy Fool legend which draw from a Christian model – itself based upon earlier mythological paradigms.

The whole world is changed at the moment of Resurrection as the involutionary arc becomes an evolutionary way of return.[5] The Vault, like the famous House of the Holy Spirit, is not fixed in one location. Just as the Ship of Solomon is really the Barque of Faith which transports the wood of Eden's Tree in the shape of a canopied bed that it might become the Tree of Golgotha in a later time, so the Vault is a treasury from which later ages can draw. The astonishing impulse behind the defence of Jerusalem during the Crusades was the desire to protect the Holy Sepulchre: 'He is not here. He is risen'. The importance is not the empty tomb but the one who occupied it so briefly, his teaching and his Resurrection. These are timeless tabernacles which we must explore if we wish to see our own likeness to the hero-initiate. Our imaginations can recreate their reality as initiaton-chambers, but we will have to follow the pattern of the Holy Fool.

The Vault may be timelessly present within our imaginations, yet we cannot remove the brass plate without first preparing ourselves. Even as the original discoverers of the Vault kept their curiosity in check, sleeping and consulting their Lullian Rota first, so the women at the Sepulchre returned home to keep the Sabbath before returning to open the tomb and anoint the body of their Lord. What miraculous resurrections occur in this quiet time of preparation?

We step into the microcosm of the Vault. What is this sun which shines in the centre of the ceiling? Whence is its light? We are told: 'although the Sun never shines in this Vault, nevertheless it was enlight-ened with another sun, which had learned this from the sun'. Light of this kind can only be kindled by a prior light; yet at the centre of the earth there is no light. If this is the Midnight Sun which shines for the initiate in the sanctuary, how is it still shining for us, who are not adepts? It must have its source of kindling from a previous initiate who brings the greatest light of all.

The source of all light is the Creator who brings light out of dark-ness, though darkness cannot comprehend it. The Creator therefore manifests in order to bring a light which can be comprehended – even by the ignorant and simple.

I will bear witness
That tho this bairn was ybore, there blazed a star

That all the wise of this world in o wit accorded
That such a bairn was ybore in Bethlehem the citee
That man's soul should save and sin destroy.
And all the elements ... hereof bearen witness.
That he was God that all wrought the wolkne [heavens] first showed
Though that were in heaven token stella comata
And tendered her as a torch to reverence his birth;
The light followed the Lord into the low earth.[6]

The Star of Bethlehem is distilled as dew[7] in the Virgin's womb, humbly
and insignificantly becoming manifest. Alchemically, Christ is the rose
flowering on the cross of the elements in one last blaze of glory. Then
the light is extinguished:

The sonne was clips and dark in every rem [realm]
When Christ Jesu five welles list unclose
Towards Paradis called the rede strem [stream],
Of whose five woundes print in your hert a rose.[8]

The descent of Christ's light into the dark places of the earth must here
break off. We cannot look upon this light of the Vault any longer; it
dazzles us, and we are unprepared to explore further

It is Shere Thursday and Venus Day already.[9] The tomb is sealed; the
King is laid to rest. Whether for three days or a hundred and twenty
years, we must wait. 'Of the upper part [of the vault] you shall understand no more at this time.'[10]

3. A Porter in Hell

I have descended into the bosom of the Mistress
– Orphic inscription

So we return to the vault to view the body of our master, C.R.. There is
a sense of timeslip as we gaze within. We are but the latest successors
who look through the doors of time into the Otherworld reality of the
Inner dimension. As Seth is allowed three glimpses of Paradise when he
goes back to the Garden to gain the Oil of Mercy for the dying Adam,[11]
and looks back into a world before the Fall; as the women look into the
empty Sepulchre and wonder on Easter Morning, seeing time reversed
and its laws overset; as Parzival gazes upon the aged Titurel who lies in

the same room as the Grail within the Fisher King's Castle and sees his predecessor – so we look into the vault upon our master, C.R..

C.R. himself was famed for opening a certain door – that door of iron inscribed with copper writing which proclaims the resting place of the Lady Venus. The light within her vault is described as 'the most precious thing that Nature ever created.'[12] When he looks upon her naked form, C.R. looks through another door of time, back to the foundation mysteries of which the Goddess is mistress. Those who have the temerity to look through such doors bind themselves irrevocably to what lies beyond them. C.R., though he is 'a grain buried in the bosom of Jesus', is also a votary of Venus. How may this be reconciled?

We look upon his incorrupt body and mentally rehearse the two accounts that have traditionally come down to us. The grave and reverend character of the *Fama* seems to bear little resemblance to the C.R. of the *Chymical Wedding*. The *Fama* is the official history of C.R. compiled by serious aspirants who stress the solid achievements of their master and recount by what means he has laid up such a treasury of knowledge. Here is recounted a parallel life to that of Christ – the respectful account, told in hushed tones. C.R. has a secret middle life in which he consults learned men (as Christ does in the Temple or, apocryphally, on his journey to Britain to learn of Druids or of Essene teachers). C.R. is acclaimed as one of the wise, he is 'the expected one' (Christ is recognized as Messiah). C.R. goes into Egypt and, like Lull before him, recognizes the kernel of wisdom at the heart of the non-Christian mysteries (Christ is 'called out of Egypt'). The Christly parallel belies any correspondence with the mysteries of the Goddess. Strikingly absent from the *Fama* is any 'Passion Narrative' wherein the earlier mystery resonances are always touched.

We need to turn from the official to the unofficial history of C.R. – the *Macgnimartha* (Youthful Exploits) or *Mabinogi*[13] of our hero in which his full mythos is clearly delineated. If the *Fama* is unhelpful, then the *Chymical Wedding* has all the clues we need to answer this riddle. The *Chymical Wedding* is a rosary – a mystical sequence of seven beads – in which C.R. gathers the roses of Venus' wealth. Each day is one petal in the seven petalled rose which surrounds him – the rose which we have called the vault. In the middle of this rose is celebrated the hierogamy of C.R. and the Lady Venus for, despite the fact that the Chymical Wedding of C. R. is assumed to be about the wedding of the royal persons, the title is actually self-descriptive and accurate as it stands.

If we turn the pages which lead up to C.R's secret hierogamy we glimpse the real C.R. who, though his hair is grey and he accounts himself as no longer young, shares the same innocent earnestness as Perceval at the outset of the Grail Quest. Here is one who would sell all he had for the possession of the pearl of wisdom and who suffers the rigours of his initiation into wisdom with the greatest humility and determination. His approach is the ideal candidate's towards initiation, unaware that, though he has been invited to a Royal Wedding, *he himself is the groom.*[14]

C.R. suffers the lot of all men: he is thrust into incarnation, into the captivity of matter, where he is yoked to his fellows. This is clearly seen in Day One of the *Chymical Wedding* where he dreams that he emerges from his dungeon by the help of 'an ancient matron'. He is wounded in such a manner that blood covers him from head to foot. He has indeed 'descended into the bosom of the Mistress', into the Taurobolium whence the initiate of Cybele's mysteries emerges 'washed in the blood of the bull'.[15] He is released from his dungeon and told by the ancient matron that he should be proud of his wounds and 'keep them for my sake'. The lamentation of the *Dies Sanguinem* is forsaken in favour of the Hilaria.[16]

C.R. arrays himself in his wedding-garments, in the manner of a morris dancer, with crossed red bands over his chest and four red roses in his hat. These roses proclaim his loyalty, for, though they may be symbolic of wounds, they are also the tokens of the Goddess. He is dressed in the emblems of his name: the cross and rose. For all its Protestant veneer, the *Chymical Wedding* is an exposition of the Mysteries of Venus, which can be traced back to the goddesses of pagan Europe whose influence underlies this narrative drama.

We have opened the door of the Vault and, like the Golden Dawn initiate before us or C.R. who enters the fateful copper-inscribed door, we are committed to all that lies beyond. But whose door have we come through? That of the Lady Venus. She is our way in and also our way out of incarnation as we shall relate. Bewildered, we see that our Vault has within it the receding image of vault inside vault, like a nest of boxes. We must go further on and further in. We watch our master, C.R., uncover the Lady Venus and we begin to realize the consequences of his action. When the mysteries of the Goddess are discovered by the initiate-hero, all her treasures lie open to him; now he must guard her mysteries like the priest of Diana in the grove of Nemi.[17] He is sequestered to remain as porter in the Castle but, instead of engaging in combat with the previous porter, he merely succeeds to the role. Nor may he forgo his duties until another comes to take his place.[18] Since C.R. is no longer young he concludes that he will die in harness. Nowhere is it told how C.R. relinquished his service to the Lady Venus for here the account of the *Chymical Wedding* breaks off.

As we ponder on this unresolved mystery we see the Vault changing before our eyes. C.R. has been pricked by Cupid within Venus' vault; like a *gallus* of Cybele – the Asiatic Venus – he has descended into the subterranean chamber of Magna Mater, into the bosom of the Mistress. As Persephone on earth is called *Kore* – Maiden – so her title in Hades is altered to *Despoina* – Mistress. He has proclaimed his allegiance in his heart and lies upon the nuptial *pastos* in the *cubiculum*, paying his tithe to hell or to the subterranean mother. The hierogamy of C.R. and the Lady Venus takes place but, for us, the veil descends in a rosy mist and we see patterned before us the symbolic wedding in another guise.

The strains of Wagner's overture to *Tannhauser* are heard, but even music is subject to variance and timewarp in the Vault, and it changes to the medieval ballad of the poet-knight Tannhauser and we hear the story unfolding yet another thread in the complex life of C.R.

Tannhauser lived in Venusberg with Lady Venus, enjoying the pleasures of her Otherworld. Yet, being a Christian knight, he was aware that his life was unblessed by his faith. Repenting, he journeyed to the Pope to gain absolution. 'It would be easier', said the Pope, 'for my staff to flower than that you could be forgiven.' Disconsolate, Tannhauser returned to Venusberg and his former mistress. Yet, no sooner had he left Rome than the papal staff burst into flower. The messengers despatched after him arrive too late to find Tannhauser entered into his unholy but blessed hill forever.[19]

The shards of this primal image are scattered throughout Germanic oral tradition from its appearance in the thirteenth century right up to the present with Thomas Mann's *Zauberberg* (The Magic Mountain). We realize that the Rosicrucian manifestos were written in awareness of the Tannhauser story which shares a common source with the Faery Otherworld of Celtic tradition.

The Venus of the Tannhauser legend is nearer in conception to Holda or Freia – the ancient goddess of the earth and underworld than to the Classical Venus. Tannhauser feasts with his mistress as the wanderer into Faeryland feasts in the Happy Otherworld with Queen

Mab, Morgan le Fay or the Queen of Faery. Tannhauser means 'forest-dweller' and may derive from Wotanhauser, the mountain where Freia and Wotan lived. We read in *Die Morin* by Herman von Sachsenheim (1453) how a hero travels to Faery and encounters Queen Venus and King (!) Tannhauser. Wotan has been replaced by this precursor of C.R.. Just prior to the publication of the Rosicrucian texts, Heinrich Kornmann collected together a series of legends about Venus entitled *Mons Veneris, Fraw Veneris Berg*, published in 1614. All the pagan elements are assembled ready to become the vehicle of the Rosicrucian impulse.

Thomas of Erceldoune and Thomas the Rhymer in Scottish Faery tradition both enter Faeryland to companion its queen; C.R. becomes the vassal of the Lady Venus. As he has lifted her veil, so he becomes her 'porter in hell' – not a Christian hell, but a pagan underworld. He becomes custodian of the previous mysteries, for no new movement can go forward without initiation from the Wise Ones who have trodden the road before him. He marries the Lady Venus to learn of her wisdom, just as those Walkers-between-the-Worlds enter Faery to be initiates of the Otherworldly wisdom.[20]

This Happy Otherworld, the timeless realm, can be dimly discerned in the Vault. We must follow the footsteps of our master C.R. closely in order to see it. The sword-bridge or turning door which leads to the pagan Otherworld is ever present but has been obscured to later ages. C.R. himself is the bridge by which we can see into it; and only he can travel thither because he agrees to do his portering in hell for the love of the Lady Venus. There must always be porters willing to carry across the wisdom of past ages: the hero-initiates who harrow hell, who marry the lady at the centre of life's maze, and are resurrected to fly out of the weary wheel only when another guardian/porter comes to take their place. C.R. has his example in Tannhauser – the medieval precursor whose pagan successors can be recognized in the Celtic tradition – but he also has the example of Christ whose substitution is on behalf, not just of the next guardian, but of all who come after.

C.R. lies incorrupt in the Vault which is tomb, womb and *cubiculum* – wedding chamber. Like Taliesin he remains for certain periods within the Spiral Castle of the Mother, and emerges having passed through all possible experiences, knowing all wisdom.[21] Thomas Vaughan's *Lumen de Lumine* (1651) shows such a personage in the underworld coils of an ourobic dragon: he sits secure and safe, with his rosary culled from

Venus' treasury. '*Non nisi parvulis*' is written over him: Christ's dictum, 'Unless you become as a little child you will never enter the kingdom of heaven.' (Matthew 18:3) We must each enter the necessity of the Mother and, being created, must endlessly give birth, wax, wane and die.

The Otherworld melts away before our eyes, and we see before us the Vault of the Lady Venus through the eyes of C.R.. He reads, 'When the fruit of my tree shall be quite melted down then I shall awake and be the mother of a king.' What does it mean? Will our master C.R. be reborn of this lady as Gwion was born as Taliesin from the womb of Ceridwen? This is a formula to discover the true nature of the Hidden Stone, but it cannot be worked out here. How can the body of C.R. be resurrected? The greatest mystery lies beyond: a story known to all, so open that its secrets are ignored, holds the answer.

4. A Dazzling Darkness

Our Lord is the fruit, our Lady is the tree:
Blessed be the blossom that sprang, Lady, of thee!
– Medieval anon (B. M. Harley 541, f228b. c. 1475–1500)

We have looked into successions of receding vaults, back to the birth of time. Our sight is blurred, our faculties uncertain of apprehension, yet one factor stands prominently isolated in our understanding – the sacrifice which transforms that Vault into a wedding-chamber as well as a sepulchre.

We know that the fruit of Venus' tree is her son/lover who undergoes a mystical death/marriage: unless he dies, he cannot be born again. Unless he is resurrected, creation is unfree. The pagan resonance of this symbolic action is figured everywhere in the hero-initiate's sacrificial death to the earth's fertility. He is hung upon a tree, beaten and tortured; and he eventually lets fall his blood in fructifying drops to the ground: 'fair Balder falleth everywhere'.[22] It is only when his dead carcass is laid in the tomb of the earth, that the womb of Dame Kind or Nature can give birth.

This is the way of things. The fate of the human body is to become part of the great metabolic renewal of the earth's replacement: the putrefaction of the body reduces matter to its prime constituents, which then become available for the growth of new life. In this work, Dame Kind is the Soror Mystica of God, without whom the alchemical work of creation could not take place. Christ's death follows this model closely, fulfilling the ancient patterns of ritual death. Yet there is a unique difference. While the sacrificial deaths and descents of Persephone, Attis or Orpheus perfectly match the archaic obligation, their persons remain subject to the laws of nature: their sphere of influence is felt primarily in the Otherworldly rather than the human reality. Christ breaks the circuit of the weary wheel by returning from death *in his own body* which, though glorified, is still a *human body*. This is out of accordance with the laws of Dame Kind. Even immortals must render her dues, going through the sorrows of incarnation, if they are foolish enough to take a human body. Dame Kind, the Mother, Lady Venus or Sophia – whatever we choose to call her – is bountiful and generous, yet she lives within her own fixed laws and these cannot be broken. Yet the Resurrection of Christ breaks them. How?

We left Christ hanging on the cross of the elements at the end of the first section of this essay. What occurs at the point of death, in the holy hiatus of Friday night through to Sunday morning, is the point under investigation. This central event is the meeting of many power lines: whatever their provenance before this event in time, whatever their divergence after it – all the lines lead through the mystery of the Resurrection.

It is not by accident that the crucifixion is accomplished upon Venus Day – Friday.

Et hoc in alta voce omnia elementa audierunt, et ante thronum Dei dixerunt: 'Wach! rubicundus sanguis innocentis agni in desponsatione sua effusus est.'[23]
(Then did all the Elements hear the great cry, and before the Throne of God, they said: 'O! the red flowing blood of the innocent lamb is shed on the wedding day.')

The Creed states that Christ 'suffered under Pontius Pilate, was crucified, dead and buried; he descended into hell; the third day he rose again from the dead'. As a summation of the principle seed-symbols of Christian doctrine it is an excellent précis; yet there are those who worry that textual references to the credal statements are thin on the ground or completely absent from the Bible, ignorant that many of the so-called Apocryphal Narratives were once canonical to the Christian New Testament. The expunging of these narratives from the canonical collations has left curious lacunae which can, nevertheless, be filled from oral Christian tradition and from both Apocryphal Gospels and Gnostic texts. We have only to look at the medieval mystery plays to see that the life of the Saviour (particularly his birth and death) is only slightly more emphasized than the intriguing narratives of Creation and the Harrowing of Hell. Medieval laypeople stood a better chance of understanding the mystical subtext of the creed than do laypeople today.

We have considered the pagan motif of C.R.'s sojourn in the service of Lady Venus in some depth. The hierogamy of C.R. and the Lady Venus joined the Rosicrucian impulse directly to the roots of the mystery tradition: the Goddess is mistress of the foundation mysteries. In order for these mysteries to be made manifest, the Lady Venus must become 'the mother of a king.' But even as the Rosicrucian mysteries were to be transmitted by these means, so too were the Christian mysteries. It is time to pass from the initiate, C.R., to the master on which his eyes are set – Christ – whose mysteries are established on the foundations of the Goddess's.

Now let the Vault assume its last and most awesome appearance as we listen to the Hidden Gospel which speaks of the Creation of the World and its Way of Return.[24]

> In the beginning was silence. And in the silence was God.
> God's helpmeet was Sophia, his wisdom. She fell from the
> fullness of the Pleroma and caused the creation of the world,
> becoming its guardian – the World Soul or manifest Sophia.
> In her distress she lifted up her voice and cried aloud, saying,
>   'My Father, my Father!
>   Why didst Thou create me?
>   My god 'El, 'El,
>   Why hast thou set me far away, cut me off,
>   Left me in the depths of the earth
>   And in the nether gloom of darkness
>   So that I have no strength to rise up thither?'

She had become Sophia Nigrans, the guardian of the laws of creation: the door through whom all living things must pass. (See Chap. 8)

The incarnation of Christ is through the body of Lady Mary. The Star of Bethlehem sheds its divine dew into her womb, which is the vessel of his becoming. His purpose in taking flesh is to break the incarnatory round of matter not to destroy it, but to redeem it, giving it the opportunity of taking the way of evolutionary return. He reverses the involutionary path of Sophia Nigrans' fall. So that where it is written[25] 'Pray in the place where there is no woman. Destroy the works of femaleness, not because she is another … but so that [her works] might cease from you,' the destruction of womankind or of Sophia's value is not meant to be understood – rather the reversal of involution into evolution is intended. Christ has to undergo the torments of death in order to meet with Sophia Nigrans, the ancient Mother of creation; and as her dowry, to offer her the way of return.

At the crucifixion Christ, as the emblem of Compassion, offers up his own flesh for the sake of all living flesh. He is laid in the tomb, entering the dark realm of Sophia Nigrans, who is guardian of the densest kernel of creative matter at the centre of the earth. He embraces her outcast darkness, as the hero-initiate embraces the Hag; and it is in their embrace that the spark of Resurrection is enkindled. The Star of Bethlehem blazes in the dark places of the earth. The burst of vivifying light is so strong that the shroud of Christ is forever imprinted with his image; likewise his image is imprinted upon the face of Sophia Nigrans who turns her dark face to that of her divine original – Sophia Stellarum – the bride of God and of the Stars.

Carbon liquifies into light – coal into diamond.

The philosophers have told us that 'the Stone is a black, vile, and fetid stone, and it is called the origin of the world and it springs up like germinating things.'[26] Also that, 'this stone proceeds from a sublime and most glorious place of great terror which has given over many sages to death'.[27] Yet Christ dies not, nor is the Stone 'black, vile and fetid'. It is become a 'true Crystalline Rock – a bright virgin earth without spot or darkness'.[28] The Philosopher's Stone is none other than the regenerate Sophia, now suffused and imprinted with the very potentia of all creation to return to its source.

The stone of the Sepulchre is rolled away; creation proceeds backwards at the turning point of Resurrection. And in the morning, very early, the great Epiphany of the Resurrected One takes place. Christ returns from the Underworld tomb – which is both womb and wedding chamber now – to show himself wearing the livery of Sophia Nigrans – his wounds. And she who is the Sophianic mediator upon earth, Mary Magdalene, is told, 'Do not cling to me, for I am not yet ascended to the Father.' Since the Resurrection, time is on the arc of evolutionary return. The next Sophianic embrace cannot now take place until Sophia Nigrans returns to the Pleroma – and this cannot be until the last blade of grass returns before her. Only then can Sophia Stellarum resume her rightful place as the Bride of Christ in the fullness of the Pleroma.

Until the time comes when Sophia Nigrans and Sophia Stellarum cease to polarize as the manifest and transcendent aspects of God's wisdom, the Lady Mary, Christ's Mother, sits in the place prepared for her: Mary Magdalene remains in the place of Sophianic mediator until the final apocatastasis occurs.

The subtextual gospel offered above must stand for the entire corpus of hero-initiates. Its application to the Rosicrucian Vault is universal – a microcosm corresponding in all motions to the Macrocosm', as well as 'a compendium of things past, present and to come'. The Vault is the place of incarnatory struggle, of ritual initiatic death and the place where the true nuptials of matter and spirit are enacted.

Because we have spoken here of many Just Ones – of Christ, Perceval and C.R. – we ourselves are not absolved from similar struggle, initiation or embrace. The place within the deeps of the earth, be it the realm of Sophia Nigrans, the Underworld Paradise of Venusberg, or the Rosicrucian Vault, exists in no single time. Bodily resurrection is not required of us, but the creative regeneration of the mysteries is. C.R., human and mortal like us, made his compendium of wisdom for all who came after him: he becomes a Just One – not after the manner of Christ, whose life he closely imitates, but after the manner of a prophetic light-bearer. Vaughan speaks of his body as 'being surrounded by sparkling flames which issued from his body ... Such Elijahs also are the members of this Fraternity who ... walk in the supernatural light.'[30] We too are potential light-bearers, though subject to the laws of Dame Kind. While the great initiates vanish from the earth to work in higher realms of influence, we must be potentiators of the light within our own element. Says Vaughan, 'This is the Steward of Wisdom: let him be clerk who can.'[31]

What receptacle of wisdom will each of us leave behind? The hidden treasures of our own traditions lie within vaults of our own making – they are accessible, if we take the trouble to search for them. The humility and fortitude necessary to plumb the secrets of the mysteries which precede our own time are not easily granted nor gratuitously maintained. Too often the doors of the mysteries are forced open by arrant explorers and treasure hunters to reveal a sterile tomb. The joint duty of light-bearer and pontifex is upon us, as upon C.R. The very obscurity of this task dissuades many from attempting to open 'a door to Europe'.

Not an earthly Jerusalem, a manifest mystery school with a rigid hierarchy, but a scattering of *Fidele d'amore* who pursue a solitary way within the Inner Realms is required: those who are willing to mount the cross of the elements and to learn from the sources of the Ancient Wisdom in order to enter the furthest circle of the heavenly rose.

The Rosicrucian manifestos state plainly that their function is to draw together men and women of goodwill into a common bond where details and differences are set aside: in this, Rosicrucianism proclaims itself a mystery school. The mystery narratives of C.R. are shown to be transmitters of the Ancient Wisdom, for which the Vault itself is a symbolic paradigm. Yet, in our own time, these emblematic mysteries have been constrained into manifest schools of Rosicrucian wisdom, and the true Rosicrucian impulse is not free to flow. The true Rosicrucian remains invisible, except in his or her effect. Only those who go down into the sepulchre of the Vault may aspire to build the Temple of Wisdom. Only those who make the sacrifice of the unreserved dedication may enter the seven pillared house where Wisdom has spread her table and mixed her wine. Only those who die to themselves may sit down to eat with her at the Wedding Feast of the Lamb.

Notes

1 John Matthews, Christopher Bamford, Joscelyn Godwin et al., *The Rosicrucian Enlightenment Revisited* (Lindisfarne Books, Hudson, 1999).
2 *Apocatastasis* is Greek for 'The End or Restoration of All Things.' It is a concept familiar to Qabalists as the *Tikkun*. Origen's use of this theory in his cosmological speculation is mirrored in Valentinian Gnosis.
3 An Orphic inscription; a common theme in Classical mystery schools. See Joscelyn Godwin, *Mystery Religions in the Ancient World* (Thames & Hudson, 1981).
4 *Queste del San Graal*, ed. & trans. P. Matarasso (Penguin, 1969).
5 The way of involution and evolution is clearly expounded in Gareth Knight, 'Esoteric Training in Everyday Life', in *Quadriga*, No. 14, Summer 1980.
6 William Langland, *The Vision of Piers Plowman* (Dent & Sons, 1978), *passus* XVIII, lines 231–40. Spelling modernized by C. Matthews.
7 The ancients believed dew to be the sweat of the stars. The emblem of dew permeates medieval Christian tradition. The antiphon for the time of

Advent and Christ's coming, is '*Rorate Caelie desuper*': Ye heavens, let fall your dew from above and let the clouds rain down the just One: The medieval carol,

He came all so still,
Where his mother was,
As dew in April
That falleth on the grass

beautifully conveys this concept of conception. In Qabalistic tradition, dew is shed from the Tree of Life which will revive the dead.

8 John Lydgate (1370–1450), 'Like A Midsummer Rose', in *The Oxford Book of Medieval English Verse* (Oxford University Press, 1970).

9 Shere Thursday is Maunday Thursday, the day upon which, variously, people were shriven or shaved their beards preparatory to Easter Day. Also the title of a magnificent poem by David Jones in his *Anathamata* (Faber, 1952). Friday of course, derives from Freya's Day, the Norse Venus.

10 Frances A. Yates, *Fama Fraternitatis*, in *The Rosicrucian Enlightenment* (Paladin, 1975).

11 This story appears in the Greek Apocryphal Acts Of Pilate (cf. M.R. James, *The Apocryphal New Testament*, Oxford University Press, 1924). It is a motif which reoccurs in the Grail texts, particularly in *Queste del San Graal*, op. cit. Seth sees through Eden's gates a dry tree, a serpent hanging in a dry tree, and a child sitting in a green tree, each image being a prefiguring of Christ. Similarly C.R. and companions go to the Tower of Olympus in *The Chymical Wedding* in order to heal the Royal Persons: a typos of Paradise.

12 Gareth Knight and Adam MacLean, Commentary on *The Chymical Wedding of Christian Rosenkreutz* (Edinburgh: Magnum Opus Hermetic Sourceworks, 1984).

13 These were, respectively, Irish and Welsh titles of a genus of story dealing with the Youthful Exploits of the hero: an art-form in its own right as was the medieval French genre, the *enfances*. In Christian Ireland and Wales, the same kind of stories were told about Christ: in Wales, the Christ-Child is still called Mabon.

14 This is irresistibly reminiscent of *Alice in Wonderland* and *Through the Looking Glass*, where Alice progresses from Pawn to Queen. In the light of this, the parable of the Wedding Guest (Matthew 22:1–24) can be seen as a species of initiatory story.

15 Initiates of both Mithraic and Cybelene mysteries partook of this rite, wherein a bull was slain so that its blood flowed through a perforated floor onto the candidate in a pit below the sacrifice. The cult of Cybele is more

apposite to the Rosicrucian impulse, as her initiates were men who castrated themselves in her honour – a total allegiance. See Maarten J. Vermaseren, *Cybele and Attis* (Thames & Hudson, 1977).

16 The *Dies Sanguinem* commemorated the ritual flagellation of Cybele's priests, in mourning for Attis. A *taurobolium* was also held on this day – 22 March. The lenten rituals of Spain retain elements of this cult. The *Hilaria* commemorated the mystic resurrection of Attis on 25 March. It is not difficult to make the analogy between these celebrations and those of Holy Week.

17 The priest of Nemi held his office until successfully overcome in combat by another candidate. See J. G. Frazer, *The Golden Bough* (Macmillan, 1922).

18 The theme of a substitute porter is curiously common in oral tradition. A story gathered by the Grimm Brothers, 'The Devil with the Three Golden Hairs' tells of 'a foolish boy who knew everything', who is sent to hell to obtain three golden hairs of the devil, by his wicked father-in-law. On the borders of hell he meets a ferryman who is weary of his endless duty. The boy promises to relieve him of his duty if he will help him perform his task. By a series of clever questions and answers, the boy returns from hell, and spins a yarn about the amount of gold to be found there, so that his father-in-law goes thither. The ferryman relinquishes his paddle into the wicked father-in-law's hands and is thus released, leaving the dupe to fulfil the office of Charon.

The folksong 'The Maid and the Palmer' – a variant of the Cruel Mother – charges a mother who has slain her children that her punishment will be 'seven long years a-portering in hell' (*Child Ballads* 20 and 21)

We may consider the way in which Perceval himself succeeds to the role of Keeper of the Grail Castle after he ceases to be a seeker of the Grail.

19 J.W. Thomas, *Tannhauser: Poet and Legend* (University of North Carolina Press, 1974).

20 See further: John and Caitlín Matthews, *The Western Way*, vol. 1 (Routledge & Kegan Paul, Spring 1985), for a discussion of the native shamanic role.

21 Lady Charotte Guest, *The Mabinogion* (Dean & Sons, 1906).

22 David Jones, *In Parenthesis* (Faber, 1937).

23 Caitlín Matthews (trans.) From a sequence, *O Ecclesia*, in honour of St Ursula by Abbess Hildegard of Bingen (1098–1179). A record with this sequence is available: *A Feather on the Breath of God* (Gothic Voices, Hyperion A66039).

24 Lest I be accused of fabricating this narrative, I refer the reader to the *Apocryphal New Testament* (op. cit.) and the *Nag Hammadi Library* (Brill, 1977), as well as to *Gnosis* by Kurt Rudolph (T.T. Clark Ltd., 1983). The symbolic resonances and their relevant texts will be found therein, as well as in the works of Thomas Vaughan, *The Works of Thomas Vaughan*, ed. A.E. Waite (New York: University Books, 1968).

25 'Dialogues of the Saviour', in *Nag Hammadi Library* (op.cit.). There is a textual lacuna in this question.

26 Vaughan, Thomas, 'Lumen de Lumine', in *The Works of Thomas Vaughan*, ed. A.E. Waite (New York: University Books, 1968).

27 *Theatrum Chemicum* (1659).

28 Vaughan, op. cit., 'Anima Magica Abscondita'.

29 The Two Maries – the Virgin and the Magdalene are manifest examples of Sophia Stellarum and Sophia Nigrans, and mediators of those specific energies: as vehicles of Christ's incarnation and ministry, their position is pivotal. Christian tradition has always esoterically understood both figures in their true sense: exoteric tradition has worked hard to simplify the roles into those of virgin and whore, but even these bare titles are significantly appropriate.

30 Vaughan, op. cit., 'Anima Magica Abscondita'.

31 Vaughan, op. cit., 'Eugenius Philalathes: his Magical Aphorisms'.

PART THREE:

THE NEW GRAIL QUEST

~ 13 ~

The School of The Grail

John Matthews

The real inner history of the Grail has yet to be written.[1] Yet there are those who have already contributed chapters to the continuing story, some of whom are dealt with in this book, and especially in the chapters which follow.

The Grail has played a part in the esoteric life of Britain for a long time. From the moment that Robert de Boron wrote how Christ spoke to Joseph of Arimathea 'holy words that are sweet and precious, gracious and full of pity, and rightly are they called Secrets of the Grail',[2] he assured that seekers would come who would desire to know these secrets, even to imagine they knew them when they did not.

In the Middle Ages, at the height of the Grail fever which attended the appearance of more and more texts dealing with the quest for the sacred vessel, both the Cathars and the Knights Templar were thought to possess the Grail in some form. In fact the idea of the saintly 'pure men' of the Albigensian heresy possessing any physical object is unlikely – though they certainly seem to have known of the inner mystery which the Grail expresses.[3] The Templars, according to more than one authority,[4] may have guarded for a time the Mandylion, a sacred relic which may have concealed the famous Shroud of Turin. It has been noted that the description of the folded Shroud, protected by a frame which showed only the face, is consistent with descriptions of 'the head in the dish' found in certain Grail works then circulating. Whether the Templars actually possessed any secret knowledge of the Grail is less easy to prove, since so much calumny was directed at them at the time of their fall, and actual documents are few and far between.

Modern Templar Orders exist which claim the wisdom of the Grail as part of their heritage:

> It is a fundamental belief of the Templar tradition, a belief backed by long experience, that if a seeker after truth begins to work seriously on himself, he will start to radiate light on the inner levels ... Every man and woman who is stirred by stories, legends or films of noble heroes is merely reacting to the promptings of the True Knight who sleeps within the heart ... The task of awakening the True Knight within us is not an easy one. We will need first of all to look honestly at ourselves and then take the first steps with courage and determination. The spiritual impulses of the Age of Aquarius will then certainly respond to the light of our aspiration and reveal to us that True Will which will guide us inevitably to the Grail.[5]

Modern Cathar movements have also made an appearance in recent times, and have declared themselves to be founded very firmly in Grail spirituality. In particular the Lectorium Rosicrucianum, founded by J. van Rijckenborgh and Catharose da Petri in 1952, has continued to grow and disseminate ideas. A full account of it is to be found in *The Treasure of Montségur* by Walter Birks and R.A. Gilbert.[6] A guiding light in its early days was Antonine Gadal, who later changed his name to Galaad, after the greatest of the Grail knights, and who founded a centre in the Pyrenees (also called Galaad) devoted to the restoration of Cathar ideals and (possibly) to the discovery of the Grail itself. His book *Sur le Chemin du Saint Graal*[7] makes fascinating reading and is full of insights into the inner meaning of the Grail mysteries.

One of Gadal's associates for a time was the Irish writer on esotericism named Francis Rolt-Wheeler, who later made his own contribution to Grail literature in his book *Mystic Gleams from the Holy Grail*,[8] in which he gave an account of the stories from a generally esoteric viewpoint, including some unprovable connections and links with the past which nevertheless have a ring of (inner) truth about them.

> The Legend of the Holy Grail glows ... with an inner light of esoterism (sic). Few, indeed, be those who have sought to follow the silver thread of Spiritual Initiation in this strange and mysterious cycle of miracle, of faerie, of chivalry, and of a super-sacrament. Consequently, in this mystical legend, there is a glimpse of the unknown; the reader may lose his way in a thicket of visions ... This Way will lead us into the astral world and into the kingdoms of Faerie, where Merlin, the enchanter, serves as guide. Those who know how to read the Book of Nature will find the link of Celtic Initiation in these sagas, and may even hear the tread of 'the Lordly Ones'.

Despite Rolt-Wheeler's rather colourful style, there is much in his book which reinforces the fascination with the inner mysteries of the Grail among modern esotericists.

Another source of inspiration was the Rosicrucian movement, beginning in the seventeenth century from roots in the Renaissance. More than one writer has seen the Rosicrucians as the inheritors and propounders of the Grail material. In particular Manley Palmer Hall, who founded the Philosophical Research Society in the United States in 1936, linked the mysterious group with the Grail, stating that 'it is evident that the story of ... the symbolic genealogy of the Grail Kings relate[s] to the descent of Schools or Orders of initiates. Titurel [the Grail King] represents the ancient wisdom and, like the mysterious Father C[hristian] R[ose] C[ross] is the personification of the Mystery Schools which serve the Shrine of Eternal Truth.[9]

The prestigious Hermetic Order of the Golden Dawn were working with Arthurian archetypes as long ago as 1896, and after them, several offshoots, including Dion Fortune's Society of the Inner Light (see Knight pp. Ch. 14), the Stella Matutina, and the Servants of the Light, have all utilized the deeply mystical elements within the story to form working magical systems.

A.E. Waite, himself one of the founding members of the Golden Dawn, first wrote of a 'Secret School of the Grail' in his 1933 volume *The Holy Grail: Its Legends and Symbolism.*[10] Here he finds the presence of a mystical body of thought, almost without form, but threading its way throughout the literature of the Grail, in some way 'a Grail behind the Grail'.

> The presence of this ... Secret Church is like that of angels unawares. In the outer courts there are those who are prepared for Regeneration and in the *adyta* there are those who have attained it: these are the Holy Assembly. It is the place of those who, after the birth of flesh, which is the birth of the will of man, have come to be born of God ... it is the place of the Waters of Life, with the power to take freely. It is like the still, small voice: it is heard only in the midst of the heart's silence, and there is no written word to tell us how its Rite is celebrated; but it is like a Priesthood within the Priesthood and harmony, wherein is neither haste nor violence. There are no admissions – at least of the ceremonial kind – to the Holy Assembly: it is as if in the last resource a Candidate inducts himself. There is no Sodality, no Institution, no Order which throughout the Christian centuries has worked in silence ... it is not a revelation but an inherence ... It does not come down: more correctly it draws up; but it also inheres. It is the place of those who have become transmuted and tinging (sic) stones.

Despite Waite's words, which should be understood in a mystical rather than a literal way, other groups and individuals have continued to work along the lines which assume the existence of such a school.

The Anthroposophical Movement, founded by Rudolf Steiner as a breakaway from the Theosophists, has had the Grail at the heart of its operations from the beginning. Steiner himself wrote a considerable amount on the subject, which repays study, including this prophetic passage from his *An Outline of Occult Science*:

> The 'hidden knowledge' flows, although quite unnoticed at the beginning, into the mode of thinking of the men of this period ... The 'hidden knowledge' which from this side takes hold of mankind now and will take hold of it more and more in the future, may be called symbolically 'the wisdom of the Grail' ... The modern initiatives may, therefore, also be called initiates of the Grail. [and] The way into the supersensible worlds ... leads to the 'science of the Grail'. [thus] The 'concealed knowledge of the Grail' will be revealed; as an inner force it will permeate more and more the manifestations of human life ... We see that the highest imaginable ideal of human evolution results from the 'knowledge of the Grail': the spiritualization that man acquires through his own efforts.[11]

During the 1930s and 1940s Christine Hartley and Charles Seymour worked together under the aegis of the Stella Matutina lodge of the Golden Dawn, forming a Merlin Temple and pursuing their studies of Arthurian archetypes and the Grail. A partial account of their activities is to be found in two recent books: *Dancers to the Gods*[12] by Alan Richardson and *Ancient Magics for a New Age*[13] by Richardson and Geoff Hughes. The latter also contains an account of Hughes' own more recent work in the tradition of the Merlin Temple.

More recently the Servants of the Light School of Esoteric Science have utilized specifically Arthurian and Grail materials as the foundation of their inner work.[14] Some privately issued papers give an idea of the range involved: *Grail Centres, Alexandria, Gnostics and the Grail* are anonymous works, while the Grail Lectures by S.F. Annett includes *The Grail Tests* and *The Gnostic Hypostases and the Grail Legend*. The former examines the initiations of Arthurian knighthood, with especial emphasis on the chivalry of the Grail, which the writer finds central to the concept of inner strength and

Self Reverence, Self Knowledge, Self Control
These three alone raise man to sovereign power.

Other esoteric groups who have continued to work with the Grail are the Aurum Solis, or Order of the Sacred Word, originally founded by Charles Kingold and George Stanton in 1897, and more recently continued by Melita Denning and Osborn Phillips, who have released some of the order's papers in the form of a series of books published under the general title of *The Magical Philosophy*.[15]

In America, the Sangreal Sodality, founded by the British occultist William G. Gray, until recently operated a correspondence course based upon Gray's ongoing series of books. These included a study of Kabbalah, of the background to the Western Inner Tradition, and a series of ceremonials and sacraments loosely based on the Grail Mysteries.[16]

This is a prime example of a modern mystery school deeply founded upon the matter of the Grail. At Hawkwood College in Gloucestershire, Gareth Knight has lead a number of weekend workshops which brought into being a company very like that described by Waite above – having no constitution, sodality or initiation beyond that of simple presence and participation in the work involved. A ritual 'Catechism of the Grail', first performed in 1981, is still in regular use among those who were privileged to be present at these latter-day Arthurian Mysteries.[17]

All of this gives some idea of the richness of the tradition still in operation, not only in Britain but elsewhere in the world, which draws upon the Grail stream for its inspiration and energy.

Charles Williams, who is the subject of a later chapter in this book, himself a member of the Golden Dawn, founded the Order of the Co-inherence within an immediate circle of friends. This was something again closer to Waite's idea, and was more of a mystical brother and sisterhood than a proper magical order. Williams wrote about it at the end of his study of the Holy Spirit, in the following terms:

> The apprehension of this order, in nature and in grace, without and within Christendom, should be, now, one of our chief concerns; it might indeed be worth the foundation of an Order within the Christian Church [where …] the pattern might be stressed, the image affirmed. The Order of the Co-inherence would exist only for that, to mediate and practise it … the Order would have no easy labour. But, more than can be imagined, it might find that, in this present world, its labour was never more needed, its concentration never more important, its profit never perhaps more great.[18]

This is to speak of a need for the Grail to be at work in the world. That it is so seems apparent, for despite the dark times in which we live there are certain gleams of light which betray the presence of the active principle of light still at work in the world.

Notes and References

1 J. Matthews, *Elements of the Grail Tradition* (Shaftesbury: Element Books, 1990).
2 M. Schlauch, *Medieval Narrative* (New York: Gordian Press, 1969).
3 J. Matthews, op. cit., 1989.
4 N. Currer-Briggs, *The Shroud and the Grail* (London: Weidenfeld, 1987).
5 G. Delaforge, *The Templar Tradition in the Age of Aquarius* (Vermont: Threshold Books, 1987).
6 W. Birks & R.A. Gilbert, *The Treasure of Montségur* (Wellingborough: Crucible, 1987).
7 A. Gadal, *Sur le Chemin de Saint Graal* (Harlaam: Rosenkruis-Pers, 1979).
8 F. Rolt-Wheeler, *Mystic Gleams from the Holy Grail* (London: Rider, n.d.).
9 M.P. Hall, *The Adepts in the Western Esoteric Tradition* (Los Angeles: Philosophical Research Soc., 1949).
10 A.E. Waite, *The Holy Grail, its Legends and Symbolism* (London: Rider, 1933).
11 R. Steiner, *An Outline of Occult Science* (New York: Anthroposophic Press, 1972).
12 A. Richardson, *Dancers to the Gods* (Wellingborough: Aquarian Press, 1985).
13 A. Richardson & G. Hughes, *Ancient Magicks for a New Age* (Minnesota: Llewellyn Press, 1989).
14 For further information about the Qabalistic correspondence course, write to Servants of the Light, PO Box 215, St Helier, Jersey, Channel Islands, UK.
15 M. Denning & O. Phillips, *The Magical Philosophy*, 5 vols (Minnesota: Llewellyn Press, 1974–9).
16 W.G. Gray, *Western Inner Workings* (1982); *The Sangreal Sacrament* (1983); *Concepts of Qabalah* (1985); *Sangreal Ceremonies and Rituals* (Maine: Weiser, 1986).
17 This esoteric work is continued and visually portrayed by Caitlín & John Matthews in *The Arthurian Tarot* and *Hallowquest* (Wellingborough: Aquarian Press, 1990).
18 C. Williams, *The Descent of the Dove* (London: Faber & Faber, 1939).

~ 14 ~

Dion Fortune and The Graal

Gareth Knight

*Of the many esotericists who have worked with the matter of Arthur, Merlin
and the Grail, perhaps the most important was Dion Fortune (Violet Mary
Firth). The details supplied by Gareth Knight, himself a sometime member of
the Society of the Inner Light, the order founded by Dion Fortune in c.1922,
show something of the depths and power of the work she undertook. Much of that
work has since become public property through her own publications and those
of her associates – including Gareth Knight's own seminal books* The Secret
Tradition in Arthurian Legend *(Aquarian Press, 1983) and* The Rose Cross
and the Goddess *(Aquarian Press, 1985).*

*At another level altogether, her insights have filtered through to popular
fiction, such as Marion Zimmer Bradley's* Mists of Avalon *(Michael Joseph,
1987) and more recently the trilogy of works by Stephen Lawhead:* Taliesin,
Merlin *and* Arthur *(Lion Books, 1987–9). Each of these works has picked up on
Dion Fortune's connection of the Arthurian Grail tradition with the ancient
concept of Atlantis. Whether or not this is accepted by the more sceptical readership of our own or these later books is not important. What matters is that from
this synthesis comes a degree of inner contact rarely equalled. The Grail has
from its beginnings lent itself easily to esoteric interpretation; in the future it
must surely become more widely developed in this area, with what results we
must wait to see.*

Dion Fortune is a key figure in the history of modern occultism, for she
marks a transition from nineteenth-century to late twentieth-century
occult thinking and practice.

She was born in the early 1890s, when the attitudes of occult
fraternities in the West still reflected the past. On the one hand they
tended to be antiquarian discussion groups with a mystical symbolic
bent, or enclosed orders with secret ceremonies of initiation that

borrowed much from the Freemasonry of the previous two hundred years. Of these, the Hermetic Order of the Golden Dawn exercised a considerable influence, and it was within an offshoot of this organization that Dion Fortune received much of her early training.

Most of the secret ceremonies of the Golden Dawn have now been exposed to the public eye, and for the practising occultist they have a certain period charm. The rituals do have a considerable residual power within them and there remain small groups of enthusiasts who apparently derive some benefit from working them.

No one in those days could have foreseen the present widespread interest in altered and expanded states of consciousness. Nowadays, what was once reserved for the innermost inner of the old time fraternities is relatively freely available in books, cassettes, videos, and a whole host of weekend workshops and conferences.

Much of this is presented under the banner of psychology, as indeed much of it is, although the subject is rather more extensive than psychology in the narrower sense. It is the opening of doors of perception into very real 'inner worlds' that have an objectivity of their own, and are by no means confined to the contents of one's own head – any more than the physical world is despite the fact that it comes to us filtered by the interpretations of the mind upon what is received by the physical senses. The inner worlds are sources of equally objective events that happen to be perceived by inner or psychic senses. These psychic senses are more common, and natural, than many people realize.

Dion Fortune was attracted to occultism via psychology, through the study of Freudian psychoanalysis. She later stated that she sought in occultism the key to certain phenomena of the mind that psychology failed to explain. Two of her early works, under her maiden name of Violet Firth, were in fact books of popular psychology – *The Machinery of the Mind* and *The Psychology of the Servant Problem* – although their very titles indicate that they are now somewhat dated.

Her first works of fiction, however, under the pen-name of Dion Fortune, were short stories under the title of *The Secrets of Dr Taverner*, where the protagonist was a very special kind of psychologist, who ran a strange nursing home for the treatment of psychic disorders. In this, and her related non-fiction work, *Psychic Self-Defence*, it might well be thought that she wrote up the cases with considerable artistic licence to make a good story. She always maintained, however, that she toned them down to make them acceptable to the general public. However, her main contribution to occultism lay not in the psychopathologies of the subject, which in fact are relatively rare, but in the more positive field of psychospiritual development, to which end she strove to re-establish, as well as she could, the ancient mystery tradition of the West.

She did indeed, as other leading occultists of the time such as Israel Regardie, welcome the developments of Jungian psychology, which came very much to public notice in the early 1930s, with its psychological interpretation of much traditional symbolic material. Indeed, when I joined her society in 1953 one of the essential textbooks was on Jungian psychology. However, analytical psychology was never an end in itself, but rather a means to an end.

In any practical occult work that is more than what W.E. Butler used to refer to as 'pussy cat occultism', its practitioners have to learn to cope with quite considerable psychic pressures that may come up from the subconscious or from inner objective sources. Failure to cope with such forces results in phenomena that are usually termed in psychoanalytic circles 'transference' or 'projection', i.e. quite disproportionate loves, hates, obsessions or antipathies directed towards individuals or groups. The history of occult and spiritual movements is littered with anecdotes of the bizarre behaviour of its protagonists, much of which is diligently recorded by biographers for the titillation of their readers. Often the reporting itself is inaccurate because the evidence is taken from one of the parties who is suffering from such a bout of transference or projection. Hence no leader of any group is likely to stand much chance of a good press if left to the memoirs of discontented associates. The main problem of such psychological unbalance is that it takes a great deal of experience to discern when it is happening. Hence the Delphic injunction 'know thyself'.

After her death, the group which Dion Fortune founded continued to try to improve the quality of its members by various psychological techniques, but gradually Jungian psychology was abandoned, a full analysis being both too time-consuming and expensive for practical purposes, and all attempts to train a member to be a kind of resident group analytical psychologist foundered for one reason or another. There is in fact a profound gap between the basic premises of practical occultism and Jungian psychology, despite the common interest in traditional symbolism. The one is firmly based on spiritual philosophy, the other on scientific materialism. The Divine Ideas of Plato or of the

Qabalistic Rabbis are a far cry from the archetypes of the unconscious of C.G. Jung.

However, this problem was little understood in Dion Fortune's day, and has only become apparent in the light of more recent experience.

Another powerful influence upon the occultism of her time was that of the East. There has always been a strong tradition of occult theory and practice in the Orient because the various religions lend themselves more to direct inner experience than has ever been countenanced by the institutional churches in the West, where even great mystics of unimpeachable orthodoxy have been regarded with considerable suspicion, and those outside orthodoxy have been roundly persecuted.

Madame Blavatsky's *The Secret Doctrine*, published in 1888, did much to open up a flood of popular interpretation of Eastern esoteric doctrines, which was given even greater impetus by the efforts of pioneering stalwarts to the Theosophical Society such as Annie Besant and C.W. Leadbeater. So pervasive was this influx that most esoteric students in the West have taken in various concepts from it lock, stock and barrel. One will, for example, hear even pagan loyalists of the old Western native traditions happily chattering about *karma*, *kundalini* and *reincarnation*.

Dion Fortune, no less than most others of her generation, took this on board, but she stuck to the fundamentally important line that there is also a Western Esoteric Tradition which, although fragmented through historical circumstance, is every bit as valid and important as anything coming from the East.

She was also one of the first to take a stand against the obsession with occult secrecy that was perhaps a natural consequence of the long tradition of persecution of unorthodox belief and practice in the West. One will, nonetheless, find it difficult to find precise practical instruction in any of her classic textbooks, whether *The Mystical Qabalah*, *The Esoteric Orders and their Work*, *The Training and Work of an Initiate* or *Sane Occultism*, although there are plenty of hints. However she did go out of her way to try and make some of the practicalities evident in her novels, particularly the later ones, *The Winged Bull*, *The Sea Priestess* and *Moon Magic*, although how far she succeeded in this is open to debate. Certainly the public did not beat a path to her door to buy them; the second had to be published by herself out of her own pocket, and the last one did not see the dignity of print until after her death. It was indeed only in her series of weekly War

Letters, during the period of national emergency from 1939 to 1942, that she came out with specific practical instruction in an extended meditation group. This type of work might be considered fairly commonplace now, some half a century later, but it marked a considerable milestone then. Oddly enough, the letters have not, to this date, been published in volume form, but they tell a lot of Dion Fortune and of practical occultism in her day, despite being obviously dated as to some of the references to contemporary events.

The great strength and contribution of Dion Fortune was her synthesizing ability, and this was not always apparent even to her contemporaries – some of whom saw her as too mystically Christian, and others as too obsessed with power lines and sacred sites, while to yet others her concern with ceremonial magic seemed to dominate all else.

She saw three strands to the Western Esoteric Tradition, which had to be worked together into one strong thread. These three strands were sometimes referred to by colours, as the Green Ray, the Blue Ray and the Purple Ray. That is respectively, the Nature contacts, the Hermetic or magical tradition, and Christian mysticism.

Each has its various modes of expression. The Green Ray can be said to include all the neo-pagan movements, yet also nature mystics such as Richard Jeffries, and in its most modern manifestation it would certainly include ecological concern and the appreciation of the planet as a living organism. Indeed most aspects of 'the return of the Goddess' come under the Green Ray, including the current interest in ley-lines, sacred sites and centres, megaliths and so on. Above all, as far as Dion Fortune was concerned, were the powerful Elemental contacts she picked up, not only at Glastonbury, where she lived, but in the great parks of the city.

The Blue Ray or Hermetic Tradition is more of an intellectual approach that seeks to categorize the inner dynamics of creation and to formulate various ground maps and plans for inner exploration. Such maps are for instance the Tree of Life of the Qabalah and its associated symbolism. An important side of it is the practical, however, without which all theory is useless, either in physical ceremonial ritual or in similar patterned formal work by directed meditation upon an inner level.

The Purple Ray is that of devotional mysticism, which in the West is predominantly Christian, and is certainly of major importance to us in our consideration of Dion Fortune as a member of the 'Household of the Grail.' In the native traditions of the British Isles it embraces the insights of the old Celtic Christianity and the Glastonbury legends of Joseph of Arimathea coming to these islands, and even the Christ child too.

Her Green Ray work is, perhaps because of its very nature, the least well documented. An important plank not only within it but in the foundation of all her work was an Elemental contact that came to her at Pentecost in 1926, on Glastonbury Tor, at the foot of which she had founded her small group a few weeks earlier at Easter.

In those days she had tended to work in full trance, and her colleague C.T. Loveday, who wrote up the occasion, records that the Fire and Air contacts came through with considerable power, the repetitions gliding up the scale in quarter tones and ever increasing volume, whilst those of Earth and Water were of a soft and sweeter nature, tending gradually to diminish in tone.

Short excerpts of the repetitive chant of the Fire and Air Elementals run as follows:

> *The wind and the fire work on the hill.*
> *The wind and the fire work on the hill.*
> *The wind and the fire work on the hill.*
> *Invoke ye the wind and the fire …*

And of the Earth and Water Elementals:

> *Earth and water are friendly and kind.*
> *Earth and water are friendly and kind.*
> *Earth and water are friendly and kind …*

This eventually broke into declamatory prose that concluded:

> Come in the Name of the White Christ and the Hosts of the Elements. Come at our bidding and serve with us the One Name above all Names – the Lover of Men and of the Elemental Peoples – the Great Name of JEHOSHUA – JESU!

In later exegesis that same evening they were told:

> You must develop the Green Ray contacts. You need them. Without them your group is imperfect … The time has arrived when you can handle it. That is why you have been given this house at the very centre of these

Forces. It is not for nothing that you came to the Tor, and have built on the Tor, not for nothing believe me. Here you have the Air and Fire contracts. You will have your devotional aspect in the city, and you will have your Nature contacts here. The Elemental Forces will co-operate with you and give you the aid of their Powers.

The prophetic statement that they would have a devotional centre in the city came to pass four years later in the foundation of the Guild of the Master Jesus (also called in those early days the Church of the Graal), of which more anon. But the relevance of the Christian mysteries to the Elemental powers was further elaborated upon in the statement that in the three days between the Crucifixion and the Resurrection, when Christ is said to have preached to the spirits in prison, these spirits included the creatures of the Elements and to them also the Christ gave the power to become 'sons and daughters of God'. Thus, in Elemental eyes, the Risen Lord loved the Elementals, and so it is in the sign of the Risen Lord that human beings can and should contact the children of the Elements.

All this became part of a system of allocating the various hills of Glastonbury to the Elemental contacts; the Tor to Air and Fire, Chalice Hill to Water, and Wearyall Hill to Earth.

With regard to Dion Fortune's commitment to the Blue Ray or Hermetic Tradition, little need be said, as her published work remains as a permanent memorial. *The Mystical Qabalah*, published in volume form in 1936, remains a classic and certainly one of the most readable books on the subject of the Tree of Life. She was also well into the practicalities of the subject with the system of initiation that she founded with graded rituals for progress through the Fraternity. On a more philosophical level her cosmological treatise *The Cosmic Doctrine*, although by no means easy reading, is a continuing source of inspiration and study to discerning Hermetic students. This she also received at Glastonbury in an impressive display of mediumship, which she always claimed was the source of power for any practical occult group, although this *modus operandi* is generally regarded now as somewhat passé, and the tendency now is to work a round table rather than Bee Hive formula, i.e. to develop group intuitive insights by mutual interchange, rather than have a group of lesser workers relying on the psychic contacts and abilities of one central individual.

As to the Purple Ray of devotional mysticism, Dion Fortune's commitment came largely from inner experience and somewhat against her natural inclinations. This stemmed, as in so many cases of Christian conversion, from a deeply impressive vision that she had, wherein she was taken to a high place by one of the leading magical figures of the day, the inner plane adept known as the Master Rakoczi, and given firmly into the keeping of the Lord Jesus, somewhat, it should be said, to her chagrin!

This commitment brought her into conflict with certain members of the Theosophical Society of the day in whose eyes the Lord Jesus was a minor master inhabiting a physical body somewhere in Syria. It was felt that the Eastern conception of the Lord Maitreya had rendered Christian mysticism somewhat outmoded. Dion Fortune was quite unable to accept this view, and withdrawing from the Christian Mystic Lodge of the Theosophical Society she formed the Guild of the Master Jesus which held public services at her headquarters. This was in one sense a fulfilment of what had been predicted at Glastonbury some four years earlier from the unlikely source of the Elemental contacts. It also emphasized the threefold basis of her work in that it was conducted in its services on classical Hermetic lines. To revert to the earlier instructions at Glastonbury, it was said:

> You must balance the Rays in your training, and you will find in each tradition the elements which connect it with all the other traditions.
>
> On the Green Ray – the Celtic nature Ray – you will find the connection with the Purple Ray through the Celtic Saints, such as St Bride, St Columba and many others. You will find the link with the Hermetic tradition also, through the Mage Merlin, who is very important, and is the Master of the Celtic Ray in these islands.

Correspondingly it is stated:

> On the Christian Ray you will find the link with the Celtic tradition through Grail legends and the Arthurian cycle; and with the Hermetic tradition through the Mysteries.

And thirdly:

> In the Hermetic tradition you will find the link with Christian aspects through the Rose and the Cross, and with the Celtic aspect through Merlin again.

Thus, particularly through the Arthurian cycle we find common ground, and to follow Dion Fortune's personal Quest for the Graal we should perhaps start back at the beginning again – in Glastonbury.

* * * * *

Dion Fortune's interest in the Graal tradition had its most obvious foundation in her commitment to Glastonbury. It was there that she founded her headquarters at the foot of the Tor, on a plot of ground called Chalice Orchard and just across the lane from the famous Chalice Well where the water runs red from the Chalybeate spring which in those days used to run freely down the side of the road.

Her appreciation of Glastonbury and of the Graal tradition with which it is inseparably entwined is to be found at length in the series of articles she wrote that were published in 1934 in volume form as *Avalon of the Heart*.

Indeed, in her opening chapter to this book she recalls the legendary role of Chalice Hill, and tells how it is reputed to have been the home of the guardian of the Graal, the Fisher King, who kept it in his secret treasury at the heart of the hill.

She goes on in fact to identify two traditions in Glastonbury that have intermingled. One she refers to as Avalon of the Cup and the other as Avalon of the Sword, the Cup being the Holy Graal, and the Sword, King Arthur's Excalibur.

The Excalibur tradition she identifies with the pre-Christian faith of the ancient Britons before the legends of the Fisher King became associated with Chalice Hill. Then, she says, 'dark Morgan le Fay, half-sister of Arthur and pupil of Merlin' dwelt there; and she conjures the vision of the still surface of the well 'with its great gouts of blood stained fungus' used by Morgan as a magic mirror for her visions.

This is very much a primitive and evocative vision that shows Dion Fortune's awareness of the dark forces of the Inner Earth as well as the spiritual insights and revelations of Christian mysticism. We may well conclude that she was speaking from practical experience when she says, 'that spirit it is that broods over the well and wakes the eyes of vision in the souls of those who gaze into it.'

In Avalon she also sees the Lady of the Lake and her sister queens as guardians of the Magic Sword and forerunners of the three pure maidens who later guarded the Sacred Cup of the Fisher King.

Avalon of the Cup is enshrined in the legends of Joseph of Arimathea who came to Glastonbury bearing the Cup of the Last Supper in which had been caught the drops of blood that fell from the side of the Saviour of the World, wounded by the spear of the centurian Longinus. Thus was Glastonbury fittingly called 'the holyest erthe in Englande', where the first little mud and wattle church bore the Cup of the Last Supper, or the Holy Graal with the Sacred Blood, upon its altar.

Later, as the legend told by Dion Fortune goes, the Dark Ages encroached and the relic was withdrawn from the outer world by the Fisher King, to be kept in an underground chamber, guarded by three pure maidens who watch over it day and night. Whoever drinks from it will never thirst again for it is a well spring of the Waters of Life of the soul.

Here, in Dion Fortune's vision, came the questing knights who, after an all-night vigil at the chapel of St Bride at Beckary, just over the Pons Perilous on the River Brue, came to the secret chamber to drink of the Cup. Many were never seen again, for they were translated by this very act into another world.

Then as times became more evil the Sacred Cup was concealed at the heart of a spring that rises between Chalice Hill and the Tor, which is why the waters, rising from an immense depth, run blood-red into the sacred well.

This is the legendary background that helped to draw Dion Fortune to Glastonbury, and it was here that she made her own first important contacts with inner power sources that led her to establish her own group. The gist of much of these contacts was contained in a series of papers called 'The Words of the Masters' in her society's magazine *The Inner Light*, and also in the cosmological treatise published much later as *The Cosmic Doctrine*. They were also the background inspiration to much of her other works and papers reserved for members of her group.

It is from this source that she put forward the idea that the ancient tradition of the legend of lost Atlantis was part and parcel of the Mysteries of Britain. To this end she devotes a chapter to it in *Avalon of the Heart*, where she links the memories of a lost land of Lyonesse off the coast of Cornwall with the legend of a far more ancient land in the mid-Atlantic.

This engrafting process builds resonances of old legend onto those yet more ancient, on a thesis that one is a folk memory of the other. Thus we have the idea of Merlin being an emigré of the lost continent, arriving in these islands of Britain soon after the cataclysm, and embarking upon a plan to engender a dynasty of priest kings or god kings after the manner that is well known in the history of the Orient and even Ancient Egypt.

This does not conflict with the idea of Merlin also being a much later Druid, or one who was a confidant of a legendary historical Romano-British Arthur. Rather they are all resonating parallel strings upon the harp of the legends of ancient time.

However, is the streak of psychism, the second sight, she asks, that particular gift of the Celtic people, a strain of the old Atlantean blood that gave clairvoyant gifts to its aristocratic priesthood and thus the ability to be guided by superior intelligences – thus giving another dimension to the conception of the San Graal, or *Sang Real* as 'blood royal'.

Merlin, in this scenario, which closely follows the standard tale that has come to us through Sir Thomas Malory, is the guardian and teacher of Arthur Pendragon and Morgan le Fay. In Malory it is Merlin who brings about the conception of Arthur by enabling King Uther Pendragon to lie with Ygraine, the wife of the Duke of Cornwall, and who claims the child immediately after its birth so that he can oversee its upbringing. This was a uniting of the ancient British royal line with the Atlantean blood-line of the Duchess of Cornwall, who according to this tradition was originally a princess of Atlantis. Her daughter Morgan le Fay is rather quaintly described by Malory as being sent to a nunnery so that she can study 'nigromancy'. This strange nunnery for the study of the black arts would seem to be a garbled medieval interpretation of an ancient school of initiation, run by such as Merlin – at any rate, so Dion Fortune chooses to think, and she melds the figure of Morgan with other legendary characters, describing her as 'the dark Lilith of our island legend, sometimes identified with the Lady of the Lake'. Although this apparently free interpretation of ancient legendary material may seem somewhat arbitrary and even fantastical, it does have a degree of validity for occultists working with this level of tradition. In such a context we cannot use the same criteria as the outer rules of material evidence. As Dion Fortune wrote in an early note upon her group and its work:

> I had to teach a great many things I could not verify, but which I could not afford to scrap because I should have brought the whole structure down if I

had pulled them out ... there was, moreover, always the saving grace of
intuition which sensed the presence of light and power behind the tumble-
down structure of conventional tradition. This faith was ultimately justi-
fied, for I eventually discovered that historical fables were psychological
truths, and merely required to be re-stated in terms of modern thought to
be accurate working models of things ineffable. Trouble comes, however,
when the fables and the framework are taken at their face value, for then
they are very misleading and hampering.

This is very much the statement of an empirical working occultist, and
another reason why she chose to couch a proportion of her teaching in
the guise of fiction. It is an attitude that puts results before accepted
theory, and is in line with the ancient navigators who discovered new
worlds by ignoring the accepted and seemingly obvious reasoning that
those who sailed too far south or west would either be roasted or fall off
the edge of the world. It might also be viewed as a fitting attitude for
any who are actively on the quest of the Graal.

Anyhow, it was an aid to those who sought the direct experience of
the Graal that Dion Fortune founded her Guild of the Master Jesus.
This was an inherent part in the work of her Fraternity, which she went
out of her way to stress in the following words:

> ...the Guild is not a thing apart in the system of the Inner Light, but simply
> a different set of symbols applied to the elucidation of the same ineluctable
> truths and to the guilding of the soul by the same paths of immemorial
> mystical experience. It is exceedingly important to our concept and method
> that the Guild should be seen as part, or aspect, of an undivided whole. All
> the ministrants of the Guild have been through the Hermetic training
> which teaches them the technical methods of the Mysteries. These
> methods, applied to the traditional Christian symbolism, make the Way of
> the Cross a true initiatory Path of the Lesser Mysteries, precisely paralleling
> the coveted Hermetic training.

Thus we see that we have a *magical* technique being applied to induce,
in those who might not otherwise come to it, a *mystical* experience.
(We use the term 'mystical' to refer to an experience of the Uncreate
Realities, the direct experience of God, or Eternity, whilst 'magical'
refers to techniques of the visual imagination and other inner faculties
of the adept. These same techniques were used by Ignatius of Loyola
to train his Jesuits and it is also the *modus operandi* of Rosicrucian
symbolism as correctly understood.)

In the Guild ceremony the heart of the matter was the building of a mighty Chalice upon the higher ethers, about which Dion Fortune writes quite categorically, 'We are functioning as adepts in a magical ceremony; we are making a channel of evocation.'

And she advised those who attended to assist in the building of this imagery by visualizing a mighty golden chalice, greater than the stature of a man, suspended in the air over the celebrant, who stood in the centre of a zodiacal circle in the midst of the sanctury. It was to be seen at such a height that a man standing upright could reach up and lay a hand on its base at arm's length. Thus it would be seen there throughout the whole ceremony, above the heads of the participants in the sanctuary, where, she said 'those who have psychic powers will be interested to observe the astral phenomena connected with it.' And the nature and power of its contents would be experienced in the charged atmosphere at the giving of the bread and wine across the sanctuary rails which represented the divide between the inner and the outer planes.

Of its function and symbolism Dion Fortune wrote:

> The Cup is the mystically exalted soul of man, held up to receive the influx of the Holy Ghost; and when receiving this influx from on high we stand with our feet set firm in the very heart of Nature, thus affirming the natural basis of all things in the Earth our Mother.

At the outbreak of war in 1939 the public meetings of the society had to come to an end, and Dion Fortune started a system to meet the exigencies of the war situation. This was to have a private Sunday meeting of a few chosen members consciously linked up with all those, scattered across the country, to whom her weekly letter had been sent the previous mid-week. This letter contained a subject for meditation and a couple of quarto sides of comment about it.

This started off as something of an experiment but quickly gathered power and momentum during the winter of 1939 and spring of 1940. Certain images began spontaneously to arise, at first in the form of a triangle, with a powerful figure at each point.

At one point in a sphere of red was the figure of a mailed warrior on horseback wielding a drawn sword. This was identified as King Arthur. At an opposite point in a sphere of blue was a figure seated on a throne wielding a diamond sceptre, and this was identified as Merlin. And at the third point, in a sphere of purple, there built up the figure of the Christ holding a chalice, or the Graal.

Students of the Qabalah may note that we have here a figure that will fit readily upon the Tree of Life, with the points of the triangle at Geburah, Chesed and Yesod, the red, blue and purple spheres respectively.

After a while the image took on a three-dimensional aspect, with the figure in the purple sphere holding the Graal becoming the Virgin, and the figure of the Christ forming the apex of a pyramid in a sphere of bright light. Again, Qabalistic students will see how this also fits the Tree of Life, with the figure of the Christ in the Sun sphere of Tiphereth.

This work with spontaneous magical images that built up in the group mind that they had formed continued through the duration of the national emergency, and included also the cooperation with an angelic patrol about the shores of Britain which it may be recalled is traditionally known as Merlin's Enclosure.

After the middle of 1942 the weekly letters had served their practical purpose and became more philosophical in tone. Eventually they were reduced to a monthly basis, and reverted to a more generalized teaching role. The Graal and Arthurian work went on, however, within the confines of the group. Here the gifted mediation of Margaret Lumley Brown played a part, and a considerable amount of material was brought through and worked with, known as 'The Arthurian Formula', the greater part of which was used, with permission, as source material in my book *The Secret Tradition in Arthurian Legend*, published in 1983.

Much of this material was the work of the later war years and after, and again when I joined in 1953 another of the required textbooks was *Le Morte d'Arthur* of Sir Thomas Malory. A number of the inner group were known by Arthurian nicknames, 'Morgan', 'Merlin', or `Dragon', and until the early 1960s a staple ritual of the Greater Mystery group was the Graal Ritual, which has been constructed by Dion Fortune's successor as Warden, Arthur Chichester. This was based upon a familiar four-fold pattern of Lance, Cup, Sword and Stone, and had as a basic principle the same legend espoused by Dion Fortune in her early Glastonbury writings, about how the new Christian faith was welcomed by the Druids and flourished in the Celtic Church.

Thus it is possible to trace, from the first contacts of Dion Fortune with Glastonbury, how the Graal and Arthurian tradition developed in her mind and work, to be taken up by her group after her death, and thence by those yet to come and those beyond it. For now we see a running tide of interest in the whole field, extending it ever further. Thus apart from my own public workings concerned with the calling of King Arthur and the raising up of Merlin from the enchantment of Nimuë, Bob Stewart has brought new insights with his Merlin Festivals and his work on the *Prophecies* and *Life of Merlin* by Geoffrey of Monmouth, so long neglected. John Matthews has edited and collated material on the Graal itself, of which this book forms a part, and Caitlín Matthews has done much to elucidate and reconstruct the ancient mysteries of Mabon enshrined in *The Mabinogion*. There have been many others contributing to this work, each in their own way, and with varying degrees of power and direction of emphasis. No one has a monopoly on any of this universal material. And yet, if truth were told, all this published work and even the practical work associated with it, some known and some known only to a few, is but the tip of a mighty iceberg, whose hulk floats deep in the hidden memories, historical and paradisal, of the Mysteries of Britain, of Arthur, Merlin and the Holy Graal.

~ 15 ~

The Grail as Bodily Vessel

Bob Stewart

The themes of renewal and restoration which are such a crucial part of Grail literature all point towards the supreme example of the Vessel expressed in human terms – the Virgin who bears the body and blood of the Saviour within her own body. Here the image is taken further, into the realm of genetic manipulation, and though the author's own statements make it clear that we must be wary of placing too much emphasis on the words, an abiding truth can be found in the statement that `the physical vessel of the body is also the spiritual vessel of renewal.' For here is an essential matter of the Grail: that within the symbolic vessel is a reality which transcends physical fact, and that within each person who succeeds in the quest a spiritual alchemy must take place.

I

Among the many obscure and fascinating documents relating to the Grail, the diligent reader may find references to two lesser vessels: 'And when our lorde in the dendony was drest, This blode in two cruettes Joseph dyd take' (*The Life of Joseph of Arimathea*); 'Joseph has with him in his sarcophagus two white and silver cruets, filled with the blood and sweat of the Prophet Jesus' (Maelgwyn of Avalon: *Historia de Rebus Britannicus*). We shall return to these curious statements later, as they form part of a persistent oral tradition which manifests to the present day. The main proposition of this analysis of certain aspects of Grail lore is not, as one might expect, identical to the subject suggested by the title. Before the reader accuses the author of false pretences, and tears the pages from the book, this use of the stump of tradition as a peg upon which to hang the shield of reflection must be explained.

The external appearance of any subject is seldom sufficient to prove its origin and identity, and this is especially true when we examine ancient and obscure traditions, tales, legends, songs and accumulated expositions and commentaries upon such lore. In several portentous and wonderful publications that have appeared amidst loud fanfares in recent years, tradition has been represented as an occult and political conspiracy. The message of the following pages is that tradition is neither a material conspiracy to be unravelled by television documentaries, nor a reliquary of eccentric old gew-gaws, but a catalytic mode of alteration of individual and group awareness. In this respect, tradition may be passive, as the group vehicle of inter-related symbols preserved and passed on through time by various means, or it may be active. The activation occurs through an enlivening of the basic symbols within imagination, a process which we shall refer to again when considering symbols from the Grail lore itself.

Any writer who makes such a suggestion stands as a helpless guardian of the entrance to Tophet, the burial place of forbidden and cursed gods. It was customary for the Hebrews to spit at the very name of this place, which is identical to the Celtic Underworld of Annwn in many respects, the same place in which the Grail may be found. Why helpless? Because the steady stream of pseudo-academic looters that bustles back and forth does not consider such a theory worthy of their spittle; it 'proves' nothing.

The Grail is a vessel of the Underworld, no matter what upper route it has travelled in the hands of exalted intellects. Qabalists may understand this paradox instantly, but it will be more difficult for orthodox Christians or those who follow eastern paths adapted for the use of westerners.

Familiarity with the source material is essential, and the suggestions offered are meaningless unless related to the early and basic 'Grail' texts, or other sources mentioned in context. The main source is *The Quest of The Holy Grail* (translated by P. Matarasso, Penguin, 1976). No amount of retrospective commentary can replace the actual legends themselves; they are the vehicle of a living, powerful, and ultimately undeniable inner transformation. As tradition implies, this transformation ferments from within to express itself outwardly, and not in any mere political or religious or ephemeral form.[1]

One of the hallmarks of a great symbol, such as the Grail, is that it may manifest in a number of different ways to human perception, yet each manifestation will be attuned to the nature of the original. Such a definition is not identical to suggestions that the Grail is 'all things to all men' or that it may be 'whatever we wish it to be'. A great symbol or key to altered awareness has limits, even if we cannot perceive them, and we may presume that the Grail is no exception to this rule.

The activation of a great symbol, or arch-symbol, can cause numerous effects within apparent serial time, all of which are analogous to their original, albeit with different modes of expression. The relationship between such manifestations cannot be deduced by mere lists of their correspondences, but by a deep realization that they are simultaneous expressions of one original model.

Careful consideration of this process suggests that whereas the ramifications of a great symbol may indeed be countless in expression, no one of these units alone can be true to the original. To be defined by material expression involves limitation, but we should not blandly assume that if we patch all the limited expressions together the resulting whole will be a sum of all parts! When this mechanical approach to symbolism is attempted, the potency and clarity of the original is inevitably lost.

Paradoxically, perhaps, it is one of the major operational laws of magic that the whole may operate through one part, even though the total accretion of parts can never make the whole. Understanding of this simultaneous diversity in unity was common to the philosophy, metaphysics, and ritual of the ancients; it is currently undergoing a considerable intellectual revival.

The pagan and early Christian symbolists were eminently practical. They expected, even demanded, that their most potent symbols should manifest through the physical body. It is in this context that we shall consider the Grail, always bearing in mind that its manifestation as a bodily vessel, a human being, is identical in essence (but not in mode of expression) to manifestation in any other consensual form.

The most dramatic and far-reaching religious variant of this potent manifestation may be found within orthodox Christianity, modulated through the individual preference for cult expressions of the primary original faith. The Christian Incarnation was founded upon a well-known and widespread system of magic, available not only to so-called 'initiates' but also to everyday common folk.

While adherents of esoteric Christianity will dispute that the Incarnation was of a higher order or degree than those of similar pagan rituals, they cannot reasonably suggest that the symbolism of virgin birth was not of long standing and well established before, during, and after the appearance of the Saviour. Orthodox religion, of course, does not allow such considerations at any price, even in the light of factual historical evidence such as classical literature, archaeological proof, or comparative religion and mythology.

Of particular interest in our present context is the repeated evidence that such an ancient system may still operate today, or rather that people believe that it still operates. Whether or not such a system is in any way effective or valid for the twentieth century is a separate discussion.

Within the popular revival of interest in ancient and racial lore, a revival which occurs with almost every generation, acceptance of the Grail as a Celtic and early Christian symbol has become commonplace. Despite the ever-increasing mass of literature that examines the manuscript and folklore evidence relating to the subject, there are several curious aspects of what might be termed 'Grail lore' that spill over into British tradition, and these should be considered within the broader context of magical practices and both pagan and Christian symbology.

While our analysis will revolve around one brief and specific tradition, it will not be limited to that subject alone, and will not adopt the typical approach of literary comparison, or semi-scientific folklore. Much of the material offered will probably be familiar to the reader, but some of the conclusions may be startling.

The tradition from which we begin is pleasantly short, appearing in literary form early in the thirteenth century, in the work of Robert de Boron. The reference, to two vessels or 'cruets' associated with the Grail, is a feature of the familiar tale of Joseph of Arimathea, and his association with the holy ground of Glastonbury. The endless argument about the origins and validity of this material is well known, but the absorption within popular and esoteric tradition is worthy of close examination. (*Joseph d'Arimathie*, Robert de Boron, *c.* 1200.)

No better way can be found to emasculate old traditions than to find a 'proof' of their origins. What is seldom grasped by the pernicious peddlers of 'proof' is that many apparently fabricated traditions find their way into the common imagination, and are openly accepted for centuries after the originators (or presumed originators) are dust.

Before proceeding any further, we must make clear to the reader that we have no intention of 'proving' anything. It is unnecessary to prove traditional lore; if it could be proven it would be valueless. We are concerned only with the undeniable fact that a tradition exists, and that the many branches of that tradition (literary, folklore, and esoteric) all offer similar information, though in confused and fragmented forms.

To treat such material as a mere detective problem, to suggest that there were or are actual secret 'orders' preserving lore into the present era for purposes of world domination, is to utterly degrade the value of traditional lore, and effectively reveals the petty mentality of the authors of such theories.

One cannot 'own' the Grail; nor can one 'prove' a Tradition.

Sources for the pattern of tradition under analysis are numerous, and references may be found within:

1 orthodox Christian teaching and scripture. Old and New Testaments;
2 pagan parallels to Christian mythology;
3 folklore parallels, in native British and European tales, songs, ballads and games or ritual dramas;
4 the main body of Grail literature from the twelfth and thirteenth centuries, which offers heretical Christian and pagan traditions in profusion;
5 esoteric traditions, as taught in European and British schools or systems of magic. These include the so-called 'inner-plane' teachings, devolving from sources not of this world, but are well represented in oral teaching, ranging from revived witchcraft through to various forms of Qabalah.

Once again we should state, at the risk of being repetitive, that the following pages are not offered as a 'proof' of anything whatsoever; nor do they necessarily constitute a statement of belief or practice on the part of the author. The true value of esoteric or symbolic lore is not found within its content, but through the effect of that content upon awareness.

Setting aside the matter of social or historical, or even literary, validity, we must consider the power of traditional material to shape and develop individual and group consciousness. In certain cases, that power acts suddenly, dynamically, and irrevocably.

Eastern systems of altered consciousness have gained considerable attention, and the use of certain tales and sayings, such as the famous Zen 'koan' are now well known. Keys of this sort work by jolting the awareness of the individual into new and previously unexperienced modes. This catalytic power may be experienced to very deep levels through the Mystery of the Grail.

Within the overall Mystery, there are a number of lesser but significant mysteries which devolve from it, which we might call sub-symbols. Such sub-symbols are useful means of approach to the greater symbol, and often act as short-cuts or secret ways to understanding, by-passing corrupted or authoritarian routes.

It is within such a context that we should consider the esoteric traditions that suggest possible physical descendants of Jesus Christ. Such traditions are not required to be factual, though they may very well be so, and are utterly prostituted when treated as seamy press scandals.

They are, in fact, operative as 'koans' or as parables. The realization of a traditional genetic inheritance, a magically activated bloodline, was intended to shock the awareness of the initiate into new modes or realms of reality. The initial jolt may have been great indeed, in the face of stultifying orthodoxy, but the process of association and absorption resulting from the first shock attunes to a level of awareness that runs under religious propaganda, and provides a continuing tradition.

More significant, from a practical approach, is that the potent catalysing effect is not triggered by mere verbal or literary analysis; it comes as a surprising and inward certainty, through participation in the symbolic language of the Grail Mystery. To this end, popular works aimed at earning money from bowdlerizing tradition and esoteric keys may not, in fact, do as much damage as one thinks.

During previous centuries, however, the realizations under discussion were regarded as secrets, not in themselves, but in their linking or bridging function between esoteric practices and the mass, group, or racial consciousness. These secrets, which were punishable heresy to preach, were regarded as games, jokes, and silly tales. The myth-historian Geoffrey of Monmouth, for example, went to great lengths to tell us repeatedly that his material was full of puns, even at the risk of being accused of mocking his noble patrons. The Grail legends, however serious in their intent, contain this same child-like accumulation of traditional lore.

The precedents for such an approach are ancient indeed, and are firmly stated in Luke XVIII: verse 17. 'Verily I say unto you, Whosoever shall not receive the kingdom of God as a little child shall in no wise enter therein.'

While there is no firm evidence of coherent or secret teaching being perpetuated through the centuries, there is evidence of a recurring tradition which is protean and indestructible. From a magical standpoint, and even from the grossly materialist suppositions of modern psychology, we find that lore connected to 'genetic magic' arises spontaneously through contact, real or imagined, with certain branches of the Western Mysteries.

It is lore of this sort that advises that the 'cruets' mentioned by de Boron were offspring of Jesus of Nazareth; male and female vessels of seed and blood. In both orthodox and esoteric symbolism, 'water' is a euphemism for seed or semen in certain contexts.

This esoteric tradition may be communicated by word of mouth, and may also occur as a 'communication' from non-physical entities, who teach a coherent and applicable body of lore combining pagan and Christian enlightenment within a physical Mystery framework, aimed at manifestation through human reproduction and reincarnation.

The validity of this teaching is of no importance, but its repeated occurrence within individual and group awareness even to the present day is of great significance. It shows the operation of certain symbolic modes of consciousness through the interpretation of the emotions and the intellect into physical expression.

This same 'mystery' has occurred for thousands of years, and has many variant expressions in the main body of Grail lore. It may be fashionable from time to time to 'prove' that the mystery has been faked or forged, or that it is real and exists through the occult activity of secret organizations. The truth may be more simple, rooted in the regeneration of such concepts within group awareness. That which does not regenerate is not the Grail.

The European development of symbolism expressing a vessel of regeneration may be traced to famous manuscript references, reporting ancient Celtic tradition. These in turn compare favourably with classical references, and with remains from the Roman-Celtic period as early as the first century AD. Sites such as Aquae Sulis, with its Celtic-Roman Temple of Sul Minerva, offer practical working models of pagan belief in regeneration within the Underworld or Otherworld.

This regeneration motif is present in folklore and folksong collected from oral tradition during the twentieth century, though references are widely diffused, and the word 'grail' never occurs.

The heretical Grail lore of the twelfth and thirteenth centuries binds pagan and early Christian beliefs with a strong thread of monastic influence in interpretation. This interpretation, which is not always orthodox, acts as a cement that enabled the pagan and rather 'dangerous' native lore to hold together. Whereas in the work of Geoffrey of Monmouth, the various mythical traditions were combined upon an old 'after the cataclysm' model, in 'The Quest Of the Holy Grail' such traditions are linked by a 'redemption of the world' model.

We know from sources which noted Welsh lore in the Middle Ages that the Celts believed in a Cauldron of Immortality. This vessel restored dead men to life, though they were sometimes dumb, and renewed pork joints from old bones. It was part of the sacred feast of the dead ancestors, and was employed in a ritual which was aimed at conferring divine knowledge and immortality. This theme was also found in Greek mythology and ritual.

The magical vessel had its home underground, and all wells, springs and lakes were regarded as Gateways to the Underworld. A much-quoted Welsh poem, *Preiddeu Annwn* records a magical raid upon the Underworld by a band of heroes and this theme of theft from the depths recurs in various forms throughout folklore, magic, and religion. The poem is likely to be an early example of the Grail quest.

The foundation of belief in a vessel of power, and its place in the Underworld lay in the pagan concept of exchange between the human and otherworlds, a concept still important in ritual magic today. Duality of death and life was unknown, they were manifestations of one power, not entities in conflict.

A most obvious vessel for magical power in the outerworld is the human being, and this is reflected in the constant belief in exchange found in period inscriptions from the Celtic-Roman culture, and from classical accounts of the Celtic attitude to physical death. Humankind bargained with the Underworld.

It is in this context of exchange and interplay between human and otherworld powers that practices of human sacrifice arose. Such practices were inseparable from systems of controlled birth or potential reincarnation.

Although this system is generally bandied about in modern works on magic, and much of the material concerned is vague and nonsensical, there is a strong suggestion of its continuity in esoteric traditions and in folk or rural magical practices. The modern revival of witchcraft, although essential and praiseworthy in its attempts to recapture a fresh relationship with nature powers, has tended to cloud perception of the magical systems concerned by claiming traditions without recourse to the metaphysics which underpinned their operation. While the Christians attempted to use the conceptual models of the ancients without allowing the generative magic that gave such models life, the modern pagans have picked up the cast-off generative organs without considering that they are fallen from a great and divine body of wisdom. Little wonder, in the face of such a conflict, that the prototype of the maimed Fisher King should have been pierced through the thighs, losing his ability to reproduce. This type of symbolism refers not only to spiritual imbalance or sickness, but to actual physical illness and reproductive processes.

In its simplest form, we have a story of heroes who raid the mysterious otherworld to gain a great prize; in its most complex form we have the quest for the Grail. In both cases, there is a powerful motif connected with fertility; not fertility in a merely sexual reproductive sense, but a through line of fertility, reaching from the Underworld, to the physical body, to the mental, emotional, and spiritual fertility of the individual and of the tribe or race.

That which does not regenerate is not the Grail.

Celtic practices of ancestor worship (the cult of the dead) involved the spirit passing into the otherworld or underworld, and then communicating with a seer or seeress who still lived in the outer or human world. This system was so widespread in the ancient cultures that it merely needs to be mentioned here, as the reader will have access to numerous works which speculate upon it in great detail. The esoteric practices of controlled fertility and timed conception were aimed at specific reincarnations of certain ancestors. Over a considerable period of time, a theoretical reservoir of illuminated souls became available to the mysteries which operated in this manner. It was believed that any particular king was literally the vehicle of all his ancestors, and this is reflected in examples from Irish tradition.

The widespread pre-Christian system, often called the rituals of the sacred king in modern literature, permeated through orthodox religion well into historical time, and much of its subtle practical operation is enshrined in the Grail legends. This enshrinement takes two forms; as specific almost offhand examples of apparently unrelated incidents, and as a continual theme reflecting upon the value of divinely given qualities of nobility.

We should not be surprised, therefore, when one branch of this material suggests that actual children were born to Jesus of Nazareth, and that they should be of the blood of the dark myth-woman of Christianity, Mary Magdalene.

The type of tradition outlined may be horribly unorthodox in the crude authoritarian sense, yet it harmonizes with some deep and persistent myth that is rooted in the group consciousness expressed within the Western Mysteries. The physical vessel of the body is also the spiritual vessel of renewal, either in the timeless experience of inspiration, or through numerous reincarnations, depending upon the will, beliefs and culture of the individual.

In Celtic imagination, there is little to separate the dead, the ancestors, the fairies or otherworld powers, and those about to be born. Similar beliefs were held by many pagan cultures, often refined to great sophistication and complexity.

All such arbitrary selection of lore might indeed be regarded as superficial, were it not for several undeniable facts that support our curious conclusions, without ever proving them. The most important indication is the persistence of certain themes both in and out of manuscript or print, particularly as folklore or as esoteric teachings, maintained by oral traditions.

The second significant element is the relatively modern science of genetics. Knowledge of this field may have been applied by the ancients, but based upon a rather different primary model to that of deductive and experimental science.

If we dare to encapsulate this complex subject, we might define genetics as one of the major factors in the construct that appears as a 'human being'. Genetics form one of the matrices that enable the entity to operate through many levels of function in manifestation. Specialists are still researching the relative values of genetics, environment, conditioning, innate response and so forth, but the genetic inheritance is as proven as any workable scientific theory, and new applications are constantly being discovered for genetic theories.

In short, science instructs us that we inherit something of our ancestors, as was common knowledge to the ancestors themselves. Such a concept is central to the practice of ritual magic; orthodox authority was able to charge pagans and heretics with necromancy. Geoffrey of Monmouth tells us that the British King Bladud 'spread necromancy throughout the land', which is merely another way of saying that his forefathers were ancestor worshippers. Both archaeology and classical sources confirm Geoffrey's statement.

The Celtic lore in Geoffrey is only superficially concealed, and the reader will find many parallels to the later Grail legends in *The History of the British Kings* (translated by Aaron Thompson, 1718, or the more modern translations, such as that of Sebastian Evans). While Geoffrey used to be popular as a 'source' for the Grail legends, as his work 'predated their appearance', scholars now suggest that all such material may be derived from general sources within oral lore ... a concept which has always been understood by teachers of esoteric traditions, and by modern folklorists.

It is significant that Geoffrey applies a genealogical proof to his post-cataclysm mythical history.

How is the genetic inheritance communicated? Through the interaction of male and female characteristics. In magical language these factors have long been expressed as The Seed and The Blood. The Celtic obsession with genealogy is not entirely a claim for social superiority. In the not too distant past, it was the equivalent of the modern genetic chart; a statement of direction with respect to the future, confirmed by the records of the past.

Readers who are familiar with the Christian Bible will remember the two distinct genealogies offered for Jesus Christ, by Matthew and Luke, in their opening chapters. Matthew gives an orthodox male line of inheritance, whereas Luke shows a female line, including miraculous births of both Jesus and John the Baptist brought about by the mediation of the Archangel Gabriel upon the 'daughters of Aaron', Elisabeth and Mary.

In many ancient cultures, the matrilinear line is primary in the definition of race, tribe, inheritance of property and other matters, and this emphasis is found in a great deal of Celtic folklore. Although modern revivalist pagans often take this, perhaps rightly, as evidence of a once dominant Goddess culture, it also reflects the magical and metaphysical concern with genetic lines.

Many of the clearly emphasized incidents within the Grail cycle involving female lines of descent, blood, and mysterious conceptions should be analysed in the light of modern genetic science. They are likely to be a magical analogy or operative model which uses a different vocabulary, but relates to the same processes as the modern expositions. This comparison should not be taken too literally, however, for the magical or metaphysical models were concerned only with the inheritance of otherworld power through the physical body, and were based upon long cycles of observation and correlation linked to seer-ship. These are the very cycles that are referred to in both genealogies of Jesus, and which appear again in the replication of Christ in the form of Galahad.

The special role of Jesus in replacing the hero who raids the otherworld is emphasized in several ways in Celtic Christian mythology, the earliest form of Christianity native to Britain.

Scottish Highlanders retained the ancient tradition that Jesus was fostered by the native goddess Brigit, the most powerful beneficial goddess of the Celtic pantheon. In early social structures, the foster mother and midwife were as important as the blood mother; in magical terms that which brings a child from the womb will powerfully affect the outer life of that child. The birth of the Saviour was associated with the blessing of the most important culture goddess of the pagan world, Brigit to the Celts, and Minerva to the Romans, patroness of so many heroes who plundered the dark powers of the Underworld, slew monsters, and brought special aid to their people.

As a result of this significant midwifery, which may be interpreted in several ways, Jesus fulfilled his expected duty by the so-called Harrowing of Hell – his journey through the Underworld. It would have been unthinkable that such a divine hero might pass from the outer world without reproducing his line; the blood line carries the message of the experience of his role as Mediator and Saviour. The power is passed *directly* through the body, bypassing all other mental and emotional routes.

It is not surprising that this heretical aspect of early Christian belief should be rigorously suppressed – the aim of the later church was to control and suppress the power, not to scatter it broadcast as a universal seed. Esoteric tradition advises us that sensuality may be a snare, but that specific reproduction along certain special lines may be beneficial to us all. Concepts of this sort are subject to considerable abuse, and historic manifestations up to and including the present century have frequently been of the worst possible nature. The abuse comes through literal attempts to 'prove' the system by 'purifying' human groups, a quite absurd and impossible venture, which utterly ignores the complex time-scales inherent in magical work, and wilfully rejects the spirit of true grace and enlightenment which blows where it will.

Despite the obvious abuses, against which we might choose to weigh the appalling career of the orthodox churches in their abuse of humanity at large, we may indulge in a few (idle) speculations. If Jesus of Nazareth had been initiated in the ancient mysteries, or as an Essene, or during his traditionally avowed youth in Druid Glastonbury, he would have had a clear understanding of the magical lore of sacred breeding and reincarnation. Indeed, the fragments of the suppressed Gnostic gospels suggest that he tried to apply this knowledge in rather specific ways which aimed at removing the enlightened from the physical matrix of consensual reality through the practice of magical chastity. We will return to this disappearing act shortly, in later and lesser variants.

It might not be too wildly imaginative to suggest that there could be no better way of perpetuating a spiritual revolution in a fallen world than to plant its seed within the blood of following generations. Such is the esoteric tradition which deals with the two Vessels or Cruets associated with the Grail.

II

It is difficult for the retrospective analyst of folklore or of period embodiments of tradition in manuscript to decide exactly what the true nature of the subject matter may be. This is why we gain such endless occupation in the study of early literature and of oral tales and songs.

Material may be classified into units of local, national, and even international currency as motifs, but this does little more than show a crude statistical summary, a preliminary organization which tidies up the sweepings ready for real examination.

Ultimately it is the personal belief of the student of any school or body of lore that enlivens and colours interpretation. Some modern writers regard all ancient lore as nothing more nor less than the inevitable product of economic and social struggles; many folklorists insist that apparent evidence of early magical or pagan lore in modern folk sources is either an illusion on the part of the interpreter, or an intrusion culled from nasty literature. Regrettably, they are often correct in their insistence.

During our analysis, we have made the monstrous presumption that a great deal of ancient matter is incorporated within oral tradition and that this matter is available to the present day, in numerous though attenuated forms. We have capped this presumption with an even greater one; that a careful comparison of standard folklore and song, magical symbolism and pagan philosophy will reveal many practical insights into the Grail legends.

Any student of magic who reaches beyond the superficial levels so profusely available in publication will have realized that magic is somehow concerned with 'genetics'. Our ancestors, from whom we inherit our magic as well as our physical characteristics, were most concerned to perpetuate certain blood lines that held special abilities. If the Grail legends are considered in this light, they are found to be replete with indications of genetic magic, especially aimed at spiritual regeneration attuned to physical regeneration.

As we mentioned above, *The History of The Kings of Britain* assembled traditional magical and religious motifs upon a mythical 'post-cataclysm' framework, a rationalization of myth in the classical form of the fall of Troy, and the flight of a band of heroes. The Grail legends, on the other hand, deal with the Fall and Redemption. By the time alchemical works had begun to appear, based upon the common symbolism found within the Grail and pagan lore, and later refined by the great hermetic philosophers of the fifteenth, sixteenth and seventeenth centuries, the esoteric tradition as a whole had begun to concern itself with the redemption and regeneration or restoration of the Fallen World. It is in this atmosphere that the monumental works of Christian metaphysics allied to magical practices appeared. The perceptive reader may detect a similar cycle, expressed in different modes, from the eighteenth century to the present day, distributing the three phases over a shorter time scale.

A few obvious examples of genetic magic within the 'Quest' would be:

1 Lancelot, whose excellence is the product of his breeding and not of his own inward efforts. He falls into sin and despair through the squandering of his natural gifts, and suffers considerable hardship before he attempts to develop his spiritual essence or true nature and attune his physical inheritance and prowess to its proper end. A believer in reincarnation might suggest that Lancelot lives off the capital of previous lives, without fully becoming aware of his function in the present life. He is, in this sense, an example of everyman, though a highly amplified and noble example in many respects.

2 Galahad, the product of a mysterious liaison between Lancelot and a maiden. Galahad seems to be a model of perfection, so much so that his father asks why he does not aid him in his spiritual plight. The esoteric answer to this question is that if Lancelot and Galahad are to become spiritually free, each to his own degree, then they must transcend the old genetic cycles of magical work, and realize a truly spiritual inspiration.

3 Arthur, the offspring of a union arranged by magical illusion, and traditionally said to be under the protection of the enchanter Merlin during his childhood.

Most important of all, however, is the master model that explains many of the lesser examples and characters in the Grail legends, so we will move straight to this without listing further individuals, especially as such lines may be found clearly stated within the 'Quest' itself.

The major key is, of course, the tale of the 'Tree of Life', which clearly offers the salvation of humankind through the action of the power of woman. This tale should be studied in detail, and compared to topological models such as the Qabalistic Tree of Life, a mathematical structure which shows the interrelationship between metaphysics and human energies through various conceptual worlds. It also shows the pattern of genetics and relationships which have been 'discovered' by modern science and psychology.

Of particular relevance to our suggestion that the Grail may manifest as ancestor worship or necromancy is the action of Solomon in the legend of 'The Tree Of Life'. Through meditation upon the quality of womanhood, Solomon, the model or archetype of wisdom, achieves the revelation that 'there shall come a woman through whom man shall know joy greater an hundred times than is your sorrow; and she shall be born of your inheritance.'[2]

Delighted by this knowledge, Solomon studies 'every sign according him, whether waking or in dream, in the hope of coming at the truth of the ending of his line'.

Finally, having discovered that The Virgin shall be his descendant, and that the last male of his line shall be even more valorous than Josiah, he decides to send a message through time to his descendants.

The resulting magical ship, needless to say, is devised by his scheming wife, who uses the three sports of the Tree of Life in its symbolism; Red, White and Green. While the male struggles to send his knowledge through time, the female provides the means whereby this might be realized, and a third and mysterious power activates the vessel and casts it off upon the ocean of life. (See Ch. 6, pp. 111–112)

The entire venture is a simple restatement of the Celtic application of ancestor lore, magical genetics, and divination; science-arts which were held in common by the advanced peoples of the ancient world, and which persist to the present day in diffused forms.

One factor which is easily overlooked in consideration of the Grail legends is that their originals were from an oral tradition; the reader of, or rather the listener to, the Grail stories would have been comfortably able to relate their content to a large store of similar tales, songs and entertainments which were widespread in all levels of society.

It is only in relatively recent years that an understanding of folklore has enabled scholars to realize the nature of the Grail material; it is combined and edited from a common stock of lore, and doubtless contains innumerable cross-references, themes and motifs which the modern reader cannot glimpse, or which have been lost.

Such themes, however, cannot be 'traced to originals', for they are the currency of communication in the dream-like process of the group imagination. It cannot be over-emphasized that Grail lore was intentionally fused from parts in common regular use in the general imagination; it cannot be denied that this fusion created a new and powerful imaginative entity that works as a vehicle for transformation when activated. The works of Homer are directly comparable.

In modern jargon, we could suggest that the Grail legends, and the related works such as *The History of the Kings of Britain* and *The Prophecies of Merlin*, are models of the racial psychology; but they are also maps of the magical physiology of the relationship between the Ancestors, the Land, and the Underworld.

Primitive examples of this type of symbolism were operative as rituals during the early part of the twentieth century, and a few still persist today. A list of such examples from folklore would be long indeed, but one of the most famous examples, 'The Cutty Wren', involves a ritual hunt for a mythical bird (represented by a real wren), and its cooking in 'a bloody great brass cauldron'. The remains are so large, that the poor can be fed with the spare ribs alone.

Promoters of the theory of sacrificial kingship often use this folksong and ritual as proof of survival, but setting such a complex argument aside, we can observe identical motifs to those of the raid upon the

Underworld in the poem *Preiddeu Annwn* mentioned above. For while the gap in time between the two is many centuries, the message has been sent down through time in the vessel of the common tradition.

The genetic flow, or pattern of communication with the ancestors in the otherworld, is intimately linked to the persistence of a common tradition which expresses itself in song, story and ritual, carrying material that appears to be retained from ancient cultural and magical sources. We would emphasize the apparent or superficial nature of this similarity, which is more likely to be the result of a deeply regenerative power of group consciousness than of active preservation and policy.

The legend of the 'Tree of Life' also gives an insight into the nature of magical or spiritual virginity, an esoteric understanding which greatly pre-dates the Christian emphasis of its appearance in the Grail lore. Maidenhood, we are advised, is a mere physical circumstance, but virginity is a state of awareness, a mode of consciousness. The collator of the Grail stories is intentionally stating a central and powerful magical law – something which must be fully realized before any type of magical work becomes truly effective. It has very little to do with morality and physical chastity, and a 'virgin' in ancient terminology need not be a 'maiden'. This applies equally to males and females, as the Grail legends repeatedly state.

Virginity is a primal or spiritual state, whereas maidenhood is the physical mirror of that state, which occurs through renewal of the body in reincarnation. Conversely, a maiden may not be virgin, but maidens who are not virgin are of little use in magic, contrary to popular opinion and fiction.

This metaphysical law was clearly stated by Jesus: 'But I say unto you, that every one that looketh upon a woman to lust after her hath committed adultery with her already in his heart' Matthew V: verse 28. Regrettably, subtle magical laws of this sort have been deliberately poisoned and misrepresented, leaving modern men and women with a dismal heritage of separation from their true power of relationship.

When we are advised that both the mother of Jesus and the mother of John the Baptist were 'the daughters of Aaron' and conceived as virgins, we are experiencing a mythical reworking of the magical rituals common to the pagans, whereby special breeding was aimed at bringing forth certain powerful ancestral or otherworld beings by the purity of the male and female partners, synchronized to specific times and places. Such a suggestion, however, in no way challenges or lessens the religious or spiritual power of the Virgin, as She is the essence, the Virgin of all virgins, and the human manifestation of the Grail.

With this point, we have come full circle in our argument, and repeat that a great symbol, such as the Holy Grail, may manifest in several different modes simultaneously. The difference is actually in the perception or level of consciousness of the recipient, as is clearly shown at the conclusion of the 'Quest'.

Although we have found a convenient circularity in the exposition, it does not suggest that all Mysteries are identical in operation or results, even if they use identical methods and key symbols. In the case of 'genetic magic' esoteric tradition supposes several sources for magical lines of descent, initiation, and communication from otherworld beings. These vary from widely published (but little understood) sources such as the lost continent of Atlantis, to quite obscure individuals with utterly localized traditions. Royal and noble families are often included, though pedigree is no guarantee of magical and spiritual power. As a mere aside, the perceptive student of history will have realized that most, if not all, of the ancient European blood lines have been usurped.

To express the matter crudely, not all members of the Mysteries are descendants of Jesus Christ, but there is a symbolic tradition that implies that any one of them *might be*. The corollary, that any one of us might be a descendant of some lesser divine hero or sacred king, is almost equally important.

It is this imaginative potential that acts as the super-catalyst to fire the consciousness into new realms, and the resulting changes will be shaped by the matrix which contains the imaginative energies at the moment of transition or translation. This method is radically different from the standard concepts of prayer, faith, or even of meditation, and is one of the true magical or esoteric 'secrets' handed down to us by our native tradition. An understanding of this pattern of human consciousness, this method of transformation, enabled the early Christian authorities to sink certain programmes of control very deeply into the group mind, by tapping the collective symbols and merely reconnecting them in a slightly, but deliberately, confused manner.

If, as genetic science informs us, there is a set of co-ordinates that defines the physical entity derived from our ancestors; if, as modern psychology suggests by vaguely plagiarizing the philosophy of the ancients, there is a deep fund of group or racial memory, how may we awaken this knowledge, wisdom and understanding, locked within our very cells and our hidden depths of consciousness? Might not the deep memories and the bodily pattern be one and the same thing?

Magical tradition avers that this is indeed the case, and offers a full and effective method for such an arousal.

Folk tradition supports this with accounts of certain persons who made trips to the otherworld while still in bodily form. Some of these returned as seers or seeresses, while others remain lost but not dead. One typical example of this class of magical disappearance is the Reverend Robert Kirk of Aberfoyle (1644–?), the first translator of the Bible into Gaelic, and collector of an early set of examples of fairy lore and the Second Sight. People were still attempting to rescue Kirk from fairyland only a generation ago, as the result of a local tradition that had continued for almost three hundred years.

Religious tradition offers us the example of Enoch, who walked with God and 'was not', and, more relevant to the Grail, the Roman Catholic belief in the physical ascent of the Virgin into Heaven.

Similar examples might be enumerated at great length, but their significance in our present context is that the belief was attached to historical persons, such as Kirk, Thomas of Erceldoune, and others within British or Celtic tradition. It is this demanding of literal physical manifestation (or perhaps we should say un-manifestation) that is close to the inmost heart of Western magic; this same deep intuition that the divine powers must flow through the body has led to popular misconceptions of the work of the alchemists, magicians and metaphysicians of past centuries. More subtly, it leads to the common complaint against 'magic', that the art does not work, for the experimenter had no physical results to be observed or experienced.

The demand that magic work upon the outer matrix or physical world is no mere puerile materialist plea; it runs ancient and deep, and is actually the result of our most potent collective intuition about apparent reality; that it can be changed.

Firm attempts to combine magical power, blood lines, and temporal power have frequently appeared in history, such as the foundation of The Order of the Garter, based upon Grail symbolism. Such organizations, dependent upon hierarchies of beings similar to those of the orthodox church, inevitably fail.

The true value of such traditions as those outlined briefly above lies in a full absorption of the symbolism, and its subsequent activation to create a revolutionary alteration of awareness. This revolution is not limited to politics, religion, or even personal mental activity, but runs through each and every aspect of the human entity, manifesting through the physical body, and transforming utterly. No hierarchical authority can exist or function against the blowing of the spirit.

One final suggestion, which seems inevitable, is that the subsequent destruction of the kingdom, in which Arthur and his knights are defeated after the quest, is the result of their seeking the Grail. That this destruction should arise through Arthur's own seed in the form of his magically inspired offspring of incest is hardly surprising, if we follow the concepts of genetic magic through carefully.

The willed pursuit of the power of the spirit brings breakdown and change (Matthew X:34), and in the earliest version of the Grail quest, the vessel was stolen from the Underworld, the realm of seething, ever changing energy. Unless this energy is contained by perfect balance and purity within the outer world, it will rotate according to cycles of creation and destruction, the only way in which its essential nature may be expressed in manifestation. This cyclical pattern of ancient lore repeats itself in the Grail legends, despite the higher order of Salvation offered by the Saviour.

We are promised, however, that Arthur is not dead, but merely sleeping or waiting within the otherworld for the correct time to return. Not wise, indeed, to seek the grave of any of our true kings, virgins or heroes, for they live on within each and every one of us, waiting to be aroused by the power of the spirit, the regeneration offered through The Holy Grail.

Notes

1 For those who seek academic cross references, such delights occur in abundance in the footnotes of any good research work upon medieval or traditional tales. For the present a short list of works is here appended. All have been used extensively in the preparation of this essay. P. Matarasso, *The Quest of The Holy Grail* (Harmondsworth: Penguin, 1969, translation). J. Cable, *The Death of King Arthur* (Harmondsworth: Penguin, 1971, translation). J. Gantz, *The Mabinogion* (Harmondsworth: Penguin, 1976, translation). Rev. C.C. Dobson, *Did Our Lord Visit Britain?* (London: Covenant, 1974). H. Jennings, *The Rosicrucians* (London: George Routledge, 1907). Rev. R. Kirk, *The Secret Commonwealth*, Sanderson

(ed.) (Cambridge, N.J.: Brewer/Rowman & Littlefield, 1976). A. & B. Rees, *Celtic Heritage* (London: Thames & Hudson, 1978). A. Ross, *Pagan Celtic Britain* (London: Cardinal, 1974). A. Ross, *Folklore of the Scottish Highlands* (London: Batsford, 1976). H.M. Porter, *The Celtic Church in Somerset* (Bath: Morgan, 1971). E. Pagels, *The Gnostic Gospels* (London: Weidenfeld & Nicolson, 1980). R. Steiner, *The Occult Significance of Blood* (London: Steiner Publishing Co.). G.R.S. Mead, *The Hymn of Jesus* (London: Watkins, 1963). L.C. Wimberley, *Folklore in the English and Scottish Ballads* (New York: Ungar, 1959).

2 Matarasso, op. cit., pp. 222–35. The position of this legend relative to the other material of *The Quest* is interesting, for it comes almost as a retrospective key to many of the events and relationships in the preceding adventures. In this key explanatory role, it prepares the reader for the revelations that are to follow.

~ 16 ~

Charles Williams and The Grail

John Matthews

Charles Williams was a poet, novelist, historian, biographer and theologian with equal skill and remarkable perception. He was also a long-time student of the Arthurian myths, who delved deeply into their origins and from there projected his own unique vision of the Grail. Through the medium of poetry, he produced two extraordinary volumes, Taliessin Through Logres *and* The Region of the Summer Stars, *which together form a cycle unequalled for its sensitivity and depth among any Arthurian or Grail text in the present age. Working from the thousand-and-one clues scattered throughout the literally hundreds of medieval re-tellings, Williams formed many new and exciting theories, which together gave a wholly new dimension into the matter of the Grail. Without his work, which deserves to be better known than at present, our view of the Grail would be very different, and so much the poorer.*

I

When Charles Walter Stansby Williams was born in London in 1886, William Morris was still living and had not long since written his *Defence of Guinevere*. The pre-Raphaelite School of painters and designers were still active, recreating, in their own unique terms, the world of Arthur and the Grail. It was a world that Williams was to make his own, both in what he wrote and in the way the myth interpenetrated his own life. He was to leave behind a legacy unique in Grail literature since the Middle Ages, and which changed the shape of the myth so profoundly that once one has encountered his work it is no longer possible to see the old stories in quite the same way again.

Williams worked for most of his life at the Oxford University Press, first in London and later in Oxford itself, where he came into contact with a group of writers who met regularly to discuss their work in progress. Known as the Inklings,[1] the most famous and influential members of the group were undoubtedly J.R.R. Tolkien, author of *The Lord of the Rings*, and C.S. Lewis, Christian apologist, critic and novelist. Charles Williams has not attained anything like the status of the above named, but his work has continued to attract attention and to find an increasingly enthusiastic readership.

Without doubt the majority of this readership comes from among students of the Arthurian legends, and of the Grail in particular; and although Williams wrote over 40 books, in the fields of fiction, criticism, theology, and history, as well as several brilliant and much neglected plays, it is the four titles in which he dealt with Arthur and the Grail which are most likely to survive.

These four books, in order of publication, are a novel, *War in Heaven*,[2] two volumes of poetry, *Taliessin Through Logres*,[3] and *The Region of the Summer Stars*,[4] and a posthumously published prose study of the Arthuriad entitled *The Figure of Arthur* which was edited, along with a commentary of the poetry, by C.S. Lewis as *Arthurian Torso*.[5] To these must be added an essay, 'Malory and the Grail Legend', originally published in *The Dublin Review* in 1944,[6] an early volume of poetry, *Heroes and Kings*,[7] in which many of the ideas developed in the later volumes first appeared, and several poems printed in William's *Three Plays*[8] in 1931.

But his first foray into the realm of the Grail comes in the novel, and we should begin by looking at this in detail, since it gives an in-depth idea of Williams's thinking at this point in time.

Williams wrote seven novels in all – he called them 'spiritual shockers' and dismissed them as money-spinners. But they are much more than that – in fact they are probably the finest examples of modern occult fiction to date, better written than either Dion Fortune or Dennis Wheatley, and more steeped in the reality of the inner worlds and higher powers. They are, in fact, commentaries on the action of magic and the supernatural in the everyday world.

Williams peoples his stories with everyday people, familiar objects and characters which have a *symbolic* reality – for example the policeman in his novel of the Tarot, *The Greater Trumps*,[9] who stands for Justice. In another novel, *The Place of the Lion*,[10] Platonic archetypes enter the world through a magical accident and are let loose to create havoc – their sheer reality is too much for our dimension, which is mere shadow compared to the huge aliveness of the dwellers in the archetypal realms. In *War in Heaven*, the Graal is the archetypal object found within the world. Its actions are the subject of the book, together with the struggle for its possession by the forces of good and evil.

The book begins memorably: 'The telephone bell was ringing wildly but without result, since there was no one in the room but the corpse.' This corpse is the beginning of a fantastic modern quest, undertaken by a publisher's clerk, an archdeacon of the Anglican Church and a member of the peerage, who each, in his own way, corresponds generally to the three most famous Grail knights – Galahad, Perceval and Bors.

We are introduced to these three in turn. First there is Kenneth Mornington, who works for the publisher in whose office the corpse is found. He is a pleasant enough chap, with a fine disregard for everything, no obvious religious beliefs and a rather superior manner. Yet he is nonetheless an essentially 'good' man, a lover of poetry and literature and a believer in the moral standards of the time (the novel is set in the 1930s). He is, perhaps, the Bors of the book.

The second member of the group is Julian Davanant, Archdeacon of Castra Parvelorum, the Camp of the Children, which has become more widely known as Fardles. He is a simple, almost saintly man, though with a very human sense of humour and a sharp eye for the darker side of human nature. He is given to singing little snatches of hymns of psalms aloud to himself – he is most clearly identified as Galahad.

The third member of the group is the Duke of the West Ridings, a staunch Catholic from an old family which numbers both the Norfolks and the Howards in its ancestors. He is also a poet and a deeply religious man – perhaps nearest to the figure of Perceval in Williams' scheme of things.

Ranged against this unlikely trio are three servants of the negative side of creation: Gregory Persimmons, a long-time practitioner of small evils, petty hateful things which have finally drawn him to become part of a greater evil. He seeks the left-hand path with a great willingness, desiring to become one with the God he worships, who is Satan, leader of all the hosts of darkness. He is the murderer of the man found in Kenneth Mornington's room at the start of the book, and he desires the Graal to use as a talisman of power to bind the soul of a child to his own perverted way.

Persimmons' associates are Manasseh, a Jew who is dedicated to the destruction of the Graal, and a mysterious Greek, Demitri Lavrodopolous, who is so far down the path of destruction that he has almost no human characteristics at all – he is simply an expression of the supreme negativity of evil, which desires nothing unless it be total absorption into the dark nothingness of Hell.

Each of this trio of anti-Graal figures represents to some extent Williams' depiction of evil. For him it was complex, intricate, convoluted; good was simple, direct, uncluttered – above all ordered. Order was the most central part of his hieratic world. As C.N. Manlove puts it in his book *The Impulse of Fantasy Literature*:[11]

> His vision of reality is of an ordered dance in which all things, from the most evil to the most good, and from the most magnificent to the most sordid, offer in their own modes delight to the beholder and praise to the Creator.

In *War in Heaven*, the balance between good and evil is maintained by the Graal itself, which is capable of being used to destroy as well as to create; in the hands of the 'good' people of the book it can heal and defeat the forces of darkness; in their hands it could, potentially, destroy everything.

After the discovery of the corpse in the publishing house the police declare themselves baffled. The murder seems totally motiveless, and there are no identifying marks either on the body or its clothing. But stranger things are afoot. By chance Kenneth Mornington makes the acquaintance of the Archdeacon, who has a book to offer for publication, and by chance when he visits the publishing house to discuss this with Kenneth, the Archdeacon happens to catch sight of a set of uncorrected proofs of a book called *Historical Vestiges of Sacred Vessels in Folklore* by Sir Giles Tumulty. In fact Tumulty is a friend of Gregory Persimmons, who also happens to own the publishing company. He is a thoroughly unpleasant man who has travelled the world and seen, and possibly been involved with, many strange and not always pleasant things. He has stumbled on the fact that in all probability the Graal is now kept in the Archdeacon's own church at Fardles. He has conveyed this fact to Gregory who has requested him to remove the reference from his book. By chance the Archdeacon sees a set of proofs which still have the passage. His thoughts about the Graal at this time are that it is unimportant, though undoubtedly interesting for the energies it may have absorbed from its use as the Cup of the Last Supper and for having received the blood of Christ after the Crucifixion.

Immediately after this, Persimmons himself, who has taken a large house close at hand, visits the rectory and tries unsuccessfully to buy the chalice from the Archdeacon. When this fails an attempt is made to steal it, causing the Archdeacon finally to believe there might be something more to the suggestion that the chalice is indeed the Graal.

Meanwhile, Persimmons visits a strange chemist's shop somewhere off the Finchley Road, where he encounters the Greek and purchases a strange ointment. That night he uses it to send him on a terrifying interior journey to meet his master. Williams' description, here as elsewhere, conveys a disturbingly real sense of what it actually feels like to work magic. (He was an active member of the Hermetic Order of the Golden Dawn for a number of years.) In this case it is a dark magic, and we are left in no doubt as to its effects or to the nature of the man working it.

Meanwhile, the Archdeacon, having decided that the chalice may indeed be the Graal, decides to take it to London, and to his Archbishop. Within sight of Fardles, however, he is knocked unconscious by Persimmons' chauffeur and the Graal is stolen.

Kenneth Mornington, having decided to take a walking holiday in the country and to call upon the Archdeacon on the way, encounters the Duke of North Ridings in a storm and the two arrive together at Fardles in time to hear of the Archdeacon's adventures. The police subsequently arrive, having been called to investigate the attack on the Archdeacon. He, reluctantly, tells of his suspicions and is even more reluctantly persuaded to go to Persimmons and confront him. Once there, events move fast. The Archdeacon, along with Mornington and the Duke, steal back the Graal and flee to London, where the cup is subjected to an occult attack and is successfully defended by the Graal's new guardians.

This latest attempt having failed, the enemy set about obtaining the Graal by other means. But a new character is now brought into the action, in the shape of a young man in grey, who appears without warning in Gregory Persimmons' garden and addresses him in such a way that it is clear that he knows what is afoot and that he is the Graal's true guardian.

Unshaken by this, Persimmons continues with his plan. He has invited to stay, in a cottage in the grounds, another employee of the publishing house named Lionel Rackstraw, together with his wife, Barbara, and their young son, Adrian. Gregory's desire is to use Barbara as a means of obtaining the Graal, and at the same time to steal Adrian in order to bind his soul to the ways of evil. He manages to inflict a small wound on Barbara Rackstraw's arm and anoints it with some of the evil ointment. Its effects on the innocent woman are as one would expect; faced with interior images of evil too subtle for her innocent nature, she appears to go mad.

Having taken charge of Adrian, Gregory attempts to use him as a medium to find out more concerning the young man in grey, but finds that he encounters a force greater and stranger than anything he knows.

Undeterred, Gregory suggests to Lionel that if the Graal were to be offered to a certain doctor he knows of (who is in fact the Jew Manasseh), a cure might be found for Barbara, and a desperate Lionel calls on the Archdeacon for help. He of course responds willingly, though not without grave doubts on the part of the Duke. In the end, another agency releases Barbara, though in the confusion of the moment the Archdeacon still gives Manasseh the Cup.

Meanwhile, Sir Giles, who is about to leave, having realized that all may not be going Persimmons' way, meets the young man in grey, who finally reveals his identity:

> I am Prester John, I am the Graal and the Keeper of the Graal. All enchantment has been stolen from me, and to me the vessel itself shall return.

In the outside world, a series of small clues have led the police investigating the murder of the man found in Mornington's office towards an unlikely suspect, the publisher Mr Gregory Persimmons. The police begin to close in on the chemist shop, where plans continue to pervert the Graal to evil use. At this juncture the Duke and Kenneth arrive on the scene, bent upon retrieving the Graal. They are unprepared for the strength of the evil face, and Kenneth dies in the attempt to win back the Cup. But other and higher matters are yet to come. The enemy themselves are scarcely aware that they are caught up in a greater struggle than that for the Graal – war in Heaven has indeed been joined ...

The police search now for the house where the chemist shop should be, but it has been hidden. The Archdeacon, called to the aid of his fellows and not knowing of Kenneth's death, is now held captive. A terrible fate awaits him as Gregory and his associates prepare to 'marry' his soul to that of the murdered man, whom Gregory had slain as an offering to his god. Then the police, still searching for the house in a strange fog, receive a surprise. For suddenly, the strange mist concealing the shop parts and Gregory emerges to give himself up for the murder.

How has this come about? The last two chapters of the book are required reading for all who wish to see Williams at his best and most powerful. They contain some of the most powerful descriptions of magical acts ever written. For, as the Archdeacon is about to be sacrificed, the young man in grey appears and overcomes all opposition. The forces of evil are utterly overthrown and the Archbishop, the Duke and the innocent Adrian are returned to their homes, together with the Graal.

Next day in the church of Castra Parvelorum the Archdeacon, the Duke, and Lionel Rackstraw and his family gather, there to perceive, each in his or her own way, the Higher Mysteries once perceived by Galahad, Perceval and Bors in the Holy City of Sarras, which we see now is also the Kingdom of Prester John. Here the Final Things take place, as the Priest King (who is also in some senses Christ) celebrates the Mass of the Graal.

> He stood; He moved His hands. As if in benediction He moved them, and at once the golden halo that had hung all this while over the Graal dissolved and dilated into spreading colour; and at once life leapt in all those who watched and filled and flooded and exalted them. 'Let us make man,' he said, 'in Our image, after Our likeness,' and all the church of visible and invisible presences answered with a roar: 'In the image of God created He him: male and female created He them.' All things began again to be. At a great distance Lionel and Barbara and the Duke saw beyond Him, as he lifted up the Graal, the moving universe of stars, and then one flying planet, and then fields and rooms and a thousand remembered places, and all in light and darkness and peace.

Heroes and Kings appeared in the same year as *War in Heaven*, showing that Williams had already advanced far upon the path to the Grail even though his poetic establishment of it had still some way to go. These poems display the strengths and weaknesses of Williams' early writings – the rhythms are less sure and the verse style is still that of the Georgian school of the 1920s rather than the harder, more sinewy line which he developed later on, but the sense of the numinous is already present. It is, however, to the later works that we must turn for a full appreciation of Williams' work on the Arthur myth.

II

Williams' poems are often described as difficult, and, to be sure, they are not light reading. However, most of the complexities disappear once a working knowledge of the underlying story is arrived at. C.S. Lewis's commentary is invaluable, as are the various (sadly, fragmentary) clues scattered throughout Williams' own writings.[12]

Lewis gives a list of the poems in the order which he believes they should be read in order to best understand the structure of the cycle:

From *The Region*:	The Calling of Taliessin
From *Taliessin*:	The Calling of Arthur
	The Vision of the Empire
	Taliessin's Return to Logres
	Mount Badon
	The Crowning of Arthur
	Taliessin's Song of the Unicorn
	Bors to Elayne: the Fish of Broceliande
	Taliessin in the School of the Poets
	Taliessin on the Death of Virgil
	Lamorack and the Queen Morgause of Orkney
	Bors to Elayne: on the King's Coins
	The Star of Percevale
	The Ascent of the Spear
	The Sister of Percevale
From *The Region*:	The Founding of the Company
	Taliessin in the Rose Garden
	The Departure of Dindrane
	The Queen's Servant
From *Taliessin*:	The Son of Lancelot
	Palomides Before His Christening
	The Coming of Galahad
	The Departure of Merlin
	The Death of Palomides
	Perceval at Carbonek
From *The Region*:	The Son of Lancelot
From *Taliessin*:	The Last Voyage
From *The Region*:	The Prayers of the Pope
From *Taliessin*:	Taliessin at Lancelot's Mass[13]

This gives an idea of the richness and detail of the work, which will bear more than one such rearrangement of material. Williams' own statement, in the preface to *The Region of the Summer Stars*, states the 'argument' of the work as clearly as one could wish.

> The Theme is what was anciently called the Matter of Britain; that is, the reign of King Arthur in Logres and the Achievement of the Grail. Logres is Britain regarded as a province of the Empire with its centre at Byzantium. The time historically is after the conversion of the Empire to Christianity but during the expectation of the Return of Our Lord (the Parousia). The Emperor of the poem, however, is to be regarded rather as operative Providence. On the south-western side of Logres lies the region of Broceliande, in which is Carbonek where the Grail and other Hallows are in the keeping of King Pelles and his daughter Helayne. Beyond the seas of Broceliande is the holy state of Sarras. In the antipodean seas is the opposite and infernal state P'o-l'u.

Another quotation, from *The Figure of Arthur*, might stand as an introduction to the whole of the work as it would have existed if William had lived to complete it.

> [The] theme is the coming of two myths, the Myth of Arthur and the Myth of the Grail; of their union; and of the development of that union.[14]

We should realize at the outset that for Williams the Grail was, beyond question, a Christian myth. It may have subsumed elements from Celtic story and oriental symbolism,[15] but the essential story 'came from, and with Christ, and it came with and from no one else'.[16] This is an extreme view and one which many scholars would question, but it sets Williams's Grail myth firmly in context. He intended it to serve as a paradigm of the union of Christianity with the civilization of the West – Hellenic, Roman, Indo-European.

For Williams the way of the Grail was made straight by the complexities of doctrinal argument throughout the period immediately before and during the growth of the Grail in literature. The attempt to define the doctrine of the Blessed Sacrament, culminating in the Doctrine of Transubstantiation, whereby the species of Bread and Wine used at the Mass were said to contain the actual body and blood of Christ, is central to the manifestation of the Grail in the medieval world as Charles Williams saw it.

Another essential set of keys to an understanding of Williams' Arthurian works is a knowledge of certain symbols and characters which run throughout the entire cycle. The most important of these is the Forest of Broceliande, in which it could be said that most of the events described take place. Williams himself described it in *The Figure of Arthur* as a Western forest which 'was to expand on all sides until presently it seemed as if Camelot and Caerleon and even Carbonek were both temporary clearings within it'.[17]

It lies to the West of the Arthurian kingdom of Logres, with its feet in the sea and touching the terrible land of P'o-L'u, Williams' image of Hell, where the 'Headless Emperor' walks in a place where land and sea, forest and water merge.

The second important aspect of Williams' vision is centred not in an abstract symbol but in the figure of Taliessin, the King's poet, who is called to visit first of all Byzantium, where he has a vision of the future and is sent back to Logres-in-Britain in search of the great events to come.

The bard Taliessin (or, as he is more usually spelled, Taliesin) is known to have lived in sixth-century Wales, and thus to have been more or less contemporary with the historical figure of Arthur. He left behind a body of extraordinary lapidary verse which has only recently begun to be properly understood.[18] There is no doubt that his writings influenced Williams in a remarkable way, for although the latter eschews the Celtic element within the Grail myth, images such as 'the Region of the Summer Stars' are taken directly from the work of the Welsh bard – albeit transformed.

In the opening poem Arthur defeats the opposing forces which threaten his new, young kingdom, concentrated into the figure of King Cradlemas, one-eyed and leering, in 'a mask o'ergilded' which covers 'his wrinkled face'. The kingdom is established and the Round Table Fellowship, the 'household of Arthur' comes into being.

An important aspect of Williams' symbolism is that of the human body, which is equated with the landscape of the poems throughout the later part of the cycle. The endpapers to the original edition of *Taliessin Through Logres* depict the naked body of a woman superimposed upon the map of the Western world. The head is Logres, the breasts are at Paris, giving the 'milk of learning'; the hands are at Rome, signifying those of the Pope dispensing blessing; the navel is Byzantium, the centre of the Empire; while the loins, which generate life, are at

Jerusalem, the buttocks are at Caucasia, and the feet rest on or in the anti-realm of P'o-L'u. The importance of this plan is that it enables Williams to relate the various zones within the forest to the events taking place both at Camelot and Carbonek, cities at once of chivalry and of the Grail.

The unified Catholic world of the Emperor lies East of Logres; West is Broceliande, the Forest of potentialities. Here Nimuë (Nature) lives and rules through her children Merlin (Time) and Brisen (Space), who perform a magical operation to bring about the foundation of the Kingdom of the Grail. In effect they seek to unify Carbonek (the Grail) with Byzantium (the Emperor) in Camelot (Arthur). Britain (or Logres) is an important part of the Empire, its foundation resting upon Byzantium in the East and Rome, the place of the Pope, in the West. These two points control the rest, seeking an 'organic whole', of which Logres represents the head, where will come about the 'union' of mind and spirit.

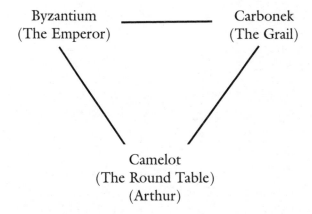

Byzantium   Carbonek
(The Emperor)   (The Grail)

Camelot
(The Round Table)
(Arthur)

If the plan had been successfully carried out, and all the perfections of the kingdom been established as the great powers intended, the intention then was that

> ... the King Pelles, the Keeper of the Hallows, was at the proper time, when Merlin had brought Arthur into his royalty and Logres had been cleared and established, to emerge from Carbonek into Logres ... [as] the prelude of the Second Coming. Logres was to be blessed thus, and he who said Mass in Sarras would say it in Caerleon and Camelot as he did in Jerusalem.[19]

Within Broceliande lies the Wounded King. He receives his hurt from the pagan knight Balm le Sauvage, who rides in search of vengeance. In the castle of Carbonek he seizes the Spear which wounded Christ on the Cross and strikes a blow in self-defence which brings about the wound which will not heal and the Waste Land which surrounds the place of the Grail until the Quest is achieved. The Dolorous Blow, as this is called, becomes for Williams the image of the Fall, and is followed by Balin's death at the hands of his own brother, the coming of the Waste Lands, and, somewhere, the beginning of the Quest.

> Balin the Savage in ignorance kills his own brother Balan, and Balan him. The natural pieties begin to be lost, and there is incivility in the blood. It is in fact the further externalization of the Wounded King. But the disorder spreads further. In the first tales Mordred was the king's nephew, in later versions he became the King's son by incest, but unknown incest. The Queen Morgause of Orkney, the wife of King Lot, was Arthur's sister. But he does not know this when she comes to the court, and he tempts her to lie with him. The birth of that incestuous union is Mordred, and the fate of the Round Table comes into the world almost before the Table has been established … (AT 86)[20]

From here on the pattern is set. Arthur must choose between power (the Kingdom) and spiritual love (the Grail). He chooses power. Lancelot, on the other hand, must choose between carnal love (Guinevere) and the Grail. He chooses the Queen. Arthur becomes, as nearly always in the myth, passive; while Lancelot, his soul's twin, becomes active both in his love of the Queen and the power he exercises on behalf of the Round Table. Guinevere herself fails to represent fully 'the glory [of herself] to the Women of Logres' (Rose Garden) and instead, as Williams puts it, has nothing to do but 'sit and work at embroideries and love'. She is contrasted unfavourably with Dindrane, Perceval's sister, who gives her blood for the healing of another, while at best Guinevere can only rise to the level of remarking to Taliessin, in 'The Poet in the Rose Garden', 'Has my lord dallied with poetry among the roses?'

Dindrane indeed is Taliessin's great love – though we would suppose hopeless since he says of himself 'no woman would wish to bed me'. Dindrane is Williams' ideal of womanhood: saintly yet human, an almost Beatrician figure who is alone permitted the grace of being buried in Sarras, the Land of the Trinity and the place of the Grail. Williams conflates her with the usually unnamed sister of Perceval, and

Blanchfleur, the Woman of the Tent, with whom Perceval falls in love in Chrétien de Troyes *Conte del Graal* (see Paxson).

Williams' use of the three knights, Galahad, Perceval and Bors, to show three very different approaches towards wholeness is fascinating. Galahad is made for his task, but both Perceval and Bors have to struggle on the long journey from the temporal to the spiritual order. The Quest...

> is the tale of the mystical way; but it is also the tale of the universal way ...
> Bors is in the chapel at Sarras as well as Galahad and Perceval. This is what
> relates the Achievement to every man. The tale must end, and that part of it
> when the holy thing returns again to earth – when Galahad is effectually in
> Bors as Bors is implicitly in Galahad – cannot be told until the cause of the
> Lord's Prayer is fulfilled and the kingdom of heaven is come upon earth ...[21]

The union of opposites, which is one of the themes most consistently dealt with by Williams, takes place within the Grail. There, Galahad and Bors 'exchange places' and act out each other's roles and experiences. Finally, the Grail can only manifest through the intermediary of the Atonement, which Christ enacted for all men. Galahad, as a type of Christ, brings the Grail into manifestation and takes it back out again, leaving the way open for others as yet unborn who will one day set out upon the Quest. Thus Williams hints that Galahad is indeed a manifestation of the Parousia, the Second Coming, mentioned in the introduction to the poems.

Behind this lies Williams' idea of 'co-inherence'. It implies, simply, that all things in creation, no matter how large or small, are intimately connected, so that no single act can take place which does not have its concomitant effect elsewhere. Thus the acts of the Emperor, or the Pope, are what holds the Empire together in a kind of temporal stability – a stability which is broken when the Round Table and the realm of Logres is 'broken' by internal strife, the head no longer knowing what the hands are doing, acting in estrangement from the laws of the heart.

The second important theme, and an extension of the first, is that of 'exchange', which is defined as the ability of all created beings to take upon themselves responsibility for the lives and deaths of each other. The Incarnation of Christ is the prime example of this. Christ 'exchanges' the love of God for Man, and of Man for God through the act of the Crucifixion and the Resurrection, of which the Grail is an outward symbol. As the Archdeacon in *War in Heaven* notes, the Grail 'had been nearest the Divine and Universal heart'.

In the re-worked myth, the coming of Galahad is a supreme example of the way of Exchange. Even as early as the poems contained in *Heroes and Kings* we find this theme expressed in a poem entitled '*The Song of the Riding of Galahad*', in which the Grail knight speaks of his coming to the court of Camelot, and of his parentage.

Though I be in great fame
Who hath called me by name?
Though I sit at the Table Round
Who hath seen me or found?
What Bishop or King or Knight
Hath spoken of me right?
Though I be greatly styled
The Champion, the Merciful Childe,
The High Prince Dom Galahad,
Yet most shall they be glad
That none have at all forgot
I am also Lancelot.
I am no faery's son,
No ghastly myrmidon
Loosed from the thick profound
Shadows of underground
Wherein Apollyon roars,
Nor cherub from the doors
Of heavenly beauty sent
To herald God's advent,
Not elemental Knight
Made human but to right:
I am all men, I wot,
And born of Lancelot.

For my lord Sir Lancelot
In a marvel me begot
On my mother the lady Helayne,
Whom, our fair Christ did ordain
For a covering and a shrine
For the body that is mine:
From his joy and agony
Then I began to be,
His love being a fair thing
Had holy assoiling

By the heaven's council and plot
I also am Lancelot ...[22]

Already the importance of Galahad's relationship to his father is established. This was to remain a central image of Williams' work. He wrote of it again in *The Descent of the Dove: A Short History of the Holy Spirit in the Church.*[23]

> There was built up, in the romances called the *Lancelot* and the *Queste del Saint Graal*, a world of chivalry and love in order to be overthrown by the creation of another world of religion, contrition, and sanctity; and as in that world the Grail shone defined, the same and yet (in effect) other than the Eucharist, so in proportion to its pure glory Lancelot was barred from achieving it. But by what has been one of the greatest moments of imagination ever permitted to man, he was allowed and compelled, in an enchantment and supposing himself to be with the queen, to beget upon the predestined mother the shape of the High Prince.

Thus the 'sin' of Lancelot and Guinevere is transformed, 'exchanged' into good. Galahad comes. The Quest begins. And Taliessin, standing outside the castle sees:

> ... through the unshuttered openings of stairs and rooms the red flares of processional torches and candles winding to the king's bed; where instead of Arthur Galahad that night should lie, Helayne's son instead of the king's, Lancelot's instead of Guinevere's ...[24]

Here an entire complex of themes is brought together. Galahad should have been Arthur's and Guinevere's son; instead he is the product of Lancelot's obsession with the Queen, which is caused to bring about the creation of Galahad. Thus do Merlin and Nimuë prepare for the possibility of failure in the perfect kingdom they have helped establish, arranging the begetting of Galahad who, even though the rest fail, will bring about his own apotheosis and move beyond – perhaps, like Christ, experiencing the joy of the Grail for the sake of all. (Thus in Williams' version the final achievement takes place as Arthur prepares for battle with Mordred. The dream of the kingdom is over, but the dream of the Grail continues.)

We see only fragmentary glimpses of the quest from here on. Through the experiences of the quest knights we watch the development of the myth, remaking some, all but destroying others.

In the end, Logres, the ideal world devised by Merlin and Brisen, fails. Lancelot and Guinevere are discovered, Arthur banishes his greatest knight and condemns the Queen to the stake. In the inevitable rescue operation Lancelot accidentally kills two of Gawain's brothers, setting in motion a vendetta which culminates in Arthur following him to France and making war upon him. Meanwhile, Mordred dreams of taking power from his father and thinks of the Grail that he needs no such 'faery mechanisms' and that if it existed he would send a dozen of his knights to destroy it. Once his father is away he overthrows the kingdom and declares himself king. It is a victory for the anti-Grail powers, and the Pope, awaiting good news from the West, hears only

> ... of bleak wars between Arthur and Lancelot.
> Gawain set to seek his heart's vengeance,
> The king's son gone whoring with fantasies,
> and mobs roaring through Camelot ...[25]

Williams' theme of the unification of the ideals of Christianity with those of civilization proves to be unattainable in Arthur's Logres, which slips back to 'mere Britain'. Charles Moorman, in his valuable study of Williams' Arthuriad, sums up:

> ... this order is constantly frustrated by man's desire for self-sufficiency and independence. The main theme of the cycle thus becomes the battle between order and charity and cupidity, love and pride, exchange and possession.[26]

Charles Williams was a remarkable man by any standards. It was not enough for him to recreate the myths of Arthur and the Grail in written form. He wished to bring the insights he possessed into the spiritual lives of his characters to the world of everyday existence. To this end he formed 'The Company of the Co-inherence', made up of friends and colleagues. He saw Sir Humphrey Milford, the then head of Oxford University Press, very much as he saw Arthur in the myth. Others were allotted other parts. He himself seems to have identified with Taliessin. Lois Lang-Sims, in *Letters to Lalarge*, her as yet unpublished account of her friendship with Williams, describes the way in which this worked, and describes him as 'a writer so passionately and personally involved in his own thought-world, even to the extent of manipulating his friends into fulfilling the roles created for them in his private myth'.[27]

Alice Mary Hadfield, who worked with Williams at the Oxford University Press, notes also that his office life 'was always on the point of becoming the opening of one of his own novels. Every morning when I went to work I had a fluttering feeling that it might happen, and although my office was on the floor below I would make sure I got into the plot.'[28]

In his *The Descent of the Dove*, which is dedicated to 'The Companions of the Co-inherence', appears the passage quoted on p. 235 of this book. It shows the depths of the idea as it permeated all of Williams' life and work. This extraordinary sense of identification with the spiritual realities represented by the Arthurian characters, as by real people, are what gives Williams' work such power and immediacy. There is a constant sense of urgency behind all that he wrote, as though he indeed awaited the Second Coming at every moment (as perhaps he did in truth). For him the myth of the Grail was a reality which transcended the world of form. Of all the multitude of modern writers on the subject he perhaps more than any has re-shaped the myth in which the Grail resides, making it different for all who come after. As his work becomes gradually better known, its influence will certainly be keenly felt in the lives of those who still seek the wholeness implicit within the stories of the divine vessel.

Notes and References

1 Humphrey Carpenter, *The Inklings* (London: Allen & Unwin, 1978).
2 Charles Williams, *War in Heaven* (London: Gollancz, 1930).
3 —— *Taliessin Through Logres* (Oxford Univ. Press, 1938).
4 —— *Region of the Summer Stars* (Oxford Univ. Press, 1944).
5 C.S. Lewis, 'The Figure of Arthur' in *Arthurian Torso* (Oxford Univ. Press, 1948).
6 Charles Williams, 'Malory and the Grail Legend' in *Dublin Review*, April 1944.
7 —— *Heroes and Kings* (The Sylvan Press, 1930).
8 —— *Three Plays* (Oxford Univ. Press, 1931).
9 —— *The Greater Trumps* (London: Gollancz, 1932).
10 —— *The Place of the Lion* (London Gollancz, 1931).
11 C.M. Manlove, *The Impulse of Fantasy Literature*.

12 Charles Williams, *The Image of the City and Other Essays*, ed. Anne Ridler (Oxford Univ. Press, 1958).

13 C.S. Lewis, *The Arthurian Torso* (Oxford Univ. Press, 1948).

14 Ibid.

15 John Matthews, *Elements of the Grail Tradition* (Shaftesbury: Element Books, 1990).

16 Lewis, *The Arthurian Torso*.

17 Ibid.

18 John Matthews, *Taliesin: Shamanic Mysteries in Britain & Ireland* (London: Unwin Hyman, 1990).

19 Lewis, *The Arthurian Torso*.

20 Ibid.

21 Ibid.

22 Williams, *Heroes and Kings*.

23 —— *The Descent of the Dove* (London: Faber & Faber, 1939).

24 —— *Taliessin Through Logres*.

25 —— *The Region of the Summer Stars*.

26 Charles Moorman, *Arthurian Triptych* (Russell & Russell, 1960).

27 Lois Lang-Sims, *Letters to Lalage: A Correspondence with Charles Williams* (unpublished MS).

28 Alice Hadfield, 'The Relationship of Charles Williams' Working Life to his Fiction', in *Shadows of Imagination*, ed. M.R. Hillegas (Southern Illinois Univ. Press, 1969).

17

Joseph Campbell and The Grail Myth

Jules Cashford

Joseph Campbell was arguably the greatest mythographer of our age. In seminal works such as Hero With a Thousand Faces, Masks of God *and the best-selling* Power of Myth, *based on the hugely successful TV series of the same name, which had audiences in the USA glued to their TV sets over the six weeks of its screening in 1987, Campbell reawoke a latent fascination with the subject which has been present in mankind from the earliest times. Throughout his life he 'followed the bliss' of his innermost dreams much as the Grail knights followed their obsession. He brought fresh and illuminating insights to the myth which have opened it up for a fresh generation of students. His influence has reached far, even into Hollywood, where the director of the* Star Wars *trilogy drew heavily on the* Hero With a Thousand Faces *for the overall shape of his epic. No better contender could be found to end this collection, for if any man could be called one of the Household of the Grail, Joseph Campbell is he.*

For Joseph Campbell, the Grail myth was the beginning of Europe. The unprecedented sense of yearning and striving towards an unknown end, not knowing what to look for or how to look for it, while at the same time believing that whatever is to be discovered must be found inside the seeker's own heart – this inaugurated the characteristically Western living of life which we inherit. The age-old theme of the quest had now turned irrevocably inwards; the inspiration, motive, direction and guide are for the first time wholly individual and utterly unique. There is no authorized way or teacher to be followed, for all ways already found, known and proven, are wrong ways, since they are not the person's own.

In the thirteenth-century legend *La Queste del Saint Graal*, when the vision of the veiled Grail appears to the knights in Arthur's banquet hail to summon them each to their quest of unveiling it, the knights decide to ride forth singly, for to go in a group would have been shameful. This is the point which Campbell – the greatest mythologist of this century – holds up as testimony to a new moral initiative that is of the essence of European spirituality. When all the knights had put on their arms, attended Mass and expressed their gratitude to their king, they 'entered into the forest, at one point and another, there where they saw it to be thickest, *all in those places where they found no way or path ...*' (his italics) (CM, 540). So they start their journey as individuals, each trusting to their own authority and to the mysterious power of their calling. As it transpired, though, in this story written by a Cistercian monk, there was finally only one way to be followed, the 'straight path to Paradise', and so the orthodox Christian opposition of the spiritual and the physical worlds – the world of God distinct from the world of nature – remained unchallenged. The Grail is revealed as a symbol of a supernatural grace dispensed by way of sacraments, not a blessing upon the choice and persistence in the dark and lonely path.

Wolfram von Eschenbach's *Parzival* was the book which inspired Campbell beyond all the other stories of the Grail. For him it was not only the greatest book of the Middle Ages, beyond even Dante, but also 'the first sheerly individualistic mythology of the human race'. (CM, 553) It is Wolfram's achievement to have taken a Christian symbol – with all the customary associations of an historical and literal interpretation – and to have opened it out to its universal and psychological meaning, so becoming the first example in world literature of a consciously developed secular Christian myth. (CM, 476)

The crowning moment is Parzival's failure. He honours the code and he dishonours his heart, and thus a new ethic is disclosed. As Campbell tells the tale in his book *Creative Mythology* (the last of four volumes of his monumental work *The Masks of God*), Parzival is the one figure through whom this crucial distinction between individual and collective can be worked out. Like the meaning of his name 'right through the middle', he is destined to get to the centre of things. For he has been brought up in the country by a mother, disillusioned of the court, who wanted her son to know nothing of its elaborate rules and codes of conduct. His life is lived in terms of the dynamic of his own natural impulses, and when he first sees three knights riding by on their prancing horses he falls to the ground on his knees imagining they are angels. Then he received teaching from the knight Gurnemanz – never to lose the sense of shame, to be compassionate to the needy, not to ask too many questions, and so on – and when he has mastered these the prince then offers him his daughter in marriage. But Parzival says, 'No, I must earn a wife, not be given a wife,' passing the first spiritual test of both Wolfram and Campbell.

Having later earned his true bride, whom he loves, he rides to the next test a married man, and is eventually conducted to the Castle of the Grail. There he sees the Grail resting on its deep green cloth of gold-threaded silk and he shares the cup of its infinite sweetness with his suffering and melancholy host who, resting on a litter unable to sit or stand or lie, tells him God has maimed him. And Parzival thought, remembering Gurnemanz: 'He counselled me, in sincerity and truth, not to ask too many questions.'

'For that I pity him,' Wolfram comments, 'and I pity too his sweet host, whom divine displeasure does not spare, when a mere question would have set him free.' (CM, 446)

Parzival's fault was not to act on his impulse of compassion. He was moved to ask, 'What ails you, Uncle?' But he quells his spontaneous moment of sympathy, the natural opening of the human heart to another human being, believing it to be more important to obey the rule of courteous restraint given to him by his teacher who had helped him come this far. Yet his question was an expression of compassion, and as a truly individual human feeling could not fall under any general notion of society. It was not curiosity – 'another' question – not one of 'too many'; it was *the* Question, his question.

Parzival does not fully understand what he has done wrong until, poised for the glory of acceptance at the Round Table of King Arthur, the summit and consummation of knightly virtue, he is shamed before the meal begins by the dog-nosed, boar-tusked Cundrie, who curses him for his empty heart. She shames him because, Campbell explains, she is the messenger of a deeper sphere of values and possibilities than was yet sensed or understood by his socially conscious mind, but which, in the dreamlike, visionary image of the Castle of the Grail, had appeared to him as the first sign of a kingdom still to be earned, beyond the sphere of the world's flattery, proper to his own unfolding life. (CM, 454) It was his own inward knowledge, but he did not yet know it. Parzival takes up Cundrie's challenge: 'I am resolved to know no joy until I have seen again the Grail,' he declares, in defiance now of the rule that proclaims there are no second chances. Then, in answer to Gawain's gentle wish that God would give him good fortune in battle, he makes this momentous reply:

> Alas, what is God? Were He great, He would not have heaped undeserved disgrace on us both. I was in his service, expecting His grace. But I now renounce Him and His service. If He hates me, I shall bear that. Good friend, when your own time comes for battle, let a woman be your shield. (CM, 452)

Parzival's denunciation of God, or of what he takes to be God – the god-image 'up there' reported by his mother and the knightly code – marks, Campbell says, 'a deep break in the spiritual life not only of this Christian hero, as a necessary prelude to his healing of the Maimed King and assumption of the role without inheriting the wound, but also of the Gothic age itself and thereby Western man.' (CM. 452) For Parzival has now to confront directly the void without and within, where, as Nietzsche tells, the dragon of 'Thou Shalt' is to be slain. By saying No to the social, collective morality, and No to the image he takes to be God, he casts himself into the wilderness where he wanders desolate for five years, but in so doing he frees his own authentic experience, since that has become the only thing and everything he has.

Only the Grail can redeem the Wasteland, yet what is the Wasteland but the absence of the Grail? Before this, Parzival lived in the Wasteland, but did not suffer it; now he experiences the anguish of that life and so takes on symbolically the wound of the Grail king whose maiming is the expression of the Wasteland. For only when Parzival has healed himself will he be able to heal Anfortas and take upon himself the role of king. But what is the Wasteland? For Campbell it is simply the inauthentic life, a state of being which is barren of the truth of who you are. Wolfram could see it all around him in the twelfth century, but it belongs to any age or person who lives a life handed down by society and does not take up the challenge of his or her own destiny. In practice, this means that you put what (you think) is expected or required of you (the social 'ought') before the impulse of your own heart, wherever it may lead. This is exactly parallel to Jung's radical distinction between the individual and the collective life, which is the life you inherit – the ideals, beliefs, perspectives – you have not yet made your own. The appeal of the collective sensibility is clear with Parzival: why should he be blamed, he protests, when he only behaved courteously, as any true knight would? And in Wolfram's ironic aside, he had indeed been 'true to the dictates of good breeding'. But the often beguilingly reasonable claims of the society are never valid, Campbell insists. To be persuaded that they are is the third temptation of the Buddha – 'Perform your Duty to Society'. Your duty to society is no good, he persists, unless it is you. First, you have to be an individual, and it takes a hero to be one.

In 1949, Campbell wrote a book called *The Hero with a Thousand Faces*, which is a book not just to learn from but one which lives and grows as the reader's own understanding of its meaning and implications deepens. There, the world of myth comes brilliantly alive:

> Throughout the inhabited world, in all times and under every circumstance, the myths of man have flourished; and they have been the living inspiration of whatever else may have appeared out of the activities of the human body and mind. It would not be too much to say that myth is the secret opening through which the inexhaustible energies of the cosmos pour into human cultural manifestation. (H, 3)

The images and symbols of mythology are not, therefore, manufactured; they are natural phenomena, born out of and rooted in the human imagination.

> They cannot be ordered, invented, or permanently suppressed. They are spontaneous productions of the psyche, and each bears within it, undamaged, the germ power of its source. (H, 4).

How, then, are the images of myth different from the images of a dream?

> Dream is the personalized myth, myth the depersonalized dream; both myth and dream are symbolic in the same general way of the dynamics of the psyche. But in the dream the forms are quirked by the peculiar troubles of the dreamer, whereas in myth the problems and solutions shown are directly valid for all mankind. (H, 19)

The essential drama of mythology is the visionary quest which is the myth of the hero. The particular function of the hero myth is to carry the human spirit forward, offering the model and guide by means of which people may be assisted across 'those difficult thresholds of transformation that demand a change in the patterns not only of conscious but also of unconscious life.' (H, 10) For while the passage of the mythological hero may be overground, incidentally:

> Fundamentally it is inward – into depths where obscure resistances are overcome, and long lost forgotten powers are revivified, to be made available for the transfiguration of the world. (H, 29)

All heroes follow a characteristic path. Whether Prometheus, Jason, Theseus, Odysseus, Aeneas, the Buddha, Jesus or Parzival, they all fall into the same pattern of *Separation-Initiation-Return*. The first task of the hero is to turn away from his society – the false, restrictive consciousness entranced with the infinitely various and bewildering spectacle of phenomena. So, dying to the world, he must venture bravely forth into the lonely realm of night – the belly of the whale, the underworld, the descent to hell – a region, typically, of supernatural wonder where fabulous forces are encountered. Suffering first the trials and then the victories of initiation, often with the unsuspected assistance that comes to one who has undertaken his proper adventure, the hero is reborn into his own true nature, and thereby into the nature of the wonder of being. Finally, he returns once again to the society he had originally to leave behind, bearing now his gift of a vision transformed.

Campbell calls Parzival the Grail Hero, and here his immense range of study into the mythologies of the world allows him to discern the universal dimension within the specific cultural ideas of medieval Europe. It was essential, he taught, to distinguish the 'ethnic' or 'folk ideas' of a particular time and place from the 'elementary ideas', (in Bastian's term), or the 'archetypes of the collective unconscious', (in Jung's term), which are the mythic motifs common to all human beings. For a recognition of the two aspects, a universal and a local, in the constitution of sacred stories everywhere – whether called myths, religion, literature, or even history – prevents the fruitless debate on which one is 'right'. Mythology, he declares, 'is psychology, misread as biology, history, cosmology.' (H, 256)

Parzival's separation from Arthur's Court and his refusal of the courtly God marks, then, the first stage of the hero's solitary journey to fulfilment, that lonely dangerous quest, which is the only way to an individual life. As a boy, he was first 'called' away from his childhood by the knightly messengers – 'angels', as he thought. Later, a knight himself, after his loving marriage to Condwiramurs and his unwitting visit to the Castle of the Grail, he was ritually conducted to Arthur's Table by the gentlest knight of all, Gawain, the only one who understands his gazing at the drops of blood upon the ground to be the trance of love. The second messenger who summons him, this time away from the rewards of his worldly goal, and sets him irrevocably on the inward, visionary quest, is no angel of light but the dark apparition of the Loathly Damsel, Cundrie, richly arrayed and ugly as a hog.

The Loathly Damsel or Ugly Bride is a familiar figure in Celtic legend and fairy-tale, a maiden who is seen as ugly by the wicked and as fair by the good, and whom a loving kiss can transform from ugly to beautiful in an instant. (Compare the Russian tale of the Toad Bride, *Beauty and the Beast*, and also the play on this motif by Papagena in Mozart's *The Magic Flute*.) In the Celtic folk-tale, this mythic figure appears as the daughter of the King of the Land of Youth, who was cursed with the head of a pig, but, when boldly kissed, became beautiful and granted her saviour the kingship of her timeless realm. Here, buried in the image of Cundrie's boar tusks, is a vital clue to the nature of the Kingdom of the Grail, and one, furthermore, that would most likely be overlooked without the kind of mythic reach that Campbell offers. For, he argues, the Kingdom of the Grail is such a land as is suggested by this image: 'To be achieved only by one capable of transcending the painted wall of space-time with its foul and fair, good and evil, true and false display of the names and forms of merely phenomenal pairs of opposites.' (CM, 455) Consequently, the image prepares us for a passage beyond the known bounds and forms of space, time and causality to a domain of vision, where time and eternity are at one: in Parzival's case, the Grail Castle, and in Gawain's – summoned at the same time, as though they were soul brothers – the enchanted Château Merveil.

Entering, then, the Wasteland of their own disoriented lives, the next stage of trial begins in the enchanted underworld, and here the story passes to Gawain who, having lifted the spell on the enchanted castle, then meets the Lady Orgeluse, sitting by a spring. Seeing in her the reflection of the moving principle of his life, his lifelong service to love in general is irreversibly transformed into a service to that particular love. His spiritual test is now to hold to that *one* experience in loyalty and love beyond both fear and desire for distraction, the model already established in the Buddha's holding to the 'immovable point' beneath the Bodhi Tree, which neither fear nor desire could move. Again, the mythic resonance is necessary to transform our perception of the image: 'The sense of such a female by a spring is of an apparition of the abyss: psychologically, the unconscious; mythologically, the Land below Waves, Hell, Purgatory or Heaven. She is a portion of oneself, one's destiny.' (CM, 489) The larger point being made here, and one which is essential to an understanding of the meaning of the Grail, is that 'initiations transpire through the revelations of chance, according to the readiness of the psyche.' (CM 484) Campbell frequently refers to James Joyce's *Ulysses* as a parallel contemporary myth, comparing Stephen Dedalus and Parzival as the solitary introverts moved by a sense of purpose, and Bloom and Gawain as love-questing extroverts. So similarly, Joyce writes of Dedalus: 'He found in the world without as actual what was in his world within as possible.' (CM 197) Since, in the case of both Gawain and Parzival, their trials were proper to their own lives, they were consequently their match. And so the second heroic stage of Initiation was achieved.

What then, finally, is the Holy Grail? Campbell did not leave the symbol vague and general, in the bafflingly opaque terms of the cup of transformation which would grant eternal life. In all the Grail stories, the Grail is the supreme spiritual value, but which one? Since, also, 'it is a law of symbolic life that the god beheld is a function of the state of consciousness of the beholder', (CM 566) it is a matter of some consequence which author is doing the beholding. In the monastic version of the Grail story (*La Queste del Saint Graal*), the Grail is exclusively associated with Christ's passion, as it is in Wagner's opera *Parzival* and Tennyson's *Idylls of the King*: The Grail is the chalice of the Last Supper and the chalice that received Christ's blood when he was taken down from the cross. Thus the reference of the symbol remains enclosed within the Christian orthodox tradition, dependent on the dualistic opposition of spirit and nature, and on belief in the sacraments as administered by the Church. Here the source of the Grail's gift is imagined as coming from outside nature, so nature is still inherently fallen, or cursed, not itself, even potentially, divine. So the reawakening to nature that was springing up everywhere in the twelfth and thirteenth centuries was, in this work, reversed, and the supernatural reimposed as the proper authority, leaving, as Campbell characteristically puts it, 'nature, man, history, and all womankind except baptized nuns, to the Devil'. (CM, 566)

It is hardly surprising that one who was not just a comparative mythologist but who practically 'invented' comparative mythology as an independent study should place the claims of psychology beyond those of any particular theology. Campbell's criterion for evaluating the different Grail myths was always their relation to the archetypal order. Does the local, specific image become translucent to a universal truth? Is it a statement about the nature of humanity, valid for the whole human race? For the ultimate reference of mythology is to the human being as human. So it was to Wolfram's *Parzival* that he again turned for an understanding of the Grail as a symbol of a metaphysical truth. Wolfram tells a story of the origins of the Grail in which it was once carried from heaven to earth by the angels who had remained neutral when Satan opposed God and there was war in heaven. These were the angels in the middle, between the warring factions, and so the Grail here stands for that spiritual path that is between pairs of opposites, between fear and desire, black and white, good and evil (hence the meaning of Parzival's name). As he says at the beginning of his tale: 'Every act has both good and evil results.' Between these opposites, where the Grail is to be found, is the spontaneous *natural* impulse of a noble heart.

The Grail, as Campbell describes it, drawing on the meaning of Wolfram's image, is then the inexhaustible vessel, the centre of life continuously coming into being, energy pouring into creation, energy as creation, out of which civilizations arise, mountains are formed – the unquenchable fountain of the source. If we relate that image to ourselves, it is the place in us where life comes into being inside us – 'the still point of the turning world', as T.S. Eliot calls it in *The Four Quartets* – which is a place before or beyond desiring and fearing, just pure becoming. This is an image which emerges in very different cultures separated by time and space, and so must be a reflection of certain powers or spiritual potentialities in the psyche of every one of us. Furthermore, by contemplating this and other mythic images, we evoke their powers in our own lives.

In Celtic mythology, for instance – the immediate origins of all Arthurian Romance – there was not a chalice but a cauldron of plenty in the mansion of the god of the sea, Manannan Mac Lir, himself the Northern Celtic counterpart of the Roman Neptune and the Greek

Poseidon, who in turn was the Occidental counterpart of the Oriental Shiva. Beneath the waves, Manannan served the flesh of pigs that, killed today, were alive tomorrow, and an ambrosial ale which bestowed immortality on all his guests, enacting, in the ceaseless ebb and flow of the tides of the sea, the continual filling and emptying of the celestial cup of the moon above. These are the images that point, in turn, to the distant roots of the mythology of the Celts in the most ancient native European mythological tradition: that of the old Megalithic, Bronze Age Goddess of many names, mother of all creation – gods and humans – and the immanent power of all nature: the earth, not as dust (as it became in the Judeo-Christian tradition), but as the source, the living body which was herself, out of whom all things proceed and to whom they return at peace.

Nearer to Celtic myth, in place and time, was Germanic myth. And there, similarly, the life-giving vessel is central. Odin (Wotan) gave an eye for a sip from the Well of Wisdom at the foot of the World Ash, Yggdrasil, where it was guarded by the dwarf, Mimir; while high above in Valhalla, the warrior dead drank a mead, served by the Valkyries, which restored them to life and joy. The late Classical Orphic sects (themselves rooted in the earlier Bronze Age Mother Goddess cultures of Mesopotamia, Crete, Egypt and Old Europe), also conducted their mystery rites through the drinking of liquid from sacramental bowls, though the symbols there were read in the inward anagogical way that is proper to symbols, not reduced to a literal sense and referred outward to supposed, actual or possible historical events. These cults were carried by the Roman armies as they advanced into northern Europe in the Gallo-Roman period, when at the same time the native Celto-Germanic gods which they encountered in the lands they occupied were identified with their Greco-Roman counterparts, allying, thereby, the classical mystery tradition with local Celtic myth and ritual.

Wolfram linked his central symbol to both these traditions – the Celtic and the Classical – and their ancient sources, as well as extending its reference to include Islam. For in his work, while the Grail acts *like* a vessel – in its presence whatever anyone stretched out their hands for it was waiting for, food and drink alike – it was actually a stone, the 'Wish of Paradise', called 'lapsit exillis', the name of the Philosophers' Stone of the alchemists, but also suggesting the Ka'aba of Islam. The Grail, which 'was the very fruit of bliss, a cornucopia of the sweets of this world and such that it scarcely fell short of what they tell us of the

Heavenly Kingdom', (P, 127) was a symbol which unified the different, even warring, traditions in a new image of the human being released from any one ecclesiastical authority, serving the world through individual love.

In his television conversations with Bill Moyers, entitled *The Power of Myth*, and in the book of the same name in which many of these conversations are recorded, Campbell interprets these myths of the vessel, bowl and cauldron, or the Grail stone as cornucopia, as meaning that it is out of the depths of the unconscious that the energies of life come to us, the bubbling spring from which all life proceeds. And not only the unconscious of the race – the collective unconscious, as Jung calls it – but also the vale of the world. It is not just the psyche and it is not just the world; it is from the depths of both that life comes irrepressibly forth, since one is the reflection of the other. There had been other images of the inexhaustible source of creation, but no myth before this had linked that image to the spontaneous outpouring of an individual heart, rendering the outward Grail consubstantial with the inward point of becoming life in the human being.

Then how is the Grail attained? Wolfram's answer, conveyed first through Parzival's failure and then through the terms on which he and Gawain finally succeed, is that it is won through the act of compassion that comes spontaneously out of an individual who lives his or her own authentic life. The Maimed Grail King, Anfortas, had not earned his castle or his throne; they had come to him as a gift, and for this reason he could not withstand the lance of the pagan, the Muslim knight, who rode at him in the woods. The Grail King's lance kills the pagan, but the pagan's lance castrates the Grail King. What this means, Campbell explains, is that 'the Christian separation of matter and spirit, of the dynamism of life and the realm of the spirit, of natural grace and super-natural grace, has really castrated nature ... The true spirituality, which would have come from the union of matter and spirit, has been killed.' (PM, 197) For the pagan represents the natural man, and yet, astonishingly, the word 'Grail' was written on the head of his lance: 'That is to say,' he continues, 'nature intends the Grail. Spiritual life is the bouquet, the perfume, the flowering and fulfilment of a human life, not a supernatural virtue imposed upon it.' (PM, 197).

This battle is in a sense re-enacted between Parzival and the pagan knight, his half-brother Feirfiz, whose nobility (and compassion) in fighting (throwing away his sword when Parzival's had broken) allows a recognition to take place between them, after which Cundrie appears to summon Parzival to heal the King and receive the Grail along with his wife and son. When the moment arrives, Feirfiz cannot see the Grail but only the eyes of her who carried it, the Queen Repanse de Schoye, and he was urged to be baptized and to renounce his gods if he would marry her (Parzival's aunt, as it turned out). In a lecture that he gave on the Grail myth which was taped, Campbell, telling the story to a room already resounding with laughter, expostulates at this point: 'Good God, I thought, is Wolfram going to let me down here at the end of the story?' But it was all right; Wolfram played with the idea of baptism and the one true god. Feirfiz asks: 'Is your god her god?' 'Yes,' says Parzival. 'Then for the sake of your aunt's god, let me be baptized,' says Feirfiz with much enthusiasm. (CM, 563)

Courtly love, Campbell explains, is exemplified in this idea of putting the loved person before any other authority in utmost particularity. For it is not the two impersonal relations of *Eros* and *Agape* – earthly and spiritual love, neither of which require a personal relationship between two unique people – but *Amor*, the specific, discriminating love that both Parzival and Gawain achieve for the one person who could be no other, and who is loved for who she is. One of Parzival's tests was at the marriage of Gawain when he chose to leave the scene of festivities because of his love for Condiramors – she who leads him to love. His pagan brother simply loves the god in his lady, whoever it is.

Now when the newly baptized heathen sees the Grail with his own eyes, he sees written upon the Grail a hitherto unprecedented statement of compassion extended to the political world: 'If any member of the Grail Company should, by the grace of God, be given mastery over a foreign folk, he must not speak to them of his race or of his name, and must see to it that they gain their rights.' (FG, 221)

In the lecture, and in many places in his books, Campbell turns to Schopenhauer for an understanding of the power and meaning of compassion. In *The Foundation of Morality*, Schopenhauer asks the question: How is it that a human being can so participate in the pain and danger of another that, forgetting his own self-protection, he moves spontaneously to the other's rescue? How is it that what we think of as the first law of nature – self-protection – is suddenly dissolved and another law asserts itself spontaneously? Schopenhauer answers: this is the breakthrough of a metaphysical truth – that you and the other are one, and that separateness is a secondary effect of the way our minds experience the world in the frame of time and space. At the meta-physical level, we are all manifestations of that consciousness and energy which is the consciousness and energy of life. This is Schopenhauer:

> The experience that dissolves the distinction between the I and the Not I ... underlies the mystery of compassion, and stands, in fact, for the reality of which compassion is the prime expression. That experience, therefore, must be the metaphysical ground of ethics and consist simply in this: that one individual should recognize in another, himself in his own true being ... Which is the recognition for which the basic formula is the standard Sanskrit expression, 'Thou are that', *tat tvam asi*. (CM, 75)

When Parzival can ask 'what ails you?' he has experienced the other in himself. If this is the impulse which wins the Grail, then the Grail, in its widest implication, is an image of the unity of creation – the reality of which compassion is in humanity the prime expression.

*   *   *   *   *

Campbell's own life could itself be seen as an enactment of the Grail myth. His whole life is marked with the passion of the hero on his visionary quest, and, retrospectively at least, the events of his life would seem to fall into the imaginative pattern of the hero's journey of transfiguration and return for the enlightenment of the human tribe. He lived his own description of the hero as 'the one who, while still alive, knows and represents the claims of the superconsciousness which throughout creation is more or less unconscious'. (H, 259)

Mythology was the way that was most truly his own. It was not simply a lifelong study of a subject which he also taught; it was a profound religious position, one that refused the doctrine of a divinity transcendent to nature: 'The great realization of mythology,' he said, 'is the immanence of the divine.' (OL, 32) He often quoted the saying of Jesus from the Gnostic *Gospel of Thomas*: 'See the Kingdom of Heaven is spread out upon the earth, and men do not see it.' By contrast, religion, in the orthodox sense of unilateral belief, was best defined as 'a misinterpretation of mythology', where 'the misinterpretation consists precisely in attributing historical references to symbols which properly are spiritual in their reference'. (OL, 79) The mythic image is here, now, and always; myths are great poems which render insights into the wonder and miracle of life. Though they are deeply meaningful, they do not offer meaning or answers so much as delight and the longing to participate in the mystery of this finally inscrutable universe. As a union of psyche and metaphysics, myths put you in touch with your hearts.

Later in his life, in conversations on TV and taped dialogues, Campbell was often asked how to live the authentic life of an individual, how even to begin to try. To this he had one answer which remained constant throughout his life: 'Follow your Bliss.'

> I feel that if one follows what I call one's bliss – the thing that really gets you deep in the gut and that you feel is your life – doors will open up. They do! They have in my life and they have in many lives that I know of. (OL, 24)
> If you follow your bliss you put yourself on a kind of track that has been there all the while, waiting for you, and the life that you ought to be living is the one you are living. When you can see that, you begin to meet people who are in the field of your bliss, and they open the doors to you. I say, follow your bliss and don't be afraid ... (PM, 120)

He came to this idea of bliss, he explains, because of three terms in Sanskrit, which is the great spiritual language of the world: *Sat, Chit, Ananda. Sat* means being; *Chit* means consciousness; *Ananda* means bliss or rapture, and these terms represent the brink, the jumping-off place to the ocean of transcendence. 'I thought,' he said, 'I don't know whether what I know of my being is my proper being or not; but I do know where my rapture is. So let me hang on to my rapture, and that will bring me both my consciousness and my being.' (PM, 120)

Yet it is not always easy to hang on to your rapture, and here the hero myth, and specifically the Grail myth, offers a guide. If the Call comes – the feeling that there is an adventure there for you – the risk must be taken. In *An Open Life*, a compilation of taped interviews with Michael Toms from 1975–85, Campbell speaks from the experience of an idea he has personally tested: 'When I wrote about the Call forty years ago (in *The Hero with a Thousand Faces*), I was writing out of what I had read. Now that I've lived it, I know it's correct ... These mythic clues work.' (OL, 26) Elsewhere, he adds: 'I always tell my students, go where your body and soul want to go. When you have the feeling, then stay with it, and don't let anyone throw you off.' (PM, 118) When you follow your bliss, you come to bliss. But how to find your bliss, if it has not called you? 'We are having experiences all the time which may on occasion render some sense of this, a little intuition of where your bliss is. Grab it. No one can tell you what it is going to be. You have to learn to recognize your own depth.' (PM, 118)

When still at an early age, Campbell had to take on the challenge of seeing things differently from those around him. While he was brought up in the Roman Catholic faith, which he took very seriously, he was at the same time going with his father to see the Museum of Natural History with its rooms of totem poles, learning about the American Indians. So he was comparing virgin births, deaths and resurrections in both mythological systems at an early age. When he was a kid, he said, he never let anyone push him off course, and in this his family always supported him.

In his university years, he studied the literature of the Middle Ages and classical mythology, finding the same images which occurred in the Christian tradition, but inflected towards the more universal point of view. Graduate work in medieval literature took him first to Paris, in 1927, where he discovered James Joyce, and also modern art – particularly, Picasso and Klee. Then, in 1928–9, he went to Germany, to the University of Munich to study philology – the history of language – which brought him to Sanskrit, and introduced him to the whole world of the Orient. He had met Krishnamurti by chance (or synchronicity) on a boat to Europe in 1924, and had been given a book on the life of the Buddha, which prepared him for his later translating and editing of the *Upanishads* and *The Gospel of Sri Ramakrishna* with Swami Nikhilananda.

In Germany he discovered Thomas Mann, and also Freud and Jung who opened up for him a new psychological dimension in the field of mythology. When he wrote *The Hero with a Thousand Faces*, the two men were equal in his thinking, Freud relating to (what Jung calls) the personal unconscious and Jung to the collective unconscious. But in the years following, Jung became more and more eloquent for him: 'Freud tells us what myths mean to neurotics. On the other hand, Jung gives us clues as to how to let the myth talk to us in its own terms, without putting a formula on it.' (OL, 121) Jung's *Symbols of Transformation* was 'one of those things that sends all the lights up in all directions.' (OL, 50) Campbell and Jung both saw mythology as the expression of the collective unconscious (though Campbell was more interested in diffusion and relationships historically than Jung was), and when they met, years later, it was as co-editors of the work of Heinrich Zimmer, the great Indologist and interpretor of symbols, whom he regarded as 'supplementary to Jung'. (OL, 120) It was Zimmer who, beyond anyone, gave him the courage to interpret myths out of what he knew to be their common symbols. There's always a risk in such an interpretation, he added, pointing us to the operation of the hero myth at any moment of our lives, whatever we are doing.

When Cundrie appears to Parzival at Arthur's Table, she disrupts the vision he had of how his life would be, and he got up and left it all behind. Campbell describes an experience in the little garden of Cluny in Paris, in which he was similarly struck by an impulse to change the course of his life, one that he, like Parzival, immediately followed. He was sitting in the garden, having put some years of study into his Ph.D., when:

> It suddenly struck me: What in heaven's name am I doing? I don't even know how to eat a decent nourishing meal, and here I'm learning what happened to vulgar Latin when it passed into Portugese and Spanish and French. So I dropped work on my Ph.D. On my return I found a place in upstate New York and read the classics for 12 hours a day. I was enjoying myself enormously, and realized I would never finish my degree because it would have required me to do things I had already outgrown. In Europe, the world had opened up: Joyce, Sanskrit, the Orient, and the relationship of all these to Psychology. I couldn't go back and finish up that Ph.D. thesis; besides, I didn't have the money. And that free-wheeling maverick life gave me a sense of the deep joy in doing something meaningful to me. (OL, 125–6)

Like Parzival, he spent five years without a job! He came back from Europe in 1929, just three weeks before the Wall Street crash, which meant there were no jobs to be had, so he found a retreat up in Woodstock, New York, in 'a little chicken coop place', with no running water, and here he did most of his basic reading and work: 'It was great. I was following my bliss.' (PM, 120) When, after five years, he was invited to teach at Sarah Lawrence College, it was on his own terms: 'I would not have taken a job otherwise, just as I wouldn't take the Ph.D.' (OL, 126)

He was to stay at Sarah Lawrence College from 1934 until he retired as Professor Emeritus in 1972, pursuing his own vision, and offering it back to the many students and friends who have found his life an inspiration. He makes it sound easy, but he once shared with a friend something of what it had asked of him. They were in front of some statue, and Campbell was bringing the mythic resonances of the image to life by comparing it with similar images in other cultures, and – to temper somewhat his friend's appreciative enthusiasm – Campbell said: 'Yes, but think of all the hundreds of hours spent reading, all the days, all the parties missed ...'

The image of courtly love also played through his relationship to his wife, Jean Erdman, the dancer and choreographer, to whom he was married for 49 years. Marriage, he said, was a sacrament in which you give up your personal simplicity to participate in a relationship, but you give not so much to the other person as to the relationship. In 1984, towards the end of his life, he was perhaps speaking of his own experience of *Amor*: 'What a beautiful thing is a life together as growing personalities, each helping the other to flower, rather than just moving into the standard archetype.'

Jean Erdman writes of his work: 'Throughout his long career, Joseph Campbell endeavoured to communicate his understanding of myth – his passion. And he tirelessly pursued the task he had set himself. Besides his books and lectures, there were workshops and interviews, which he eagerly welcomed because he believed scholarship should not mean isolation.' (OL, Foreward)

Before *The Hero with a Thousand Faces* was published in 1949, which took four years to write, he had already edited the posthumous works of Heinrich Zimmer – *Philosophies of India* and *The Art of Indian Asia* – as well as six volumes of the papers from the Eranos conferences set up by Jung to explore the issues around analytical psychology, called the *Eranos Notebooks*. Next came *The Flight of the Wild Gander* (1951), which, as he wrote in his introduction, 'occupied, or rather punctuated, a period of twenty-four years, during the whole of which I was circling, and from many quarters striving to interpret, the mystery of mythology.' (FG, 3) There followed his unique discussion of the world's archetypal images of divinity in their historical contexts, called *The Masks of God*, which was published over a period of 12 years as four separate but related books: *Primitive Mythology*; *Oriental Mythology*; *Occidental Mythology*; and *Creative Mythology* (1959–1968). He also wrote *A Skeleton Key to Finnegan's Wake*, and edited *The Portable Jung* and *The Portable Arabian Knights*. *Myths To Live By* (1971) was a selection of talks on mythology delivered in New York City between 1958 and 1971. In 1975, *The Mythic Image* was published by Princeton University Press after 10 years in preparation, a book which, incidentally, sets a standard for the right relation of text to image that has never subsequently been met. In 1983, *The Way of the Animal Powers* was published as the first volume of the *Historical Atlas of World Mythology*, followed in 1988 by the second volume, *The Way of the Seeded Earth*. In 1986, a record of various lectures in San Francisco, given between 1981 and 1984, was published under the title of *The Inner Reaches of Outer Space: Metaphor as Myth and as Religion*. Since then, in 1988, his conversations with Bill Moyers on TV (collected in *The Power of Myth*) and with Michael Toms on the 'New Dimension' tapes (compiled in *An Open Life*) have shown how profoundly he lived his own myth. His great gifts of story-telling and scholarship were offered to his students and readers that they also might engage in the call of the age:

> The adventure of the Grail – the quest within for those creative values by which the Waste Land is redeemed – has become today for each the unavoidable task; for, as there is no more any fixed horizon, there is no more any fixed center, any Mecca, Rome, or Jerusalem. Our circle today is that announced, *c*. 1450, by Nicolas Cusanus (1401–64): whose circumference is nowhere and whose center is everywhere; the circle of infinite radius, which is also a straight line. (OC, 522)

The study of mythology was for Campbell a truly sacred task because it allowed a move out of the dogma of formal religion and into the spontaneous nature of one's own inward drama and vitality of being. It is inevitable, then, that his life might seem to us to be the mythic image that he taught us how to understand, for mythology and the way of his life were one. If the Grail represents, as he said, 'the fulfilment of the highest spiritual possibilities of the human consciousness', (PM, 197) then his lifelong quest of the Holy Grail may indeed have been rewarded.

Abbreviations

H	*The Hero with a Thousand Faces*, Joseph Campbell.
FG	*The Flight of the Wild Gander*, Joseph Campbell.
OC	*Occidental Mythology*, Joseph Campbell.
CM	*Creative Mythology*, Joseph Campbell.
PM	*The Power of Myth*, Joseph Campbell.

OL   *An Open Life*, Joseph Campbell.
P   *Parzival*, Wolfram von Eschenbach, trans. A.T. Hatto
            (Harmondsworth: Penguin Classics, 1980).

Bibliography

The Hero with a Thousand Faces, Bollingen Series XVII (Princeton Univ. Press, 1949).

The Flight of the Wild Gander: Explorations in the Mythological Dimensions (Gateway Edition, 1951).

The Masks of God: Primitive Mythology (New York: Viking Press, 1959).

The Masks of God: Oriental Mythology (New York: Viking Press, 1962).

The Masks of God: Occidental Mythology (New York: Viking Press, 1964).

The Masks of God: Creative Mythology (New York: Viking Press, 1968).

Myths To Live By (London: Bantam, 1972).

The Mythic Image, Bollingen Series C (Princeton Univ. Press, 1974).

The Inner Reaches of Outer Space: Metaphor as Myth and as Religion (London: St James Press, 1986).

Historical Atlas of World Mythology:
    Vol. 1, *The Way of the Animal Powers* (London: Times Books, 1984).
    Vol. 2, *The Way of the Seeded Earth* (New York: Harper & Row, 1988).

The Power of Myth, with Bill Moyers, from transcripts of the TV series (New York: Doubleday, 1988).

An Open Life In Conversation with Michael Toms. (Compilations of Interviews from 1975–85) (Larsons Publications, 1988).

The Grail Tapes of lecture given in 1982 (Living Dharma Tapes).

Completed and edited the papers of Heinrich Zimmer: *Myths and Symbols in Indian Art and Civilization*, *The King and the Corpse*, *Philosophies of India*, and *The Art of Indian Asia*.

Translated and edited, with Swami Nikhilananda, *The Upanishads* and *The Gospel of Sri Ramakrishna*.

Edited Papers from the *Eranos Yearbooks* (6 vols.), *Myths, Dreams and Religion*, *The Portable Jung*, and *The Portable Arabian Nights*.

Co-authored, with Henry Morton Robinson, *A Skeleton Key to Finnegan's Wake*.

18

David Jones and the Matter of Britain

John Matthews

Of all the contemporary writers who have influenced the way we perceive the Grail, nothing quite equals the extraordinary, lapidary and detailed evocation of the Anglo-Welsh poet and painter David Jones. The seeming obscurity of much of his work hides a deeply felt and passionate love for the ancient mythology of Britain, from which he called forth a vast world of image and idea, expressed in some of the riches and most lovely language of this or any age. There is no better way of concluding this collection than to explore the richness of David Jones' vision.

The word most often used to describe David Jones' written work is 'difficult' and, while this is generally qualified, in some instances with understanding, it retains its influence and works against the reading of this luminous and lapidary work as it should be read – with heart and mind open, receptive to the multitude of bright images drawn from sources as far and wide as any poet has ever used. The problem arises from the nature of the material – Welsh myth and legend, the Latin liturgy, geology, Old English and Arthurian literature – none of which are likely, in this day and age, to evoke a shared response. This is, in a larger sense, the problem of the age in which we live, where we have largely lost touch with our own heritage of tradition, the numinous response to the old sacred myths of the Land.

David Jones recognised this lack many years before it became a widely recognised fact. He strove to restore the numinous history of the Island of the Mighty (to use the Welsh term for Britain) in his own unique fashion – largely through a deep and abiding love for the Matter of Britain which went back to his childhood. As he wrote in the 1951 Preface to *The Anathemata*, his last complete published work:[1]

> There was in those days a children's pink paper-covered series called *Books for the Bairns* and one of the series dealt with King Arthur's knights ... that was the book I most liked hearing read.

He must have been five or six at the time, and he was still writing about and making paintings on Arthurian themes nearly seventy years later.

The twin pillars of David Jones' work are his Welshness and his Catholicism. The former gives us Arthur and the Celtic myths and legends, the latter gives us the great remembering *anamnesis* of the Mass. Between these two pillars he roves at will though the broken littoral of this country's history, from the pre-jurassic age to the time of the Roman invasion and occupation, and on to the battlefields of the 1914–18 war.

But it is the Arthurian legends, the Matter of Britain as it is called to distinguish it from the Matter of France – the legends of Charlemagne – which informs so much of his work. Throughout *In Parenthesis*, his great work about the war in which he was himself a participant, it is the writing of Thomas Malory, the fifteenth-century chronicler of Arthur and his knights, which underpins the matter of the work. Thus when he recalls the dreadful carnage of the Western Front, it is the madness of Merlin that he refers to, who ran into the wilderness after witnessing the death of family and comrades:

> *Merlin in his madness, for the pity of it; for*
> *the young men reaped like barley.* (IP, p. 24)

Here the concern is for fallen humanity; later it is the Land itself, as a sacred thing, which comes to the fore. And it is Arthur's association with the Land – as protector and ruler, which is uppermost. In 'The Hunt' and 'The Sleeping Lord', two parts of a much larger, unfinished work called 'The Roman Quarry', this is a persistent and powerful theme.

The image of quarrying indeed, of 'making a heap of all he could find', of burrowing into the past and remembering – putting back together, the half forgotten fragments of this land's traditions – is what marks out David Jones as the great artist, both in word and line, that he is. For through them he preserves the innate traditions of this land – and through them the traditions to which he himself bore witness in everything he wrote – the qualitative rather than the quantitative, the creaturely and the inspired, the present and particular, and those things which Kathleen Raine has called 'the actually known and loved'.[2]

For David Jones the myths of Britain, specifically Wales, represented a spiritual history of this land. As Blake said in a phrase often quoted by David Jones, 'The Acts of Arthur are the Acts of Albion', referring to the deeper, inner Britain, sacred Albion, whose presence is felt, though deeply buried, even now. Thus David Jones' Sleeping Lord, and Blake's Giant Albion are closely related, brothers perhaps, even father and son.

As he wrote in a letter to Harmon Grisewood:

> I tried very hard to make a lucid, impersonal statement with regard to those things which have made us *all* – of this island. (DG, 37)

References to the Matter of Arthur are so deeply and intricately threaded through the whole of David Jones' work that it would be impossible to trace them all here. All that we can hope to do is to trace some of the threads which derive directly from the Matter and show how they resonate within the works as a whole.

In Parenthesis

From the beginning *In Parenthesis* is signposted by its links with the Matter of Britain. The quotation which prefaces the whole book is from the great native Welsh myth-book known as *The Mabinogion*. It refers to the moment when one of the followers of Bendegied Vran (Bran the Blessed) having been entertained by the mysterious singing head of their Lord, is tempted to open a door which they had all been specifically forbidden to do:

> Evil betide me if I do not open the door to know if that is true which is said concerning it. So he opened the door ... and when they had looked, they were conscious of all the evil they had ever sustained, and of all the friends and companions they had lost and of all the misery that had befallen them, as if all had happened in that very spot; ... and because of their perturbation they could not rest.[3]

The reference is clear enough – this is a kind of Fall – and the writer sets out to open the door upon his own memories. These, which are often terrible, are chiefly of the Waste Land, the place where, in Malory's own words:[4]

> ... there increased neither corn, nor grass, nor well-night no fruit, nor in the water was here found any fish. Therefore men called it ... the Waste Lande. (Bk. XVII, ch. 3.)

In David Jones work this becomes a metaphor for the war-scarred land-scape of the trenches, whose blasted trees and broken buildings are so powerfully described in his own paintings. This landscape has a voice of its own, one which David Jones laboured to express in his writing. Thus in the preface to *In Parenthesis* he says:

> I think the day by day in the Waste Land, the sudden violences and long stillnesses, the sharp contours and unformed voids of that mysterious exis-tence, profoundly affected the imagination of those who suffered it. It was a place of enchantment. It is perhaps best described in Malory, book iv, chapter 15 – that landscape spoke 'with a grimly voice'. (IP, pp. x–xi)

This is echoed later in section 3 of the work, 'Starlight Order' where the platoon of soldiers make a long night-march to the trenches. As they proceed, with mounting terror and discomfort, through the deadly waste, Jones refers directly to Malory's description of Lancelot at the Chapel Perilous, a dreaded testing place for any knight who came near it, where skeletal figures with glowing eyes rush out of the night with levelled swords:

> *Past the little gate*
> *into the field of upturned defences,*
> *into the burial yard –*
> *the grinning and the gnashing and the sore dreading – nor saw he any light in*
> *that place.* (IP, p. 31)

This episode, together with a later one in the sequence of the Grail Quest, were especially important to David Jones. During the time he was in Flanders, he came upon a ruined farm building and looked though a hole in the battered wall. Inside a Catholic priest was celebrating the Mass. In a letter to Rene Hague, he wrote:

I can't recall at what part of the Mass it was I looked through that squint-hole and I didn't think I ought to stay long as it seemed rather like an uninitiated bloke prying on the Mysteries of a Cult. (DGC, p. 249)

This image, which he later caught in the painting entitled *A Latere Dextro* (1943–49) clearly recalled the episode of Lancelot who, standing before the chapel of the Grail, sees the priest struggling to hold up the body of a crucified man, and desiring nothing more than to help, rushes forward. He is struck down by a tongue of fire and temporarily blinded. It was not appropriate for a sinful man to enter this place of Holy mysteries. That David Jones felt this passage deeply is reflected in this passage from the later poem *The Grail Mass*:

> *Lake-wave Lawnslot*
>   *beats against that*
> *varnished pine*
>   *his quillon'd* cleddyf-*hilt*
> *fractures the notices for the week*
> *he would see*
>   *right through that chamber door*
> *he would be*
>   *where the Cyrenean deacon*
> *leans inward*
>   *to relive the weight*
> *he too would aid the venerable man*
>   *surcharged with that great weight ...* (RQ, p. 110)

Returning to *In Parenthesis*, later in the same sequence comes a whole thicket of Arthurian and myth-laden reference. A soldier is observed, keeping watch over his sleeping fellows. This evokes a whole series of images: of

> *Spell-sleepers, thrown about anyhow under the night.*
> *And this one's bright brow turned against your boot leather,*
> *tranquil as a* fer sidhe *sleeper, under fairy tumuli, fair as Mac Og sleeping.*
> (IP, p. 51.)

Here, Jones remarks in his own notes to the work, he was thinking of 'the persistent Celtic theme of armed sleepers under the mounds' of the *sidhe* or faery folk of Ireland, of the Mac ind Oic, the love god of Ireland, of the Greek god of time and space, Cronus who, according to

Plutarch, sleeps on a golden stone beneath an island which is identified with Britain. And of course there is Arthur himself. In the first of many references to the Sleeping Lord – culminating in the fragment of that name not published until 1967 – Jones makes reference to the idea of the mighty leader who sleeps beneath the land awaiting his country's call to arms.

This is an important theme both in Arthurian myth and in the writings of David Jones. It is tied to the belief that the person of the king is sacred, and that its sacredness must remain inviolate. Thus, in Celtic tradition, when the king is wounded or maimed the land over which he rules suffers also.

This is the meaning of the theme in the Matter of Britain which refers to the Wounded King. In Malory we read how this comes about through the actions of the pagan knight Balin le Sauvage who, while on a quest set him by Arthur, encounters Garlon, a knight who rides 'invisibly' and uses his gift to attack and kill his enemies. When Balin discovers him in the castle of King Pellam, he attacks without warning and dispatches the cowardly knight. However, unbeknownst to Balin, Garlon is the King's brother, and Pellam now pursues him through the rooms of the castle. In one of these Balin discovers:

> … a table of clean gold with four pillars of silver that bare up the table, and upon the table stood a marvellous spear strangely wrought. (Bk II, Ch. xv.)

Having lost his sword, Balin takes up the spear and uses it to defend himself. He strikes down King Pellam, wounding him through the thighs – a term generally accepted to mean in the generative organs – which renders him impotent and at the same time causes the Waste Land. This stroke, we learn, leaves the king with a wound that will only heal when the Grail is achieved, specifically when a ritual question is asked which will 'free the waters', healing land and king.

This is the Dolorous Stroke referred to several times in *In Parenthesis*, particularly in the section titled 'King Pellam's Launde', where at the very beginning we find a reference to Pellam's Castle, who falls down as a result of the Dolorous Stroke. The quotation referring to this, which opens this section, is again from Malory:

> So thus he sorrowed till it was day and heard the foules sing, then somewhat he was comforted. (IP, p. 59)

But it is in the famous passage towards the end of this section, which is generally known as 'Dai's Boast' that the references begin to coalesce, and to draw upon the imagery of the Grail Quest.

The character of Dai is important to the structure of the work as a whole, because in this long section, David Jones gathers together many of the strands with which he has been working, and signposts a whole cluster of mythological references.

The boast itself is meant to recall the supposedly boastful nature of the Welsh bards, as well as a most famous boast – that of the sixth-century Welsh poet Taliesin, a number of whose poems are extant. In particular Jones refers to the *Hanes Taliesin*, a fourteenth-century poem attributed to the ancient bard, in which is listed a lengthy catalogue of places, things and events which the poet has variously been, seen or experienced. A passage will serve to illustrate both style and content:

> *Primary chief poet*
> *Am I to Elffin.*
> *My native country*
> *Is the place of the Summer Stars.*

> *John the Divine*
> *Called me Merlin,*
> *But all future kings*
> *Shall call me Taliesin ...*

> *I was the instructor*
> *To the whole universe.*
> *I shall be until judgement*
> *On the face of the earth.*
> (*Hanes Taliesin*, My trans.)

Set alongside 'Dai's Boast' the similarities are obvious.

> *I was the spear in Balin's hand*
>   *that made waste King Pellam's land ...*
>   *I the adder in the little bush*
> *whose hibernation-end*
> *undid,*
> *unmade victorious toil:*
> *In ostium fluminis.*

At the four actions in regione Linnuis
    by the black waters.
At Bassas in the shallows.
At Cat Coit Celidon.
At Guinnion redoubt, where he carried the Image.
In urbe Ligionis.
By the vallum Antonini, at the place of boundaries, at the
    toiling estuary and strong flow called Tribruit.
By Agned mountain.
On Badon Hill, where he bore the Tree … (IP)

After the reference to the Dolorous Stroke comes this long list of battles. All are attributed to Arthur in the few historical documents concerning him which have survived. At Guinnion, he is said to have carried a shield on which was painted an icon of the Virgin (the 'Image' of the poem); at Badon, the great battle in which the historical Arthur finally routed the invading Saxons, his shield bore the image of the crucified Christ. In this battle Arthur carried all before him. The other reference, which significantly comes before the list of Arthur's victories – to the 'adder in the little bush' refers to the last battle fought by Arthur, in which he received his death-wound. It began when an adder woke and bit the heel of a knight, who drew his sword and thus precipitated the conflict. Arthur's end is thus seen to have been laid down even before his victories, and in the poem we learn of the reason – Arthur's overweening pride.

The passage reads as follows:

I saw the blessed head set under
    that kept the narrow sea inviolate.
To keep the Land,
to give the yield:
    under the White Tower
        I trowelled the inhuming mortar.
    They learned me well the proportions due –
by water
by sand
by slacked lime.
    I drest the cist –
the beneficent artisans knew how well to keep
the king's head to keep
the land inviolate.
    The Bear of the Island: he broke it in his huge pride,
and overreach of his imperium.
The Island Dragon.

The Bull of Battle
(this is the third woeful uncovering).
Let maimed kings lie – let be
O let the guardian head
keep back – bind savage sails, lock the shield-wall, nourish the sowing.
The War Duke
The Director of Toil –
he burst the balm-cloth, unbricked the barrow
(cruel feet march because of this
ungainly men sprawl over us).
O Land! – O Bran lie under. (IP, pp. 81–2)

This refers again to the story, found in *The Mabinogion*, of the great Celtic hero-god Bran, who has the epithet 'bendegied' (blessed). He bears this because, when he is wounded with a poisoned dart – much like the Maimed King of the Grail myths, whom he predates – he orders his head cut off by his own followers and after various adventures, instructs them to bury it beneath the White Mount, now the site of the Tower of London. It was to be set in place with the face towards France – because of which no enemy will ever overcome this land.

This is done, but when Arthur is king he orders the head exhumed, because no one but he should guard the kingdom. In the collection of gnomic wisdom collected under the title of *The Welsh Triads*[5] this is reference to as 'one of the three woeful uncoverings' – because, of course, the Island is overrun by the Saxons for a time, and after Arthur completely so.

There is a sense here that David Jones is making a parallel between the pride of Arthur – Bull of Battle, Director of Toil, Island Dragon: all are titles from the Celtic stories – and the subsequent overrunning of the Island of the Mighty by the Saxons, with the wastefulness of the war-effort, which sacrificed so many for the cause of National pride, and which so nearly ended with a new invasion of 'Saxon' enemies.

There are other Arthurian references in *In Parenthesis*. To the failure of Lancelot in the Quest for the Grail, from which he is turned back because of his sinful relationship with Arthur's Queen. This, as we have seen, was a matter of some moment to David Jones, who saw it as a parallel to human failure in general. In addition there are references to the great hunt of the boar Twrch Trwyth, which was later to become the subject of another of the fragments collected under the title of *The Sleeping Lord*.

But by far the most extended and powerful Arthurian references appear in the final section of *In Parenthesis*, 'The Five Unmistakable Marks'. Again, as elsewhere throughout the work, the opening quotation is from the old Welsh heroic poem 'The Gododdin',[6] which tells of a hopeless assault by a handful of Celtic tribesmen against a vastly superior force. This in fact gives a backbone of reference to the whole work, which parallels it in many ways.

Arthurian and Celtic references inform the whole of the battle described in this section. Aneurin Lewis, the gunner whose death is recorded here, 'sleeps in Arthur's Lap', while the battle itself is compared both to Catraeth (the battle described in 'The Gododdin') and to Camlan, the last battle fought by Arthur against his son Mordred. Lancelot's fearful encounter at the Chapel Perilous is invoked next, then the Dolorous Stroke – though the latter is dismissed as irrelevant – 'who gives a bugger for the Dolorous Stroke' – in the face of the naked extremity of War. A list of chiefly Arthurian heroes follows, including:

> *Tristan,*
> *Lamorack de Galis*
> *Alisander le Orphelin*
> *Beaumains who was the youngest …*
> *or the sweet brothers Balin and Balan*
> *embraced beneath their single monument.*

The latter, a reference to the mutual deaths of these two brothers, who slew each other, not knowing, until too late, their truer identities, adds to the catalogue of worthless death, while the enemy, 'lurkers who pounce', are 'like Garlon's truncheon that struck invisible.' Almost the last image in the book, which refers to

> *Oeth and Annoeth's hosts …*
> *who in the night grew*
> *younger men*
> *younger striplings'* (IP, p. 187)

This is a complex reference to the graves of the heroes listed in *The Englyns of the Graves*,[7] a twelfth-century Welsh text which lists the resting places of many Arthurian heroes, and perhaps also to the Cauldron of Annwn, which gave back life to dead warriors, restored in all but speech.[8]

The Matter of Britain can be seen to underpin a great deal of the imagery of *In Parenthesis*. It provides a deeply-laid structure which gives a degree of meaning to the senseless carnage of the war. It is as though, by remembering Malory and the heroes of ancient Celtic Britain, David Jones found a way to unprocess the horror and devastation he had witnessed.

However, *In Parenthesis* is not about the glory of war, still less about its victory. It is about he futility of war in the face of the Eternal. As Thomas Dilworth writes in *The Liturgical Parenthesis of David Jones*, 'Liturgy endows life with meaning by uniting in a dramatised hypothesis the ordinary experiences of life with the fullness of belief and desire.'[9]

This makes it clear that what David Jones meant to write about was the way in which the 'creaturely' is subsumed in the world of order, brought into harmony like a ground string resonating in sympathy with subtle counterpoints being played outside the range of human hearing or understanding. Meaningless acts – such as the deaths of thousands on the field of battle – become meaningful within the framework of the Mass. Even the apportioning of rations becomes an instance of the Eucharist:

> *Come off it, Moses – dole out the issue.*
> *Dispense salvation,*
> *strictly apportion it,*
> *let us taste and see,*
> *let us be renewed.*

No action is too mean not to have its liturgical counterpart. In some places the liturgy is not always Christian, but shadows an older experience. The men are fodder for a darker sacrifice:

> *for the northern Cybele.*
> *The hanged, the offerant:*
> *himself to himself*
> *on the tree.*

In the references to Arthur there are more echoes of the sacrificed Lord.

Attis, Odin, Christ or Arthur, the sacrifice is indistinguishable, and here the quality of David Jones' faith is most interesting: profound sympathy between man and his fellow being, the relationship of man with beast or inanimate object is mirrored forth in his understanding of the immanance of redemption. The times and foreshadowings of Christ's sacrifice were known to David Jones, who saw them as prophetic forerunners and as necessary signs of understanding. Wherever compassion and love set their sign, wherever worship spontaneously arose, there too was Christ.

The Anathemata

In his next published work, *The Anathemata*, the presence of the Matter of Britain is still there, still felt, but has gone deeper. The whole poem is concerned with the act of remembering of *anamnesis*, made by the priest during the saying of the Roman Mass, who is himself prefigured by 'the cult-man' who performs a ritual of his own which is also a prophetic recollection of the history of the Island of Britain. The epigraph which appears on the title pages makes this clear – it is a quotation from *King Lear*: 'This prophecy Merlin shall make for I live before his time'.

The first section, 'Rite and Fore-Time', evokes this older figure who

> ... stands alone in Pellam's land: more precariously than he knows he guards the *signa*: the pontifex among his house-treasures, (the twin-*urbes* his house is) he can fetch things new and old: the tokens the matrices, the institutes, the ancilla, the fertile ashes – the paladdic foreshadowings: the things come down from heaven together with the kept memorials, the things lifted up and the venerated trinkets. (AN, p. 50)

Pellam is the Lord of the Grail, its guardian. And, in guarding the *signa*, the signs or sacred things, the Hallows of the Land, he guards more than he knows. For these things, of which the Grail is one, are nothing less than the memorials of time and place which lie in the landscape itself, the hills upon which, in ancient times, rituals took place which honoured the land as Mother.

These are the same *'colles Arthuri'* (the Hills of Arthur) beneath which Cronos, Bran, and Arthur himself are said to sleep. They are also the 'Buarth Meibion Arthur', 'The Enclosure of the Children of Arthur' where lie 'dragons and old Pendragons', the ancestors of Arthur himself. 'Searching where the kitchen midden tells of the decline which with the receding cold marked the recession of the Magdalenian splendours' uncovers not only the disjecta of ancient times, but the living bones of myth:

> *... the dish*
> > *that holds no coward's food*
> *... the hound-bitches*
> > *of the stone kennels of Arthur*
> *that quested the hog and the brood of the hog*
> > *from Pebidiog to Aber Gwy?*

These references are to the beginnings of the Matter of Britain, specifically to the ancient ninth-century poem 'The Spoils of Annwn', in which Arthur, accompanied by seven fabled heroes, stages a raid on the Underworld itself, to bring back the Cauldron of Annwn, a vessel which 'will not boil the food of a coward' and which, when dead men are put into it, gives them back living – but dumb, unable to speak of what they have seen; and to the great hunt of the boar Twrch Trwyth, the subject of David Jones' later work 'The Hunt'.

All of these references build into a vast pattern of association with Arthur, the Grail, and the spirit of place itself. For, it is impossible to remember one without the other, to perceive any single sign without becoming aware of the power of *all* signs to place those who honour them into a special state of being – what we might choose to call a state of grace.

The fifth section, 'The Lady of the Pool', is really a long reminiscence of the history of London, or Lud's Town as it is here called after its legendary founder. But the lady herself is clearly one of the Ladies of the Lake who appear at so many crucial points in the history of Arthur, advising, beguiling, betraying and supporting according to their lights. Thus we hear of 'Taffy Merlin's mistress' who is Nimuë, the maiden upon whom the great magician is said to have doted, and who, by dint of offering him her favours, acquired his secrets and then shut him beneath a stone – where he becomes yet another 'voice of the land' calling plaintively 'the cri du Merlin', from his place of imprisonment.

Such are themselves guardians, re-memberers, who, like Arthur and Bran, lie under the earth but eternally guard the walls of the city and the land, and who, as the Lady tells us:

> *... have ward of us that be his townies –*
> *and certain THIS BOROUGH WERE NEVER FORCED,*

cap-tin!! ...
  and these slumberers
was great captains, cap'n:
tyrannoi come in keels from Old Troy
    requiescant.
For, these fabliaux say, of one other such quondam king
rexque futurus. (IP, 195)

Here Arthur is the 'quondam King', upon whose tomb the words were written, 'Hic Jacet Arthurus Rex quondam Rexque futurus' – here lies Arthur, the once and future king'. So that he is another who exists both in 'the fore-time' and in the future time, the time which is, as the poet tells us 'the sagging end and chapters close' of Western history.

In 'Mabinog's Liturgy' comes a remarkable and unforgettable description of Gwenhwyfar (Guinevere), Arthur's Queen, who is compared to Selene, the Blessed Virgin, and Helen of Troy. Her elaborate costume is described in such sensuous detail that one can almost feel it.

Physically, she is described in terms of barley, marble, and pale Welsh gold.

If her gilt, unbound
(for she was consort of a *regulus*) and falling below her
sacral bone, was pale as standing North-Humber barley-corn,
here, held back in the lunula of Doleucothi gold, it was
paler than under-stalks of barley, held in the sickle's lunula.
So that the pale gilt where it was by nature palest, together
with the pale river-gold where it most received the pallid candle-sheen,
rimmed the crescent whiteness where it was whitest. (AT, 196ff)

This is taken up directly by the description of the linen which drapes the altar-stone on which is the Chalice and the holy things of the Mass. The connection with the Arthurian Grail mysteries and the parallels between Arthur and Christ, and between Christ and Apollo, and the Grail Winner, who frees the waters of the wasteland, are then evoked:

What says his mabinogi?
  Son of Mair, wife of jobbing carpenter
  in via nascitur
  lapped in hay, parvule.
But what does his Boast say?
  Alpha es et O
    that which

the whole world cannot hold.
Atheling to the heaven-king.
Shepherd of Greekland
Harrower of Annwn.
Freer of the waters.
Chief Physician and
dux et pontifex. (AN, p. 207)

Finally, we come to 'Sherthursday and Venus Day', which at once evokes the Arthurian connection with the Grail story, which is linked closely to the Mass throughout. 'Sherthursday', the old name for Maunday Thursday, is a direct reference to Malory, where Christ, appearing to the Grail winners says of the vessel that: 'this is the holy dish wherein I ate the lamb on Sherthursday' (Bk XVII, Ch. 20).

In the passage beginning:

Grown in stature
he frees the waters ...

Peredur, the Welsh form of Perceval, is conflated with Christ, and his childhood in the forest, where he is brought up, in ignorance of human ways, becomes a pattern of innocence. But the youth encounters two of Arthur's knights, whom he thinks are angels, and from that moment will not settle until he has himself become a *miles*, a knight. He thus puts on the armour of a man, and takes his place in the world. This act will result in the death of his mother, from sorrow, but also, ultimately, brings about the healing mystery of the Grail. For Peredur, or Perceval, is he who asks the all important question: whom is it that the Grail serves, which reverse the effects of the Dolorous Stroke and 'frees the waters which in turn cause the refructification of the Waste Land.'

All of this is summed up in the passage which reads:

Her Peredur
vagrant-born, earth-fostered
acquainted with the uninhabited sites.
His woodland play is done, he has seen the
questing milites, *he would be a* miles *too.*
Suitor, margaron-gainer.
Tryst-keeper
his twelve-month-and-a-day
falls tomorrow.

He would put on his man's lorica.
  He has put it on
his caligae on
    and is gone
to the mark-land ...
Unless he ask the question
  how shall the rivers run
or the suitors persuade their lovers
or the erosion of the land cease? (AN, 225–6)

Finally, the poem reaches an almost elegiac close. The sacring of the Mass, the oblation, the offering of gifts, is depicted, as Christ himself says mass with the Holy Cup:

Here, in this place
  as in Sarras city
(where the maim was ended
    at the voyage end)

Here, in this high place
  into both hands
he takes the stemmed dish
  as in many places
by this poured and that held up
whatever their directing glosses read:
  Here he takes the victim.
At the threshold-stone
    lifts the aged head?
can the toothless beast from stable come
    discern the Child
in the Bread? (AN, p. 242)

In 'The Hunt' and 'The Sleeping Lord' – both parts of a longer work provisionally entitled 'The Roman Quarry' and left unfinished at the time of his death – David Jones returned again to the Matter of Britain in an even more direct fashion. Taking up themes which had been mentioned both in *In Parenthesis* and *The Anathemata*, he extends the parallels between Arthur and Christ and Arthur as guardian of the sacred Land. 'The Hunt', his most clearly Arthurian work, returns to the theme of the hunting of the great boar Twrch Trwyth, described in the medieval story of 'Culhwch and Olwen'. In the notes to a recording made in 1967 he prefaced the work as follows:

The great boar is the personification of destructive potency, so that the tale is largely one of the immemorial struggle between what is salvific and what is inimical – 'cosmos' against 'chaos' ... I tried to evoke something of the feel of the stress, urgency and effort of the war-bands of the island lead by an Arthur-figure in pursuit of their formidable quarry across the whole of South Wales. What distinguishes this native prose-tale from the subsequent great medieval Arthurian Romance-Cycles is its vivid sense of the particular, of locality and site ... Though the theme itself is a common mythological theme stretching back to remote prehistory, here in this Welsh tale, its setting is a knowable, factual, precisely defined tract of country.

In short, for all its marvels and numinous powers, its many strata of mystery, its narration 'proceeds from the known to the unknown ...'[10]

Here the wonderfully rich strata of Celtic and Arthurian myth are evoked and overlaid with a background of emergent Christianity. The war-bands learn from the Cumaean Sybyl 'the Change Date and the Turn of Time' when the message of Christ comes to Britain; and the whole of the long description of Arthur's riding across the land forms a striking picture of both the Wounded King, the 'stricken numen of the woods', and the crucified saviour.

Arthur rides:

> *with the trophies of the woods*
> > *upon him*
> *who rode*
> > *for the healing of the woods*
> *and because of the hog.* (SL, p. 69)

This beast has become, like Garlon or the Dolorous Stroke, the active principle of evil, the cause of the Waste Land, which must be healed. Arthur, as its guardian must suffer also, and thus his riding causes him to be wounded, like Christ, for the sake of the land and its people. He is:

> > *the speckled lord of Prydain*
> *in his twice-embroidered coat*
> > *the bleeding man in the green*
> *and if through the trellis of green*
> > *and between the rents of the needlework*
> *the whiteness of his body shone*
> > *so did the dark wounds glisten.* (SL, p. 68)

In 'The Sleeping Lord' this parallels has become even stronger. The themes of the Waste Land and the Wounded King are explored through the notion that the king must be perfect in every limb before he can rule, and that if he is wounded then the land is also. The whole of the poem is really a huge single image. The Lord, be he Arthur or Christ or Bran, sleeps beneath the land – *is* the land. He is invoked by these named and others: Cunedda Wledig, proto-ancestor of the Celts, Ambrosius Aurelianus, the last of the Roman lords of Britain and Arthur's uncle, Cronos the sleeper who is imprisoned beneath the Island of Britain, Mabon the *puer eternis* of the Celts, who shared his imprisonment with Arthur ... These and all the

> many, many more whose names are, for whatever reason, on the diptycha of the Island; and vastly many more still, whether men or womankind, of neither fame nor recorded *nomen*, whether bond or freed or innately free, of far back or of but recent decease, whose burial mounds are known or unknown or for whom no mound was ever raised or any mark set up of even the meanest sort of show the site of their interment ... (SL, p. 85)

Thus the Sleeping Lord becomes a container of memory, a living *anamnesis* who recalls, within himself, the history and myth and story of the land. It is David Jones' purest statement of his art, and it is rooted most deeply on the Land that gave birth to Arthur. In the final passage from the poem, this is set forth as a series of great questions, which are one with the Grail question, and with the great Question of life itself.

With this David Jones brings into focus all the themes he has been exploring from *In Parenthesis* onward: the question of the ordinary and the particular, the named and the un-named, the nature of salvific signs, the re-membering, the wasted land and the search for the Great Theme which is the human quest for meaning, which was for him found in the life and teachings of Christ.

In these works, and in paintings such as *The Lord of Venedotia*, *Lancelot and the Three Queens*, *Trystan ac Essylt*, and *Lancelot in the Queen's Chamber*, David Jones distilled the whole of his understanding of the Matter of Britain. In so doing he also showed how it fit within the pattern of a greater whole, the heritage of Western Spirituality and history, and the literary heritage of the Middle Ages. For this alone we owe him a great debt.

What makes David Jones the great poet and artist that he was (he preferred the term 'maker') arises out of his concern with the outwardly obscure, inwardly bright – to the degree that he transcends the problem of obscurity by transmuting the base elements (the stuff of creation itself) into work of the highest imaginal quality. He was an alchemist who worked in images both plastic and literary – the coin of his genius being mined from that rarest of Welsh gold – the substrata of history and belief. He clothed his raw materials not with shoddy, transitory likeness, but with true, vibrant colours, bringing out their inherent numinosity so that they spoke directly to the spiritual apprehension of the viewer or reader. In this way his craftsmanship was of the highest order, he explored the path of the solitary image in an age which had already begun to be fascinated by the exterior shell alone.

Here the artist is less 'maker' than 'revealer'. He shows us the particularity of all things, the burden of tradition, the loss we suffer if the sacred memorials are allowed to fail. He sounds a warning note amid the wreckage of Western civilisation. If we allow ourselves to forget the great patterns of older times, if we reject them in pursuit of the New, we shall suffer the consequences – consequences we can indeed see all around us. In the precise memorials of his written and painted works David Jones left a record of one man's vision – a vision which strove to be always impersonal, and which was defined by the shining images and signs of the Matter of Britain and the cloudy glory of the Grail.

I can think of no better way to end than with words written by David Jones himself, forming a prayer which sums up, for me, all of his work. It comes from the fragmentary poem 'Cailleach' (Old Woman) published posthumously in *The Roman Quarry* and the reference is once again to that moment where Lancelot, standing before the entrance to the Grail Chapel, sees the 'venerable priest' lifting the body of the crucified man at the oblation of the Mass. It might well stand as a fitting epitaph not only to David Jones himself but to all artists and writers living at the 'sagging end and chapters close' of the twentieth century:

Holy and Eternal Lord, Gwledig Nef, I ask but that one microscopic fraction of this world's time of you, who within the vast Wheel of Eternity created time as not illusory but of *realitas*. No more I ask but that, not any amelioration of what is adjudged me, on the *in favilla* day, As David and the Sibyl have it. *Nil intultum remanbit* – but I too would aid the venerable man surcharged with that great weight, and it is but for that brief moment I ask it. (RQ, p. 105)

Notes

1 All quotations from the writings of David Jones are from the following editions:

In Parenthesis (Faber & Faber, 1963)	(IP)
Anathemata (Faber & Faber, 1952)	(AN)
The Sleeping Lord (Faber & Faber, 1974)	(SL)
Dai Great Coat (Faber & Faber, 1980)	(DGC)
The Roman Quarry (Agenda Editions, 1981)	(RQ)
The Kensington Mass (Agenda Editions, 1983)	(KM)

2 *David Jones & the Actually Loved & Known* (Golgonooza Press, 1978).

3 *The Mabinogion*, ed. Lady Charlotte Guest (J.M. Dent, 1906).

4 All quotations are from Sir Thomas Malory, *Le Morte D'Arthur*, ed. John Matthews (Orion, 1999).

5 *Triodd Ynys Prydein*, ed. & trans. Rachel Bromwich (Cardiff: Univ. of Wales Press, 1978).

6 *The Gododdin*, trans. A.O.H. Jarman.

7 'The Stanzas of the Graves' in *Proceedings of the British Academy*, vol. 63, ed. & trans. T. Jones, 1967.

8 Cf. the ninth-century Welsh poem: 'The Prieddeu Annwn' in *Taliesin: Shamanism & The Bardic Mysteries in Britain & Ireland*, trans. John Matthews (Inner Traditions, 2002).

9 Thomas Dillworth, *The Liturgical Parenthesis in David Jones*.

10 Argo recording, No ALP 1093. London, 1967.

INDEX